*The Best of the Best
American Science Writing*

THE BEST AMERICAN SCIENCE WRITING

EDITORS

The Best
of the Best American

SCIENCE WRITING

INTRODUCTION BY JEROME GROOPMAN

Series Editor: Jesse Cohen

An Imprint of HarperCollinsPublishers

Contents

2007
Editor: Gina Kolata

2008
Editor: Sylvia Nasar

2009
Editor: Natalie Angier

Introduction

IMAGINE THAT YOU AND I UNEXPECTEDLY RECEIVE AN invitation to a unique gathering. We suspect that we were on the guest list because of our love of science. Indeed, it is hard for us to enter a bookstore or peruse a magazine stand without our eyes stopping on a title about the natural world. Our scientific interests are eclectic. Often we delve into subjects that probe deeply into the human experience, our biology and our psychology. There are other times when we prefer not to navel gaze but turn our heads upward to the heavens to ponder the awesome forces that control the cosmos.

The invitation appears especially engaging because we readily recognize many names on the guest list. They are prominent writers about natural science and medicine. But there is a novel twist. The party – because now you realize that this gathering is not going to be a dry and sober affair, but rich and animated with a spectrum of personalities and perspectives – has a unique format. Each of the "bold face names," those readily recognizable authors whom we relish, has been asked to bring two of his or her favorite friends. We know that the choices were challenging, not easily made. There are so many friends whom they would want to bring along, and, in fact, would be terrific additions. But the rules are strict, limiting each to only two picks. And that makes it even more fun, because we appreciate that whom they choose to bring as their guests will not only enliven the gathering with points of view that are surprising and sharp, but we will learn something about those bold face names based on their selections.

By now, I suspect you realize that the gathering and its animated and engaging conversation is in your hands. Each of the editors of *The Best of American Science Writing*, from the initiation of the series in 2000 through the decade ending in 2009, was asked by the relentless Jesse Cohen to carefully consider each of their collections and choose two articles for this *Best of the Best American Science Writing*. Such choices are always subjective, and, as mentioned earlier, tell us as much about the chooser as the chosen. But, since I had the opportunity to preview the gathering of these extraordinary talents before the party was open to the public, I can testify that you will be elated, inspired, challenged, and enlightened. Most importantly, the topics that the writers tackle are far from stale. Quite the contrary: they have ripened like the most precious grapes on the vine to provide the kind of wine that intoxicates the thirsty spirit. None of the subjects addressed in this book has been "settled." Indeed, the debate around each has expanded. Reading them now provides a perspective from the recent past that points to a path in future.

It is fitting that we move through the reception line in chronological order, greeting each editor and his chosen companions according to the date of his or her publication. James Gleick is an accomplished science writer who worked for a decade as an editor and reporter for *The New York Times*. His landmark book, *Chaos*, was the finalist for both National Book Award and the Pulitzer Prize. It is not surprising that a writer with a taste for order and disorder would choose as his two guests to bring to the party Atul Gawande and Sheryl Gay Stolberg. Gawande, my colleague at *The New Yorker* magazine, is a practicing surgeon and health policy expert who brought to the fore the issue of medical mistakes. His compelling piece on clinical errors in *The New Yorker* followed a report from the National Academy of Sciences indicating that such mistakes could cause up to 100,000 deaths a year. In the current efforts around health care reform, the nation is debating how to safeguard hospitals and change this sad and frightening statistic. Here, Dr. Gawande succeeds in bringing the reader deep into the inner sanctum of the hospital, transforming remote numbers on medical mistakes into palpable human tragedies. Similarly, Gleick chose Sheryl Gay Stolberg, a prolific writer for *The New York Times*, who details the death of Jesse Gelsinger, an 18-year-old volunteer who received an experimental gene treatment. How patients and their families evaluate new therapies, how risks and rewards presented by researcher physicians, and the extent of oversight by government and hospitals over clinical trials of cutting edge technologies, are all issues that continue in the national conversation.

Timothy Ferris, our next editor, is truly a Renaissance man. Professor Ferris has taught in five disciplines: astronomy, English, history, journalism, and philosophy. His pedagogy illuminated four different universities, and he is currently an emeritus professor at the University of California, Berkeley. I imagine Ferris's wide-ranging interests led him to invite Freeman Dyson, the Princeton physicist who writes like a dream and consistently enriches our understanding of science in society. At this gathering, Dyson is talking about "green and gray technologies," the aim of environmental science to improve life on the planet, and the benefits of mechanical advances that have flourished since the industrial revolution. What makes Dyson's eye so sharp is his unalloyed vision of both the benefits and the dangers that man can introduce to society in exploiting new knowledge from the green and the gray sciences. Ferris also chose Ernst Mayr, who explores Darwin, specifically his extraordinary impact on modern thought. Mayr shows how evolutionary biology has greatly influenced not only natural science but every corner of intellectual endeavor in our modern world.

Now, I happen to know Matt Ridley. In 2002, we shared the platform at an event at the 92nd Street Y in New York heralding his wonderful edition of this series. Ridley grew up on the playing fields of Eton. But his empire is not one of imperialism; rather, it is the marvels of zoology. As it happens, his choice of the article by Lauren Slater on plastic surgery, its appeal and its disturbing trends, has been a regular feature of the literature seminar I teach at Harvard College for freshmen (and yes, each student buys the book). Ridley's love of the contrarian is evident in Slater's profile of a surgeon at Dartmouth who wants to go beyond facelifts and tummy tucks to carve humans with wings. Oy vey! And speaking of tummy tucks, Matt Ridley also brought along Gary Taubes. His article on how conventional wisdom about dietary fat was turned on its head (if not its stomach) teaches us a great deal about how politics and wishful thinking foster medical urban legends. Obesity is a hot topic in health care reform, as is the call for evidence-based medicine; Taubes alerts us to the truth that analysis of evidence is never fully objective. We all bring our biases to bear when deciding what is "significant" with statistics. Prejudices deeply color our conclusions, and we are susceptible to wanting to believe what is pleasing. H.L. Mencken famously said that for every complex problem there is a clear and direct solution that is wrong. The battle over the genesis and cure of obesity, over how Americans are expanding horizontally and what they should do to shrink their waistlines, certainly call to mind Mencken's dry wit and Taubes's keen eye.

Oliver Sacks was my inspiration to begin writing. I suspect he was the inspiration to many other scientists and physicians – and he continues to be. A polymath, with the kind of mind that ranges from the taxonomy of ferns to the vibrations of the flute, and the kind of soul that reaches deep into the science to find the marvel of humanity, Sacks occupies a unique place in today's pantheon of medical scribes. So his choice of guests takes on a particular resonance. Danielle Ofri's article is poignant and rivetting, moving to the climax of a physician revealing her deepest secrets to the reader and, in a larger sense, to all those in need of compassionate connection. Her writing is an act of courage, as so much outstanding writing is at its core. Sacks also invited Floyd Skloot who describes his beloved mother with Alzheimer's. She lacks for words but still holds the melodies of her life. Sacks's exploration of the brain and, most recently, its relationship to music, are prefigured in his inclusion of Skloot's marvelous telling of how song can still unite us with the ailing aged.

We have received from the pen of editor Dava Sobel enriching accounts of how man mapped the earth and worked to understand the heavens. A fluid writer, Sobel has not only produced important works in print but transformed them into films and plays. Sobel's choice of Michael Benson's tale of adventure enlightens us about the determined effort to send a spaceship half a billion miles away to Jupiter's moons. Her other choice is William Langewiesche's indepth piece about the tragedy of the space shuttle *Columbia*, specifically the challenges, risks, and potential rewards of NASA's endeavor. Written in compelling prose, the article is still heartbreaking and informative after all these years.

Our next editor is Alan Lightman, who stands with one foot firmly planted in hard science, specifically physics, and his other foot in the arts. His contributions to astronomy and relativity are legion, and his gifts to a lay audience include critically acclaimed novels and essays. Lightman graciously brought along Robin Marantz Henig, who certainly electrifies the gathering by bringing up the often taboo topic of race. One of the marvelous characteristics of science writing is that it is fearless. Henig addresses the contentious question of what race means after decoding the human genome, and how to best advance medical treatments among diverse populations in a culturally sensitive way. Some five years after Henig's piece first appeared, the subject continues to vex physicians and ethicists alike. Similarly, Lightman's focus on the nexus of culture and science is evident in his invitation to David Quammen. Some may joke about the flat-earth society, but the tenacious belief in creationism has real ramifications in the education of our youth. I am one who holds both religious sensibilities and a rigorous scientific perspective, certainly a form of cognitive dissonance, but I separate science that describes the physical world and faith that speaks in metaphors to the spiritual domain. As Quammen rightly points out, those metaphors of the Bible must give way to scientific data, and he marshals cogent arguments about evolution in a powerful and compelling way in his article.

Atul Gawande invited two guests who illuminate issues of bias and of technology. Gawande has written about how he is a product of a proud Indian family, raised in Ohio, in touch with culture of the small town Midwest; he is also an urban sophisticate who has lived on both coasts. Jack Hitt, in "Mighty White of You," tackles the problem of how not-so-subtle racism can drive revisionist theories about the first Americans, positing that they were Europeans rather than people from Asia. And Tom Mueller, in "Your Move," explores Gawande's other interest, technology. Mueller describes how computers advance strategies in chess, that most cerebral form of war, on a battlefield that may have been created by man but is now being completely remapped by machine.

Gina Kolata is certainly familiar to readers for her compelling contributions to *The New York Times*. Her books show a mastery of topics that range from the great influenza pandemic of 1918 to the myths and truths of dieting. Kolata has long been a sharp observer of the culture of competitive science, and her selection of Jennifer Couzin-Frankel's article "Truth and Consequences," shows the painful fallout from scientific cheating on those most vulnerable, the trainees. It is a chilling and cautionary tale. Kolata also invited her colleague Dr. Lawrence K. Altman, the dean of medical reporters, who brings us into the operating room at a dramatic pivotal moment in the life of a celebrated heart surgeon, Michael DeBakey. One component of the current health care debate centers on limits on patient choice and control – who decides at such life-and-death times to proceed or to let go. Altman gives us a story of heroic measures for a heroic surgeon, and like all outstanding writing, raises questions that have no single or simple answer.

Full disclosure: I do not personally know Sylvia Nasar, but have greatly admired her as a writer, the author of *A Beautiful Mind*. She chose my *New Yorker* article on the controversy about the diagnosis and treatment of bipolar disorder in children, "What's Normal?" I humbly leave it to the reader to decide on its merits, but merely point out that the issue of the pharmaceutical industry medicalizing human behavior, and the desperate need for families to diagnose troubled children when there are no objective measures, continue to spark sharp debate and controversy. Ms. Nasar also brought along Amy Harmon, who describes in haunting prose the pain and poignancy of "Facing Life with a Lethal Gene." Her subject will become mainstream as researchers continue to unravel everyone's risk for deadly diseases in our double helix.

Last to arrive at the gathering, but most warmly welcomed, is Natalie Angier. A Pulitzer Prize–winning science journalist at *The New York Times*, Ms. Angier's writing is acclaimed for its colorful imagery and playful tone, all the while communicating keen insights about the biological world. She chose Margaret Talbot, a prolific writer who graces the pages of *The New Yorker*. In Talbot's contribution, we meet Alex, an African gray parrot whose language skills seized the mind and stole the heart of the cognitive scientist Irene Pepperberg, but also raised the hackles of other researchers who felt that the bird was far from proof of animal intelligence. You judge for yourself after listening to Talbot's balanced telling. And Karen Olsson, in "The Final Frontier," puts a spotlight on a dimension of science that is rarely seen, specifically salesmanship. There is a famous phrase in the Talmud, "Without grain, there is no learning." Science is a costly endeavor requiring much "bread," whether it be the pursuit of dark energy with expensive astronomic instruments, as Ms. Olsson describes, or the costly equipment and reagents to clone genes and purify proteins. Her article on how serious scientists must hustle and sell their dreams will be familiar to those in the field, and likely new to those who only know research from its results.

The event is about to begin. Like any gathering, feel free to circulate as you like. Some may want to go from the front of the group to the back, while others skip around. But all will savor the offerings, nourished in mind and spirit. You will not be disappointed. Rather, deeply delighted.

2000

Editor: JAMES GLEICK

ATUL GAWANDE

When Doctors Make Mistakes

FROM *THE NEW YORKER*

> *A study released by the National Academy of Sciences in November 1999 reported that medical errors caused between 44,000 and 98,000 deaths a year. Congress held hearings to investigate its findings and President Clinton ordered hospitals to monitor errors and report them to a federal agency. Months before, readers of* The New Yorker *were introduced to the subject through the courageous reporting of a young surgical resident. Atul Gawande's bracing first-person account of life-and-death decision-making in the emergency room puts a human face on this complex and urgent issue.*

I—CRASH VICTIM

At 2 A.M. on a crisp Friday in winter, I was in sterile gloves and gown, pulling a teenage knifing victim's abdomen open, when my pager sounded. "Code Trauma, three minutes," the operating-room nurse said, reading aloud from my pager display. This meant that an ambulance would be bringing another trauma patient to the hospital momentarily, and, as the surgical resident on duty for emergencies, I would have to be present for the patient's arrival. I stepped back from the table and took off my gown. Two other surgeons were working on the knifing victim: Michael Ball, the attending (the staff surgeon in charge of the case), and David Hernandez, the chief resident (a general surgeon in his last of five years of training). Ordinarily, these two would have come later to help with the trauma, but they were stuck here. Ball, a dry, imperturbable forty-two-year-old Texan, looked over to me as I headed for the door. "If you run into any trouble, you call, and one of us will peel away," he said.

I did run into trouble. In telling this story, I have had to change significant details about what happened (including the names of the participants and aspects of my role), but I have tried to stay as close to the actual events as I could while protecting the patient, myself, and the rest of the staff. The way that things go wrong in medicine is normally unseen and, consequently, often misunderstood. Mistakes do happen. We think of them as aberrant; they are anything but.

The emergency room was one floor up, and, taking the stairs two at a time, I arrived just as the emergency medical technicians wheeled in a woman who appeared to be in her thirties and to weigh more than two hundred pounds. She lay motionless on a hard orange plastic spinal board—eyes closed, skin pale, blood running out of her nose. A nurse directed the crew into Trauma Bay 1, an examination room outfitted like an O.R., with green tiles on the wall, monitoring devices, and space for portable X-ray equipment. We lifted her onto the bed and then went to work. One nurse began cutting off the woman's clothes. Another took vital signs. A third inserted a large-bore intravenous line into her right arm. A surgical intern put a Foley catheter into her bladder. The emergency-medicine attending was Samuel Johns, a gaunt, Ichabod Crane–like man in his fifties. He was standing to one side with his arms crossed, observing, which was a sign that I could go ahead and take charge.

If you're in a hospital, most of the "moment to moment" doctoring you get is from residents—physicians receiving specialty training and a small income in exchange for their labor. Our responsibilities depend on our level of training, but we're never entirely on our own: there's always an attending, who oversees our decisions. That night, since Johns was the attending and was responsible for the patient's immediate management, I took my lead from him. But he wasn't a surgeon, and so he relied on me for surgical expertise.

"What's the story?" I asked.

An E.M.T. rattled off the details: "Unidentified white female unrestrained driver in high-speed rollover. Ejected from the car. Found unresponsive to pain. Pulse a hundred, B.P. a hundred over sixty, breathing at thirty on her own . . ."

As he spoke, I began examining her. The first step in caring for a trauma patient is always the same. It doesn't matter if a person has been shot eleven times or crushed by a truck or burned in a kitchen fire. The first thing you do is make sure that the patient can breathe without difficulty. This woman's breaths were shallow and rapid. An oximeter, by means of a sensor placed on her finger, measured the oxygen saturation of her blood. The "O_2 sat" is normally more than ninety-five percent for a patient breathing room air. The woman was wearing a face mask with oxygen turned up full blast, and her sat was only ninety percent.

"She's not oxygenating well," I announced in the flattened-out, wake-me-up-when-something-interesting-happens tone that all surgeons have acquired by about three months into residency. With my fingers, I verified that there wasn't any object in her mouth that would obstruct her airway; with a stethoscope, I confirmed that neither lung had collapsed. I got hold of a bag mask, pressed its clear facepiece over her nose and mouth, and squeezed the bellows, a kind of balloon with a one-way valve, shooting a litre of air into her with each compression. After a minute or so, her oxygen came up to a comfortable ninety-eight percent. She obviously needed our help with breathing. "Let's tube her," I said. That meant putting a tube down through her vocal cords and into her trachea, which would insure a clear airway and allow for mechanical ventilation.

Johns, the attending, wanted to do the intubation. He picked up a Mac 3 laryngoscope, a standard but fairly primitive-looking L-shaped metal instrument for prying open the mouth and throat, and slipped the shoehornlike blade deep into her mouth and down to her larynx. Then he yanked the handle up toward the ceiling to pull her tongue out of the way, open her mouth and throat, and reveal the vocal cords, which sit like fleshy tent flaps at the entrance to the trachea. The patient didn't wince or gag: she was still out cold.

"Suction!" he called. "I can't see a thing."

He sucked out about a cup of blood and clot. Then he picked up the endotracheal tube—a clear rubber pipe about the diameter of an index finger and three times as long—and tried to guide it between her cords. After a minute, her sat started to fall.

"You're down to seventy percent," a nurse announced.

Johns kept struggling with the tube, trying to push it in, but it banged vainly against the cords. The patient's lips began to turn blue.

"Sixty percent," the nurse said.

Johns pulled everything out of the patient's mouth and fitted the bag mask back on. The oximeter's luminescent-green readout hovered at sixty for a moment and then rose steadily, to ninety-seven percent. After a few minutes, he took the mask off and again tried to get the tube in. There was more blood, and there may have been some swelling, too: all the poking down the throat was probably not helping. The sat fell to sixty percent. He pulled out and bagged her until she returned to ninety-five percent.

When you're having trouble getting the tube in, the next step is to get specialized expertise. "Let's call anesthesia," I said, and Johns agreed. In the meantime, I continued to follow the standard trauma protocol: completing the examination and ordering fluids, lab tests, and X-rays. Maybe five minutes passed as I worked.

The patient's sats drifted down to ninety-two percent—not a dramatic change but definitely not normal for a patient who is being manually ventilated. I checked to see if the sensor had slipped off her finger. It hadn't. "Is the oxygen up full blast?" I asked a nurse.

"It's up all the way," she said.

I listened again to the patient's lungs—no collapse. "We've got to get her tubed," Johns said. He took off the oxygen mask and tried again.

Somewhere in my mind, I must have been aware of the possibility that her airway was shutting down because of vocal-cord swelling or blood. If it was, and we were unable to get a tube in, then the only chance she'd have to survive would be an emergency tracheostomy: cutting a hole in her neck and inserting a breathing tube into her trachea. Another attempt to intubate her might even trigger a spasm of the cords and a sudden closure of the airway—which is exactly what did happen.

If I had actually thought this far along, I would have recognized how ill prepared I was to do an emergency "trache." Of the people in the room, it's true, I had the most experience doing tracheostomies, but that wasn't saying much. I had been the assistant surgeon in only about half a dozen, and all but one of them had been non-emergency cases, employing techniques that were not designed for speed. The exception was a practice emergency trache I had done on a goat. I should have immediately called Dr. Ball for backup. I should have got the trache equipment out—lighting, suction, sterile instruments—just in case. Instead of hurrying the effort to get the patient intubated because of a mild drop in saturation, I should have asked Johns to wait until I had help nearby. I might even have recognized that she was already losing her airway. Then I could have grabbed a knife and started cutting her a tracheostomy while things were still relatively stable and I had time to proceed slowly. But for whatever reasons—hubris, inattention, wishful thinking, hesitation, or the uncertainty of the moment—I let the opportunity pass.

Johns hunched over the patient, intently trying to insert the tube through her vocal cords. When her sat once again dropped into the sixties, he stopped and put the mask back on. We stared at the monitor. The numbers weren't coming up. Her lips were still blue. Johns squeezed the bellows harder to blow more oxygen in.

"I'm getting resistance," he said.

The realization crept over me: this was a disaster. "Damn it, we've lost her airway," I said. "Trache kit! Light! Somebody call down to O.R. and get Ball up here!"

People were suddenly scurrying everywhere. I tried to proceed deliberately, and not let panic take hold. I told the surgical intern to get a sterile gown and gloves on. I took a bactericidal solution off a shelf and dumped a whole bottle of yellow-brown liquid on the patient's neck. A nurse unwrapped the tracheostomy kit—a sterilized set of drapes and instruments. I pulled on a gown and a new pair of gloves while trying to think through the steps. This is simple, really, I tried to tell myself. At the base of the thyroid cartilage, the Adam's apple, is a little gap in which you find a thin, fibrous covering called the cricothyroid membrane. Cut through that and—voilà! You're in the trachea. You slip through the hole a four-inch plastic tube shaped like a plumber's elbow joint, hook it up to oxygen and a ventilator, and she's all set. Anyway, that was the theory.

I threw some drapes over her body, leaving the neck exposed. It looked as thick as a tree. I felt for the bony prominence of the thyroid cartilage. But I couldn't feel anything through the rolls of fat. I was beset by uncertainty—where should I cut? should I make a horizontal or a vertical incision?—and I hated myself for it. Surgeons never dithered, and I was dithering.

"I need better light," I said.

Someone was sent out to look for one.

"Did anyone get Ball?" I asked. It wasn't exactly an inspiring question.

"He's on his way," a nurse said.

There wasn't time to wait. Four minutes without oxygen would lead to permanent brain damage, if not death. Finally, I took the scalpel and cut. I just cut. I made a three-inch left-to-right swipe across the middle of the neck, following the procedure I'd learned for elective cases. I figured that if I worked through the fat I might be able to find the membrane in the wound. Dissecting down with scissors while the intern held the wound open with retractors, I hit a vein. It didn't let loose a lot of blood, but there was enough to fill the wound: I couldn't see anything. The intern put a finger on the bleeder. I called for suction. But the suction wasn't working; the tube was clogged with the clot from the intubation efforts.

"Somebody get some new tubing," I said. "And where's the light?"

Finally, an orderly wheeled in a tall overhead light, plugged it in, and flipped on the switch. It was still too dim; I could have done better with a flashlight.

I wiped up the blood with gauze, then felt around in the wound with my fingertips. This time, I thought I could feel the hard ridges of the thyroid cartilage and, below it, the slight gap of the cricothyroid membrane, though I couldn't be sure. I held my place with my left hand.

James O'Connor, a silver-haired, seen-it-all anesthesiologist, came into the room. Johns gave him a quick rundown on the patient and let him take over bagging her.

Holding the scalpel in my right hand like a pen, I stuck the blade down into the wound at the spot where I thought the thyroid cartilage was. With small, sharp strokes—working blindly, because of the blood and the poor light—I cut down through the overlying fat and tissue until I felt the blade scrape against the almost bony cartilage. I searched with the tip of the knife, walking it along until I felt it reach a gap. I hoped it was the cricothyroid membrane, and pressed down firmly. Then I felt the tissue suddenly give, and I cut an inch-long opening.

When I put my index finger into it, it felt as if I were prying open the jaws of a stiff clothespin. Inside, I thought I felt open space. But where were the sounds of moving air that I expected? Was this deep enough? Was I even in the right place?

"I think I'm in," I said, to reassure myself as much as anyone else.

"I hope so," O'Connor said. "She doesn't have much longer."

I took the tracheostomy tube and tried to fit it in, but something seemed to be blocking it. I twisted it and turned it, and finally jammed it in. Just then, Ball, the surgical attending, arrived. He rushed up to the bed and leaned over for a look. "Did you get it?" he asked. I said that I thought so. The bag mask was plugged onto the open end of the trache tube. But when the bellows were compressed the air just gurgled out of the wound. Ball quickly put on gloves and a gown.

"How long has she been without an airway?" he asked.

"I don't know. Three minutes."

Ball's face hardened as he registered that he had about a minute in which to turn things around. He took my place and summarily pulled out the trache tube. "God, what a mess," he said. "I can't see a thing in this wound. I don't even know if you're in the right place. Can we get better light and suction?"

New suction tubing was found and handed to him. He quickly cleaned up the wound and went to work.

The patient's sat had dropped so low that the oximeter couldn't detect it anymore. Her heart rate began slowing down—first to the sixties and then to the forties. Then she lost her pulse entirely. I put my hands together on her chest, locked my elbows, leaned over her, and started doing chest compressions.

Ball looked up from the patient and turned to O'Connor. "I'm not going to get her an airway in time," he said. "You're going to have to try from above." Essentially, he was admitting my failure. Trying an oral intubation again was pointless—just something to do instead of watching her die. I was stricken, and concentrated on doing chest compressions, not looking at anyone. It was over, I thought.

And then, amazingly, O'Connor: "I'm in." He had managed to slip a pediatric-size endotracheal tube through the vocal cords. In thirty seconds, with oxygen being manually ventilated through the tube, her heart was back, racing at a hundred and twenty beats a minute. Her sat registered at sixty and then climbed. Another thirty seconds and it was at ninety-seven percent. All the people in the room exhaled, as if they, too, had been denied their breath. Ball and I said little except to confer about the next steps for her. Then he went back downstairs to finish working on the stab-wound patient still in the O.R.

We eventually identified the woman, whom I'll call Louise Williams; she was thirty-four years old and lived alone in a nearby suburb. Her alcohol level on arrival had been three times the legal limit, and had probably contributed to her unconsciousness. She had a concussion, several lacerations, and significant soft-tissue damage. But X-rays and scans revealed no other injuries from the crash. That night, Ball and Hernandez brought her to the O.R. to fit her with a proper tracheostomy. When Ball came out and talked to family members, he told them of the dire condition she was in when she arrived, the difficulties "we" had had getting access to her airway, the disturbingly long period of time that she had gone without oxygen, and thus his uncertainty about how much brain function she still possessed. They listened without protest; there was nothing for them to do but wait.

II—THE BANALITY OF ERROR

To much of the public—and certainly to lawyers and the media—medical error is a problem of bad physicians. Consider some other surgical mishaps. In one, a general surgeon left a large metal instrument in a patient's abdomen, where it tore through the bowel and the wall of the bladder. In another, a cancer surgeon biopsied the wrong part of a woman's breast and thereby delayed her diagnosis of cancer for months. A cardiac surgeon skipped a small but key step during a heart-valve operation, thereby killing the patient. A surgeon saw a man racked with abdominal pain in the emergency room and, without taking a C.T. scan, assumed that the man had a kidney stone; eighteen hours later, a scan showed a rupturing abdominal aortic aneurysm, and the patient died not long afterward.

How could anyone who makes a mistake of that magnitude be allowed to practice medicine? We call such doctors "incompetent," "unethical," and "negligent." We want to see them punished. And so we've wound up with the public system we have for dealing with error: malpractice lawsuits, media scandal, suspensions, firings.

There is, however, a central truth in medicine that complicates this tidy vision of misdeeds and misdoers: *All* doctors make terrible mistakes. Consider the cases I've just described. I gathered them simply by asking respected surgeons I know—surgeons at top medical schools—to tell me about mistakes they had made just in the past year. Every one of them had a story to tell.

In 1991, *The New England Journal of Medicine* published a series of landmark papers from a project known as the Harvard Medical Practice Study—a review of more than thirty thousand hospital admissions in New York State. The study found that nearly four percent of hospital patients suffered complications from treatment which prolonged their hospital stay or resulted in disability or death, and that two-thirds of such complications were due to errors in care. One in four, or one percent of admissions, involved actual negligence. It was estimated that, nationwide, a hundred and twenty thousand patients die each year at least partly as a result of errors in care. And subsequent investigations around the country have confirmed the ubiquity of error. In one small study of how clinicians perform when patients have a sudden cardiac arrest, twenty-seven of thirty clinicians made an error in using the defibrillator; they may have charged it incorrectly or lost valuable time trying to figure out how to work a particular model. According to a 1995 study, mistakes in administering drugs—giving the wrong drug or the wrong dose, say—occur, on the average, about once for every hospital admission, mostly without ill effects, but one percent of the time with serious consequences.

If error were due to a subset of dangerous doctors, you might expect malpractice cases to be concentrated among a small group, but in fact they follow a uniform, bell-shaped distribution. Most surgeons are sued at least once in the course of their careers. Studies of specific types of error, too, have found that repeat offenders are not the problem. The fact is that virtually everyone who cares for hospital patients will make serious mistakes, and even commit acts of negligence, every year. For this reason, doctors are seldom outraged when the press reports yet another medical horror story. They usually have a different reaction: *That could be me.* The important question isn't how to keep bad physicians from harming patients; it's how to keep good physicians from harming patients.

Medical-malpractice suits are a remarkably ineffective remedy. Troyen Brennan, a Harvard professor of law and public health, points out that research has consistently failed to find evidence that litigation reduces medical-error rates. In part, this may be because the weapon is so imprecise. Brennan led several studies following up on the patients in the Harvard Medical Practice Study. He found that fewer than two percent of the patients who had received substandard care ever filed suit. Conversely, only a small minority among the patients who did sue had in fact been the victims of negligent care.

And a patient's likelihood of winning a suit depended primarily on how poor his or her outcome was, regardless of whether that outcome was caused by disease or unavoidable risks of care.

The deeper problem with medical-malpractice suits, however, is that by demonizing errors they prevent doctors from acknowledging and discussing them publicly. The tort system makes adversaries of patient and physician, and pushes each to offer a heavily slanted version of events. When things go wrong, it's almost impossible for a physician to talk to a patient honestly about mistakes. Hospital lawyers warn doctors that, although they must, of course, tell patients about complications that occur, they are never to intimate that they were at fault, lest the "confession" wind up in court as damning evidence in a black-and-white morality tale. At most, a doctor might say, "I'm sorry that things didn't go as well as we had hoped."

There is one place, however, where doctors can talk candidly about their mistakes, if not with patients, then at least with one another. It is called the Morbidity and Mortality Conference—or, more simply, M. & M.—and it takes place, usually once a week, at nearly every academic hospital in the country. This institution survives because laws protecting its proceedings from legal discovery have stayed on the books in most states, despite frequent challenges. Surgeons, in particular, take the M. & M. seriously. Here they can gather behind closed doors to review the mistakes, complications, and deaths that occurred on their watch, determine responsibility, and figure out what to do differently next time.

III—SHOW AND TELL

At my hospital we convene every Tuesday at five o'clock in a steep, plush amphitheatre lined with oil portraits of the great doctors whose achievements we're meant to live up to. All surgeons are expected to attend, from the interns to the chairman of surgery; we're also joined by medical students doing their surgery "rotation." An M. & M. can include almost a hundred people. We file in, pick up a photocopied list of cases to be discussed, and take our seats. The front row is occupied by the most senior surgeons: terse, serious men, now out of their scrubs and in dark suits, lined up like a panel of senators at a hearing. The chairman is a leonine presence in the seat closest to the plain wooden podium from which each case is presented. In the next few rows are the remaining surgical attendings; these tend to be younger, and several of them are women. The chief residents have put on long white coats and usually sit in the side rows. I join the mass of other residents, all of us in short white coats and green scrub pants, occupying the back rows.

For each case, the chief resident from the relevant service—cardiac, vascular, trauma, and so on—gathers the information, takes the podium, and tells the story. Here's a partial list of cases from a typical week (with a few changes to protect confidentiality): a sixty-eight-year-old man who bled to death after heart-valve surgery; a forty-seven-year-old woman who had to have a reoperation because of infection following an arterial bypass done in her left leg; a forty-four-year-old woman who had to have bile drained from her abdomen after gall-bladder surgery; three patients who had to have reoperations for bleeding following surgery; a sixty-three-year-old man who had a cardiac arrest following heart-bypass surgery; a sixty-six-year-old woman whose sutures suddenly gave way in an abdominal wound and nearly allowed her intestines to spill out. Ms. Williams's case, my failed tracheostomy, was just one case on a list like this. David Hernandez, the chief trauma resident, had subsequently reviewed the records and spoken to me and others involved.

When the time came, it was he who stood up front and described what had happened.

Hernandez is a tall, rollicking, good old boy who can tell a yarn, but M. & M. presentations are bloodless and compact. He said something like: "This was a thirty-four-year-old female unrestrained driver in a high-speed rollover. The patient apparently had stable vitals at the scene but was unresponsive, and brought in by ambulance unintubated. She was G.C.S. 7 on arrival." G.C.S. stands for the Glasgow Coma Scale, which rates the severity of head injuries, from three to fifteen. G.C.S. 7 is in the comatose range. "Attempts to intubate were made without success in the E.R. and may have contributed to airway closure. A cricothyroidotomy was attempted without success."

These presentations can be awkward. The chief residents, not the attendings, determine which cases to report. That keeps the attendings honest—no one can cover up mistakes—but it puts the chief residents, who are, after all, underlings, in a delicate position. The successful M. & M. presentation inevitably involves a certain elision of detail and a lot of passive verbs. No one screws up a cricothyroidotomy. Instead, "a cricothyroidotomy was attempted without success." The message, however, was not lost on anyone.

Hernandez continued, "The patient arrested and required cardiac compressions. Anesthesia was then able to place a pediatric E.T. tube and the patient recovered stable vitals. The tracheostomy was then completed in the O.R."

So Louise Williams had been deprived of oxygen long enough to go into cardiac arrest, and everyone knew that meant she could easily have suffered a disabling stroke or been left a vegetable. Hernandez concluded with the fortunate aftermath: "Her workup was negative for permanent cerebral damage or other major injuries. The tracheostomy was removed on Day 2. She was discharged to home in good condition on Day 3." To the family's great relief, and mine, she had woken up in the morning a bit woozy but hungry, alert, and mentally intact. In a few weeks, the episode would heal to a scar.

But not before someone was called to account. A front-row voice immediately thundered, "What do you mean, 'A cricothyroidotomy was attempted without success?'" I sank into my seat, my face hot.

"This was my case," Dr. Ball volunteered from the front row. It is how every attending begins, and that little phrase contains a world of surgical culture. For all the talk in business schools and in corporate America about the virtues of "flat organizations," surgeons maintain an old-fashioned sense of hierarchy. When things go wrong, the attending is expected to take full responsibility. It makes no difference whether it was the resident's hand that slipped and lacerated an aorta; it doesn't matter whether the attending was at home in bed when a nurse gave a wrong dose of medication. At the M. & M., the burden of responsibility falls on the attending.

Ball went on to describe the emergency attending's failure to intubate Williams and his own failure to be at her bedside when things got out of control. He described the bad lighting and her extremely thick neck, and was careful to make those sound not like excuses but merely like complicating factors. Some attendings shook their heads in sympathy. A couple of them asked questions to clarify certain details. Throughout, Ball's tone was objective, detached. He had the air of a CNN newscaster describing unrest in Kuala Lumpur.

As always, the chairman, responsible for the over-all quality of our surgery service, asked the final question. What, he wanted to know, would Ball have done differently? Well, Ball replied, it didn't take long to get the stab-wound patient under control in the O.R., so he probably should have sent Hernandez up to the E.R. at that point or let Hernandez close the abdomen while he himself came up. People nodded. Lesson learned. Next case.

At no point during the M. & M. did anyone question why I had not called for help sooner or why I had not had the skill and knowledge that Williams needed. This is not to say that my actions were seen as acceptable. Rather, in the hierarchy, addressing my errors was Ball's role. The day after the disaster, Ball had caught me in the hall and taken me aside. His voice was more wounded than angry as he went through my specific failures. First, he explained, in an emergency tracheostomy it might have been better to do a vertical neck incision; that would have kept me out of the blood vessels, which run up and down—something I should have known at least from my reading. I might have had a much easier time getting her an airway then, he said. Second, and worse to him than mere ignorance, he didn't understand why I hadn't called him when there were clear signs of airway trouble developing. I offered no excuses. I promised to be better prepared for such cases and to be quicker to ask for help.

Even after Ball had gone down the fluorescent-lit hallway, I felt a sense of shame like a burning ulcer. This was not guilt: guilt is what you feel when you have done something wrong. What I felt was shame: *I* was what was wrong. And yet I also knew that a surgeon can take such feelings too far. It is one thing to be aware of one's limitations. It is another to be plagued by self-doubt. One surgeon with a national reputation told me about an abdominal operation in which he had lost control of bleeding while he was removing what turned out to be a benign tumor and the patient had died. "It was a clean kill," he said. Afterward, he could barely bring himself to operate. When he did operate, he became tentative and indecisive. The case affected his performance for months.

Even worse than losing self-confidence, though, is reacting defensively. There are surgeons who will see faults everywhere except in themselves. They have no questions and no fears about their abilities. As a result, they learn nothing from their mistakes and know nothing of their limitations. As one surgeon told me, it is a rare but alarming thing to meet a surgeon without fear. "If you're not a little afraid when you operate," he said, "you're bound to do a patient a grave disservice."

The atmosphere at the M. & M. is meant to discourage both attitudes—self-doubt and denial—for the M. & M. is a cultural ritual that inculcates in surgeons a "correct" view of mistakes. "What would you do differently?" a chairman asks concerning cases of avoidable complications. "Nothing" is seldom an acceptable answer.

In its way, the M. & M. is an impressively sophisticated and human institution. Unlike the courts or the media, it recognizes that human error is generally not something that can be deterred by punishment. The M. & M. sees avoiding error as largely a matter of will—of staying sufficiently informed and alert to anticipate the myriad ways that things can go wrong and then trying to head off each potential problem before it happens. Why do things go wrong? Because, doctors say, making them go right is hard stuff. It isn't damnable that an error occurs, but there is some shame to it. In fact, the M. & M.'s ethos can seem paradoxical. On the one hand, it reinforces the very American idea that error is intolerable. On the other hand, the very existence of the M. & M., its place on the weekly schedule, amounts to an acknowledgment that mistakes are an inevitable part of medicine.

BUT WHY DO THEY HAPPEN so often? Lucian Leape, medicine's leading expert on error, points out that many other industries— whether the task is manufacturing semiconductors or serving customers at the Ritz-Carlton—simply wouldn't countenance error rates like those in hospitals. The aviation industry has reduced the frequency of operational errors to one in a hundred thousand flights, and most of those errors have no harmful consequences. The buzzword at General Electric these days is "Six Sigma," meaning that its goal is to make product defects so rare that in statistical terms they are more than six standard deviations away from being a matter of chance—almost a one-in-a million occurrence.

Of course, patients are far more complicated and idiosyncratic than airplanes, and medicine isn't a matter of delivering a fixed product or even a catalogue of products; it may well be more complex than just about any other field of human endeavor. Yet everything we've learned in the past two decades—from cognitive psychology, from "human factors" engineering, from studies of disasters like Three Mile Island and Bhopal—has yielded the same insights: not only do all human beings err but they err frequently and in predictable, patterned ways. And systems that do not adjust for these realities can end up exacerbating rather than eliminating error.

The British psychologist James Reason argues, in his book *Human Error*, that our propensity for certain types of error is the price we pay for the brain's remarkable ability to think and act intuitively—to sift quickly through the sensory information that constantly bombards us without wasting time trying to work through every situation anew. Thus systems that rely on human perfection present what Reason calls "latent errors"—errors waiting to happen. Medicine teems with examples. Take writing out a prescription, a rote procedure that relies on memory and attention, which we know are unreliable. Inevitably, a physician will sometimes specify the wrong dose or the wrong drug. Even when the prescription is written correctly, there's a risk that it will be misread. (Computerized ordering systems can almost eliminate errors of this kind, but only a small minority of hospitals have adopted them.) Medical equipment, which manufacturers often build without human operators in mind, is another area rife with latent errors: one reason physicians are bound to have problems when they use cardiac defibrillators is that the devices have no standard design. You can also make the case that onerous workloads, chaotic environments, and inadequate team communication all represent latent errors in the system.

James Reason makes another important observation: disasters do not simply occur; they evolve. In complex systems, a single failure rarely leads to harm. Human beings are impressively good at adjusting when an error becomes apparent, and systems often have built-in defenses. For example, pharmacists and nurses routinely check and counter-check physicians' orders. But errors do not always become apparent, and backup systems themselves often fail as a result of latent errors. A pharmacist forgets to check one of a thousand prescriptions. A machine's alarm bell malfunctions. The one attending trauma surgeon available gets stuck in the operating room. When things go wrong, it is usually because a series of failures conspire to produce disaster.

The M. & M. takes none of this into account. For that reason, many experts see it as a rather shabby approach to analyzing error and improving performance in medicine. It isn't enough to ask what a clinician could or should have done differently so that he and others may learn for next time. The doctor is often only the final actor in a chain of events that set him or her up to fail. Error experts, therefore, believe that it's the process, not the individuals in it, which requires closer examination and correction. In a sense, they want to industrialize medicine. And they can already claim one success story: the specialty of anesthesiology, which has adopted their precepts and seen extraordinary results.

IV—NEARLY PERFECT

At the center of the emblem of the American Society of Anesthesiologists is a single word: "Vigilance." When you put a patient to sleep under general anesthesia, you assume almost complete control of the patient's body. The body is paralyzed, the brain rendered unconscious, and machines are hooked up to control breathing, heart rate, blood pressure—all the vital functions. Given the complexity of the machinery and of the human body, there are a seemingly infinite number of ways in which things can go wrong, even in minor surgery. And yet anesthesiologists have found that if problems are detected they can usually be solved. In the nineteen-forties, there was only one death resulting from anesthesia in every twenty-five hundred operations, and between the nineteen-sixties and the nineteen-eighties the rate had stabilized at one or two in every ten thousand operations.

But Ellison (Jeep) Pierce had always regarded even that rate as unconscionable. From the time he began practicing, in 1960, as a young anesthesiologist out of North Carolina and the University of Pennsylvania, he had maintained a case file of details from all the deadly anesthetic accidents he had come across or participated in. But it was one case in particular that galvanized him. Friends of his had taken their eighteen-year-old daughter to the hospital to have her wisdom teeth pulled, under general anesthesia. The anesthesiologist inserted the breathing tube into her esophagus instead of her trachea, which is a relatively common mishap, and then failed to spot the error, which is not. Deprived of oxygen, she died within minutes. Pierce knew that a one-in-ten-thousand death rate, given that anesthesia was administered in the United States an estimated thirty-five million times each year, meant thirty-five hundred avoidable deaths like that one.

In 1982, Pierce was elected vice-president of the American Society of Anesthesiologists and got an opportunity to do something about the death rate. The same year, ABC's *20/20* aired an exposé that caused a considerable stir in his profession. The segment began, "If you are going to go into anesthesia, you are going on a long trip, and you should not do it if you can avoid it in any way. General anesthesia [is] safe most of the time, but there are dangers from human error, carelessness, and a critical shortage of anesthesiologists. This year, six thousand patients will die or suffer brain damage." The program presented several terrifying cases from around the country. Between the small crisis that the show created and the sharp increases in physicians' malpractice-insurance premiums at that time, Pierce was able to mobilize the Society of Anesthesiologists around the problem of error.

He turned for ideas not to a physician but to an engineer named Jeffrey Cooper, the lead author of a ground-breaking 1978 paper entitled "Preventable Anesthesia Mishaps: A Study of Human Factors." An unassuming, fastidious man, Cooper had been hired in 1972, when he was twenty-six years old, by the Massachusetts General Hospital bioengineering unit, to work on developing machines for anesthesiology researchers. He gravitated toward the operating room, however, and spent hours there observing the anesthesiologists, and one of the first things he noticed was how poorly the anesthesia machines were designed. For example, a clockwise turn of a dial decreased the concentration of potent anesthetics in about half the machines but increased the concentration in the other half. He decided to borrow a technique called "critical incident analysis"—which had been used since the nineteen-fifties to analyze mishaps in aviation—in an effort to learn how equipment might be contributing to errors in anesthesia. The technique is built around carefully conducted interviews, designed to capture as much detail as possible about dangerous incidents: how specific accidents evolved and what factors contributed to them. This information is then used to look for patterns among different cases.

Getting open, honest reporting is crucial. The Federal Aviation Administration has a formalized system for analyzing and reporting dangerous aviation incidents, and its enormous success in improving airline safety rests on two cornerstones. Pilots who report an incident within ten days have automatic immunity from punishment, and the reports go to a neutral, outside agency, NASA, which has no interest in using the information against individual pilots. For Jeffrey Cooper, it was probably an advantage that he was an engineer, and not a physician, so that anesthesiologists regarded him as a discreet, unthreatening interviewer.

The result was the first in-depth, scientific look at errors in medicine. His detailed analysis of three hundred and fifty-nine errors provided a view of the profession unlike anything that had been seen before. Contrary to the prevailing assumption that the start of anesthesia ("takeoff ") was the most dangerous part, anesthesiologists learned that incidents tended to occur in the middle of anesthesia, when vigilance waned. The most common kind of incident involved errors in maintaining the patient's breathing, and these were usually the result of an undetected disconnection or misconnection of the breathing tubing, mistakes in managing the airway, or mistakes in using the anesthesia machine.

Just as important, Cooper enumerated a list of contributory factors, including inadequate experience, inadequate familiarity with equipment, poor communication among team members, haste, inattention, and fatigue.

The study provoked widespread debate among anesthesiologists, but there was no concerted effort to solve the problems until Jeep Pierce came along. Through the anesthesiology society at first, and then through a foundation that he started, Pierce directed funding into research on how to reduce the problems Cooper had identified, sponsored an international conference to gather ideas from around the world, and brought anesthesia-machine designers into safety discussions.

It all worked. Hours for anesthesiology residents were shortened. Manufacturers began redesigning their machines with fallible human beings in mind. Dials were standardized to turn in a uniform direction; locks were put in to prevent accidental administration of more than one anesthetic gas; controls were changed so that oxygen delivery could not be turned down to zero.

Where errors could not be eliminated directly, anesthesiologists began looking for reliable means of detecting them earlier. For example, because the trachea and the esophagus are so close together, it is almost inevitable that an anesthesiologist will sometimes put the breathing tube down the wrong pipe.

Anesthesiologists had always checked for this by listening with a stethoscope for breath sounds over both lungs. But Cooper had turned up a surprising number of mishaps—like the one that befell the daughter of Pierce's friends—involving undetected esophageal intubations. Something more effective was needed. In fact, monitors that could detect this kind of error had been available for years, but, in part because of their expense, relatively few anesthesiologists used them. One type of monitor could verify that the tube was in the trachea by detecting carbon dioxide being exhaled from the lungs. Another type, the pulse oximeter, tracked blood-oxygen levels, thereby providing an early warning that something was wrong with the patient's breathing system. Prodded by Pierce and others, the anesthesiology society made the use of both types of monitor for every patient receiving general anesthesia an official standard. Today, anesthesia deaths from misconnecting the breathing system or intubating the esophagus rather than the trachea are virtually unknown. In a decade, the over-all death rate dropped to just one in more than two hundred thousand cases—less than a twentieth of what it had been.

And the reformers have not stopped there. David Gaba, a professor of anesthesiology at Stanford, has focused on improving human performance. In aviation, he points out, pilot experience is recognized to be invaluable but insufficient: pilots seldom have direct experience with serious plane malfunction anymore. They are therefore required to undergo yearly training in crisis simulators. Why not doctors, too?

Gaba, a physician with training in engineering, led in the design of an anesthesia-simulation system known as the Eagle Patient Simulator. It is a lifesize, computer-driven mannequin that is capable of amazingly realistic behavior. It has a circulation, a heartbeat, and lungs that take in oxygen and expire carbon dioxide. If you inject drugs into it or administer inhaled anesthetics, it will detect the type and amount, and its heart rate, its blood pressure, and its oxygen levels will respond appropriately. The "patient" can be made to develop airway swelling, bleeding, and heart disturbances. The mannequin is laid on an operating table in a simulation room equipped exactly like the real thing. Here both residents and experienced attending physicians learn to perform effectively in all kinds of dangerous, and sometimes freak, scenarios: an anesthesia-machine malfunction, a power outage, a patient who goes into cardiac arrest during surgery, and even a cesarean-section patient whose airway shuts down and who requires an emergency tracheostomy.

Though anesthesiology has unquestionably taken the lead in analyzing and trying to remedy "systems" failures, there are signs of change in other quarters. The American Medical Association, for example, set up its National Patient Safety Foundation in 1997 and asked Cooper and Pierce to serve on the board of directors. The foundation is funding research, sponsoring conferences, and attempting to develop new standards for hospital drug-ordering systems that could substantially reduce medication mistakes—the single most common type of medical error.

Even in surgery there have been some encouraging developments. For instance, operating on the wrong knee or foot or other body part of a patient has been a recurrent, if rare, mistake. A typical response has been to fire the surgeon. Recently, however, hospitals and surgeons have begun to recognize that the body's bilateral symmetry makes these errors predictable. Last year, the American Academy of Orthopedic Surgeons endorsed a simple way of preventing them: make it standard practice for surgeons to initial, with a marker, the body part to be cut before the patient comes to surgery.

The Northern New England Cardiovascular Disease Study Group, based at Dartmouth, is another success story. Though the group doesn't conduct the sort of in-depth investigation of mishaps that Jeffrey Cooper pioneered, it has shown what can be done simply through statistical monitoring. Six hospitals belong to this consortium, which tracks deaths and complications (such as wound infections, uncontrolled bleeding, and stroke) arising from heart surgery and tries to identify various risk factors. Its researchers found, for example, that there were relatively high death rates among patients who developed anemia after bypass surgery, and that anemia developed most often in small patients. The fluid used to "prime" the heart-lung machine caused the anemia, because it diluted a patient's blood, so the smaller the patient (and his or her blood supply) the greater the effect. Members of the consortium now have several promising solutions to the problem. Another study found that a group at one hospital had made mistakes in "handoffs"—say, in passing preoperative lab results to the people in the operating room. The study group solved the problem by developing a pilot's checklist for all patients coming to the O.R. These efforts have introduced a greater degree of standardization, and so reduced the death rate in those six hospitals from four percent to three percent between 1991 and 1996. That meant two hundred and ninety-three fewer deaths. But the Northern New England cardiac group, even with its narrow focus and techniques, remains an exception; hard information about how things go wrong is still scarce. There is a hodgepodge of evidence that latent errors and systemic factors may contribute to surgical errors: the lack of standardized protocols, the surgeon's inexperience, the hospital's inexperience, inadequately designed technology and techniques, thin staffing, poor teamwork, time of day, the effects of managed care and corporate medicine, and so on and so on. But which are the major risk factors? We still don't know. Surgery, like most of medicine, awaits its Jeff Cooper.

V—GETTING IT RIGHT

It was a routine gallbladder operation, on a routine day: on the operating table was a mother in her forties, her body covered by blue paper drapes except for her round, antiseptic-coated belly. The gallbladder is a floppy, finger-length sac of bile like a deflated olive-green balloon tucked under the liver, and when gallstones form, as this patient had learned, they can cause excruciating bouts of pain. Once we removed her gallbladder, the pain would stop.

There are risks to this surgery, but they used to be much greater. Just a decade ago, surgeons had to make a six-inch abdominal incision that left patients in the hospital for the better part of a week just recovering from the wound. Today, we've learned to take out gallbladders with a minute camera and instruments that we manipulate through tiny incisions. The operation, often done as day surgery, is known as laparoscopic cholecystectomy, or "lap chole." Half a million Americans a year now have their gallbladders removed this way; at my hospital alone, we do several hundred lap choles annually.

When the attending gave me the go-ahead, I cut a discreet inch-long semicircle in the wink of skin just above the belly button. I dissected through fat and fascia until I was inside the abdomen, and dropped into place a "port," a half-inch-wide sheath for slipping instruments in and out. We hooked gas tubing up to a side vent on the port, and carbon dioxide poured in, inflating the abdomen until it was distended like a tire. I inserted the miniature camera. On a video monitor a few feet away, the woman's intestines blinked into view. With the abdomen inflated, I had room to move the camera, and I swung it around to look at the liver. The gallbladder could be seen poking out from under the edge.

We put in three more ports through even tinier incisions, spaced apart to complete the four corners of a square. Through the ports on his side, the attending put in two long "graspers," like small-scale versions of the device that a department-store clerk might use to get a hat off the top shelf. Watching the screen as he maneuvered them, he reached under the edge of the liver, clamped onto the gallbladder, and pulled it up into view. We were set to proceed.

Removing the gallbladder is fairly straightforward. You sever it from its stalk and from its blood supply, and pull the rubbery sac out of the abdomen through the incision near the belly button. You let the carbon dioxide out of the belly, pull out the ports, put a few stitches in the tiny incisions, slap some Band-Aids on top, and you're done. There's one looming danger, though: the stalk of the gallbladder is a branch off the liver's only conduit for sending bile to the intestines for the digestion of fats. And if you accidentally injure this main bile duct, the bile backs up and starts to destroy the liver. Between ten and twenty percent of the patients to whom this happens will die. Those who survive often have permanent liver damage and can go on to require liver transplantation. According to a standard textbook, "injuries to the main bile duct are nearly always the result of misadventure during operation and are therefore a serious reproach to the surgical profession." It is a true surgical error, and, like any surgical team doing a lap chole, we were intent on avoiding this mistake.

Using a dissecting instrument, I carefully stripped off the fibrous white tissue and yellow fat overlying and concealing the base of the gallbladder. Now we could see its broad neck and the short stretch where it narrowed down to a duct—a tube no thicker than a strand of spaghetti peeking out from the surrounding tissue, but magnified on the screen to the size of major plumbing. Then, just to be absolutely sure we were looking at the gallbladder duct and not the main bile duct, I stripped away some more of the surrounding tissue. The attending and I stopped at this point, as we always do, and discussed the anatomy. The neck of the gallbladder led straight into the tube we were eying. So it had to be the right duct. We had exposed a good length of it without a sign of the main bile duct. Everything looked perfect, we agreed. "Go for it," the attending said.

I slipped in the clip applier, an instrument that squeezes V-shaped metal clips onto whatever you put in its jaws. I got the jaws around the duct and was about to fire when my eye caught, on the screen, a little globule of fat lying on top of the duct. That wasn't necessarily anything unusual, but somehow it didn't look right. With the tip of the clip applier, I tried to flick it aside, but, instead of a little globule, a whole layer of thin unseen tissue came up, and, underneath, we saw that the duct had a fork in it. My stomach dropped. If not for that little extra fastidiousness, I would have clipped off the main bile duct.

Here was the paradox of error in medicine. With meticulous technique and assiduous effort to insure that they have correctly identified the anatomy, surgeons need never cut the main bile duct. It is a paradigm of an avoidable error. At the same time, studies show that even highly experienced surgeons inflict this terrible injury about once in every two hundred lap choles. To put it another way, I may have averted disaster this time, but a statistician would say that, no matter how hard I tried, I was almost certain to make this error at least once in the course of my career.

But the story doesn't have to end here, as the cognitive psychologists and industrial-error experts have demonstrated. Given the results they've achieved in anesthesiology, it's clear that we can make dramatic improvements by going after the process, not the people. But there are distinct limitations to the industrial cure, however necessary its emphasis on systems and structures. It would be deadly for us, the individual actors, to give up our belief in human perfectibility. The statistics may say that someday I will sever someone's main bile duct, but each time I go into a gallbladder operation I believe that with enough will and effort I can beat the odds. This isn't just professional vanity. It's a necessary part of good medicine, even in superbly "optimized" systems. Operations like that lap chole have taught me how easily error can occur, but they've also showed me something else: effort does matter; diligence and attention to the minutest details can save you.

This may explain why many doctors take exception to talk of "systems problems," "continuous quality improvement," and "process reëngineering." It is the dry language of structures, not people. I'm no exception: something in me, too, demands an acknowledgment of my autonomy, which is also to say my ultimate culpability. Go back to that Friday night in the E.R., to the moment when I stood, knife in hand, over Louise Williams, her lips blue, her throat a swollen, bloody, and suddenly closed passage. A systems engineer might have proposed some useful changes. Perhaps a backup suction device should always be at hand, and better light more easily available. Perhaps the institution could have trained me better for such crises, could have required me to have operated on a few more goats. Perhaps emergency tracheostomies are so difficult under any circumstances that an automated device could have been designed to do a better job. But the could-haves are infinite, aren't they? Maybe Williams could have worn her seat belt, or had one less beer that night. We could call any or all of these factors latent errors, accidents waiting to happen.

But although they put the odds against me, it wasn't as if I had no chance of succeeding. Good doctoring is all about making the most of the hand you're dealt, and I failed to do so. The indisputable fact was that I hadn't called for help when I could have, and when I plunged the knife into her neck and made my horizontal slash my best was not good enough. It was just luck, hers and mine, that Dr. O'Connor somehow got a breathing tube into her in time.

There are all sorts of reasons that it would be wrong to take my license away or to take me to court. These reasons do not absolve me. Whatever the limits of the M. & M., its fierce ethic of personal responsibility for errors is a formidable virtue. No matter what measures are taken, medicine will sometimes falter, and it isn't reasonable to ask that it achieve perfection. What's reasonable is to ask that medicine never cease to aim for it.

SHERYL GAY STOLBERG

The Biotech Death of Jesse Gelsinger

FROM *THE NEW YORK TIMES MAGAZINE*

By early 2000, gene therapy—using healthy genes to replace faulty ones—was at the center of an explosive public-health debate. After the death of an eighteen-year-old volunteer, Jesse Gelsinger, during the clinical trial of a new gene treatment, federal agencies placed new scrutiny on gene therapy, and the U.S. Congress launched an investigation into the safety of this potentially promising but still unproven technique. Sheryl Gay Stolberg, whose reporting for the New York Times *has helped shape public opinion on this issue, tells the story of how the search for a scientific breakthrough led to an unforeseen tragedy.*

THE JAGGED PEAK OF MOUNT WRIGHTSON TOWERS 9,450 feet above Tucson, overlooking a deep gorge where the prickly pear cactus that dots the desert floor gives way to a lush forest of ponderosa pine. It is said that this is as close to heaven as you can get in southern Arizona. Jesse Gelsinger loved this place.

So it was here, on a clear Sunday afternoon in early November, that Paul Gelsinger laid his eighteen-year-old son to rest, seven weeks after a gene-therapy experiment cost him his life.

The ceremony was simple and impromptu. Two dozen mourners—Jesse's father; his mother, Pattie; his stepmother, Mickie; and two sisters, a brother, three doctors, and a smattering of friends—trudged five miles along a steep trail to reach the rocky outcropping at the top. There, Paul Gelsinger shared stories of his son, who loved motorcycles and professional wrestling and was, to his father's irritation, distinctly lacking in ambition. Jesse was the kind of kid who kept $10.10 in his bank account. "You need $10 to keep it open," Gelsinger explained but those assembled on the mountaintop agreed that he had a sharp wit and a sensitive heart.

At Gelsinger's request, the hikers had carried Jesse's medicine bottles filled with his ashes, and now they were gathered at the edge of the peak. Steve Raper, the surgeon who gave Jesse what turned out to be a lethal injection of new genes, pulled a small blue book of poetry from his pocket. "Here rests his head upon the lap of Earth," Raper read, reciting a passage from an elegy by Thomas Gray, "a youth to Fortune and Fame unknown. / Fair Science frowned not on his humble birth." Then the surgeon, the grieving father and the rest scattered Jesse's ashes into the canyon, where they rose on a gust of wind and fell again in a powerful cloud of fine gray dust. "I will look to you here often, Jess," Paul Gelsinger said sadly.

Jesse Gelsinger was not sick before he died. He suffered from ornithine transcarbamylase (OTC) deficiency, a rare metabolic disorder, but it was controlled with a low-protein diet and drugs, thirty-two pills a day. He knew when he signed up for the experiment at the University of Pennsylvania that he would not benefit; the study was to test the safety of a treatment for babies with a fatal form of his disorder. Still, it offered hope, the promise that someday Jesse might be rid of the cumbersome medications and diet so restrictive that half a hot dog was a treat. "What's the worst that can happen to me?" he told a friend shortly before he left for the Penn hospital, in Philadelphia. "I die, and it's for the babies."

As far as government officials know, Jesse's death on September 17 was the first directly related to gene therapy. The official cause, as listed on the death certificate filed by Raper, was adult respiratory distress syndrome: his lungs shut down. The truth is more complicated. Jesse's therapy consisted of an infusion of corrective genes, encased in a dose of weakened cold virus, adenovirus, which functioned as what scientists call a vector. Vectors are like taxicabs that drive healthy DNA into cells; viruses, whose sole purpose is to get inside cells and infect them, make useful vectors. The Penn researchers had tested their vector, at the same dose Jesse got, in mice, monkeys, baboons, and one human patient, and had seen expected, flulike side effects, along with some mild liver inflammation, which disappeared on its own. When Jesse got the vector, he suffered a chain reaction that the testing had not predicted—jaundice, a blood-clotting disorder, kidney failure, lung failure, and brain death: in Raper's words, "multiple-organ-system failure." The doctors are still investigating; their current hypothesis is that the adenovirus triggered an overwhelming inflammatory reaction—in essence, an immune-system revolt.

What they do not understand yet is why.

Every realm of medicine has its defining moment, often with a human face attached. Polio had Jonas Salk. In vitro fertilization had Louise Brown, the world's first test-tube baby. Transplant surgery had Barney Clark, the Seattle dentist with the artificial heart. AIDS had Magic Johnson. Now gene therapy has Jesse Gelsinger.

Until Jesse died, gene therapy was a promising idea that had so far failed to deliver. As scientists map the human genome, they are literally tripping over mutations that cause rare genetic disorders, including OTC deficiency, Jesse's disease. The initial goal was simple: to cure, or prevent, these illnesses by replacing defective genes with healthy ones. Biotech companies have poured millions into research—not for rare hereditary disorders but for big-profit illnesses like cancer, heart disease, and AIDS. As of August, the government had reviewed 331 gene-therapy protocols involving more than 4,000 patients. Just 41 were for the "monogeneic," or single-gene, defect diseases whose patients so desperately hoped gene therapy would be their salvation.

At the same time, the science has progressed slowly; researchers have had trouble devising vectors that can carry genes to the right cells and get them to work once they are there. Four years ago, Dr. Harold Varmus, the director of the National Institutes of Health, commissioned a highly critical report about gene therapy chiding investigators for creating "the mistaken and widespread perception of success." Since then, there have been some accomplishments: a team at Tufts University has used gene therapy to grow new blood vessels for heart disease patients, for instance. But so far, gene therapy has not cured anyone. As Ruth Macklin, a bioethicist and member of the Recombinant DNA Advisory Committee, the National Institutes of Health panel that oversees gene-therapy research, says, bluntly, "Gene therapy is not yet therapy."

On December 8, the "RAC," as the committee is called, will begin a public inquiry into Jesse's death, as well as the safety of adenovirus, which has been used in roughly one-quarter of all gene-therapy clinical trials. The Penn scientists will report on their preliminary results, and investigators, who at the RAC's request have submitted thousands of pages of patient safety data to the committee, will discuss the side effects of adenovirus. Among them will be researchers from the Schering-Plough Corporation, which was running two experiments in advanced liver cancer patients that used methods similar to Penn's. Enrollment in those trials was suspended by the Food and Drug Administration after Jesse's death. The company, under pressure from the RAC, has since released information showing that some patients experienced serious side effects, including changes in liver function and blood cell counts, mental confusion and nausea; two experienced minor strokes, although one had a history of them. Once all the data on adenovirus are analyzed at the December 8 meeting, the RAC may recommend restrictions on its use, which will almost certainly slow down some aspects of gene-therapy research.

* * *

THE MEETING WILL BE IMPORTANT for another reason: it will mark an unprecedented public airing of information about the safety of gene therapy—precisely the kind of sharing the RAC has unsuccessfully sought in the past. Officials say gene therapy has claimed no lives besides Jesse's. But since his death, there have been news reports that other patients died during the course of experiments—from their diseases, as opposed to the therapy—and that the scientists involved did not report those deaths to the RAC, as is required. This has created a growing cloud of suspicion over gene therapy, raising questions about whether other scientists may have withheld information that could have prevented Jesse's death. That question cannot be answered until all the data are analyzed. But one thing is certain: four years after the field was rocked by Varmus's highly critical evaluation, it is now being rocked again, this time over an issue more fundamental than efficacy—safety. "I think it's a perilous time for gene therapy," says LeRoy Walters, a bioethicist at Georgetown University and former chairman of the RAC. "Until now, we have been able to say, 'Well, it hasn't helped many people, but at least it hasn't hurt people.' That has changed."

No one, perhaps, is more acutely aware of gene therapy's broken promise than Mark Batshaw, the pediatrician who proposed the experiment that cost Jesse Gelsinger his life.

At fifty-four, Batshaw, who left the University of Pennsylvania last year for Children's National Medical Center, in Washington, is tall and gangly with slightly stooped shoulders and a shy smile that gives him the air of an awkward schoolboy, which he once was. As a child, Batshaw struggled with hyperactivity: He didn't read until the third grade; in the fourth, his teacher grew so irritated at his constant chatter that she stuck his chair out in the hall. The experience has left him with a soft spot for developmentally disabled children, which is how he has become one of the world's foremost experts in urea-cycle disorders, among them OTC deficiency.

The urea cycle is a series of five liver enzymes that help rid the body of ammonia, a toxic breakdown product of protein. When these enzymes are missing or deficient, ammonia—"the same ammonia that you scrub your floors with," Batshaw explains—accumulates in the blood and travels to the brain, causing coma, brain damage, and death. OTC deficiency is the most common urea-cycle disorder, occurring in one out of every 40,000 births. Its genetic mutation occurs on the X chromosome, so women are typically carriers, while their sons suffer the disease.

Severe OTC deficiency is, Batshaw says, "a devastating disease." Typically, newborns slip into a coma within seventy-two hours of birth. Most suffer severe brain damage. Half die in the first month, and half of the survivors die by age five. Batshaw was a young post-doctoral fellow when he met his first urea-cycle–disorder patient in 1973, correctly diagnosing the disease at a time when most other doctors had never heard of it. Within two years, he and his colleagues had devised the first treatment, a low-protein formula called keto-acid. Later, they came up with what remains standard therapy to this day: sodium benzoate, a preservative, and another type of sodium, which bind to ammonia and help eliminate it from the body.

But the therapy cannot prevent the coma that is often the first sign of OTC and ravages the affected infant. By the time Batshaw joined the faculty at Penn in 1988, he was dreaming of a cure: gene therapy. Patients were dreaming, too, says Tish Simon, former co-president of the National Urea Cycle Disorders Foundation, whose son died of OTC deficiency three years ago. "All of us saw gene therapy as the hope for the future," Simon says. "And certainly, if anybody was going to do it, it had to be Mark Batshaw."

GENE THERAPY BECAME A REALITY on September 14, 1990, in a hospital room at the National Institutes of Health, in Bethesda, Maryland, when a four-year-old girl with a severe immune-system deficiency received a thirty minute infusion of white blood cells that had been engineered to contain copies of the gene she lacked. Rarely in modern medicine has an experiment been filled with so much hope; news of the treatment ricocheted off front pages around the world. The scientist who conducted it, Dr. W. French Anderson, quickly became known as the father of gene therapy. "We had got ourselves all hyped up," Anderson now admits, "thinking there would be rapid, quick, easy, early cures."

Among those keeping a close eye on Anderson's debut was Jim Wilson, a square-jawed, sandy-haired midwesterner who decided to follow his father's footsteps in medicine when he realized he wasn't going to make it in football. As a graduate student in biological chemistry, Wilson had taken a keen interest in rare genetic diseases. "All I did," he says, "was dream about gene therapy."

Today, as director of the Institute for Human Gene Therapy at the University of Pennsylvania, Wilson is in an excellent position to make that dream a reality. Headquartered in a century-old building amid the leafy maple trees and brick sidewalks of the picturesque Penn campus, the six-year-old institute, with 250 employees, state-of-the-art laboratories and a $25 million annual budget, is the largest academic gene-therapy program in the nation. In a field rife with big egos, Wilson is regarded as first-rate. "Present company excluded," Anderson says, "he's the best person in the field."

Batshaw was banging on Wilson's door even before Wilson arrived at Penn in March 1993, and within a month they were collaborating on studies of OTC-deficient mice. Their first task was to develop a vector. Adenovirus seemed a logical choice.

There had been some early problems with safety—a 1993 cystic fibrosis experiment was shut down when a patient was hospitalized with inflamed lungs—but Wilson and Batshaw say they figured out how to make a safer vector by deleting extra viral genes. Adenovirus was the right size: when its viral genes were excised, the OTC gene fit right in. It had a "ZIP code" on it, Batshaw says, that would carry it straight to the liver. And while its effects did not last, it worked quickly, which meant that it might be able to reverse a coma, sparing babies from brain damage. "It wasn't going to be a cure soon," Batshaw says, "but it might be a treatment soon."

The mouse experiments were encouraging. Mice that had the therapy survived for two to three months even while fed a high-protein diet. Those that lacked the treatment died. "It wasn't subtle," Wilson says. "We felt pretty compelled by that." But when the team contemplated testing in people, they ran smack into an ethical quandary: Who should be their subjects?

To Wilson, the answer seemed obvious: sick babies. Arthur Caplan, the university's resident bioethics expert, thought otherwise. Caplan says parents of dying infants are incapable of giving informed consent: "They are coerced by the disease of their child." He advised Wilson to test only stable adults, either female carriers or men like Jesse, with partial enzyme deficiencies. The National Urea Cycle Disorders Foundation agreed. When Batshaw turned up at their 1994 annual meeting asking for volunteers, so many mothers offered to be screened for the OTC gene that it took him four hours to draw all the blood.

BY THE TIME MARK BATSHAW and Jim Wilson submitted their experiment to the Recombinant DNA Advisory Committee for approval, the panel was in danger of being disbanded. Varmus, the NIH director, who won the Nobel Prize for his discovery of a family of cancer-causing genes, had made no secret of his distaste for the conduct of gene-therapy researchers. He thought the science was too shoddy to push forward with human testing, and it bothered him that so few experiments were focusing on genetic diseases. It irked him to have to sign off on protocols the RAC approved, and it irked him even more to see biotech companies touting those approvals, like some kind of NIH imprimatur, in the business pages of the papers. "Some days," says Dr. Nelson Wivel, the committee's former executive director, who now works for Wilson at Penn, "it felt as though the RAC was helping the biotech industry raise money. Dr. Varmus hated that."

At the same time, the pharmaceutical industry and AIDS activists were complaining that the RAC was redundant: the FDA already reviewed gene-therapy proposals. So in mid-1995, after seeking the advice of an expert panel, Varmus reorganized the RAC, slashing its membership from twenty-five to fifteen and stripping it of its approval authority—a decision that, some say, has enabled gene-therapy researchers to ignore the panel and keep information about safety to themselves. "The RAC," complains Dr. Robert Erickson, a University of Arizona medical geneticist who served on the panel, "became a debating society."

The Batshaw-Wilson protocol was among the last the committee would ever approve. The plan was for eighteen adults (nineteen eventually signed up, including Tish Simon, but the last patient was never treated, because of Jesse's death) to receive an infusion of the OTC gene, tucked inside an adenovirus vector, through a catheter in the hepatic artery, which leads to the liver. The goal was to find what Wilson calls "the maximum tolerated dose," one high enough to get the gene to work, but low enough to spare patients serious side effects. Subjects would be split into six groups of three, with each group receiving a slightly higher dose than the last. This is standard fare in safety testing. "You go up in small-enough increments," Wilson explains, "that you can pull the plug on the thing before people get hurt."

The experiment stood in stark contrast to others that had earned Varmus's scorn. It was paid for by NIH, which meant it had withstood the rigors of scientific peer review. It was aimed at a rare genetic disease, not cancer or AIDS. It was supported by plenty of animal research: Wilson and his team had performed more than twenty mouse experiments to test efficacy and a dozen safety studies on mice, rhesus monkeys and baboons. Still, it made Erickson, one of two scientists assigned by the RAC to review the experiment, uneasy.

He was troubled by data showing that three monkeys had died of a bloodclotting disorder and severe liver inflammation when they received an earlier, stronger version of the adenovirus vector at a dose twenty times the highest dose planned for the study. No one had injected adenovirus directly into the bloodstream before, either via the liver or otherwise, and the scientists admitted that it was difficult to tell precisely how people would respond. They planned to confine the infusion to the right lobe of the liver, so that if damage occurred it would be contained there, sparing the left lobe. And they outlined the major risks: bleeding, from either the gene-therapy site or a subsequent liver biopsy, which would require surgery; or serious liver inflammation, which could require an organ transplant and might lead to death.

Both Erickson and the other scientific reviewer thought the experiment was too risky to test on asymptomatic volunteers and recommended rejection. But in the end, Batshaw and Wilson prevailed. They offered up Caplan's argument that testing on babies was inappropriate. And they agreed to inject the vector into the bloodstream, as opposed to putting it directly into the liver. That decision, however, was later reversed by the FDA, which insisted that because the adenovirus would travel through the blood and wind up in the liver anyway, the original plan was safer.

The RAC, in such disarray from Varmus's reorganization that it did not meet again for another year, was never informed of the change. Jesse Gelsinger was seventeen when his pediatric geneticist, Dr. Randy Heidenreich, first told him about the Penn proposal. He wanted to sign up right away. But he had to wait until he was eighteen.

Paul Gelsinger was also enthusiastic. A trim forty-seven-year-old with intense blue eyes, Gelsinger, who makes his living as a handyman, gained custody of his four children nine years ago, when he divorced their mother, who suffers from manic depression. He had been having some difficulty with Jesse then; the boy was in the midst of an adolescent rebellion and was refusing to take his medicine. "I said: 'Wow, Jess, they're working on your disorder. Maybe they'll come up with a cure.'"

Jesse's was not a typical case of OTC deficiency: his mutation appears to have occurred spontaneously in the womb. His disease having been diagnosed when he was two, Jesse was what scientists call a mosaic—a small portion of his cells produced the missing enzyme. When he watched what he ate and took his medicine, he was fine. But one day last December, Paul Gelsinger arrived home to find his son curled up on the couch. He had been vomiting uncontrollably, a sign, Paul knew, that Jesse's ammonia was rising. Jesse landed in the hospital, comatose and on life support. When he recovered, he never missed another pill.

On June 18, the day Jesse turned eighteen, the Gelsingers—Paul, Mickie, and the children—flew to Philadelphia to see Paul's family. They played tourists, visiting the Liberty Bell and the Rocky statue, where Jesse was photographed, fists raised, a picture that would circulate in the newspapers after his death. On the twenty-second, they went to the University of Pennsylvania, where they met Raper, the surgeon, who explained the experiment and did blood and liver-function tests to see if Jesse was eligible. He was, and his treatment was scheduled for the fall. Jesse would be the youngest patient enrolled.

On September 9, Jesse returned to Philadelphia, this time alone. He took one duffel bag full of clothes and another full of wrestling videos. Paul Gelsinger planned to fly in a week later for the liver biopsy, which he considered the trial's most serious risk.

The treatment began on Monday, September 13. Jesse would receive the highest dose. Seventeen patients had already been treated, including one woman who had been given the same dose that Jesse would get, albeit from a different lot, and had done "quite well," Raper says. That morning, Jesse was taken to the interventional-radiology suite, where he was sedated and strapped to a table while a team of radiologists threaded two catheters into his groin. At 10:30 A.M., Raper drew 30 milliliters of the vector and injected it slowly. At half past noon, he was done.

That night, Jesse was sick to his stomach and spiked a fever, 104.5 degrees. Raper was not particularly surprised: other patients had experienced the same reaction. Paul Gelsinger called; he and Jesse talked briefly, exchanging I love yous. Those were the last words they ever spoke.

Early Tuesday morning a nurse called Raper at home; Jesse seemed disoriented. When Raper got to the hospital, about 6:15 A.M., he noticed that the whites of Jesse's eyes were yellow. That meant jaundice, not a good sign. "It was not something we had seen before," Raper says. A test confirmed that Jesse's bilirubin, a breakdown product of red blood cells, was four times the normal level. Raper called Gelsinger, and Batshaw in Washington, who said he would get on a train and be there in two hours.

Both doctors knew that the high bilirubin meant one of two things: either Jesse's liver was failing or he was suffering a clotting disorder in which his red blood cells were breaking down faster than the liver could metabolize them. This was the same disorder the scientists had seen in the monkeys that had been given the stronger vector. The condition is life-threatening for anyone, but particularly dangerous for someone with Jesse's disease, because red blood cells liberate protein when they break down.

By midafternoon Tuesday, a little more than twenty-four hours after the injection, the clotting disorder had pushed Jesse into a coma. By 11:30 P.M., his ammonia level was 393 micromoles per liter of blood. Normal is 35. The doctors began dialysis.

Paul Gelsinger had booked a red-eye flight. When he arrived in the surgical intensive care unit at 8:00 Wednesday morning, Raper and Batshaw told him that dialysis had brought Jesse's ammonia level down to 72 but that other complications were developing. He was hyperventilating, which would increase the level of ammonia in his brain. They wanted to paralyze his muscles and induce a deeper coma, so that a ventilator could breathe for him. Gelsinger gave consent. Then he put on scrubs, gloves, and a mask and went in to see his son.

By Wednesday afternoon, Jesse seemed to be stabilizing. Batshaw went back to Washington. Paul felt comfortable enough to meet his brother for dinner. But later that night Jesse worsened again. His lungs grew stiff; the doctors were giving him 100 percent oxygen, but not enough of it was getting to his bloodstream. They consulted a liver-transplant team and learned that Jesse was not a good candidate. Raper was beside himself. He consulted with Batshaw and Wilson, and they decided to take an extraordinary step, a procedure known as ECMO, for extracorporeal membrane oxygenation, essentially an external lung that filters the blood, removing carbon dioxide and adding oxygen.

It had been tried on only 1,000 people before, Raper says. Only half had survived.

"If we could just buy his lungs a day or two," Raper said later, they thought "maybe he would go ahead and heal up."

The next day, Thursday, September 16, Hurricane Floyd slammed into the East Coast. Mickie Gelsinger flew in from Tucson just before the airport closed. (Pattie Gelsinger, Jesse's mother, was being treated in a psychiatric facility and was unable to leave.) Batshaw spent the day trapped outside Baltimore on an Amtrak train. He ran down his cell phone calling Raper; when it went dead, he persuaded another passenger to lend him his. The ECMO, Raper reported, appeared to be working. But then another problem cropped up: Jesse's kidneys stopped making urine. "He was sliding into multiple-organ-system failure," Raper says.

That night, at his hotel, Paul Gelsinger couldn't sleep. He left his wife a note and walked the half mile to the Penn medical center to see Jesse. The boy was bloated beyond recognition; even his ears were swollen shut. Gelsinger noticed blood in Jesse's urine, an indication, he knew, that the kidneys were shutting down. How can anybody, he thought, survive this?

On the morning of Friday the seventeenth, a test showed that Jesse was brain dead. Paul Gelsinger didn't need to be told: "I knew it already." He called for a chaplain to hold a bedside service, with prayers for the removal of life support.

The room was crowded with equipment and people: seven of Paul's fifteen siblings came in, plus an array of doctors and nurses. Raper and Batshaw, shellshocked and exhausted, stood in the back. The chaplain anointed Jesse's forehead with oil, then read the Lord's Prayer. The doctors fought back tears.

When the intensive-care specialist flipped two toggle switches, one to turn off the ventilator and the other to turn off the ECMO machine, Raper stepped forward. He checked the heart-rate monitor, watched the line go flat and noted the time: 2:30 P.M. He put his stethoscope to Jesse's chest, more out of habit than necessity, and pronounced the death official. "Good-bye, Jesse," he said. "We'll figure this out."

WILSON REPORTED THE DEATH IMMEDIATELY, drawing praise from government officials but criticism from Arthur Caplan, who says they should have made the news public, in a news conference. In the weeks since, the Penn team has put every detail of Jesse's treatment under a microscope. It has rechecked the vector to make certain it was not tainted, tested the same lot on monkeys, reexamined lab and autopsy findings. Wilson's biggest fear was that Jesse died as a result of human error, but so far there has been no evidence of that. "That's what's so frightening," French Anderson says. "If they made a mistake, you would feel a little safer."

The death has rattled the three doctors in various ways. Wilson has asked himself over and over again whether he should have done anything differently. "At this point, I say no, but I'm continuing to re-evaluate constantly." He has been besieged by worry, about the morale of his staff, about whether his institute's financial sponsors would pull out, about whether patients would continue to volunteer, about whether he would lose his bravado—the death knell for a scientist on the cutting edge. "My concern," he confessed, over dinner one night in Philadelphia, "is, I'm going to get timid, that I'll get risk-averse."

Raper has thrown himself into his work, trying to live up to his promise to "figure this out." There are a number of possible explanations, he says: the vector may have reacted badly with Jesse's medication; Jesse's status as a mosaic may have played a role; or perhaps the early testing in monkeys, which showed that the stronger vector had deleterious side effects, was more of a harbinger of danger than the doctors realized. An answer may take months, but he is determined to find one; only by understanding what happened to Jesse, and how to prevent it in others, can the research continue. "That," Raper says, "would be the best tribute to Jesse."

Of the three, Batshaw seems to have taken it the hardest. He is not a particularly religious man, but a few days after Jesse died he went to synagogue to say Kaddish, the Jewish mourner's prayer. He struggles with the idea of personal responsibility. He has cradled many a dying child in his career, but never before, he says, has a patient been made worse by his care. "What is the Hippocratic oath?" Batshaw asks rhetorically, looking into the distance as his fingers drum the tabletop. He pauses, as if to steel himself, and says, "I did harm."

Paul Gelsinger does not hold the doctors responsible, although he is acutely interested in knowing what other scientists knew about adenovirus before Jesse died. He has experienced a deep spiritual awakening since losing his son; in dying, he says, Jesse taught him how to live. He speaks frequently of God, and of "purity of intent," which is his way of saying that Jesse demonstrated an altruism the rest of us might do well to emulate. "I hope," he said on the mountaintop that Sunday afternoon, "that I can die as well as my son has died."

2001

Editor: TIMOTHY FERRIS

FREEMAN J. DYSON

Science, Guided by Ethics, Can Lift Up the Poor

FROM *THE INTERNATIONAL HERALD TRIBUNE*

Innovations in biotechnology promise to transform our world for the better—but only, as the eminent physicist Freeman J. Dyson argues, if science maintains an ethical perspective.

THROUGHOUT HISTORY, PEOPLE HAVE USED TECHNOLogy to change the world. Our technology has been of two kinds, green and gray. Green technology is seeds and plants, gardens and vineyards and orchards, domesticated horses and cows and pigs, milk and cheese, leather and wool. Gray technology is bronze and steel, spears and guns, coal and oil and electricity, automobiles and airplanes and rockets, telephones and computers. Civilization began with green technology, with agriculture and animal-breeding, 10,000 years ago. Then, beginning about 3,000 years ago, gray technology became dominant, with mining and metallurgy and machinery. For the last 500 years, gray technology has been racing ahead and has given birth to the modern world of cities and factories and supermarkets.

The dominance of gray technology is coming to an end. During the last 50 years, we have achieved a fundamental understanding of the processes in living cells. With understanding comes the ability to exploit and control. Out of the knowledge acquired by modern biology, modern biotechnology is growing. The new green technology will give us the power, using only sunlight as a source of energy, and air and water and soil as materials, to manufacture and recycle chemicals of all kinds. Our gray technology of machines and computers will not disappear, but green technology will be moving ahead even faster.

Green technology can be cleaner, more flexible and less wasteful than our existing chemical industries. A great variety of manufactured objects could be grown instead of made. Green technology could supply human needs with far less damage to the natural environment. And green technology could be a great equalizer, bringing wealth to the tropical areas of the planet, which have most of the world's sunshine, people, and poverty. I am saying that green technology could do all these good things, not that green technology will do all these good things.

To make these good things happen, we need not only the new technology but the political and economic conditions that will give people all over the world a chance to use it. To make these things happen, we need a powerful push from ethics. We need a consensus of public opinion around the world that the existing gross inequalities in the distribution of wealth are intolerable. In reaching such a consensus, religions must play an essential role. Neither technology alone nor religion alone is powerful enough to bring social justice to human societies, but technology and religion working together might do the job.

We all know that green technology has a dark side, just as gray technology has a dark side. Gray technology brought us hydrogen bombs as well as telephones. Green technology brought us anthrax bombs as well as antibiotics. Besides the dangers of biological weapons, green technology brings other dangers having nothing to do with weapons. The ultimate danger of green technology comes from its power to change the nature of human beings by the application of genetic engineering to human embryos. If we allow a free market in human genes, wealthy parents will be able to buy what they consider superior genes for their babies. This could cause a splitting of humanity into hereditary castes. Within a few generations, the children of rich and poor could become separate species. Humanity would then have regressed all the way back to a society of masters and slaves. No matter how strongly we believe in the virtues of a free market economy, the free market must not extend to human genes.

I see two tremendous goods coming from biotechnology: first, the alleviation of human misery through progress in medicine, and second, the transformation of the global economy through green technology spreading wealth more equitably around the world. The two great evils to be avoided are the use of biological weapons and the corruption of human nature by buying and selling genes. I see no scientific reason why we should not achieve the good and avoid the evil. The obstacles to achieving the good are political rather than technical. Unfortunately a large number of people in many countries are strongly opposed to green technology, for reasons having little to do with the real dangers. It is important to treat the opponents with respect, to pay attention to their fears, to go gently into the new world of green technology so that neither human dignity nor religious conviction is violated. If we can go gently, we have a good chance of achieving within a hundred years the goals of ecological sustainability and social justice that green technology brings within our reach.

The great question for our time is how to make sure that the continuing scientific revolution brings benefits to everybody rather than widening the gap between rich and poor. To lift up poor countries, and poor people in rich countries, from poverty, technology is not enough. Technology must be guided and driven by ethics if it is to do more than provide new toys for the rich. Scientists and business leaders who care about social justice should join forces with environmental and religious organizations to give political clout to ethics. Science and religion should work together to abolish the gross inequalities that prevail in the modern world. That is my vision, and it is the same vision that inspired Francis Bacon 400 years ago, when he prayed that through science God would "endow the human family with new mercies."

Darwin's Influence on Modern Thought

FROM *SCIENTIFIC AMERICAN*

*Shortly before he died, Ernst Mayr (1904–2005), one of the twenti-
eth century's preeminent evolutionary biologists, eloquently summed
up how Darwin influenced not only science but nearly every area of
human thought.*

CLEARLY, OUR CONCEPTION OF THE WORLD AND OUR
place in it is, at the beginning of the 21st century, drastically
different from the zeitgeist at the beginning of the 19th century. But no consensus exists as to the source of this revolutionary
change. Karl Marx is often mentioned; Sigmund Freud has been in
and out of favor; Albert Einstein's biographer Abraham Pais made
the exuberant claim that Einstein's theories "have profoundly
changed the way modern men and women think about the phenomena of inanimate nature." No sooner had Pais said this, though, than

he recognized the exaggeration. "It would actually be better to say 'modern scientists' than 'modern men and women,'" he wrote, because one needs schooling in the physicist's style of thought and mathematical techniques to appreciate Einstein's contributions in their fullness. Indeed, this limitation is true for all the extraordinary theories of modern physics, which have had little impact on the way the average person apprehends the world.

The situation differs dramatically with regard to concepts in biology. Many biological ideas proposed during the past 150 years stood in stark conflict with what everybody assumed to be true. The acceptance of these ideas required an ideological revolution. And no biologist has been responsible for more—and for more drastic—modifications of the average person's worldview than Charles Darwin.

Darwin's accomplishments were so many and so diverse that it is useful to distinguish three fields to which he made major contributions: evolutionary biology; the philosophy of science; and the modern zeitgeist. Although I will be focusing on this last domain, for the sake of completeness I will put forth a short overview of his contributions—particularly as they inform his later ideas—to the first two areas.

A SECULAR VIEW OF LIFE

Darwin founded a new branch of life science, evolutionary biology. Four of his contributions to evolutionary biology are especially important, as they held considerable sway beyond that discipline. The first is the nonconstancy of species, or the modern conception of evolution itself. The second is the notion of branching evolution, implying the common descent of all species of living things on earth from a single unique origin. Up until 1859, all evolutionary proposals, such as that of naturalist Jean-Baptiste Lamarck, instead endorsed linear evolution, a teleological march toward greater perfection that had been in vogue since Aristotle's concept of *Scala Naturae*, the chain of being. Darwin further noted that evolution must be gradual, with no major breaks or discontinuities. Finally, he reasoned that the mechanism of evolution was natural selection.

These four insights served as the foundation of Darwin's founding of a new branch of the philosophy of science, a philosophy of biology. Despite the passing of a century before this new branch of philosophy fully developed, its eventual form is based on Darwinian concepts. For example, Darwin introduced historicity into science. Evolutionary biology, in contrast with physics and chemistry, is a historical science—the evolutionist attempts to explain events and processes that have already taken place. Laws and experiments are inappropriate techniques for the explication of such events and processes. Instead one constructs a historical narrative, consisting of a tentative reconstruction of the particular scenario that led to the events one is trying to explain.

For example, three different scenarios have been proposed for the sudden extinction of the dinosaurs at the end of the Cretaceous: a devastating epidemic; a catastrophic change of climate; and the impact of an asteroid, known as the Alvarez theory. The first two narratives were ultimately refuted by evidence incompatible with them. All the known facts, however, fit the Alvarez theory, which is now widely accepted. The testing of historical narratives implies that the wide gap between science and the humanities that so troubled physicist C. P. Snow is actually nonexistent—by virtue of its methodology and its acceptance of the time factor that makes change possible, evolutionary biology serves as a bridge.

The discovery of natural selection, by Darwin and Alfred Russel Wallace, must itself be counted as an extraordinary philosophical advance. The principle remained unknown throughout the more than 2,000-year history of philosophy ranging from the Greeks to Hume, Kant, and the Victorian era. The concept of natural selection had remarkable power for explaining directional and adaptive changes. Its nature is simplicity itself. It is not a force like the forces described in the laws of physics; its mechanism is simply the elimination of inferior individuals. This process of nonrandom elimination impelled Darwin's contemporary, philosopher Herbert Spencer, to describe evolution with the now familiar term "survival of the fittest." (This description was long ridiculed as circular reasoning: "Who are the fittest? Those who survive." In reality, a careful analysis can usually determine why certain individuals fail to thrive in a given set of conditions.)

The truly outstanding achievement of the principle of natural selection is that it makes unnecessary the invocation of "final causes"— that is, any teleological forces leading to a particular end. In fact, nothing is predetermined. Furthermore, the objective of selection even may change from one generation to the next, as environmental circumstances vary.

A diverse population is a necessity for the proper working of natural selection. (Darwin's success meant that typologists, for whom all members of a class are essentially identical, were left with an untenable viewpoint.) Because of the importance of variation, natural selection should be considered a two-step process: the production of abundant variation is followed by the elimination of inferior individuals. This latter step is directional. By adopting natural selection, Darwin settled the several-thousand-year-old argument among philosophers over chance or necessity. Change on the earth is the result of both, the first step being dominated by randomness, the second by necessity.

Darwin was a holist: for him the object, or target, of selection was primarily the individual as a whole. The geneticists, almost from 1900 on, in a rather reductionist spirit preferred to consider the gene the target of evolution. In the past 25 years, however, they have largely returned to the Darwinian view that the individual is the principal target. For 80 years after 1859, bitter controversy raged as to which of four competing evolutionary theories was valid. "Transmutation" was the establishment of a new species or new type through a single mutation, or saltation. "Orthogenesis" held that intrinsic teleological tendencies led to transformation.

Lamarckian evolution relied on the inheritance of acquired characteristics. And now there was Darwin's variational evolution, through natural selection. Darwin's theory clearly emerged as the victor during the evolutionary synthesis of the 1940s, when the new discoveries in genetics were married with taxonomic observations concerning systematics, the classification of organisms by their relationships. Darwinism is now almost unanimously accepted by knowledgeable evolutionists. In addition, it has become the basic component of the new philosophy of biology.

A most important principle of the new biological philosophy, undiscovered for almost a century after the publication of *On the Origin of Species*, is the dual nature of biological processes. These activities are governed both by the universal laws of physics and chemistry and by a genetic program, itself the result of natural selection, which has molded the genotype for millions of generations.

The causal factor of the possession of a genetic program is unique to living organisms, and it is totally absent in the inanimate world. Because of the backward state of molecular and genetic knowledge in his time, Darwin was unaware of this vital factor.

Another aspect of the new philosophy of biology concerns the role of laws. Laws give way to concepts in Darwinism. In the physical sciences, as a rule, theories are based on laws; for example, the laws of motion led to the theory of gravitation. In evolutionary biology, however, theories are largely based on concepts such as competition, female choice, selection, succession, and dominance. These biological concepts, and the theories based on them, cannot be reduced to the laws and theories of the physical sciences. Darwin himself never stated this idea plainly. My assertion of Darwin's importance to modern thought is the result of an analysis of Darwinian theory over the past century. During this period, a pronounced change in the methodology of biology took place. This transformation was not caused exclusively by Darwin, but it was greatly strengthened by developments in evolutionary biology. Observation, comparison, and classification, as well as the testing of competing historical narratives, became the methods of evolutionary biology, outweighing experimentation.

I do not claim that Darwin was single-handedly responsible for all the intellectual developments in this period. Much of it, like the refutation of French mathematician and physicist Pierre-Simon Laplace's determinism, was "in the air." But Darwin in most cases either had priority or promoted the new views most vigorously.

THE DARWINIAN ZEITGEIST

A 21st-century person looks at the world quite differently than a citizen of the Victorian era did. This shift had multiple sources, particularly the incredible advances in technology. But what is not at all appreciated is the great extent to which this shift in thinking indeed resulted from Darwin's ideas.

Remember that in 1850 virtually all leading scientists and philosophers were Christian men. The world they inhabited had been created by God, and as the natural theologians claimed, He had instituted wise laws that brought about the perfect adaptation of all organisms to one another and to their environment. At the same time, the architects of the scientific revolution had constructed a world-view based on physicalism (a reduction to spatiotemporal things or events or their properties), teleology, determinism, and other basic principles. Such was the thinking of Western man prior to the 1859 publication of *On the Origin of Species*. The basic principles proposed by Darwin would stand in total conflict with these prevailing ideas.

First, Darwinism rejects all supernatural phenomena and causations. The theory of evolution by natural selection explains the adaptedness and diversity of the world solely materialistically. It no longer requires God as creator or designer (although one is certainly still free to believe in God even if one accepts evolution). Darwin pointed out that creation, as described in the Bible and the origin accounts of other cultures, was contradicted by almost any aspect of the natural world. Every aspect of the "wonderful design" so admired by the natural theologians could be explained by natural selection. (A closer look also reveals that design is often not so wonderful—see "Evolution and the Origins of Disease," by Randolph M. Nesse and George C. Williams, *Scientific American*, November 1998.) Eliminating God from science made room for strictly scientific explanations of all natural phenomena; it gave rise to positivism; it produced a powerful intellectual and spiritual revolution, the effects of which have lasted to this day.

Second, Darwinism refutes typology. From the time of the Pythagoreans and Plato, the general concept of the diversity of the world emphasized its invariance and stability. This viewpoint is called typology, or essentialism. The seeming variety, it was said, consisted of a limited number of natural kinds(essences or types), each one forming a class. The members of each class were thought to be identical, constant, and sharply separated from the members of other essences.

Variation, in contrast, is nonessential and accidental. A triangle illustrates essentialism: all triangles have the same fundamental characteristics and are sharply delimited against quadrangles or any other geometric figures. An intermediate between a triangle and a quadrangle is inconceivable. Typological thinking, therefore, is unable to accommodate variation and gives rise to a misleading conception of human races. For the typologist, Caucasians, Africans, Asians, or Inuits are types that conspicuously differ from other human ethnic groups. This mode of thinking leads to racism. (Although the ignorant misapplication of evolutionary theory known as "social Darwinism" often gets blamed for justifications of racism, adherence to the disproved essentialism preceding Darwin in fact can lead to a racist viewpoint.)

Darwin completely rejected typological thinking and introduced instead the entirely different concept now called population thinking. All groupings of living organisms, including humanity, are populations that consist of uniquely different individuals. No two of the six billion humans are the same. Populations vary not by their essences but only by mean statistical differences. By rejecting the constancy of populations, Darwin helped to introduce history into scientific thinking and to promote a distinctly new approach to explanatory interpretation in science.

Third, Darwin's theory of natural selection made any invocation of teleology unnecessary. From the Greeks onward, there existed a universal belief in the existence of a teleological force in the world that led to ever greater perfection. This "final cause" was one of the causes specified by Aristotle. After Kant, in the *Critique of Judgment*, had unsuccessfully attempted to describe biological phenomena with the help of a physicalist Newtonian explanation, he then invoked teleological forces. Even after 1859, teleological explanations (orthogenesis) continued to be quite popular in evolutionary biology. The acceptance of the *Scala Naturae* and the explanations of natural theology were other manifestations of the popularity of teleology. Darwinism swept such considerations away.

(The designation "teleological" actually applied to various different phenomena. Many seemingly end-directed processes in inorganic nature are the simple consequence of natural laws—a stone falls or a heated piece of metal cools because of laws of physics, not some end-directed process. Processes in living organisms owe their apparent goal-directedness to the operation of an inborn genetic or acquired program. Adapted systems, such as the heart or kidneys, may engage in activities that can be considered goal seeking, but the systems themselves were acquired during evolution and are continuously finetuned by natural selection. Finally, there was a belief in cosmic teleology, with a purpose and predetermined goal ascribed to everything in nature. Modern science, however, is unable to substantiate the existence of any such cosmic teleology.)

Fourth, Darwin does away with determinism. Laplace notoriously boasted that a complete knowledge of the current world and all its processes would enable him to predict the future to infinity. Darwin, by comparison, accepted the universality of randomness and chance throughout the process of natural selection. (Astronomer and philosopher John Herschel referred to natural selection contemptuously as "the law of the higgledy-piggledy.") That chance should play an important role in natural processes has been an unpalatable thought for many physicists. Einstein expressed this distaste in his statement, "God does not play dice." Of course, as previously mentioned, only the first step in natural selection, the production of variation, is a matter of chance. The character of the second step, the actual selection, is to be directional.

Despite the initial resistance by physicists and philosophers, the role of contingency and chance in natural processes is now almost universally acknowledged. Many biologists and philosophers deny the existence of universal laws in biology and suggest that all regularities be stated in probabilistic terms, as nearly all so-called biological laws have exceptions. Philosopher of science Karl Popper's famous test of falsification therefore cannot be applied in these cases.

Fifth, Darwin developed a new view of humanity and, in turn, a new anthropocentrism. Of all of Darwin's proposals, the one his contemporaries found most difficult to accept was that the theory of common descent applied to Man. For theologians and philosophers alike, Man was a creature above and apart from other living beings. Aristotle, Descartes, and Kant agreed on this sentiment, no matter how else their thinking diverged. But biologists Thomas Huxley and Ernst Haeckel revealed through rigorous comparative anatomical study that humans and living apes clearly had common ancestry, an assessment that has never again been seriously questioned in science. The application of the theory of common descent to Man deprived man of his former unique position.

Ironically, though, these events did not lead to an end to anthropocentrism. The study of man showed that, in spite of his descent, he is indeed unique among all organisms. Human intelligence is unmatched by that of any other creature. Humans are the only animals with true language, including grammar and syntax. Only humanity, as Darwin emphasized, has developed genuine ethical systems. In addition, through high intelligence, language, and long parental care, humans are the only creatures to have created a rich culture. And by these means, humanity has attained, for better or worse, an unprecedented dominance over the entire globe.

Sixth, Darwin provided a scientific foundation for ethics. The question is frequently raised—and usually rebuffed—as to whether evolution adequately explains healthy human ethics. Many wonder how, if selection rewards the individual only for behavior that enhances his own survival and reproductive success, such pure selfishness can lead to any sound ethics. The widespread thesis of social Darwinism, promoted at the end of the 19th century by Spencer, was that evolutionary explanations were at odds with the development of ethics.

We now know, however, that in a social species not only the individual must be considered—an entire social group can be the target of selection. Darwin applied this reasoning to the human species in 1871 in *The Descent of Man*. The survival and prosperity of a social group depends to a large extent on the harmonious cooperation of the members of the group, and this behavior must be based on altruism. Such altruism, by furthering the survival and prosperity of the group, also indirectly benefits the fitness of the group's individuals. The result amounts to selection favoring altruistic behavior.

Kin selection and reciprocal helpfulness in particular will be greatly favored in a social group. Such selection for altruism has been demonstrated in recent years to be widespread among many other social animals. One can then perhaps encapsulate the relation between ethics and evolution by saying that a propensity for altruism and harmonious cooperation in social groups *is* favored by natural selection. The old thesis of social Darwinism—strict selfishness—was based on an incomplete understanding of animals, particularly social species.

THE INFLUENCE OF NEW CONCEPTS

Let me now try to summarize my major findings. No educated person any longer questions the validity of the so-called theory of evolution, which we now know to be a simple fact. Likewise, most of Darwin's particular theses have been fully confirmed, such as that of common descent, the gradualism of evolution, and his explanatory theory of natural selection.

I hope I have successfully illustrated the wide reach of Darwin's ideas. Yes, he established a philosophy of biology by introducing the time factor, by demonstrating the importance of chance and contingency, and by that theories in evolutionary biology are based on concepts rather than laws. But furthermore—and this is perhaps Darwin's greatest contribution—he developed a set of new principles that influence the thinking of every person: the living world, through evolution, can be explained without recourse to supernaturalism; essentialism or typology is invalid, and we must adopt population thinking, in which all individuals are unique (vital for education and the refutation of racism); natural selection, applied to social groups, is indeed sufficient to account for the origin and maintenance of altruistic ethical systems; cosmic teleology, an intrinsic process leading life automatically to ever greater perfection, is fallacious, with all seemingly teleological phenomena explicable by purely material processes; and determinism is thus repudiated, which places our fate squarely in our own evolved hands.

To borrow Darwin's phrase, there is grandeur in this view of life. New modes of thinking have been, and are being, evolved. Almost every component in modern man's belief system is somehow affected by Darwinian principles.

2002

Editor: MATT RIDLEY

Dr. Daedalus

FROM *HARPER'S MAGAZINE*

> *Whether it's a skin graft for a burn victim or a face-lift for an aging movie star, plastic surgery works in the realm that most affects our identity: our appearance. The writer and psychologist Lauren Slater profiles a plastic surgeon in Massachusetts whose radical ideas go well beyond the cosmetic—and confront our basic sense of what it means to be human.*

PART I: BEAUTIFUL PEOPLE

Joe Rosen, plastic surgeon at the renowned Dartmouth-Hitchcock Medical Center, and by any account an odd man, has a cold. But then again, he isn't sure it's a cold. "It could be anthrax," he says as he hurries to the car, beeper beeping, sleet sleeting, for it's a freezing New England midwinter day when all the world is white. Joe Rosen's nose is running, his throat is raw, and he's being called into the ER because some guy made meat out of his forefinger and a beautiful teenager split her fine forehead open on the windshield of her SUV. It seems unfair, he says, all these calls coming in on a Sunday, especially because he's sick and he isn't sure whether it's the flu or the first subtle signs of a biological attack. "Are you serious?" I say to him. Joe Rosen is smart. He graduated cum laude from Cornell and got a medical degree from Stanford in 1978. And we're in his car now, speeding toward the hospital where he reconstructs faces, appends limbs, puffs and preens the female form. "You really wonder," I say, "if your cold is a sign of a terrorist attack?"

Joe Rosen, a respected and controversial plastic surgeon, wonders a lot of things, some of them directly related to his field, others not. Joe Rosen wonders, for instance, whether Osama bin Laden introduced the West Nile virus to this country. Joe Rosen wonders how much bandwidth it would take to make virtual-reality contact lenses available for all. Joe Rosen wonders why both his ex-wife and his current wife are artists, and what that says about his deeper interests. Joe Rosen also wonders why we insist on the kinds of conservative medical restraints that prevent him from deploying some of his most creative visions: wings for human beings; cochlear implants to enhance hearing, beefing up our boring ears and giving us the range of an owl; super-duper delicate rods to jazz up our vision—binocular, beautiful—so that we could see for many miles and into depths as well. Joe Rosen has ideas: implants for this, implants for that, gadgets, gears, discs, buttons, sculpting soft cartilage that would enable us, as humans, to cross the frontiers of our own flesh and emerge as something altogether . . . what? Something other.

And we're in the car now, speeding on slick roads toward the hospital, beeper beeping, sleet sleeting, passing cute country houses with gingerbread trim, dollops of smoke hanging above bright brick chimneys; his New Hampshire town looks so sweet. We pull into the medical center. Even this has a slight country flair to it, with gingham curtains hanging in the rows of windows. We skid. Rosen says, "One time I was in my Ford Explorer with my daughter, Sam. We rolled, and the next thing I knew we were on the side of the highway, hanging upside down like bats." He laughs. We go in. I am excited, nervous, running by his bulky side with my tape recorder to his mouth. A resident in paper boots comes up to us. He eyes the tape recorder, and Rosen beams. Rosen is a man who enjoys attention, credentials. A few days ago he boasted to me, "You shouldn't have any trouble with the PR people in this hospital. I've had three documentaries made of me here already."

"Can I see them?" I asked.

"I don't know," Rosen answered, suddenly scratching his nose very fast. "I guess I'm not sure where I put them," and something about his voice, or his nose, made me wonder whether the documentaries were just a tall tale.

Now the resident rushes up to us, peers at the tape recorder, peers at me. "They're doing a story on me," Rosen says. "For *Harper's*."

"Joe is a crazy man, a nutcase," the resident announces, but there's affection in his voice.

"Why the beeps?" Rosen asks.

"This guy, he was working in his shop, got his finger caught in an electric planer. The finger's hamburger," the resident says. "It's just hamburger."

We go to the carpenter's cubicle. He's a man with a burly beard and sawdust-caked boots. He lies too big for the ER bed, his dripping finger held high in the air and splinted. It does look like hamburger.

I watch Rosen approach the bed, the wound. Rosen is a largish man, with a curly head of hair, wearing a Nordstrom wool coat and a cashmere scarf. As a plastic surgeon, he thinks grand thoughts but traffics mostly in the mundane. He has had over thirty papers published, most of them with titles like "Reconstructive Flap Surgery" or "Rhinoplasty for the Adolescent." He is known among his colleagues only secondarily for his epic ideas; his respect in the field is rooted largely in his impeccable surgical skill with all the toughest cases: shotgunned faces, smashed hands.

"How ya doin'?" Rosen says now to the carpenter. The carpenter doesn't answer. He just stares at his mashed finger, held high in the splint.

Rosen speaks softly, gently. He puts his hand on the woodworker's dusty shoulder. "Looks bad," he says, and he says this with a kind of simplicity—or is it empathy?—that makes me listen. The patient nods. "I need my finger," he says, and his voice sounds tight with tears. "I need it for the work I do."

Rosen nods. His tipsiness, his grandiosity, seem to just go away. He stands close to the man. "Look," he says, "I'm not going to do anything fancy right now, okay? I'll just have my guys sew it up, and we'll try to let nature take its course. I think that's the best thing, right now. To let nature take its course."

The carpenter nods. Rosen has said nothing really reassuring, but his tone is soothing, his voice rhythmic, a series of stitches that promises to knit the broken together.

We leave the carpenter. Down the hall, the teenage beauty lies in still more serious condition, the rent in her forehead so deep we can see, it seems, the barest haze of her brain.

"God," whispers Rosen as we enter the room. "I dislike foreheads. They get infected so easily."

He touches the girl. "You'll be fine," he says. "We're not going to do anything fancy here. Just sew you up and let nature take its course."

I think these are odd, certainly unexpected words coming from a man who seems so relentlessly anti-nature, so visionary and futuristic in his interests. But then again, Rosen himself is odd, a series of swerves, a topsy-turvy, upside-down, smoke-and-mirrors sort of surgeon, hanging in his curious cave, a black bat.

"I like this hospital," Rosen announces to me as we leave the girl's room. "I like its MRI machines." He pauses.

"I should show you a real marvel," he suddenly says. He looks around him. A nurse rushes by, little dots of blood on her snowy smock. "Come," Rosen says.

We ride the elevator up. The doors whisper open. Outside, the sleet has turned to snow, falling fast and furious. The floor we're on is ominously quiet, as though there are no patients here, or as though we're in a morgue. Rosen is ghoulish and I am suddenly scared. I don't know him really. I met him at a medical-ethics convention at which he discussed teaching *Frankenstein* to his residents and elaborated, with a little light in his eye, on the inherent beauty in hybrids and chimeras, if only we could learn to see them that way. "Why do we only value the average?" he'd asked the audience. "Why are plastic surgeons dedicated only to restoring our current notions of the conventional, as opposed to letting people explore, if they want, what the possibilities are?"

Rosen went on to explain other things at that conference. It was hard for me to follow his train of thought. He vacillates between speaking clearly, almost epically, to mumbling and zigzagging and scratching his nose. At this conference he kangaroo-leapt from subject to subject: the army, biowarfare, chefs with motorized fingers that could whip eggs, noses that doubled as flashlights, soldiers with sonar, the ocean, the monsters, the marvels. He is a man of breadth but not necessarily depth. "According to medieval man," Rosen said to the convention, finally coming clear, "a monster is someone born with congenital deformities. A marvel," he explained, "is a person with animal parts—say, a tail or wings." He went on to show us pictures, a turn-of-the-century newborn hand with syphilitic sores all over it, the fingers webbed in a way that might have been beautiful but not to me, the pearly skin stretched to nylon netting in the crotch of each crooked digit.

And the floor we're on now is ominously quiet, except for a hiss somewhere, maybe some snake somewhere, with a human head. We walk for what seems a long time. My tape recorder sucks up the silence.

Rosen turns, suddenly, and with a flourish parts the curtains of a cubicle. Before me, standing as though he were waiting for our arrival, is a man, a real man, with a face beyond description. "Sweeny,"* Rosen says, gesturing toward the man, "has cancer of the face. It ate through his sinus cavities, so I scraped off his face, took off his tummy fat, and made a kind of, well, a new face for him out of the stomach. Sweeny, you look good!" Rosen says.

Sweeny, his new face, or his old stomach, oozing and swollen from this recent, radical surgery, nods. He looks miserable. The belly-face sags, the lips wizened and puckered like an anus, the eyes in their hills of fat darting fast and frightened.

*Not his real name

"What about my nose?" Sweeny says, and then I notice: Sweeny has no nose. The cancer ate that along with the cheeks, etc. This is just awful. "That comes next. We'll use what's left of your forehead." A minute later, Rosen turns to me and observes that pretty soon women will be able to use their buttocks for breast implants. "Where there's fat," Rosen says, "there are possibilities."

THE COFFEE IS HOT AND GOOD. We drink it in the hospital cafeteria while we wait for the weather to clear. "You know," Rosen says, "I'm really proud of that face. I didn't follow any protocol. There's no textbook to tell you how to fashion a face eaten away by cancer. Plastic surgery is the intersection of art and science. It's the intersection of the surgeon's imagination with human flesh. And human flesh," Rosen says, "is infinitely malleable. People say cosmetic surgery is frivolous—boobs and noses. But it's so much more than that! The body is a conduit for the soul, at least historically speaking. When you change what you look like, you change who you are."

I nod. The coffee, actually, is too damn hot. The delicate lining of skin inside my mouth starts to shred. The burn-pain distracts me. I have temporarily altered my body, and thus my mind. For just one moment, I am a burned-girl, not a writer-girl. Rosen may be correct. With my tongue I flick the loose skin, picture it, pink and silky, on fire.

NO, PLASTIC SURGERY IS NOT just boobs and noses. Its textbooks are tomes—thick, dusty, or slick, no matter—that all open up to images of striated muscle excised from its moorings, bones—white, calcium-rich—elongated by the doctor's finest tools. Plastic surgery, as a medical specialty, is very confusing. It aims, on the one hand, to restore deformities and, on the other hand, to alter the normal. Therefore, the patients are a motley crew. There is the gorgeous blonde with the high sprayed helmet of hair who wants a little tummy tuck, even though she's thin, and then there is the Apert Syndrome child, the jaw so foreshortened the teeth cannot root in their sockets. Plastic surgery—like Rosen, its premier practitioner—is flexible, highminded, and wide-ranging, managing to be at once utterly necessary and ridiculously frivolous, all in the same breath, all in the same scalpel.

According to the American Society of Plastic Surgeons, last year more than 1.3 million people had cosmetic surgery performed by board-certified plastic surgeons, an increase of 227 percent since 1992. (These numbers do not include medically necessary or reconstructive surgeries.) The five most popular procedures were liposuction (229,588), breast augmentation (187,755), eyelid surgery (172,244), the just available Botox injections (118,452), and face lifts (70,882). Most cosmetic surgeries are performed on women, but men are catching up: the number of men receiving nose jobs—their most popular procedure—has increased 141 percent since 1997. The vast majority of patients are white, but not necessarily wealthy. A 1994 study found that 65 percent of cosmetic-surgery patients had a family income of less than $50,000, even though neither state nor private health insurance covers the cost of cosmetic surgeries. These figures alone point to the tremendous popularity and increasing acceptance of body alteration, and suggest that the slippery slope from something as bizarre as eyelid tucks to something still more bizarre, like wings, may be shorter than we think.

This medical specialty is ancient, dating back to 800 B.C., when hieroglyphics describe crude skin grafts. Rosen once explained to me that plastic surgery started as a means to blur racial differences. "A long time ago," he'd said, "Jewish slaves had clefts in their ears. And some of the first plastic surgery operations were to remove those signs of stigma."

One history book mentions the story of a doctor named Joseph Dieffenbach and a man with grave facial problems. This man had the sunken nose of syphilis, a disease widely associated with immorality. Dieffenbach, one of the fathers of plastic surgery, so the story goes, devised a gold rhinoplasty bridge for this marginal man, thus giving him, literally, a Midas nose and proving, indeed, that medicine can make criminals kings.

As a field, plastic surgery is troubled, insecure. It is a lot like psychiatry, or dentistry, in its inferior status as a subspecialty of medicine. In fact, the first plastic-surgery association, started in 1921, was an offshoot of oral practitioners. Read: teeth people. Not to digress, but the other day I woke up with a terrible toothache and rushed in to see a dentist. I said to him, just to be friendly, "What sort of training do you need for your profession?" He said, "You need A LOT of training, believe me. I trained with the same guys who cure your cancer, but I don't get the same respect."

I wonder if Rosen ever feels like my dentist, and if that's why he's so grandiose, like the little boy who is a bully. Sander Gilman, a cultural critic of plastic surgery, writes that, in this group of doctors, there are a lot of big words thrown around in an effort to cover up the sneaking suspicion that their interventions are not important. One is not ever supposed to say "nose job"; it's called rhinoplasty. Gilman writes, "The lower the perceived status of a field . . . the more complex and 'scientific' the discourse of the field becomes."

Of course, I rarely meet a doctor who doesn't like jargon and doesn't like power. Rosen may be different only in intensity. "I'm not a cosmetic surgeon," Rosen keeps repeating to me.

He says, "Really, there's no such thing as just cosmetic surgery. The skin and the soul are one." On paper, maybe, this comment seems a little overblown, but delivered orally, in a New England town when all the world is white, it has its lyrical appeal.

When Rosen cries out that he's not "just a cosmetic surgeon," he's put his finger on a real conflict in his field. Where does necessary reconstruction end and frivolous interventions begin? Are those interventions really frivolous, or are they emblematic of the huge and sometimes majestic human desire to alter, to transcend? If medicine is predicated upon the notion of making the sick well, and a plastic surgeon operates on someone who is not sick, then can the patient truly be called a patient, and the doctor a doctor? Who pays for this stuff, when, where, and how? These are the swirling questions. Over a hundred years ago Jacques Joseph, another of plastic surgery's founding fathers, wrote that beauty was a medical necessity because a person's looks can create social and economic barriers. Repairing the deformity, therefore, allows the man to function in a fully healthy way in society. Voilà. Function and form, utilitarianism and aestheticism, joined at the hip, grafted together: skin tight.

PERHAPS WE CAN ACCEPT JOSEPH'S formulation. Okay, we say. Calm down. We say this to all the hopping, hooting cosmetic surgeons who want to stake out their significance. Okay, we respect you. I'd like to say this to Rosen, but I can't. Rosen's ideas and aspirations, not to mention his anthrax concerns, go beyond what I am comfortable with, though I can't quite unearth the architecture of my concerns. After all, he doesn't want to hurt anyone. Maybe it's because Rosen isn't just talking about everyday beauty and its utilitarian aspects. He is talking EXTREMES. When Rosen thinks of beauty, he thinks of the human form stretched on the red-hot rack of his imagination, which is mired in medieval texts and books on trumpeter swans. At its outermost limits, beauty becomes fantastical, perhaps absurd. Here is where Rosen rests. He dreams of making wings for human beings. He has shown me blue-prints, sketches of the scalpel scissoring into skin, stretching flaps of torso fat to fashion gliders piped with rib bone. When the arm stretches, the gliders unfold, and human floats on currents of air. Is he serious? At least partially. He gives lectures to medical students on the meaning of wings from an engineering perspective, a surgeon's perspective, and a patient's perspective. He has also thought of cochlear implants to enhance normal hearing, fins to make us fishlike, and echolocation devices so that we can better navigate the night. He does not understand the limits we place on hands. He once met a Vietnamese man with two thumbs on one hand. This man was a waiter, and his two thumbs made him highly skilled at his job. "Now," says Rosen, "if that man came to me and said, 'I want you to take off my extra thumb,' I'd be allowed, but I wouldn't be allowed to put an extra thumb on a person, and that's not fair."

We can call Rosen ridiculous, a madman, a monster, a marvel. We could dismiss him as a techno geek or a fool or just plain immature. But then there are the facts. First of all, Rosen is an influential man, an associate professor of surgery at Dartmouth Medical School and the director of the Plastic Surgery Residency Program at the medical center. He was senior fellow at the C. Everett Koop Institute from 1997 to 1998, and he has also served on advisory panels for the navy and for NASA's Medical Care for the Mission to Mars, 2018. Rosen consults for the American Academy of Sciences committee on the role of virtual-reality technology, and he is the former director of the Department of Defense's Emerging Technology Threats work-force. In other words, this is a man taken seriously by some serious higher-ups. "Echolocation devices," Rosen explains, "implanted in a soldier's head, could do a lot to enhance our military capacity." And this isn't just about the army's fantasies of the perfect soldier. Rosen travels worldwide (he gave over a dozen presentations last year) and has had substantial impact not only scalpeling skin but influencing his colleagues' ethics in a myriad of ways. "He has been essential in helping me to conceptualize medicine outside of the box," says Charles Lucey, MD, a former colleague of Rosen's at the Dartmouth Medical School. John Harris, a medical-ethics specialist in Man-chester, England, writes in *Wonderwoman and Superman* that "in the absence of an argument or the ability to point to some specific harm that might be involved in crossing species boundaries, we should regard the objections *per se* to such practices as mere and gratuitous prejudice." Rosen himself says, "Believe me. Wings are not way off. It is not a bad idea. Who would have thought we'd ever agree to hold expensive, potentially dangerous radioactive devices up to our ears for hours on end, day after day, just so we could gossip. That's cell phones for you," he says. And smiles.

Rosen has a nice smile. It's, to be sure, a little boyish, but it's charming. Sometimes Rosen is shy. "I mumble a lot," he acknowl-edges. "I don't really like people. I don't really like the present. I am a man who lives in the past and in the future only."

Now we leave the emergency room. The snow has stopped. The roads are membraned with ice. The sun is setting in the New Hamp-shire sky, causing the hills to sparkle as though they're full of little lights and other electric things. We drive back to his house, slowly. The emergencies are over, the patients soothed or suffering, he has done what can be done in a day, and still his nose runs. He coughs into his fist. "Truth be told," he says to me, "I didn't start out wanting to be a surgeon, even though I always, ALWAYS, had big ideas. In kindergarten, when the other kids were making these little ditsy arts-and-crafts projects, I was building a room-size Seventh Fleet ship." He goes on. As a child he wanted to be an artist. In high school he became obsessed with Picasso's *Guernica* and spent months trying to replicate it in the style of Van Gogh. As a freshman at Cornell, he made a robotic hand that could crack his lobster for him, and from then on it was hands, fingers, knees, and toes. His interests in the technical aspects of the body drew him away from the arts and eventually into medical school, which was, in his mind, somewhere between selling out and moving on.

We pull into his driveway. Rosen lives in a sprawling ranch-style house. He has a pet hen, who waits for us in the evergreen tree. His second wife, Stina Kohnke, is young and, yes, attractive. I'm afraid to ask how old she is; he looks to be at least fifty-three and she looks twenty-three, though maybe that's beside the point. Nevertheless, it all gets thrown into my mental stew: grandiose man, military man, medicine man, wants to make wings, young thing for a mate. Rooster and hen. Maybe there is no story here. Maybe there's just parody. All breadth, no depth. Except for this. Everyone I tell about Rosen and his wings, his *fin de siècle* mind, widens his or her eyes, leans forward, and says, "You're kidding." People want to hear more. *I* want to hear more. His ideas of altering the human form are repugnant and delicious, and that's a potent combination to unravel. And who among us has not had flying dreams, lifted high, dramatically free, a throat-catching fluidity in our otherwise aching form, above the ocean, all green, like moving marble?

ROSEN AND HIS WIFE HAVE invited me for dinner. I accept. Stina is an artist. Her work is excellent. "Joe is an inspiration for me," she says. "He brings home pictures of his patients, and I sculpt their limbs from bronze." In her studio, she has a riot of red-bronze deformed hands clutching, reaching, in an agony of stiffness. She has fashioned drawer pulls from gold-plated ears. You go to open the breadbox, the medicine cabinet, the desk drawer, and you have to touch these things. It's at once creepy and very beautiful.

We sit at their stone dining-room table. Behind us is a seventy-gallon aquarium full of fish. Cacti, pink and penile, thrust their way into the odd air. Stina, homesick for her native California, has adorned the living room with paper palm trees and tiny live parakeets. We talk. Stina says, "Joe and I got married because we found in each other the same aesthetic and many moral equivalents. We found two people who could see and sculpt the potential in what others found just ugly."

"How did you two meet?" I ask.

"Oh, I knew Stina's sister, who was an art professor. . . . That sort of thing," mumbles Rosen.

"I kissed him first," says Stina. She reaches across the table, picks up Rosen's hand, and wreathes her fingers through his. She holds on tightly, as if she's scared. I study Stina. She is conventionally pretty. She has a perfect Protestant nose and a lithe form, and a single black bra strap slips provocatively from beneath her blouse. Rosen, a man who claims to love the unusual, has picked a very usual beauty.

"Look!" Stina suddenly shouts. I jump, startled. "Look at her ears!" she says to Rosen.

Before I know it they are both leaning forward, peering at my ears. "Oh, my God," says Stina, "you have the most unusual ears."

Now, this is not news to me. I have bat ears, plain and simple. They stick out stupidly. In the fifth grade, I used to fasten them to the sides of my skull with pink styling tape in the hope of altering their shape. I have always disliked my ears.

Rosen uncurls his index finger and touches my left ear. He runs his finger along the bumpy, malformed rim. "You're missing the *scapha*," he says. "It's a birth defect."

"I have a birth defect?" I say. I practically shout this, being someone who desires deeply not to be defective. That's why I take Prozac every day.

"Joe," says Stina, "are those not the most amazing ears. They would be so perfect to sculpt."

"They're just a perfect example," Rosen echoes, "of the incredible, delectable proliferation of life-forms. We claim most life-forms gravitate toward the mean, but that's not true. Lots of valid life exists at the margins of the bell curve. You have beautiful ears," he says to me.

"I have nice ears?" I say. "Really?"

This is just one reason why I won't dismiss Rosen out of hand. Suddenly, I see my ears a little differently. They have a marvelous undulating ridge and an intricately whorled entrance, and they do not stick out so much as jauntily jut; they are ears with an attitude. Rosen has shifted my vision without even touching my eyes. He is, at the very least, a challenger of paradigms; he calls on your conservatism, pushes hard.

That night, I do not dream of wings. I dream of Sweeny and his oozing face. I dream he comes so close to me that I smell him. Then I wake up. Sweeny is very sick. He is going to die soon. Earlier in the day, I asked Rosen when, and Rosen said, "Oh, soon," but he said it as if he didn't really care. Death does not seem to interest Rosen. Beauty, I think, can be cold.

PART II: MONSTER AND MARVELS

Today, Rosen and I are attending a conference together in Montreal. Here, everyone speaks French and eats baguettes. The conference room is old-fashioned, wainscoted with rich mahogany, ornate carvings of creatures and angels studding the ceiling, where a single light hangs in a cream-colored orb. Around the table sit doctors, philosophers, graduate students: this is a medical-ethics meeting, and Rosen is presenting his ideas. On the white board, in bold black lines, he sketches out his wings, and then the discussion turns to a patient whose single deepest desire was to look like a lizard. He wanted a doctor to split his tongue and scale his skin, and then put horns on his head. "You wouldn't do that, would you?" a bespectacled doctor asks. "Once," says Rosen, dodging in a fashion typical of him, "there was a lady in need of breast reconstruction who wanted blue areolas. What's wrong with blue areolas? Furthermore, rhinoplasty has not reached its real potential. Why just change the nose? Why not change the gene for the nose, so that subsequent generations will benefit from the surgery? Plastic surgery, in the future, can be about more than the literal body. It can be about sculpting the genotype as well."

The bespectacled doctor raises his hand. "Would you make that man into a lizard?" the doctor asks again. "What I want to know is, if a patient came to you and said, 'I want you to give me wings,' or 'Split my tongue,' would you actually do it?"

"Look," says Rosen, "we genetically engineer food. That's an issue."

"You're not answering my question," the doctor says, growing angry. Other people are growing angry, too. "Do you see any ethical dilemmas in making people into pigs, or birds?" another attendee yells out. This attendee is eating a Yodel, peeling off the chocolate bark and biting into a swirl of cream.

Rosen darts and dodges. "There is such a thing as liberty," he says.

"Yes," someone says, "but there's such a thing as the Hippocratic oath, too."

This goes on and on. At last a professor of anthropology says, "Just tell us, clearly, please. Would you give a human being wings, if the medical-ethics board allowed it?"

Rosen puts down his black marker. He rubs his eyes. "Yes," he says, "I would. I can certainly see why we don't devote research money to it. I can see why the NIH would fund work on breast cancer over this, but I don't have any problem with altering the human form. We do it all the time. It is only our Judeo-Christian conservatism that makes us think this is wrong. Who here," he says, "doesn't try to send their children to the best schools, in the hopes of altering them? Who here objects to a Palm Pilot, a thing we clasp to our bodies, with which we receive rapid electronic signals? Who here doesn't surround themselves with a metal shell and travel at death-defying speeds? We have always altered ourselves, for beauty or for power, and so long as we are not causing harm what makes us think we should stop?"

For a group of intelligent people everyone looks baffled. What Rosen has said is very right and very wrong, but no one can quite articulate the core conflicts. After all, we seem to think it's okay to use education as a way of neuronally altering the brain, but not surgery. We take Prozac, even Ritalin, to help transform ourselves, but recoil when it comes to wings. Maybe we're not recoiling. Maybe wings are just a dumb idea. No one in his right mind would subject himself to such a superfluous and strenuous operation. Yet socialite Jocelyne Wildenstein has dedicated much of her life to turning herself into a cat, via plastic surgery. She has had her lips enlarged and her face pulled back at the eyes to simulate a feline appearance. An even more well-known case is Michael Jackson, who has whitened himself, slimmed his nose, and undergone multiple other aesthetic procedures. The essential question here is whether these people are, and forever will be, outliers, or whether they represent the cutting edge of an ever more popular trend. Carl Elliott, a bioethicist and associate professor at the University of Minnesota, recently wrote in *The Atlantic* about a strange new "trend" of perfectly healthy folks who desire nothing more than to have a limb amputated, and about the British doctor who has undertaken this surgery, believing that if he doesn't amputate the patients will do it themselves, which could lead to gangrene. Elliott wonders whether amputation obsession will morph into another psychiatric diagnosis, whether, like hysteria, it will "catch on." The metaphor of contagion is an interesting one. Multiple-personality disorder "caught on"; hysteria caught on. Why then might not an unquenchable desire for wings or fins catch on, too? In any case, we use medical/viral metaphors to explain trends, and, in the case of plastic surgery, we then use medical means to achieve the trend's demands.

Rosen himself now repeats to the conferees, "We have always altered ourselves for beauty or for power. The chieftains in a certain African tribe remove their left ears, without Novocain. Other tribes put their bodies through intense scarification processes for the sake of style. In our own culture, we risk our bodies daily to achieve status, whether it's because we're bulimic or because we let some surgeon suck fat from us, with liposuction. Wings will be here," Rosen says. "Mark my words."

He suddenly seems so confident, so clear. We should do this; beauty is marvelous and monstrous. Beauty is difference, and yet, to his patients in the ER just two weeks back, he kept saying, "Let nature take its course." Perhaps he is more ambivalent than he lets on.

LATER THAT EVENING, OVER DINNER, conferees gossip about Rosen. "He's a creep," someone says. "A megalomaniac," someone else adds. For a creep or a megalomaniac, though, he's certainly commanding a lot of attention. Clearly, his notions are provocative. "The problem with wings," says someone, "is that only rich people would have them, would be able to afford them. Our society might begin to see rich people as more godly than ever."

I order a glass of wine. The waitress sets it on the table, where it blazes in its goblet, bright as a tulip. With this wine, I will tweak not only my mind but all its neuronal projections as well. My reflexes will slow down and my inhibitions will lift, making it possible for me to sound either very stupid or very smart. Is this wine an ethical problem? I ask the group that.

"Wine is reversible," someone says. "Wings aren't."

"Well, suppose they *were* reversible," someone says. "Supposing a surgeon could make wings that were removable. Then would we be reacting this way?"

"It's a question of degree," a philosopher pipes up. He is bald and skinny, with bulging eyes. "Rosen is going to the nth degree. It's not fair to lump that in with necessary alterations, or even questionably necessary alterations. Without doubt, it is very clear, diagnostically, that wings are not necessary."

I think about this. I think about what Rosen might say to this. I can imagine that his answer might have something to do with the fluidity of the concept of *necessary*. Four years ago, cell phones weren't necessary. Now they seem to be. Furthermore, he might say, if a person wants wings, if wings won't hurt a person, if they will help a person enjoy life and feel more beautiful, and if, in turn, the winged woman or man helps us to see beauty in what was before unacceptable, as we adjust and then come to love the sight of her spreading and soaring, then isn't this excellent? Later on, in my hotel room, I stand in front of the mirror, naked. My body contains eons. Once, we were single cells, then fish, then birds, then mammals, and the genes for all these forms lie dormant on their cones of chromosomes. We are pastiches at the cellular, genetic level. This may be why I fear open spaces, blank pages, why I often dream my house opens up into endless rooms I never knew were there, and I float through them with a kind of terror. It is so easy to seep, to be boundless. We clutch our cloaks of skin.

Back in Boston, I try to ascertain clearly, logically, what so bothers people about Rosen's ideas. At first glance, it might seem fairly obvious. I mean, wings. That's playing God. We should not play God. We should not reach for the stars. Myth after myth has shown us the dangers of doing so—Icarus, the Tower of Babel; absolute power corrupts absolutely. Bill Joy, chief scientist at Sun Microsystems, says, as our technological capabilities expand, "a sequence of small, individually sensible advances leads to an accumulation of great power and, concomitantly, great danger." Rosen's response to this: "So are we supposed to stop advancing? And who says it's bad to play God? We already alter the course of God's 'will' in hundreds of ways. When we use antibiotics to combat the flu, when we figure out a way to wipe smallpox off the very face of the earth, surely we're altering the natural course of things. Who says the natural course of things is even right? Maybe God isn't good."

The second objection might have to do with our notions of cate-

gorical imperatives. Mary Douglas wrote in her influential anthropological study *Purity and Danger* that human beings have a natural
aversion to crossing categories, and that when we do transgress we
see it as deeply dirty. In other words, shoes in themselves are not
dirty, but when you place them on the dining-room table they are.
When you talk about crossing species, either at the genetic or the
anatomical level, you are mucking about in long-cherished categories that reflect our fundamental sense of cleanliness and aesthetics.
Rosen's response to this, when I lob it at him in our next meeting:
"Who says taboos are anything but prejudice at rock bottom? Just
because it feels wrong doesn't mean it is. To a lot of people, racial
intermingling and miscegenation feel wrong, but to me they're fine.
I'm not a racist, and I'm not a conservative."

The third objection I can come up with has to do with the idea of
proteanism. Proteus, a minor mythological figure, could shape-shift
at will, being alternately a tiger, a lizard, a fire, a flood. Robert Lifton,
one of, I think, the truly deep thinkers of the last century, has explored in his volumes how Proteus has become a symbol for human
beings in our time. Lacking traditions, supportive institutions, a set
of historically rooted symbols, we have lost any sense of coherence
and connection. Today it is not uncommon for a human being to
shift belief systems several times in a lifetime, and with relatively
little psychological discomfort. We are Catholics, Buddhists, reborn,
unborn, artists, and dot-commers until the dot drops out of the com
and it all comes crashing down. We move on. We remarry. Our protean abilities clearly have their upsides. We are flexible and creative.
But the downside is, there is no psychic stability, no substantive self,
nothing really meaty and authentic. We sense this about ourselves.
We know we are superficial, all breadth and no depth. Rosen's work
embodies this tendency, literally. He desires to make incarnate the
identity diffusion so common to our culture. Rosen is in our face
making us face up to the fact that the inner and outer connections
have crumbled. In our ability to be everything, are we also nothing?

For me, this hits the nail on the head. I do not object to Rosen on
the basis of concerns about power, or of Mary Douglas's cross-

category pollution theory. After all, who, really, would wings reasonably benefit but the window washers among us? And as for the pollution issue, protean person that I am, I could probably adjust to a little chimerical color. Rosen's ideas and aspirations are frightening to me because they are such vivid, visceral examples of a certain postmodern or perhaps, more precisely put, post-authentic sensibility we embrace and fear as we pop our Prozacs and Ritalins and decide to be Jewish and then Episcopalian and then chant with the monks on some high Himalayan mountain via a cheap plane ticket we purchased in between jobs and just before we sold our condo in a market rising so fast that when it falls it will sound like all of the precious china plates crashing down from the cabinet—a mess. What a mess! Over and over again, from the Middle Ages on, when the theologian Pico wrote, in a direct and influential challenge to the Platonic idea of essential forms—"We have given you, Adam, no visage proper to yourself, nor endowment properly your own . . . trace for yourself the lineaments of your own nature . . . in order that you, as the free and proud shaper of your own being, fashion yourself in the form you may prefer. . . . [W]ho then will not look with awe upon this our chameleon . . . "—over and over, since those words at least, we as human beings have fretted about the question of whether there is anything fixed at our core, any set of unalterable traits that make us who we were and are and always will be. Postmodernism, by which I mean the idea of multiplicity, the celebration of the pastiche, and the rejection of logical positivism and absolutism as viable stances, will never die out, despite its waning popularity in academia. Its roots are too deep and ancient. And there has been, perhaps, no field like modern medicine, with all its possibilities and technological wizardry, to bring questions of authenticity to the burning forefront of our culture. At what point, in altering ourselves, would we lose our essential humanity? Are there any traits that make us essentially human? When might we become monsters or marvels, or are we already there? I vividly remember reading a book by a woman named Martha Beck. She had given birth to a Down's syndrome child and she wrote in a few chilling sentences that because of one tiny chromosome, her child, Adam, is "as dissimilar from me as a mule is from a donkey. He is, in ways both obvious and subtle, a different beast." Is it really that simple, that small? One tiny chromosome severs us from the human species? One little wing and we're gone?

As for me, I am an obsessive. I like my categories. I check to make sure the stove is off three times before I go to bed. I have all sorts of other little rituals. At the same time, I know I am deeply disrooted. I left my family at the age of fourteen, never to return. I do not know my family tree. Like so many of us, I have no real religion, which is of course partly a good thing but partly a bad thing. In any case, last year, in some sort of desperate mood, I decided to convert from Judaism to Episcopalianism, but when it came time to put that blood and body in my mouth I couldn't go through with it. Was this because at bottom I just AM a Jew and this amness has profundity? Or was this because I don't like French bread, which is what they were using at the conversion ceremony? In any case, at the crucial moment of incorporation, I fled the church like the proverbial bride who cannot make the commitment.

I want to believe there is something essential and authentic about me, even if it's just my ears. And although my feelings of diffusion may be extreme, I am certainly not the only one who's felt she's flying too fast. Lifton writes, "Until relatively recently, no more than a single major ideological shift was likely to occur in a lifetime, and that one would be long remembered for its conflict and soul searching. But today it is not unusual for several such shifts to take place within a year or even a month, whether in the realm of politics, religion, aesthetic values, personal relationships. . . . Quite rare is the man or woman who has gone through life holding firmly to a single ideological vision. More usual is a tendency toward ideological fragments, bits and pieces of belief systems that allow for shifts, revisions, and recombinations."

What Lifton has observed in the psyche Rosen wants to make manifest in the body. I ask Rosen, "So, do you believe we are just in essence protean, that there is nothing fundamental, or core, to being human?"

He says, "Lauren, I am a scientist. My original interests were in nerves. I helped develop, in the 1980s, one of the first computer-grown nerve chips. The answer to your question may lie in how our nervous systems operate."

PART III: THE PROTEAN BRAIN

First, a lesson. In the 1930s, researchers, working on the brains of apes, found that the gray matter contained neural representations of all the afferent body parts. Ape ears, feet, skin, hands, were all richly represented in the ape brain in a series of neural etchings, like a map. Researchers also realized that when a person loses a limb—say, the right arm—this portion of the neural map fades away. Sometimes even stranger things happen. Sometimes amputees claimed they could feel their missing arm when, for instance, someone touched their cheek. This was because the arm map had not faded so much as morphed, joined up its circuitry with the cheek map, so it was all confused.

It was then discovered, not surprisingly, that human beings also have limb maps in their brains. Neurologists conceptualized this limb map as "a homunculus," or little man. Despite my feminist leanings, I am enchanted by the idea of a little man hunched in my head, troll-like, banging a drum, grinning from ear to ear. Of course the homunculus is not actually shaped like a human; it is, rather, a kind of human blueprint, like the drawing of the house in all its minute specificity. Touch the side of your skull. Press in. Buried, somewhere near there, is a beautiful etching of your complex human hand, rich in neural web-work and delicate, axonal tendrils designed to accommodate all the sensory possibilities of this prehensile object. Move your hand upward, press the now sealed soft spot, and you will be touching your toe map. Your eye map is somewhere in your forehead and your navel map is somewhere in your cerebellum, a creased, enfolded series of cells that recall, I imagine, ancient blue connections, a primitive love.

Today, Rosen is giving a lecture. I have come up to New Hampshire to hear him, and, unlike on the last visit, the day is beautiful and bright. Rosen explains how brains are partly plastic, which comes from the Greek root meaning to mold, to shape. When we lose a limb, the brain absorbs its map or rewires it to some other center. Similarly, Rosen explains, when we gain a limb, the brain almost immediately senses it and goes about hooking it up via neural representation. "If I were to attach a sonographically powered arm to your body," Rosen explains, "your brain would map it. If I were to attach a third thumb, your brain would map it, absolutely. Our bodies change our brains, and our brains are infinitely moldable. If I were to give you wings, you would develop, literally, a winged brain. If I were to give you an echolocation device, you would develop in part a bat-brain."

Although the idea of a brain able to incorporate changes so completely may sound strange, many neurological experiments have borne out the fact that our gray matter does reorganize according to the form and function of our appendages. Because no one has yet appended animal forms to the human body, however, no studies have been done that explore what the brain's response to what might be termed an "evolutionary insult" would be. Assuming, probably wrongly but assuming nevertheless, that human beings represent some higher form of species adaptation, at least in terms of frontal-lobe intelligence, the brain might find it odd to be rewiring itself to presumably more primitive structures, structures we shed a long time ago when we waded out of the swamps and shed our scales. Rosen's desire to meld human and animal forms, and the incarnation of this desire in people like the catwoman and the lizard-man, raise some interesting questions about the intersection of technology and primitivism. Although we usually assume technology is somehow deepening the rift between nature and culture, it also can do the opposite. In other words, technology can be, and often is, extremely primitive, not only because it allows people a sort of id-like, limbic-driven power (i.e., nuclear weaponry) but also because it can provide the means to toggle us down the evolutionary ladder, to alter our brains, stuck in their rigid humanness, so that we are at last no longer landlocked.

All this is fascinating and, of course, unsettling to me. Our brains are essentially indiscriminate, able to morph—like the sea god Proteus himself—into fire, a flood, a dragon, a swan. I touch my brain and feel it flap. Now I understand more deeply what Rosen meant when he said, "Plastic surgery changes the soul." To the extent that we believe our souls are a part of our brains, Rosen is right. And, all social conflict about its place in the medical hierarchy aside, plastic surgery is really neurosurgery, because it clearly happens, at its most essential level, north of the neck. When a surgeon modifies your body, he modifies your oh-so-willing, bendable brain.

I get a little depressed, hearing this lecture. It seems to me proof at the neuronal level that we have the capacity to be, in fact, everything, and thus in some sense nothing. It confirms my fear that I, along with the rest of the human species, could slip-slide through life without any specificity, or "specieficity." Last year, I had my first child. I wonder what I will teach her, what beliefs about the body and the brain and the soul I really hold. I think, "I will show her pictures of her ancestors," but the truth is, I don't have any pictures. I think, "I will teach her my morals," but I don't know exactly what my morals are, or where they came from. I know I am not alone. Like Rosen, perhaps, I am just extreme. Now I feel a kind of kinship with him. We are both self-invented, winging our way through.

Rosen comes up to me. He is finished with his talk. "So do you understand what I mean," he asks, "about the limitlessness of the brain?" "Does it ever make you sad?" I say. "Does it ever just plain and simple make you scared?"

Rosen and I look at each other for a long time. He does seem sad. I recall him telling me once that when he envisions the future fifty years out, he hopes he is gone, because, he said, "While I like it here, I don't like it that much." I have the sense, now, that he struggles with things he won't tell me. His eyes appear tired, his face drained. I wonder if he wakes in the middle of the night, frightened by his own perceptions. Strange or not, there is something constant in Rosen, and that's his intelligence, his uncanny ability to defend seemingly untenable positions with power and occasional grace. In just three weeks he will travel to a remote part of Asia to participate in a group called Interplast, made up of doctors and nurses who donate their time to help children with cleft lips and palates. I think it's important to mention this—not only Bin Laden, bandwidth, anthrax, and wings but his competing desire to minister. The way, at the dinner table, he tousles his children's hair. His avid dislike of George W. Bush. His love of plants and greenery. Call him multifaceted or simply slippery, I don't know. All I do know is that right now, when I look at his face, I think I can see the boy he once was, the Seventh Fleet ship, the wonder, all that wonder.

"Do you and Stina want to go out for dinner? We could go somewhere really fancy, to thank you," I say, "for all your time."

"Sure," says Rosen. "Give me a minute. I'll meet you in the hospital lobby," and then he zips off to who knows where, and I am alone with my singular stretched self on the third floor of the Dartmouth-Hitchcock Medical Center. I wander down the long hallways. Behind the curtained cubicles there is unspeakable suffering. Surely that cannot be changed, not ever. Behind one of these cubicles sits Sweeny, and even if we learn to see him as beautiful, the bottom-line truth is that he still suffers. Now I want to touch Sweeny's dying face. I want to put my hand right on the center of pain. I want to touch Rosen's difficult face, and my baby daughter's face as well, but she is far from me, in some home we will, migrants that our family is, move on from sometime soon. I once read that a fetus does not scar. Fetal skin repairs itself seamlessly, evidence of damage sinking back into blackness. Plastic surgery, for all its incredible advances, has not yet been able to figure out how to replicate this mysterious fetal ability in the full-born human. Plastic surgery can give us wings and maybe even let us sing like loons, but it cannot stop scarring. This is oddly comforting to me. I pause to sit on a padded bench. A very ill woman pushing an IV pole walks by. I lift up my pant leg and study the scar I got a long time ago, when I fell off a childhood bike. The scar is pink and raised and shaped like an *o*, like a hole maybe, but also like a letter, like a language, like a little piece of land that, for now, we cannot cross over.

GARY TAUBES

The Soft Science of Dietary Fat

FROM *SCIENCE*

> *Everyone knows that eating fat is bad for you. It raises cholesterol and promotes heart disease. The message is clear: Cut down on fat and live longer. There's just one problem: Nearly fifty years of research has failed to prove conclusively that restricting dietary fat confers any health benefits. Gary Taubes, a writer with a surgeon's skill in separating scientific myth from fact, shows how politics and wishful thinking joined to create the medical equivalent of an urban legend.*

WHEN THE U.S. SURGEON GENERAL'S OFFICE SET off in 1988 to write the definitive report on the dangers of dietary fat, the scientific task appeared straightforward. Four years earlier, the National Institutes of Health (NIH) had begun advising every American old enough to walk to restrict fat intake, and the president of the American Heart Association (AHA) had told *Time* magazine that if everyone went along, "we will have [atherosclerosis] conquered" by the year 2000. The Surgeon General's Office itself had just published its 700-page landmark "Report on Nutrition and Health," declaring fat the single most unwholesome component of the American diet.

All of this was apparently based on sound science. So the task before the project officer was merely to gather that science together in one volume, have it reviewed by a committee of experts, which had been promptly established, and publish it. The project did not go smoothly, however. Four project officers came and went over the next decade. "It consumed project officers," says Marion Nestle, who helped launch the project and now runs the nutrition and food studies department at New York University (NYU). Members of the oversight committee saw drafts of an early chapter or two, criticized them vigorously, and then saw little else.

Finally, in June 1999, 11 years after the project began, the Surgeon General's Office circulated a letter, authored by the last of the project officers, explaining that the report would be killed. There was no other public announcement and no press release. The letter explained that the relevant administrators "did not anticipate fully the magnitude of the additional external expertise and staff' resources that would be needed." In other words, says Nestle, the subject matter "was too complicated." Bill Harlan, a member of the oversight committee and associate director of the Office of Disease Prevention at NIH, says "the report was initiated with a preconceived opinion of the conclusions," but the science behind those opinions was not holding up. "Clearly the thoughts of yesterday were not going to serve us very well."

During the past 30 years, the concept of eating healthy in America has become synonymous with avoiding dietary fat. The creation and marketing of reduced-fat food products has become big business; over 15,000 have appeared on supermarket shelves. Indeed, an entire research industry has arisen to create palatable nonfat fat substitutes, and the food industry now spends billions of dollars yearly selling the less-fat-is-good-health message. The government weighs in as well, with the U.S. Department of Agriculture's (USDA's) booklet on dietary guidelines, published every 5 years, and its ubiquitous Food Guide Pyramid, which recommends that fats and oils be eaten "sparingly." The low-fat gospel spreads farther by a kind of societal osmosis, continuously reinforced by physicians, nutritionists, journalists, health organizations, and consumer advocacy groups such as the Center for Science in the Public Interest, which refers to fat as this "greasy killer." "In America, we no longer fear God or the communists, but we fear fat," says David Kritchevsky of the Wistar Institute in Philadelphia, who in 1958 wrote the first textbook on cholesterol.

As the Surgeon General's Office discovered, however, the science of dietary fat is not nearly as simple as it once appeared. The proposition, now 50 years old, that dietary fat is a bane to health is based chiefly on the fact that fat, specifically the hard, saturated fat found primarily in meat and dairy products, elevates blood cholesterol levels. This in turn raises the likelihood that cholesterol will clog arteries, a condition known as atherosclerosis, which then increases risk of coronary artery disease, heart attack, and untimely death. By the 1970s, each individual step of this chain from fat to cholesterol to heart disease had been demonstrated beyond reasonable doubt, but the veracity of the chain *as a whole* has never been proved. In other words, despite decades of research, it is still a debatable proposition whether the consumption of saturated fats above recommended levels (step one in the chain) by anyone who's not already at high risk of heart disease will increase the likelihood of untimely death (outcome three). Nor have hundreds of millions of dollars in trials managed to generate compelling evidence that healthy individuals can extend their lives by more than a few weeks, if that, by eating less fat. To put it simply, the data remain ambiguous as to whether low-fat diets will benefit healthy Americans. Worse, the ubiquitous admonishments to reduce total fat intake have encouraged a shift to high-carbohydrate diets, which may be no better—and may even be worse—than high-fat diets.

Since the early 1970s, for instance, Americans' average fat intake has dropped from over 40% of total calories to 34%; average serum cholesterol levels have dropped as well. But no compelling evidence suggests that these decreases have improved health. Although heart disease death rates have dropped—and public health officials insist low-fat diets are partly responsible—the *incidence* of heart disease does not seem to be declining, as would be expected if lower fat diets made a difference. This was the conclusion, for instance, of a 10-year study of heart disease mortality published in *The New England Journal of Medicine* in 1998, which suggested that death rates are declining largely because doctors are treating the disease more successfully. AHA statistics agree: Between 1979 and 1996, the number of medical procedures for heart disease increased from 1.2 million to 5.4 million a year. "I don't consider that this disease category has disappeared or anything close to it," says one AHA statistician.

Meanwhile, obesity in America, which remained constant from the early 1960s through 1980, has surged upward since then—from 14% of the population to over 22%. Diabetes has increased apace. Both obesity and diabetes increase heart disease risk, which could explain why heart disease incidence is not decreasing. That this obesity epidemic occurred just as the government began bombarding Americans with the low-fat message suggests the possibility, however distant, that low-fat diets might have unintended consequences—among them, weight gain. "Most of us would have predicted that if we can get the population to change its fat intake, with its dense calories, we would see a reduction in weight," admits Harlan. "Instead, we see the exact opposite."

In the face of this uncertainty, skeptics and apostates have come along repeatedly, only to see their work almost religiously ignored as the mainstream medical community sought consensus on the evils of dietary fat. For 20 years, for instance, the Harvard School of Public Health has run the Nurses' Health Study and its two sequelae—the Health Professionals Follow-Up Study and the Nurses' Health Study II—accumulating over a decade of data on the diet and health of almost 300,000 Americans. The results suggest that total fat consumed has no relation to heart disease risk; that monounsaturated fats like olive oil lower risk; and that saturated fats are little worse, if at all, than the pasta and other carbohydrates that the Food Guide Pyramid suggests be eaten copiously. (The studies also suggest that trans fatty acids are unhealthful. These are the fats in margarine, for instance, and are what many Americans started eating when they were told that the saturated fats in butter might kill them.) Harvard epidemiologist Walter Willett, spokesperson for the Nurses' Health Study, points out that NIH has spent over $100 million on the three studies and yet not one government agency has changed its primary guidelines to fit these particular data. "Scandalous," says Willett. "They say, 'You really need a high level of proof to change the recommendations,' which is ironic, because they never had a high level of proof to set them."

Indeed, the history of the national conviction that dietary fat is deadly, and its evolution from hypothesis to dogma, is one in which politicians, bureaucrats, the media, and the public have played as large a role as the scientists and the science. It's a story of what can happen when the demands of public health policy—and the demands of the public for simple advice—run up against the confusing ambiguity of real science.

FEAR OF FAT

During the first half of the 20th century, nutritionists were more concerned about malnutrition than about the sins of dietary excess. After World War II, however, a coronary heart disease epidemic seemed to sweep the country. "Middle-aged men, seemingly healthy, were dropping dead," wrote biochemist Ancel Keys of the University of Minnesota, Twin Cities, who was among the first to suggest that dietary fats might be the cause. By 1952, Keys was arguing that Americans should reduce their fat intake to less than 30% of total calories, although he simultaneously recognized that "direct evidence on the effect of the diet on human arteriosclerosis is very little and likely to remain so for some time." In the famous and very controversial Seven Countries Study, for instance, Keys and his colleagues reported that the amount of fat consumed seemed to be the salient difference between populations such as those in Japan and Crete that had little heart disease and those, as in Finland, that were plagued by it. In 1961, the Framingham Heart Study linked cholesterol levels to heart disease, Keys made the cover of *Time* magazine, and the AHA, under his influence, began advocating low-fat diets as a palliative for men with high cholesterol levels. Keys had also become one of the first Americans to consciously adopt a heart-healthy diet: He and his wife, *Time* reported, "do not eat 'carving meat'—steaks, chops, roasts—more than three times a week."

Nonetheless, by 1969 the state of the science could still be summarized by a single sentence from a report of the Diet-Heart Review Panel of the National Heart Institute (now the National Heart, Lung, and Blood Institute, or NHLBI): "It is not known whether dietary manipulation has any effect whatsoever on coronary heart disease." The chair of the panel was E. H. "Pete" Ahrens, whose laboratory at Rockefeller University in New York City did much of the seminal research on fat and cholesterol metabolism.

Whereas proponents of low-fat diets were concerned primarily about the effects of dietary fat on cholesterol levels and heart disease, Ahrens and his panel—10 experts in clinical medicine, epidemiology, biostatistics, human nutrition, and metabolism—were equally concerned that eating less fat could have profound effects throughout the body, many of which could be harmful. The brain, for instance, is 70% fat, which chiefly serves to insulate neurons. Fat is also the primary component of cell membranes. Changing the proportion of saturated to unsaturated fats in the diet changes the fat composition in these membranes. This could conceivably change the membrane permeability, which controls the transport of everything from glucose, signaling proteins, and hormones to bacteria, viruses, and tumor-causing agents into and out of the cell. The relative saturation of fats in the diet could also influence cellular aging as well as the clotting ability of blood cells.

Whether the potential benefits of low-fat diets would exceed the potential risks could be settled by testing whether low-fat diets actually prolong life, but such a test would have to be enormous. The effect of diet on cholesterol levels is subtle for most individuals—especially those living in the real world rather than the metabolic wards of nutrition researchers—and the effect of cholesterol levels on heart disease is also subtle. As a result, tens of thousands of individuals would have to switch to low-fat diets and their subsequent health compared to that of equal numbers who continued eating fat to alleged excess. And all these people would have to be followed for years until enough deaths accumulated to provide statistically significant results. Ahrens and his colleagues were pessimistic about whether such a massive and expensive trial could ever be done. In 1971, an NIH task force estimated such a trial would cost $1 billion, considerably more than NIH was willing to spend. Instead, NIH administrators opted for a handful of smaller studies, two of which alone would cost $255 million. Perhaps more important, these studies would take a decade. Neither the public, the press, nor the U.S. Congress was willing to wait that long.

SCIENCE BY COMMITTEE

Like the flourishing American affinity for alternative medicine, an antifat movement evolved independently of science in the 1960s. It was fed by distrust of the establishment—in this case, both the medical establishment and the food industry—and by counterculture attacks on excessive consumption, whether manifested in gas-guzzling cars or the classic American cuisine of bacon and eggs and marbled steaks. And while the data on fat and health remained ambiguous and the scientific community polarized, the deadlock was broken not by any new science, but by politicians. It was Senator George McGovern's bipartisan, nonlegislative Select Committee on Nutrition and Human Needs—and, to be precise, a handful of McGovern's staff members—that almost single-handedly changed nutritional policy in this country and initiated the process of turning the dietary fat hypothesis into dogma.

McGovern's committee was founded in 1968 with a mandate to eradicate malnutrition in America, and it instituted a series of landmark federal food assistance programs. As the malnutrition work began to peter out in the mid-1970s, however, the committee didn't disband. Rather, its general counsel, Marshall Matz, and staff director, Alan Stone, both young lawyers, decided that the committee would address "overnutrition," the dietary excesses of Americans. It was a "casual endeavor," says Matz. "We really were totally naïve, a bunch of kids, who just thought, 'Hell, we should say something on this subject before we go out of business.'" McGovern and his fellow senators—all middle-aged men worried about their girth and their health—signed on; McGovern and his wife had both gone through diet-guru Nathan Pritikin's very low-fat diet and exercise program. McGovern quit the program early, but Pritikin remained a major influence on his thinking.

McGovern's committee listened to 2 days of testimony on diet and disease in July 1976. Then resident wordsmith Nick Mottern, a former labor reporter for *The Providence Journal*, was assigned the task of researching and writing the first "Dietary Goals for the United States." Mottern, who had no scientific background and no experience writing about science, nutrition, or health, believed his Dietary Goals would launch a "revolution in diet and agriculture in this country." He avoided the scientific and medical controversy by relying almost exclusively on Harvard School of Public Health nutritionist Mark Hegsted for input on dietary fat. Hegsted had studied fat and cholesterol metabolism in the early 1960s, and he believed unconditionally in the benefits of restricting fat intake, although he says he was aware that his was an extreme opinion. With Hegsted as his muse, Mottern saw dietary fat as the nutritional equivalent of cigarettes, and the food industry as akin to the tobacco industry in its willingness to suppress scientific truth in the interests of profits. To Mottern, those scientists who spoke out against fat were those willing to take on the industry. "It took a certain amount of guts," he says, "to speak about this because of the financial interests involved."

Mottern's report suggested that Americans cut their total fat intake to 30% of the calories they consume and saturated fat intake to 10%, in accord with AHA recommendations for men at high risk of heart disease. The report acknowledged the existence of controversy but insisted Americans had nothing to lose by following its advice. "The question to be asked is not why should we change our diet but why not?" wrote Hegsted in the introduction. "There are [no risks] that can be identified and important benefits can be expected." This was an optimistic but still debatable position, and when Dietary Goals was released in January 1977, "all hell broke loose," recalls Hegsted. "Practically nobody was in favor of the McGovern recommendations. Damn few people."

McGovern responded with three follow-up hearings, which aptly foreshadowed the next 7 years of controversy. Among those testifying, for instance, was NHLBI director Robert Levy, who explained that no one knew if eating less fat or lowering blood cholesterol levels would prevent heart attacks, which was why NHLBI was spending $300 million to study the question. Levy's position was awkward, he recalls, because "the good senators came out with the guidelines and then called us in to get advice." He was joined by prominent scientists, including Ahrens, who testified that advising Americans to eat less fat on the strength of such marginal evidence was equivalent to conducting a nutritional experiment with the American public as subjects. Even the American Medical Association protested, suggesting that the diet proposed by the guidelines raised the "potential for harmful effects." But as these scientists testified, so did representatives from the dairy, egg, and cattle industries, who also vigorously opposed the guidelines for obvious reasons. This juxtaposition served to taint the scientific criticisms: Any scientists arguing against the committee's guidelines appeared to be either hopelessly behind the paradigm, which was Hegsted's view, or industry apologists, which was Mottern's, if not both.

Although the committee published a revised edition of the Dietary Goals later in the year, the thrust of the recommendations remained unchanged. It did give in to industry pressure by softening the suggestion that Americans eat less meat. Mottern says he considered even that a "disservice to the public," refused to do the revisions, and quit the committee. (Mottern became a vegetarian while writing the Dietary Goals and now runs a food co-op in Peekskill, New York.)

The guidelines might have then died a quiet death when McGovern's committee came to an end in late 1977 if two federal agencies had not felt it imperative to respond. Although they took contradictory points of view, one message—with media assistance—won out.

The first was the USDA, where consumer-activist Carol Tucker Foreman had recently been appointed an assistant secretary. Foreman believed it was incumbent on USDA to turn McGovern's recommendations into official policy, and, like Mottern, she was not deterred by the existence of scientific controversy. "Tell us what you know and tell us it's not the final answer," she would tell scientists. "I have to eat and feed my children three times a day, and I want you to tell me what your best sense of the data is right now."

Of course, given the controversy, the "best sense of the data" would depend on which scientists were asked. The Food and Nutrition Board of the National Academy of Sciences (NAS), which decides the Recommended Dietary Allowances, would have been a natural choice, but NAS president Philip Handler, an expert on metabolism, had told Foreman that Mottern's Dietary Goals were "nonsense." Foreman then turned to McGovern's staffers for advice and they recommended she hire Hegsted, which she did. Hegsted, in turn, relied on a state-of-the-science report published by an expert but very divergent committee of the American Society for Clinical Nutrition. "They were nowhere near unanimous on anything," says Hegsted, "but the majority supported something like the McGovern committee report."

The resulting document became the first edition of "Using the Dietary Guidelines for Americans." Although it acknowledged the existence of controversy and suggested that a single dietary recommendation might not suit an entire diverse population, the advice to avoid fat and saturated fat was, indeed, virtually identical to McGovern's Dietary Goals.

Three months later, the NAS Food and Nutrition Board released its own guidelines: "Toward Healthful Diets." The board, consisting of a dozen nutrition experts, concluded that the only reliable advice for healthy Americans was to watch their weight; everything else, dietary fat included, would take care of itself. The advice was not taken kindly, however, at least not by the media. The first reports— "rather incredulously," said Handler at the time—criticized the NAS advice for conflicting with the USDA's and McGovern's and thus somehow being irresponsible. Follow-up reports suggested that the board members, in the words of Jane Brody, who covered the story for *The New York Times*, were "all in the pocket of the industries being hurt." To be precise, the board chair and one of its members consulted for food industries, and funding for the board itself came from industry donations. These industry connections were leaked to the press from the USDA.

Hegsted now defends the NAS board, although he didn't at the time, and calls this kind of conflict of interest "a hell of an issue." "Everybody used to complain that industry didn't do anything on nutrition," he told *Science*, "yet anybody who got involved was black-balled because their positions were presumably influenced by the industry." (In 1981, Hegsted returned to Harvard, where his research was funded by Frito-Lay.) The press had mixed feelings, claiming that the connections "soiled" the academy's reputation "for tendering careful scientific advice" *(The Washington Post)*, demonstrated that the board's "objectivity and aptitude are in doubt" *(The New York Times)*, or represented in the board's guidelines a "blow against the food faddists who hold the public in thrall" *(Science)*. In any case, the NAS board had been publicly discredited. Hegsted's Dietary Guidelines for Americans became the official U.S. policy on dietary fat: Eat less fat. Live longer.

Creating "Consensus"

Once politicians, the press, and the public had decided dietary fat policy, the science was left to catch up. In the early 1970s, when NIH opted to forgo a $1 billion trial that might be definitive and instead fund a half-dozen studies at one-third the cost, everyone hoped these smaller trials would be sufficiently persuasive to conclude that low-fat diets prolong lives. The results were published between 1980 and 1984. Four of these trials—comparing heart disease rates and diet within Honolulu, Puerto Rico, Chicago, and Framingham—showed no evidence that men who ate less fat lived longer or had fewer heart attacks. A fifth trial, the Multiple Risk Factor Intervention Trial (MRFIT), cost $115 million and tried to amplify the subtle influences of diet on health by persuading subjects to avoid fat while simultaneously quitting smoking *and* taking medication for high blood pressure. That trial suggested, if anything, that eating less fat might shorten life. In each study, however, the investigators concluded that methodological flaws had led to the negative results. They did not, at least publicly, consider their results reason to lessen their belief in the evils of fat.

The sixth study was the $140 million Lipid Research Clinics (LRC) Coronary Primary Prevention Trial, led by NHLBI administrator Basil Rifkind and biochemist Daniel Steinberg of the University of California, San Diego. The LRC trial was a drug trial, not a diet trial, but the NHLBI heralded its outcome as the end of the dietary fat debate. In January 1984, LRC investigators reported that a medication called cholestyramine reduced cholesterol levels in men with abnormally high cholesterol levels and modestly reduced heart disease rates in the process. (The probability of suffering a heart attack during the seven-plus years of the study was reduced from 8.6% in the placebo group to 7.0%; the probability of dying from a heart attack dropped from 2.0% to 1.6%.) The investigators then concluded, without benefit of dietary data, that cholestyramine's benefits could be extended to diet as well. And although the trial tested only middle-aged men with cholesterol levels higher than those of 95% of the population, they concluded that those benefits "could and should be extended to other age groups and women and . . . other more modest elevations of cholesterol levels."

Why go so far? Rifkind says their logic was simple: For 20 years, he and his colleagues had argued that lowering cholesterol levels prevented heart attacks. They had spent enormous sums trying to prove it. They felt they could never actually demonstrate that low-fat diets prolonged lives—that would be too expensive, and MRFIT had failed—but now they had established a fundamental link in the causal chain, from lower cholesterol levels to cardiovascular health. With that, they could take the leap of faith from cholesterol-lowering drugs and health to cholesterol-lowering diet and health. And after all their effort, they were eager—not to mention urged by Congress—to render helpful advice. "There comes a point when, if you don't make a decision, the consequences can be great as well," says Rifkind. "If you just allow Americans to keep on consuming 40% of calories from fat, there's an outcome to that as well."

With the LRC results in press, the NHLBI launched what Levy called "a massive public health campaign." The media obligingly went along. *Time*, for instance, reported the LRC findings under the headline "Sorry, It's True. Cholesterol Really Is a Killer." The article about a drug trial began: "No whole milk. No butter. No fatty meats . . ." *Time* followed up 3 months later with a cover story: "And Cholesterol and Now the Bad News. . . ." The cover photo was a frowning face: a breakfast plate with two fried eggs as the eyes and a bacon strip for the mouth. Rifkind was quoted saying that their results "strongly indicate that the more you lower cholesterol and fat in your diet, the more you reduce your risk of heart disease," a statement that still lacked direct scientific support.

The following December, NIH effectively ended the debate with a "Consensus Conference." The idea of such a conference is that an expert panel, ideally unbiased, listens to 2 days of testimony and arrives at a conclusion with which everyone agrees. In this case, Rifkind chaired the planning committee, which chose his LRC co-investigator Steinberg to lead the expert panel. The 20 speakers did include a handful of skeptics—including Ahrens, for instance, and cardiologist Michael Oliver of Imperial College in London—who argued that it was unscientific to equate the effects of a drug with the effects of a diet. Steinberg's panel members, however, as Oliver later complained in *The Lancet*, "were selected to include only

experts who would, predictably, say that all levels of blood cholesterol in the United States are too high and should be lowered. And, of
course, this is exactly what was said." Indeed, the conference report,
written by Steinberg and his panel, revealed no evidence of discord.
There was "no doubt," it concluded, that low-fat diets "will afford
significant protection against coronary heart disease" to every
American over 2 years old. The Consensus Conference officially gave
the appearance of unanimity where none existed. After all, if there
had been a true consensus, as Steinberg himself told *Science*, "you
wouldn't have had to have a consensus conference."

THE TEST OF TIME

To the outside observer, the challenge in making sense of any such
long-running scientific controversy is to establish whether the skeptics are simply on the wrong side of the new paradigm, or whether
their skepticism is well-founded. In other words, is the science at
issue based on sound scientific thinking and unambiguous data, or
is it what Sir Francis Bacon, for instance, would have called "wishful
science," based on fancies, opinions, and the exclusion of contrary
evidence? Bacon offered one viable suggestion for differentiating the
two: the test of time. Good science is rooted in reality, so it grows
and develops and the evidence gets increasingly more compelling,
whereas wishful science flourishes most under its first authors before
"going downhill."

Such is the case, for instance, with the proposition that dietary fat
causes cancer, which was an integral part of dietary fat anxiety in the
late 1970s. By 1982, the evidence supporting this idea was thought to
be so undeniable that a landmark NAS report on nutrition and
cancer equated those researchers who remained skeptical with "certain interested parties [who] formerly argued that the association
between lung cancer and smoking was not causational."

Fifteen years and hundreds of millions of research dollars later, a
similarly massive expert report by the World Cancer Research Fund
and the American Institute for Cancer Research could find neither

"convincing" nor even "probable" reason to believe that dietary fat caused cancer.

The hypothesis that low-fat diets are the requisite route to weight loss has taken a similar downward path. This was the ultimate fall-back position in all low-fat recommendations: Fat has nine calories per gram compared to four calories for carbohydrates and protein, and so cutting fat from the diet surely would cut pounds. "This is held almost to be a religious truth," says Harvard's Willett. Considerable data, however, now suggest otherwise. The results of well-controlled clinical trials are consistent: People on low-fat diets initially lose a couple of kilograms, as they would on any diet, and then the weight tends to return. After 1 to 2 years, little has been achieved. Consider, for instance, the 50,000 women enrolled in the ongoing $100 million Women's Health Initiative (WHI). Half of these women have been extensively counseled to consume only 20% of their calories from fat. After 3 years on this near-draconian regime, say WHI sources, the women had lost, on average, a kilogram each.

The link between dietary fat and heart disease is more complicated, because the hypothesis has diverged into two distinct propositions: first, that lowering cholesterol prevents heart disease; second, that eating less fat not only lowers cholesterol and prevents heart disease but *prolongs* life. Since 1984, the evidence that cholesterol-lowering drugs are beneficial—proposition number one—has indeed blossomed, at least for those at high risk of heart attack. These drugs reduce serum cholesterol levels dramatically, and they prevent heart attacks, perhaps by other means as well. Their market has now reached $4 billion a year in the United States alone, and every new trial seems to confirm their benefits.

The evidence supporting the second proposition, that eating less fat makes for a healthier and longer life, however, has remained stubbornly ambiguous. If anything, it has only become less compelling over time. Indeed, since Ancel Keys started advocating low-fat diets almost 50 years ago, the science of fat and cholesterol has evolved from a simple story into a very complicated one. The catch has been that few involved in this business were prepared to deal with a complicated story. Researchers initially preferred to believe it was simple—that a single unwholesome nutrient, in effect, could be isolated from the diverse richness of human diets; public health administrators required a simple story to give to Congress and the public; and the press needed a simple story—at least on any particular day—to give to editors and readers in 30 column inches. But as contrarian data continued to accumulate, the complications became increasingly more difficult to ignore or exclude, and the press began waffling or adding caveats. The scientists then got the blame for not sticking to the original simple story, which had, regrettably, never existed.

MORE FATS, FEWER ANSWERS

The original simple story in the 1950s was that high cholesterol levels increase heart disease risk. The seminal Framingham Heart Study, for instance, which revealed the association between cholesterol and heart disease, originally measured only total serum cholesterol. But cholesterol shuttles through the blood in an array of packages. Low-density lipoprotein particles (LDL, the "bad" cholesterol) deliver fat and cholesterol from the liver to tissues that need it, including the arterial cells, where it can lead to atherosclerotic plaques. High-density lipoproteins (HDLs, the "good" cholesterol) return cholesterol to the liver. The higher the HDL, the lower the heart disease risk. Then there are triglycerides, which contain fatty acids, and very low density lipoproteins (VLDLs), which transport triglycerides.

All of these particles have some effect on heart disease risk, while the fats, carbohydrates, and protein in the diet have varying effects on all these particles. The 1950s story was that saturated fats increase total cholesterol, polyunsaturated fats decrease it, and monounsaturated fats are neutral. By the late 1970s—when researchers accepted the benefits of HDL—they realized that monounsaturated fats are not neutral. Rather, they raise HDL, at least compared to carbohydrates, and lower LDL. This makes them an ideal nutrient as far as cholesterol goes. Furthermore, saturated fats cannot be quite so evil because, while they elevate LDL, which is bad, they also elevate HDL, which is good. And some saturated fats—stearic acid, in particular, the fat in chocolate—are at worst neutral. Stearic acid raises HDL levels but does little or nothing to LDL. And then there are trans fatty acids, which raise LDL, just like saturated fat, but also lower HDL. Today, none of this is controversial, although it has yet to be reflected in any Food Guide Pyramid.

To understand where this complexity can lead in a simple example, consider a steak—to be precise, a porterhouse, select cut, with a half-centimeter layer of fat, the nutritional constituents of which can be found in the Nutrient Database for Standard Reference at the USDA Web site. After broiling, this porterhouse reduces to a serving of almost equal parts fat and protein. Fifty-one percent of the fat is monounsaturated, of which virtually all (90%) is oleic acid, the same healthy fat that's in olive oil. Saturated fat constitutes 45% of the total fat, but a third of that is stearic acid, which is, at the very least, harmless. The remaining 4% of the fat is polyunsaturated, which also improves cholesterol levels. In sum, well over half—and perhaps as much as 70%—of the fat content of a porterhouse will improve cholesterol levels compared to what they would be if bread, potatoes, or pasta were consumed instead. The remaining 30% will raise LDL but will also raise HDL. All of this suggests that eating a porterhouse steak rather than carbohydrates might actually improve heart disease risk, although no nutritional authority who hasn't written a high-fat diet book will say this publicly.

As for the scientific studies, in the years since the 1984 consensus conference, the one thing they have not done is pile up evidence in support of the low-fat-for-all approach to the public good. If anything, they have added weight to Ahrens's fears that there may be a downside to populationwide lowfat recommendations. In 1986, for instance, just 1 year after NIH launched the National Cholesterol Education Program, also advising low-fat diets for everyone over 2 years old, epidemiologist David Jacobs of the University of Minnesota, Twin Cities, visited Japan. There he learned that Japanese physicians were advising patients to raise their cholesterol levels, because low cholesterol levels were linked to hemorrhagic stroke. At the time, Japanese men were dying from stroke almost as frequently as American men were succumbing to heart disease. Back in Minnesota, Jacobs looked for this low-cholesterol–stroke relationship in the MRFIT data and found it there, too. And the relationship transcended stroke: Men with very low cholesterol levels seemed prone to premature death; below 160 milligrams per deciliter (mg/dl), the lower the cholesterol level, the shorter the life.

Jacobs reported his results to NHLBI, which in 1990 hosted a conference to discuss the issue, bringing together researchers from 19 studies around the world. The data were consistent: When investigators tracked all deaths, instead of just heart disease deaths, the cholesterol curves were U-shaped for men and flat for women. In other words, men with cholesterol levels above 240 mg/dl tended to die prematurely from heart disease. But below 160 mg/dl, the men tended to die prematurely from cancer, respiratory and digestive diseases, and trauma. As for women, if anything, the higher their cholesterol, the longer they lived.

These mortality data can be interpreted in two ways. One, preferred by low-fat advocates, is that they cannot be meaningful. Rifkind, for instance, told *Science* that the excess deaths at low cholesterol levels *must* be due to preexisting conditions. In other words, chronic illness leads to low cholesterol levels, not vice versa. He pointed to the 1990 conference report as the definitive document on the issue and as support for his argument, although the report states unequivocally that this interpretation is not supported by the data.

The other interpretation is that what a low-fat diet does to serum cholesterol levels, and what that in turn does to arteries, may be only one component of the diet's effect on health. In other words, while low-fat diets might help prevent heart disease, they might also raise susceptibility to other conditions.

This is what always worried Ahrens. It's also one reason why the American College of Physicians, for instance, now suggests that cholesterol reduction is certainly worthwhile for those at high, short-term risk of dying of coronary heart disease but of "much smaller or . . . uncertain" benefit for everyone else.

This interpretation—that the connection between diet and health far transcends cholesterol—is also supported by the single most dramatic diet-heart trial ever conducted: the Lyon Diet Heart Study, led by Michel de Lorgeril of the French National Institute of Health and Medical Research (INSERM) and published in *Circulation* in February 1999. The investigators randomized 605 heart attack survivors, all on cholesterol-lowering drugs, into two groups. They counseled one to eat an AHA "prudent diet," very similar to that recommended for all Americans. They counseled the other to eat a Mediterranean-type diet, with more bread, cereals, legumes, beans, vegetables, fruits, and fish and less meat. Total fat and types of fat differed markedly in the two diets, but the HDL, LDL, and total cholesterol levels in the two groups remained virtually identical. Nonetheless, over 4 years of follow-up, the Mediterranean-diet group had only 14 cardiac deaths and nonfatal heart attacks compared to 44 for the "Western-type" diet group. The likely explanation, wrote de Lorgeril and his colleagues, is that the "protective effects [of the Mediterranean diet] were not related to serum concentrations of total, LDL or HDL cholesterol."

Many researchers find the Lyon data so perplexing that they're left questioning the methodology of the trial. Nonetheless, says NIH's Harlan, the data "are very provocative. They do bring up the issue of whether if we look only at cholesterol levels we aren't going to miss something very important." De Lorgeril believes the diet's protective effect comes primarily from omega-3 fatty acids, found in seed oils, meat, cereals, green leafy vegetables, and fish, and from antioxidant compounds, including vitamins, trace elements, and flavonoids. He told *Science* that most researchers and journalists in the field are prisoners of the "cholesterol paradigm." Although dietary fat and serum cholesterol "are obviously connected," he says, "the connection is not a robust one" when it comes to heart disease.

DIETARY TRADE-OFFS

One inescapable reality is that death is a trade-off, and so is diet. "You have to eat something," says epidemiologist Hugh Tunstall Pedoe of the University of Dundee, U.K., spokesperson for the 21-nation Monitoring Cardiovascular Disease Project run by the World Health Organization. "If you eat more of one thing, you eat a lot less of something else. So for every theory saying this disease is caused by an excess in x, you can produce an alternative theory saying it's a deficiency in y." It would be simple if, say, saturated fats could be cut from the diet and the calories with it, but that's not the case. Despite all expectations to the contrary, people tend to consume the same number of calories despite whatever diet they try. If they eat less total fat, for instance, they will eat more carbohydrates and probably less protein, because most protein comes in foods like meat that also have considerable amounts of fat.

This plus-minus problem suggests a different interpretation for virtually every diet study ever done, including, for instance, the kind of metabolic-ward studies that originally demonstrated the ability of saturated fats to raise cholesterol. If researchers reduce the amount of saturated fat in the test diet, they have to make up the calories elsewhere. Do they add polyunsaturated fats, for instance, or add carbohydrates? A single carbohydrate or mixed carbohydrates? Do they add green leafy vegetables, or do they add pasta? And so it goes. "The sky's the limit," says nutritionist Alice Lichtenstein of Tufts University in Boston. "There are a million perturbations."

These trade-offs also confound the kind of epidemiological studies that demonized saturated fat from the 1950s onward. In particular, individuals who eat copious amounts of meat and dairy products, and plenty of saturated fats in the process, tend not to eat copious amounts of vegetables and fruits. The same holds for entire populations. The eastern Finns, for instance, whose lofty heart disease rates convinced Ancel Keys and a generation of researchers of the evils of fat, live within 500 kilometers of the Arctic Circle and rarely see fresh produce or a green vegetable. The Scots, infamous for eating perhaps the least wholesome diet in the developed world, are in a similar fix. Basil Rifkind recalls being laughed at once on this point when he lectured to Scottish physicians on healthy diets: "One said, 'You talk about increasing fruits and vegetable consumption, but in the area I work in there's not a single grocery store.'" In both cases, researchers joke that the only green leafy vegetable these populations consume regularly is tobacco. As for the purported benefits of the widely hailed Mediterranean diet, is it the fish, the olive oil, or the fresh vegetables? After all, says Harvard epidemiologist Dimitrios Trichopoulos, a native of Greece, the olive oil is used either to cook vegetables or as dressing over salads. "The quantity of vegetables consumed is almost a pound [half a kilogram] a day," he says, "and you cannot eat it without olive oil. And we eat a lot of legumes, and we cannot eat legumes without olive oil."

Indeed, recent data on heart disease trends in Europe suggest that a likely explanation for the differences between countries and over time is the availability of fresh produce year-round rather than differences in fat intake. While the press often plays up the French paradox—the French have little heart disease despite seemingly high saturated fat consumption—the real paradox is throughout Southern Europe, where heart disease death rates have steadily dropped while animal fat consumption has steadily risen, says University of Cambridge epidemiologist John Powles, who studies national disease trends.

The same trend appears in Japan. "We have this idea that it's the Arcadian past, the life in the village, the utopia that we've lost," Powles says; "that the really protective Mediterranean diet is what people ate in the 1950s." But that notion isn't supported by the data: As these Mediterranean nations became more affluent, says Powles, they began to eat proportionally more meat and with it more animal fat. Their heart disease rates, however, continued to improve compared to populations that consumed as much animal fat but had less access to fresh vegetables throughout the year. To Powles, the antifat movement was founded on the Puritan notion that "something bad had to have an evil cause, and you got a heart attack because you did something wrong, which was eating too much of a bad thing, rather than not having enough of a good thing."

The other salient trade-off in the plus-minus problem of human diets is carbohydrates. When the federal government began pushing low-fat diets, the scientists and administrators, and virtually everyone else involved, hoped that Americans would replace fat calories with fruits and vegetables and legumes, but it didn't happen. If nothing else, economics worked against it. The food industry has little incentive to advertise nonproprietary items: broccoli, for instance. Instead, says NYU's Nestle, the great bulk of the $30-billion-plus spent yearly on food advertising goes to selling carbohydrates in the guise of fast food, sodas, snacks, and candy bars. And carbohydrates are all too often what Americans eat.

Carbohydrates are what Harvard's Willett calls the flip side of the calorie trade-off problem. Because it is exceedingly difficult to add pure protein to a diet in any quantity, a low-fat diet is, by definition, a high-carbohydrate diet—just as a low-fat cookie or low-fat yogurt are, by definition, high in carbohydrates. Numerous studies now suggest that high-carbohydrate diets can raise triglyceride levels, create small, dense LDL particles, and reduce HDL—a combination, along with a condition known as "insulin resistance," that Stanford endocrinologist Gerald Reaven has labeled "syndrome X." Thirty percent of adult males and 10% to 15% of post-menopausal women have this particular syndrome X profile, which is associated with a several-fold increase in heart disease risk, says Reaven, even among those patients whose LDL levels appear otherwise normal. Reaven and Ron Krauss, who studies fats and lipids at Lawrence Berkeley National Laboratory in California, have shown that when men eat high-carbohydrate diets their cholesterol profiles may shift from normal to syndrome X. In other words, the more carbohydrates replace saturated fats, the more likely the end result will be syndrome X and an increased heart disease risk. "The problem is so clear right now it's almost a joke," says Reaven. How this balances out is the unknown. "It's a bitch of a question," says Marc Hellerstein, a nutritional biochemist at the University of California, Berkeley, "maybe the great public health nutrition question of our era."

The other worrisome aspect of the carbohydrate trade-off is the possibility that, for some individuals, at least, it might actually be easier to gain weight on low-fat/high-carbohydrate regimens than on higher fat diets. One of the many factors that influence hunger is the glycemic index, which measures how fast carbohydrates are broken down into simple sugars and moved into the bloodstream. Foods with the highest glycemic index are simple sugars and processed grain products like pasta and white rice, which cause a rapid rise in blood sugar after a meal. Fruits, vegetables, legumes, and even unprocessed starches—pasta *al dente*, for instance—cause a much slower rise in blood sugar. Researchers have hypothesized that eating high–glycemic index foods increases hunger later because insulin overreacts to the spike in blood sugar. "The high insulin levels cause the nutrients from the meal to get absorbed and very avidly stored away, and once they are, the body can't access them," says David Ludwig, director of the obesity clinic at Children's Hospital Boston. "The body appears to run out of fuel." A few hours after eating, hunger returns.

If the theory is correct, calories from the kind of processed carbohydrates that have become the staple of the American diet are not the same as calories from fat, protein, or complex carbohydrates when it comes to controlling weight. "They may cause a hormonal change that stimulates hunger and leads to overeating," says Ludwig, "especially in environments where food is abundant. . . ."

In 1979, 2 years after McGovern's committee released its Dietary Goals, Ahrens wrote to *The Lancet* describing what he had learned over 30 years of studying fat and cholesterol metabolism: "It is absolutely certain that no one can reliably predict whether a change in dietary regimens will have any effect whatsoever on the incidence of new events of [coronary heart disease], nor in whom." Today, many nutrition researchers, acknowledging the complexity of the situation, find themselves siding with Ahrens. Krauss, for instance, who chairs the AHA Dietary Guidelines Committee, now calls it "scientifically naïve" to expect that a single dietary regime can be beneficial for everybody: "The 'goodness' or 'badness' of anything as complex as dietary fat and its subtypes will ultimately depend on the context of the individual."

Given the proven success and low cost of cholesterol-lowering drugs, most physicians now prescribe drug treatment for patients at high risk of heart disease. The drugs reduce LDL cholesterol levels by as much as 30%. Diet rarely drops LDL by more than 10%, which is effectively trivial for healthy individuals, although it may be worth the effort for those at high risk of heart disease whose cholesterol levels respond well to it.

The logic underlying population-wide recommendations such as the latest USDA Dietary Guidelines is that limiting saturated fat intake—even if it does little or nothing to extend the lives of healthy individuals and even if not all saturated fats are equally bad—might still delay tens of thousands of deaths each year throughout the entire country. Limiting total fat consumption is considered reasonable advice because it's simple and easy to understand, and it may limit calorie intake. Whether it's scientifically justifiable may simply not be relevant. "When you don't have any real good answers in this business," says Krauss, "you have to accept a few not so good ones as the next best thing."

2003

Editor: OLIVER SACKS

Common Ground

FROM *TIKKUN*

> Doctors routinely go to great lengths to care for their patients but, beyond a dose of bedside manner, maintain a professional distance from their patients' personal lives. Doing so is not always easy, however. Danielle Ofri, a doctor and writer, recollects an episode from the early days of her career when her conscience, and her own past experience, prompted her to reach out personally to a patient.

WE ARE A CATHOLIC MEDICAL CENTER, DR. OFRI." The medical director leaned back in his chair across from my desk. "Do you have any issues with that?"

His gray hair was severely parted on the right and I could trace the individual strands that were tethered down on the side by hair grease. A stethoscope peeked out of the pocket of his tailored blue suit. He had just finished his long introductory speech with me, enumerating the vast array of services and the selling points of his medical group. He was clearly trying to impress me with his institution. After all, the reason I was doing a temp assignment here was because they were short-handed and looking to hire.

I was caught off balance by the question. What could he be driving at? Was my Jewish background an issue here? Was my last name too "ethnic"? I paused and then slowly asked back, "Should I have issues?"

"Well," he replied, in his careful New England lilt, "we do not promote birth control. If a patient requests it, we will provide it. But we do not offer it, promote it, or condone it."

Before my super-ego could grab control, my New York sassiness spilled out. "So, I don't suppose you perform abortions, do you?"

I could not believe I had just said that.

The older physician did not appear fazed. "No, we do not terminate pregnancies. Nor do we permit referrals to physicians who do. If a patient requests that service, we have them call their own insurance company. Their insurance companies make the referral."

He stood up and put out his hand. "We are glad to have you aboard, Dr. Ofri. We hope you enjoy your six weeks with us. And," he paused with a smile, "we hope you consider staying longer."

I remained in my office after he left, a little confused about what I had just heard and very embarrassed about the sauciness of my retort. I finally brushed it off, attributing it to high-level politics that I was not a part of.

I had never spent much time in New England before. The town looked just as I had imagined. Regal Victorian mansions with wraparound wooden porches lined the main street. Well-tended rose bushes graced the picket fences. Manicured shrubbery lined the driveways. A river meandered through the town and I often saw kayakers as I drove over the small bridges each morning in my beige rental car. This was a different planet from my native New York City.

I had been assigned to a small private practice that was short-handed after two doctors had moved away. The staff members welcomed me warmly. They gave me a large office with three exam rooms in a separate wing of the suite, and a nurse, Karen, to work exclusively with me. At the beginning of each appointment Karen would take a brief history from the patient, check their vital signs and jot down their medications. When I entered into the room afterward to see the patient, I would find all the supplies that I might need for that particular patient neatly laid out. I learned that the walls of the examining rooms were fairly thin because when I was finished with the patient, Karen would be waiting outside with whatever vaccines or medications I had discussed with the patient.

This was nothing like Bellevue Hospital—the city hospital where I did my residency. Practicing medicine had never been so easy! I noticed that the medicine cabinet was stocked with free samples of birth control pills along with the anti-hypertensives and cholesterol medications. Apparently, no one took the contraception rule too seriously.

Nobody ever bothered Karen and me in our little corner. It was as though we had our own practice. Between patients we would share stories of her life in New England and my experiences at Bellevue. And I loved that she kept a picture of her golden retriever, Sam, on her desk.

Three weeks into my assignment I met Diana Makower, a young computer programmer at a local financial firm. She was wearing a gray suit with a purple silk blouse. A single strand of pearls hung around her neck. Her carefully applied make-up had started to smudge from the tears slipping down her cheeks. "I think I'm pregnant," she spilled out, almost before I could introduce myself. "I did one of those home pregnancy tests and it was positive. All I need from you is a blood test."

I put down my stethoscope and pulled up a chair.

"It's a complicated situation," she wept. "I am ending a relationship with my boyfriend, but it wasn't him. I have an old friend, it's never been more than that, but I think he and I might be developing a romantic relationship. We slept together just once, three weeks ago. I really think we could have a serious relationship, but it is not ready for this. I can't believe this is happening."

"If you do turn out to be pregnant," I asked, "what do you think you would do?"

"I need to have an abortion. I can't have a kid now; I'm single, I don't have a stable relationship yet. I'm not ready for it now."

"Are you sure that's what you want to do? Have you considered other options, like adoption?"

"Absolutely," she said. "I have made my decision. I just need to know where to go."

I suddenly thought of the medical director with his slicked-down gray hair. According to the rules, I was supposed to tell Diana to call her insurance company. Her insurance company? I had visions of a bored bureaucrat slurping on his coffee while dispensing advice on a delicate matter to my distraught patient. How could I send Diana into a situation like that? I excused myself and went to consult Karen.

Karen did not know which local doctors performed abortions. "I stay out of that mess," she said. The Catholic hospital that the practice was affiliated with certainly did not. She sympathized with my predicament but warned me not to let the office manager know what I was doing. "Someone else gave out a phone number once," she said, "just a phone number. It wasn't even documented in the chart, but somehow it got out and they got into trouble."

I stared out the window and could see my rental car parked in front of a clapboard house across the street. The house was painted bright yellow with pale blue trim. A wooden porch surrounded three sides of the house. It was overflowing with hanging spider plants and overripe ferns. Wicker furniture with floral cushions was arranged around a wrought-iron table. An American flag dangled from a second-story window. This Catholic medical institution might choose not to perform abortions, but what about my ethical duty to provide the care my patient needed? Sending a distressed patient to an 800 telephone number would not hold water under the Hippocratic oath.

It seemed clear to me that my duty was first to my patient, and only secondarily to some faceless institution. Unfortunately, as a stranger to this small town, I did not know the local resources. I didn't know the names of the nearby physicians to even make the referral if I had wanted to break the rules. I suddenly pined for Bellevue, where I knew all the doctors and I knew the system. If I needed help, all I had to do was dial the operator and have the appropriate doctor paged. I looked back at the yellow and blue house across the road. It seemed hostile and antagonistic. The small-town civility made me feel claustrophobic.

Grinding my teeth, I re-entered the exam room. "As you may know, this medical practice is Catholic," I told Diana, "so we cannot provide referrals for abortion. The truth is, I wouldn't know where to send you even if I could. The rule is that you are supposed to call your insurance company and get the referral yourself. I would do it for you, but I can't. However, if you get the list of possible referrals, I will call around to find out which is the best."

Diana nodded, and then asked if she could be alone. I left her with a box of tissues and told her she could stay as long as she liked.

I called Diana the next day to let her know that the repeat pregnancy test was positive. When I called, I got her voice mail at work. She had told me that it was a private line, but suddenly I felt paranoid. I did not indicate that I was a physician and I left a cryptic message about results being "confirmatory of our original data."

Diana returned my call a few hours later. Her insurance company had given her two phone numbers, without names, in the next state over. Her health plan had no gynecologists in this state who performed abortions. Nobody in the state? My patient couldn't get the care that she needed in her home state? I was horrified. How could I send her off into the unknown like that? How could I abandon her to a couple of random, blank telephone numbers in another state? I felt like we were back in the 1950s, sneaking around with code words, no names mentioned, having to go out of state for an abortion. I plowed through my roster of patients for the day, but I couldn't focus on the coughs, rashes, and shoulder pains. All I could think about was Diana. I imagined her driving over the state line, tears pressing at her lid margins. The lonesomeness in the car, the bitter highway, the directions scribbled on the back of a used envelope. I imagined her squinting at the scrawled directions, the car slipping ever so slightly out of the lane as her mind diffused focus from the highway median to the second left after the traffic light to the enormity of what lay ahead. Then she would tighten her grip and the car would even out. She'd admonish herself to watch the highway. And so she would watch the highway, look at the highway, stare at the highway, until the yellow lines would begin to quiver, then shudder, then melt into the saltiness dribbling down her face.

Between patients I paced around my office, too irritated to sit still. What kind of place was this where some administrative rule could interfere with patient care? Wasn't patient care more important than a bunch of rules? I wondered when was the last time any of those bureaucrats had actually seen a patient. When was the last time they'd sat face-to-face with a patient, watching the tension lines around the mouth tremble, smelling the moist desperation, accepting the burden and the honor of tender secrets? I fumed all afternoon, cursing the insurance companies and the politicians whose ideologies and business concerns were elbowing into my office, into the sacred space that my patient and I shared.

Then Karen told me that the wife of one of the doctors used to work at a teen clinic. Grateful for this information, I called immediately. She knew of those two out-of-state facilities and told me they had reputations for treating patients like cattle. There was, however, a private women's clinic two hours north that was professional and reliable. But most insurance companies would not cover the cost of the procedure.

I called Diana at home that evening. She had already made an appointment at one of the out-of-state clinics and was very appreciative of my "insider information." I gave her the number of the private women's clinic.

"Have you told him?" I asked.

"No. No, I can't tell him. Not yet, at least. Maybe afterward."

"Is there anyone that you'd feel comfortable talking to, a friend, a family member? Is there someone who could come with you?"

"No, not really," she replied. "I mean I have good friends, but I couldn't tell them about this. They wouldn't understand."

I winced at the thought of her going alone. There was a sense of something shameful, something to hide. "Bring your own bathrobe," I added, before we hung up. "It's more comfortable than a hospital gown."

I called her again the following day. Just to make sure she was okay. We chatted a bit and it turned out that she had grown up in New York.

"Really?" I asked, excited to uncover a fellow New York native here in the wilds of New England. "Where were you born?"

"Queens," she said, "but then we moved out to Long Island, which is where I really grew up."

"My family did something similar. I was born in Manhattan but then we moved out of the city to Rockland. I hated the suburbs, though. I never forgave my parents for leaving the city."

"Me too," Diana said. "I spent all of my high school years hanging out in the city, trying to make up for my parents' foolish flight to the 'burbs. My friends and I would take the train in on weekends and hang out in Greenwich Village."

"So did I," I said excitedly. "We used to tramp up and down Bleecker Street then go hear music at Kenny's Castaways."

"I know Kenny's Castaways. The club that never checked ID."

"That's the one. Kenny's Castaways. And you went to Le Figaro Cafe, didn't you?"

"Absolutely—southwest corner of Bleecker and MacDougal. That's where I had my first cappuccino. I couldn't bear to drink my parents' instant coffee after that."

I left work that evening and drove to my hotel. The very act of driving, of commuting by car, made me feel odd. It had been more than fifteen years since I'd relied on a car for transportation. In New York I was a regular denizen of the subway, and an avid bicyclist. I particularly relished gridlock traffic in Manhattan. I adored watching the irate drivers fume inside their cars, locked in the daily midtown mess, while I whizzed past on my ratty old ten-speed, needling my way in and out of unloading trucks, yellow cabs, and wayward pedestrians.

And now as I sat in my rental car, idling at a traffic light, I felt confined. I pined for the freedom of my bike. I yearned for the foot-based culture of New York, in which everything I needed was in walking or biking distance.

Some people feel nervous in big cities; I feel nervous in small towns. No pedestrians on the streets. No one to make eye contact with. No one to negotiate personal space on a sidewalk with. No mass of actual human beings on the street to remind you that you are alive and part of a species. Only cars.

And so I sat in my car, cut off from humanity, isolated in a metal box that rumbled with diesel heat under my feet as the traffic light languished on red. Sure, the old houses were beautiful to look at and the landscaping impressive, but there were no people. I craved people. Stuck in my car, I could think only about Diana. She was also cut off. There was no one she could confide in, no one she could bring with her. I realized that I was probably the only person in this world she had spoken to about this. In the small enclosed space of my car with that bland smell of whatever they use to make seat stuffing, the heaviness of that burden weighed onto the cramped muscles of my shoulders. There were hundreds of people tucked into similar steel automobiles who were riding along the same street as me—hundreds of cars shuttling human beings within their tiny isolated orbits—but there was only one that contained Diana Makower's confidence. As a woman, I felt an almost sisterly duty to be there for her during this uniquely feminine quandary. As her doctor I felt that I had the re-sponsibility to make sure she got the medical care she needed and felt guilty that I couldn't help her more directly. And as a human being, as the driver of the steel box that held her confidence, I felt the moral obligation to hold that dear, to treat that confidence with the utmost respect. I couldn't abandon her during this difficult and lonely period.

When I arrived back at my hotel, I called her again. Just to see how she was doing. Two days later I called Diana again. I somehow found a pretext to call her almost every day until her abortion date the following week.

I felt a bit more like a therapist than a physician and I understood why therapists are to keep their personal lives out of the therapy. Therapy is about the patient, not about the therapist.

I ached to share my own experience, but professionalism, and I suppose some lingering shame, prevented me. I'd been only seventeen at the time and just returning home from my first year in college. I had passed my calculus final exam and was pretty sure about physics. I had turned in my last organic chemistry lab report. I was about to go off to be a counselor at summer camp when I discovered that I was pregnant.

I'd had a steady boyfriend the entire year. Before we got involved I had gone to Planned Parenthood because I didn't want to be irresponsible. I remembered the long talk with the counselor in the windowless room with the overly cheery posters. We'd decided together on the diaphragm for birth control. The package insert listed a 95 percent effectiveness rate. No one ever spoke about the other 5 percent.

I lived in New York, the most liberal city in the most liberal state. My friends and parents were all liberal, pro-choice people. But I was too scared to tell anyone; it just didn't seem possible that it was happening and it didn't seem possible to tell anyone. After the pregnancy test I sat in a park and cried alone. It was a park where my family used to have picnics when I was little. My parents would buy a precooked chicken from the nearby kosher deli. We'd bring paper plates and the vegetable salad. And of course, our dog Kushi. This was her chance to run off the leash. Sitting in that park now I longed for the smell of her soft black fur. I craved her warm, all-accepting dogness to snuggle up to. Someone to whom I wouldn't have to explain all the complicated human confusions. But she'd died the previous year, just before I'd left for college.

I arranged an appointment at a local women's clinic. That night I made a long-distance call to my boyfriend. The geographical and personal gaps were apparently too vast to bridge—he couldn't quite accept what I was telling him over the phone. And he didn't offer to help me pay for it.

The next day I lied to my parents about having a party to go to so I could borrow the car. The clinic had said to bring a comfortable bathrobe. I snuck my mother's out of her closet.

The drive was eerily dissociated. The yellow lines in the road didn't seem parallel to the outer curbs. They listed and buckled, slighting the rules of Cartesian geometry. They drifted to other planes, to the odd dimensions of irrational numbers. Then they'd swing back with a jolt, clobbering into my focus.

As the car shuffled closer and closer to the clinic, I felt my body shrinking. It dwindled within itself until there was nothing left but a little girl who desperately wanted her dog.

I lugged myself, or what little was left of myself, up the steps. I registered a name—I think it was mine—and followed the nurse into the back. She instructed me to change into my bathrobe and wait in the main room until I was called. The room was filled with eight or so women in different-colored bathrobes. We could have been at a slumber party, except that no one was smiling. Some magazines were scattered on the table, but the articles were about beef casseroles and electricity-saving tips. I pulled my mother's flannel robe around me and concentrated on the orange industrial carpeting. It really was orange, although if you looked carefully, there were lonely bits of red and yellow scattered within.

They gave me a choice of general or local anaesthesia. The budding college-educated scientist wanted local, wanted to know everything that was going on, wanted to control the whole biology experiment. But the little girl who yearned for her dog immediately chose general. I didn't want to know. I didn't want to remember.

I awoke crying in another room. It was overly bright and the sheets were stiff. My stomach pulsed with an alien ache. The nurse said to stop acting like a baby, it didn't really hurt that much. I checked out and went back to the same park to cry some more.

A week later, a letter arrived from my boyfriend. He told me that he felt terribly guilty. As "penance" for himself, he said he could never be with me again. That summer was long and lonely.

In the years that have gone by I have told almost no one. Part of me feels that I should be contributing to the destigmatization of abortion by being open about my own experience. Yet another part of me feels it is something personal. Worse yet, something to hide. I feel guilty and hypocritical. Sometimes I think about the child that might have been. At seventeen, I had precious few resources to raise a child. I would never have finished college, much less gone to medical school. I might have faced a lifetime of minimum-wage jobs and food stamps. What would my child's life have been like?

I called Diana after her abortion. She told me that the staff members at the clinic were extremely kind and supportive, and that it didn't hurt too much. I breathed a sigh of relief. We spoke a few more times after that. Each time I felt the urge to share my story, but I couldn't.

I am not a politically active person. So much of what transpires in the government seems to have no bearing on my life; I just want to take care of my patients and my family. The decision about abortion is a difficult one, not one that I would wish anyone to face. But when I see teenage mothers in my clinic with minimal education, no job skills, barely mature enough to take care of themselves let alone the two or three babies on their laps, I am viscerally aware that my life was at the mercy of laws that permitted access to safe abortion. A different time or a different place and the outcome could have been vastly different.

Doctors often unconsciously separate themselves from patients— they are the sick ones and we, in our white coats, are different from them. It is humbling, and also relieving, to know that we are all made of the same stuff.

FLOYD SKLOOT

The Melody Lingers On

FROM *SOUTHWEST REVIEW*

As researchers try to get a better fix on its causes and pathology, Alzheimer's disease remains a terrifying mystery. With candor and tenderness, the poet and writer Floyd Skloot observes the toll the disease is taking on his ninety-one-year-old mother, who literally and figuratively may have forgotten the words but can remember the tune.

A T NINETY-ONE, DEEP IN DEMENTIA, MY MOTHER NO longer remembers her life. Thoughts drift as though in zero gravity, bumping occasionally against a few stray bits of memory, but nothing coheres. Her two husbands, her late son, all the cousins and community acquaintances who filled her days, her ambitions and achievements, her travels and yearnings—almost everything has floated away from her grasp, mere debris.

"Was I happily married?" she asked last week, when my wife, Beverly, and I took her out for coffee and snacks. Before I could answer, she added, "*Oh how we somethinged on the hmmm hmm we were wed. Dear, was I ever on the stage?*"

I nodded and said, "On the radio too."

"I was on the radio?" She smiled, closed her eyes and sang, "*Birds gotta swim, fish gotta fly, da-dada-da one man da-da die.*" Then she lifted a fragment of blueberry muffin and said, "Was I ever on the stage?"

It's not just her distant past that's gone. What happened two minutes ago is as lost as what happened during the twenty-seven years she lived in Manhattan, the twenty years she lived in Brooklyn or the forty-four years she lived on Long Island. Now that she's in Oregon, she doesn't know she ever lived elsewhere. Sometimes she believes her Portland nursing home is a beachfront hotel, just as she sometimes believes I am her late brother.

What's become apparent, though, is that she still knows songs. She retains many lyrics, snatches that may get confused but are easily recognizable, and when the lyrics are missing the melodies remain. She loves to sing, sings on key and with zest, and I can't help wondering why song has hung on so tenaciously while her life memories have not.

It's tempting to take the psychological approach: She never was very happy with her life, but she was happy dreaming of stardom as a torch singer. She was happy knowing she'd had a brief career singing on radio in the mid-1930s, where her five-minute program on WBNX in the Bronx aired opposite Rudy Valee. In the chemical bath of her mind, she always transformed a few years of apprentice costume work in the legitimate theater, and an assortment of roles in local community theater, into a protracted career in the *Thee-a-ter*. No question: she loved performing. I remember how extravagantly she accompanied herself on the piano, sliding along the bench to reach her notes, stomping the pedals, rising and sitting again, going through her brief repertoire before erupting with gusto at the end as a signal for applause. According to this psychological approach, my mother forgets what she needs to forget, and is left with song.

But such an explanation isn't really convincing, not when the evidence of deep organic brain damage is so apparent in her activities of daily living. She cannot dress herself, needs reminding during a meal if she is to continue eating, cannot process new information. Her failures of memory are not choices, not driven by subconscious needs. It must be that, unlike personal memories or the recall of facts, such things as song lyrics are stored in a part of her brain that has, so far, escaped the ravages of her dementia.

AS A RESULT OF ADVANCES in neuroscience, the pattern of my mother's losses can be pinpointed biologically. First, there's the sheer diminishment in her overall cognitive capacity. In his book *Searching for Memory*, Harvard psychologist Daniel L. Schacter says that "overall brain mass steadily shrinks as we enter our sixties and seventies, at roughly 5 percent to 10 percent per decade." So my mother's brain has probably lost about a quarter of its size by now. In addition, "blood flow and uptake of oxygen both decrease significantly" and there is "widespread loss of neurons in the cortex," a major site of memory storage. In Alzheimer's patients, the shrinking brain also becomes clotted with plaques and tangles, and there is further neuron loss in the hippocampus, a part of the brain associated with the ability to remember the ongoing incidents in our lives. This set of compounding pathologies explains most of her symptoms, but not the curious endurance of those songs. It's most likely that my mother's lifelong joy in performing, and the powerful emotional forces associated with it for her, have enabled the deeper storage of lyric and melody in her amygdala. This almond-shaped organ in the inner brain is critical for forming and sustaining emotional memories. Though most often spoken of in connection with persistent, enduring traumatic memories, it also is responsible for enduring positive memories. This is where our most vivid memories reside, etched there by a mix of chemical and physical processes that ensure their endurance. I suspect that my mother's amygdala has not yet been overtaken by her disease process. This would explain not only the persistence of her song repertoire, but the relative calmness and sweetness she still manifests. As David Shenk notes in his book *The Forgetting*, when the "amygdala becomes compromised, control over primitive emotions like fear, anger, and craving is disrupted; hostile emotions and bursts of anxiety may occur all out of proportion to events, or even out of nowhere."

My mother is not there yet. In trying to reduce her symptoms to these objective clinical explanations, I know I'm trying to cushion myself from the changes she's undergone and from what lies ahead. But this is my mother, not some interesting case history in a neurology text. This is the woman who fought to allow my birth, eight years after my older brother's, overcoming my father's continuing resistance. The woman who recited nonsense verse to me, sounds I still remember fifty years later though she does not, though she can no longer always remember who I am: *Nicky nicky tembo, whatso rembo, wudda wudda boosky, hippo pendro, national pom pom.* The woman, so miserable and disappointed throughout her life, filled with anger, volatile, friendless in old age, who now in dementia has grown sweet and accommodating, happy to greet the day, who has come back to song.

Those songs of hers, which routinely interrupt any effort at communication, are in fact signs of hope. They represent an enduring part of her past, connected with the rare joy in her life, which is why they linger when so much is gone. I must learn to welcome rather than be annoyed by them. In many ways, they're all we have left of her.

LIKE THE MASS OF HER brain, the physical structure of my mother's body is also shrinking. At her tallest, about 5′ 1″, the top of her head used to be level with the middle of my forehead; now she comes up to my throat. She was always wide, too, a solid and blocky woman whose flowing outfits didn't disguise her figure as she'd hoped. She took up room despite being small. But now she has lost both water and mass. Her once swollen legs have slimmed; she sags and looks frail. It's as though my mother is pulling herself in around a diminishing core, the dwindling autobiographical self she's losing touch with, and closing down before my eyes.

She was moving slowly toward our table in the coffee shop, inching her walker along, taking a few steps and stopping. When she reached the table where Beverly was placing napkins and spoons, she looked around with a smile, let go of her side rails, tilted her head heavenward and sang, "*S'wonderful, s'marvelous, la da da.*"

Her voice still comes from down near her chest, the way it's supposed to, a richly resonating smoky contralto. It's almost as deep as my own off-key tenor. But as a young singer, my mother was a soprano. There are three surviving 78 rpm records from her radio show that prove it. She was called "The Melody Girl of the Air" on a program hosted by an old family friend, and once a week she sang a few standards for him. George Gershwin was alive then and Gershwin was her favorite. There were times when she hinted at a romance with him, never going quite so far as to say they'd dated, but implying that a certain dashing young composer—whom she was not at liberty to name but who had a dowdy lyricist brother—was once very interested in her.

A solid fifty years of unfiltered Chesterfields transformed my mother's voice and, though she stopped smoking in her early seventies, those cigarettes remain audible now in her gravelly tones. But she can and does still belt out the tunes, holding nothing back. This dynamic and deeper voice is how I remember her singing. I never could make sense out of those old records, the high pitched girlishness, the piercing delivery. In my hearing, she sang dark and windy.

There was always a well-tuned mahogany piano against a living room wall in our various apartments. Its lid was shut, its music deck empty, its surfaces without dust or fingerprints. No one was allowed to sit on its bench or open the keyboard lid, much less touch the keys or press the pedals down. No examining the sheet music hidden inside the bench. She wasn't sure she wanted us even to *look* at the piano.

By the 1950s, as I was growing up, my mother's performance repertoire had been condensed to five tunes that she would play in the same order. She seldom sang more than one refrain and chorus, took no requests, brooked no singing along. She would consent to entertain at the end of small dinner parties or holiday meals, perching on the bench and holding her chin up until there was total silence. Then she struck a chord *fortissimo* and launched herself into performance. First came the Gershwin portion of the program, "They Can't Take That Away from Me," "'S Wonderful" and "Our Love Is Here to Stay." Then she did Rodgers and Hart's "Bewitched, Bothered, and Bewildered" from *Pal Joey* and finished with her signature song, Jerome Kern and Oscar Hammerstein's "Can't Help Lovin' Dat Man," from *Show Boat*. No encores. She was still, it seemed, tied to the fifteen-minute radio show format.

I see now that her songs were songs of love, joyful love. Along with fame as a performer, this was the other great unfulfilled yearning of her life. It was not there with the man she married first, who died in 1961, the man she spoke of in my hearing as "your father the butcher." Nor was it there apparently with her second husband, a kind and gentle widower, the man she spoke of as "that nice, handsome fellow." After his death, when she moved into a retirement hotel overlooking the boardwalk, my mother had a succession of boyfriends but none without glaring faults—too old and bent, too devoted to children and grandchildren, too working-class, too senile. Now, from within her own dementia, one of the main themes woven through her rambling speech is love, joyful love. Was she happily married? Does she have a boyfriend? Are Beverly and I married? Are we happy? Is the nurse married? The young man behind the Starbucks counter? Can we help my mother find a new boyfriend?

Even as a child, I sensed something that made me very uncomfortable with my mother's recitals. It wasn't just the showy way she played, or the too familiar spontaneity of her moves. It had to do with the look on her face, a rapturous hunger, and the sudden exposure of her deepest, most obsessive wishes. She leaped off her piano bench like a nearly drowned diver suddenly bursting to the surface, head back, mouth wide open, and I imagine her longing was palpable to everyone. There was something brazenly sad about her selection of romantic hits, a sadness I failed to appreciate for most of my life. She must have wanted what she could never have, what few people ever have, and she hadn't let go of the need: idealized romantic love. Her playlist was a litany of failed dreams.

Those failed dreams and her overall sense of disgruntlement seem to have shrunk now too. With the fading of memory and life story has come an apparent narrowing of mood. From the outside, seeing how she is now, this phenomenon suggests a compensation for her shattering losses, and I hope that's how it works for her. I know it could have been otherwise. Like so many people with Alzheimer's or deep dementia, she could long ago have become even angrier and more tormented, hostile and restless.

MY MOTHER LOOKED DOWN AT the coffee in her cup, unsure what to do with it. She gazed into its tawny surface and blinked. Only when she looked away did she, as though triggered by signals from a more instinctive zone of her brain, lift the cup toward her lips. I helped her steady it.

"Was I ever on the stage, dear?" she asked again.

I responded automatically: "I whistle a happy tune . . . ," and she beamed, picking up the tune itself, humming along, nodding firmly. One way to look at this, I've realized, is to consider song lyrics as my mother's native tongue. Tonal and melodious, its beauties of sound offset by the banality of its linguistic content. Well, beauties of sound when she sings it, not when I do.

"What comes next?" she asked.

"I hold my head . . . ," and she nods again, taking over, finishing out the sentence after her own fashion: "*so no one da dee da I forget.*"

From the mid-1950s to the mid-1970s, my mother was active in community theater. She was usually cast in small singing roles. I remember her playing Melba Snyder in *Pal Joey*, doing the striptease number "Zip" in the basement of our Brooklyn synagogue. She played the nanny, Gooch, in *Auntie Mame*, where she was dressed up by Mame and her friend Vera for one night as a swinger (singing "I lived! I lived! I lived!"). She was King Mongkut's first wife, Lady Thiang, in *The King and I*, shunted aside for younger wives, the romance of marriage gone though she still admires her husband and tells Anna so ("Something Wonderful"). Taking on a non-singing role, she was Yente the Matchmaker in *Fiddler on the Roof*. What these roles all have in common is their tangential relationship to passion: a cynical stripper, an unglamorous nanny spruced up for a quick taste of the sexy high life, a queen spurned and settling for grandeur instead of romance, an old woman whose business is brewing love for others. Ironically, even as she got to fulfill her desire for performing, the roles she played re-enacted romantic failure and disappointment.

I performed with her on occasion, when no reasonable excuse could be found. When she was in *The King and I*, I was ten and played one of the king's children, learning my one schoolroom speech ("What is that green over there?"), rehearsing the March of the Siamese Children, singing my brief solo ("Suddenly I'm bright and breezy") in "Getting to Know You." At thirteen, during a horrifying cabaret-style local fund-raiser, I sang a duet with her, the dutiful Sonny Boy climbing upon my mother's knee though we were the same size.

When she wasn't part of a play's cast, she still became engaged in the productions. She attended rehearsals to play the piano or read cues or kibbitz. She painted sets. Resorting to her earliest contributions to the theater, she helped design costumes.

I remember her working on hat designs for a production of *Guys and Dolls*. She would glue buttons onto blank greeting cards, paint black dots for eyes in the buttonholes and red dots for mouths, add a few ink strokes for hair. Then she snipped bits of fabric and feathers to resemble hats, pasted them onto the crowns of the buttons and made tiny adjustments with toothpicks. Below the buttons, she drew the shape of necks, then added scarves or ties. It was possible for her to devote four or five intense hours a night to this work, cigarettes smoldering in her abalone shell ashtray. The finished illustrations would be spread out over a card table to dry or for further modification. Finally, she would bring them to rehearsal, stacked in a shoe box, and get herself ready for another round.

My mother was, clearly, a trouper. I cannot remember her being as focused or as sprightly as she was at her design work or within the acting company. She saved all the reviews from our local paper, all the programs, and most of the scripts. I found them in a storage locker when she moved into the retirement hotel and, just glancing at them, felt myself swamped with the scents and sounds of her theatrical life.

As we turned onto Boundary Avenue, bringing my mother back to the nursing home after our outing, Beverly said, "This is the street where you live." Then, as though on cue, all three of us started singing Lerner and Loewe's "On the Street Where You Live": *I have often walked down the street before.* My mother's voice fractured into laughter and she could hardly keep singing. Besides, she didn't exactly have the words anymore. So she went into scat: *Doo doo doo doo do, la da dee doo da, knowing I'm doo be la doo wee oh.* We pulled up to the front door, all three of us cackling at our mutual cleverness. I've noticed during recent visits that my mother's repertoire has actually expanded. She's no longer limited to the Big Five Hits. Now she'll bring out songs I never heard her sing before, like "Fly Me to the Moon" or "Anything Goes," which I recognize from the sustained melodies more than from the snippet of lyrics she can muster. Dixon and Henderson's "Bye, Bye Blackbird" from 1926, Gus Kahn's "Makin' Whoopee" from 1928. She sings Yiddish songs, too, all new to me, songs she must have learned during her childhood, when Yiddish was spoken at home and in the Upper West Side neighborhoods where she lived. I haven't heard her speak a word of Yiddish since we moved from Brooklyn in 1957 and cannot remember her ever singing in the language that might have marked her as marginal. She also now has the melodies for some Hebrew tunes she must be picking up during Sabbath services at the nursing home. I don't believe they come from her memory tune-bank because she never went to the synagogue except for social or theatrical events, and I haven't heard her utter a word in Hebrew before.

Much as I'm amazed to hear her dredge up songs from her childhood or youth, it's the phenomenon of new songs—"Adon Olam," for instance, and "Hatikvah"—that astounds me. Perhaps this means that, because she still connects so powerfully to music, she can somehow learn and remember fresh material, at least song material, particularly melodies, though in conversation she cannot remember the question she asked a moment before, or whether we told her what state we live in, or if we're married. Asked if she has been to Sabbath services, she says, "No, they don't have them here." But they do, and she has, and the melodies have stuck.

She also comes up with songs I know she's heard in my lifetime but I hadn't realized she remembered. And she delivers them with genuine glee. *Be down to la da in a taxi baby, doo dah be-dee dee in your hay dee hay.* Gradually, I've been discovering that this is an opportunity for conversation of a sort. While it's not possible for me to ask her questions and get meaningful answers, or share information with her about the life Beverly and I are leading, or even go over memories of childhood with her, we can approximate the give and take of conversation through song. "What are those?" I'll say, pointing to the necklace of beads she's made during a crafts session. "Baubles? Bangles?" And she'll say, *"Bubbles, Bangles bright shiny beads la da dee dah."* Or I'll hum the opening notes from "If I Were a Rich Man" and she will pick up the song from there.

I'm beginning to find a solace in this exchange. We have the rhythm of conversation, if not the content. A form of give and take that enables us still to feel connected by words, or at least by meaningful sounds. "The song is ended," as her favorite songwriter wrote, "but the melody lingers on." We are holding on to the melody of contact. And they can't take that away from me, from us, at least not yet.

2004

Editor: DAVA SOBEL

MICHAEL BENSON

What Galileo *Saw*

FROM *THE NEW YORKER*

> *In 2003, the unmanned space orbiter* Galileo *burned up in the gaseous outer layers of Jupiter, ending a remarkable fourteen-year voyage through the solar system. Michael Benson recalls the unexpected triumphs of this scrappy explorer.*

FOR THE PAST EIGHT YEARS, THE VINTAGE SPACECRAFT known as the *GalileoOrbiter* has been tracing a complex path between Jupiter's four large moons. During this time, it has made detailed scientific observations and taken thousands of high-resolution photographs, beaming them to Earth, half a billion miles away. On September 21st, 2003, *Galileo*'s extended tour of Jupiter's satellites will end, and it will hurtle directly toward the immense banded clouds and spinning storms of the largest planet in the solar system.

As the orbiter plummets toward Jupiter's atmosphere, several of its observational instruments will send a live transmission to Earth, and this data stream could prove highly illuminating. *Galileo* may be able to confirm the existence of a rocky ring close to the planet—a feature that has long been suspected. Other instruments will convey information about the density and composition of the mysterious, smokelike "gossamer rings" suspended inside the orbit of Amalthea, a moonlet near Jupiter.

At 2:57 P.M. Eastern Daylight Time, *Galileo* will be travelling at a speed of thirty miles per second, and its boxy octagonal frame will start glowing red. Seconds later, it will be white-hot. By 3 P.M., many of its eighty-five thousand components will have separated from each other, and will continue to break up, becoming a hail of rapidly lique-fying shrapnel. By the time the spacecraft's remains are three hundred miles inside Jupiter's atmosphere, where the temperature is twelve hundred degrees, all its aluminum components will have vaporized. At six hundred miles, its titanium parts will disintegrate. Jupiter is a gaseous planet, with a radius of forty-four thousand miles—big enough to contain all the other planets and moons of the solar system—and *Galileo* will have hardly penetrated its outermost atmo-spheric layer. Having just crossed Jupiter's threshold, it will vanish, leaving no clues of its earthly origin or its complicated mission.

Obliteration is precisely what NASA intends for the spacecraft. The reason is that *Galileo* may still harbor some signs of life on Earth: microorganisms that have survived since its launch from the Kennedy Space Center, in Florida, in 1989. If the orbiter were left to circle Jupiter after running out of propellant (barring an interven-tion, this would likely happen within a year), it might eventually crash into Europa, one of Jupiter's large moons. In 1996, *Galileo* con-ducted the first of eight close flybys of Europa, producing breathtak-ing pictures of its surface, which suggested that the moon has an immense ocean hidden beneath its frozen crust. These images have led to vociferous scientific debate about the prospects for life there; as a result, NASA officials decided that it was necessary to avoid the possibility of seeding Europa with alien life-forms. And so the craft has been programmed to commit suicide, guaranteeing a fiery, spec-tacular end to one of the most ambitious, tortured, and revelatory missions in the history of space exploration.

* * *

ALTHOUGH EUROPA WASN'T THE ONLY target of *Galileo*'s camera during its years in space, its pictures of this weirdly fissured sphere—many of which show icebergs that apparently rafted into new positions before being refrozen into the moon's ice crust—produced euphoria among planetary scientists in the late nineties. They now speculate that Europa's global ocean may be more than thirty miles deep, which would mean that the moon has considerably more water than Earth. As Richard Terrile, a member of the NASA division that designed *Galileo*, has said, "How often is an ocean discovered? The last one was the Pacific, by Balboa, and that was five hundred years ago."

The orbiter also conducted forty flybys of planets and moons, far more than any other spacecraft. It was the first to swing close to an asteroid; the first to orbit one of the outer planets; the first to document fire fountains erupting from the surface of Jupiter's volcanic moon, Io; and the first to fly through a plume from Io, a lurid yellow-orange sphere with an estimated three hundred volcanoes erupting at any given time. In July, 1994, *Galileo* provided direct observation of fragments of the Shoemaker-Levy 9 comet slamming into Jupiter; these collisions produced explosions more powerful than that of the largest H-bomb.

In recent years, when the mission was directed from Earth by a skeleton crew on a low budget and had absorbed more than four times as much of Jupiter's fierce radiation field as it had been designed to withstand, *Galileo*'s systems faltered frequently, but it continued to make discoveries. Last November, for example, its scanner registered the presence of up to nine tiny moons orbiting close to Jupiter. In June, 2000, it oddly failed to recognize the bright star cluster Delta Velorium, which flickers in Vela, a constellation that can be seen in the Southern Hemisphere. Subsequent observations from Earth confirmed that this group of five stars contains a dual-sun system, with one of its component parts periodically eclipsing the other, resulting in the variable light output that puzzled the spacecraft's instrument. *Galileo* thus became the first interplanetary space mission ever to make an interstellar discovery.

Conceived by NASA in the early seventies, *Galileo* had a rocky beginning; its early history was marked by a series of delays. Its entire flight plan had to be redesigned five times, both because its technical specifications kept changing and because the positions of the planets shifted between launch dates. It was trucked back and forth between California and Florida, and was disassembled, cleaned, stored, and then reassembled. Although the orbiter was an extremely sophisticated piece of technology for the seventies, when it finally went into space, in 1989, many of its systems were already out of date. (Its main processors were rebuilt versions of the RCA 1802 chip, which was used to run primitive video games like Pong.)

Galileo's most critical pre-launch problem was a woefully under-powered solid-fuel booster that could barely propel the craft out of Earth's orbit. It was able to get as far as Mars or Venus, but reaching the outer planets appeared to be impossible. *Galileo* had been specifi-cally designed for shuttle deployment; after the explosion of the space shuttle *Challenger* in January, 1986, a newly safety-conscious NASA had decided that the orbiter's original, liquid-fuelled booster—which was more powerful but also potentially more dangerous than a solid-fuel device—couldn't be lofted alongside the shuttle's human cargo. The spacecraft seemed to be on the verge of a one-way trip to the Smithsonian.

Trajectory specialists at NASA's Jet Propulsion Laboratory set to work, attempting to figure out how to get *Galileo* to Jupiter with what amounted to a lawnmower engine under the hood. The man who eventually solved this puzzle was Roger Diehl.

I spoke with Diehl, who still works at the Jet Propulsion Labora-tory, in July. He told me that his first idea was to get the spacecraft to Mars, and then use that planet's gravity to hurl it all the way to Jupi-ter. "I would go to bed at night, and my wife said she could even hear me talking about trajectories in my sleep," he recalled. But he even-tually realized that because Mars had swung from its ideal position during one of *Galileo*'s launch delays, that approach wouldn't work.

"It turns out that Mars is so small that if you go out of your way to fly by Mars to get a gravity assist you usually won't get a benefit," Diehl said. "So then I said, 'Well, let's launch to Venus.'"

This was hardly an obvious solution. Venus is in the inner solar system, and Jupiter is very far in the opposite direction. Moreover, this approach posed a significant thermal problem: *Galileo* had not been designed to travel closer to the sun before heading toward the frigid space around Jupiter. "If anyone had talked to a spacecraft person, there would have been a reluctance. They would have said, 'No, don't do that,'" Diehl said, laughing.

But he came up with a daring new flight plan anyway. Galileo would fly to Venus, curve back, swing around the Earth, then fly around Earth a *second* time exactly two years later; this trajectory would act like a slingshot, flinging *Galileo* all the way to Jupiter. Diehl realized that such a course would take several more years than the original plan, but he was undeterred. "I said to myself, 'I'm going to think of the problem as doing a tour of the planets of the solar system, with the goal of getting to Jupiter,'" he recalled. "I didn't care how many years it would take."

Diehl presented his boss, Bob Mitchell, with the unlikely scheme in August of 1986. Mitchell approved the concept, which was dubbed VEEGA, for "Venus Earth Earth Gravity Assist." Within days, Jet Propulsion Laboratory designers came up with a way to save *Galileo* from the harsh temperatures near Venus: they could attach light-weight, strategically placed sun shields that would protect it from intense heat.

In the next several months, two other scientists at the Jet Propulsion Laboratory, Lou D'Amario and Dennis Byrnes, substantially improved Diehl's initial concept; for example, they expanded *Galileo*'s itinerary, modifying its trajectory to make it fly past two asteroids. In the end, the VEEGA approach would require six years to propel the spacecraft to Jupiter, double the flight time of *Galileo*'s original plan.

Diehl considers his revision of *Galileo*'s trajectory, which effectively saved the mission, the highlight of his career. "My car license plate says 'VEEGA,'" Diehl said. "Every morning, I go out and I see the word."

GALILEO WAS SUCCESSFULLY DEPLOYED FROM the space shuttle *Atlantis* on October 18, 1989, seven years after its original launch date. It spent the year making its detour to Venus. In December, 1990, *Galileo* began its "Earth-1" maneuver: the first Earth flyby. This happened to coincide with the buildup to the first Gulf War. NASA had to inform the North American Aerospace Defense Command that the blip that would appear on its radar screens on December 8th—an incredibly fast-moving object that might well seem to originate from the Middle East—was not an enemy missile but a robotic spacecraft coming from Venus.

Throughout the entire first part of its journey into space, *Galileo*'s umbrella-shaped high-gain antenna, intended to be its main communications link to the Earth from Jupiter, had remained snugly folded at one end of the craft. It was the largest such device ever to have been sent out of Earth's orbit.

The plan was to deploy it only after the orbiter had receded far enough from the sun—because it, too, had originally been designed to operate in the bitter-cold temperatures of the outer solar system. In the meantime, the spacecraft would rely on a smaller, much slower antenna that was intended to be used only close to Earth.

In April, 1991, when *Galileo* was nearing the cooler climes of the asteroid belt, which is between Mars and Jupiter, the time had come to open the high-gain antenna and begin pulsing data toward Earth, at an optimal rate of a hundred and thirty-four kilobytes per second. *Galileo* was designed to have enough bandwidth to fire home one picture per minute, while also transmitting information from its other instruments.

But when the Jet Propulsion Laboratory finally ordered *Galileo* to open this key device, it stuck. Scientists running the mission were devastated: without a means of sending back high volumes of data, *Galileo* would be severely hobbled. Within a week of the antenna failure, two engineering teams were formed at the Jet Propulsion Laboratory. One was dedicated to getting the high-gain antenna unstuck. The other had to figure out how to rescue the mission without the use of the antenna; it was made up primarily of telecommunications specialists from the Deep Space Network. This division often provided NASA with a "million-mile screwdriver"—that is, a way of fixing a spacecraft by sending radio signals from Earth.

Leslie Deutsch, then the head of research and development for the Deep Space Network, is a garrulous but precise mathematician. "This was a crisis," he recalled in a recent conversation. "I got together with a few people, and we did some brainstorming. First, we said, 'Suppose we don't change anything. What's the data rate going to be when we get to Jupiter, if we have to use this low-gain antenna?'" The answer was ten bits per second, which translated to about one picture a month—and then only if *Galileo*'s ten other scientific instruments weren't in use. Such a data rate was pitifully inadequate; in space, complex phenomena must often be photographed many hundreds of times before they can be properly understood.

Instead of attempting to change the spacecraft's hardware, the Deep Space Network rescue squad began thinking about how it could improve *Galileo*'s information-processing capabilities. There was one possibility: *Galileo*'s fundamental software could be rewritten. To accomplish this feat, the onboard computer had to be powerful enough to handle the more advanced algorithms employed in the updated code. "The computer system on *Galileo* was ancient," Deutsch said. "So we looked into what kind of microprocessors were on board, and how much memory there was. And there was good news and bad news."

The bad news was that *Galileo*'s computer processors were so old that their original designers would need to be brought out of retirement for consultation. The good news was that, shortly before being launched into space, *Galileo* had been outfitted with twice as many memory chips as its designers originally intended; engineers had been worried that they were vulnerable to damage by radiation absorbed during the long journey in space. But after nineteen months in flight all the orbiter's memory chips were still functioning, which allowed Deutsch's team to do something that had never been attempted: change all a spacecraft's software applications in midflight. Updating the software would enable the team to introduce advanced data-compression techniques, which would help make it possible for *Galileo* to send useful pictures and other valuable information from Jupiter over the low-gain antenna. *Galileo* would now be capable of sending more than two hundred pictures per month, along with other data. This rate was considerably slower than originally planned, and some of *Galileo*'s objectives would have to be modified or abandoned. But the mission could still accomplish more than seventy per cent of its goals.

It took years, but by the time the orbiter completed its first sweep around Jupiter its software had been fully replaced. It was a move with unprecedented risks—"a complete brain transplant over a four-hundred-million-mile radio link," as one team paper put it—and any error could have meant losing the spacecraft. But the update was necessary, and the code transfer was flawless.

One problem remained: *Galileo* could collect information much faster than it could send it back. Its designers needed to find a way to store images, so that they could be slowly transmitted back to Earth. The orbiter, it turned out, had a tape recorder on board. Manufactured by the Odetics Corporation, in California, it was practically indistinguishable from the reel-to-reel recorders that were attached to the higher-end stereo systems of the sixties and seventies. Though the machine was practically obsolete, it became one of *Galileo*'s most important features.

The recorder had been incorporated into the orbiter's design for one reason: to back up data from its atmospheric probe, which was scheduled to tunnel into Jupiter's clouds in 1995, when *Galileo* arrived at the planet's doorstep. This snub-nosed device would release its heat shield, deploy a parachute, and transmit information about Jupiter's atmosphere back to the orbiter as it sank into oblivion. The whole procedure was supposed to unfold over the course of an hour.

During that time, the probe's findings would be relayed from *Galileo* back to Earth.

After the failure of the high-gain antenna, however, the tape recorder became a critical instrument. *Galileo*'s handlers at the Jet Propulsion Laboratory realized that it would be necessary to store all the incoming images and other scientific data gathered by its instruments during its flybys of Jupiter's moons. That information could then be fed into *Galileo*'s computers (using the new data-compression software) and slowly transmitted back to Earth during the months-long lulls when the craft was travelling between Jupiter's moons.

The magnetic tape spooled in *Galileo*'s tape recorder became a thread on which the mission's destiny hung. The entire system had been jerry-rigged, but it worked. *Galileo* began slowly transmitting spectacular images of Jupiter and its moons to Earth, where an upgraded antenna system picked up the spacecraft's slow, faint signals.

In March, 1996, the Jet Propulsion Laboratory team assigned the task of fixing the jammed antenna finally gave up. One analysis attributes the malfunction to a design flaw that was exacerbated by vibrations sustained when the antenna was hauled repeatedly between Florida and California during the years of launch delays.

EVEN BEFORE THE SCIENTISTS AT the Jet Propulsion Laboratory finished updating *Galileo*'s software, the orbiter was not completely useless. In October, 1991, it took the first high-resolution images of an asteroid. Because the process of downloading photographs was so slow, it was instructed to send them back in fragments. Paul Geissler, a planetary geologist then at the University of Arizona's Lunar and Planetary Laboratory, was one of the few researchers allowed to view them as they came in, bit by bit. "It was wonderful— we were locked into a room and sworn to silence," Geissler said. "Because we didn't have the high-gain antenna, the data came in as what we call 'jail-bars.' *Galileo* would send down a line, and then skip twenty lines, then send down another line, and then skip twenty lines and send down another line, and the issue was, is the asteroid in the frame at all, and should we use our precious bits to send down this frame or should we save it for the next frame?"

Geissler recalled the moment when his team realized that there was a tiny moon orbiting the asteroid. "In one of these jail-bars you could see Ida, and then it dropped off back into space again, and then there was another little blip. That's all we had. These particular jail-bars had three lines and then skipped a bunch, and this blip was in all three of the lines, so we were dead certain that it wasn't a cosmic-ray hit or anything like that. We knew there was something there. But we waited until another instrument on *Galileo* had a confirmation of it, and then we announced it."

Although astronomers had long believed that some asteroids have moonlets, this was hard proof. It was also a reassuring illustration of what could still be achieved by *Galileo*, even in its extremely compromised state.

I asked Geissler, one of the leading image processors among planetary scientists, what it was like to see such unprecedented pictures before anyone else. He told me a story about the first complete shots of Ida, which had trickled in slowly, over a period of months in early 1994. "We had gotten two pictures of Ida up close, from different perspectives," he said. "As the spacecraft flew past the asteroid, it snapped a picture, at high resolution, and then it flew a little bit farther and then snapped another picture of the same region." Geissler realized that this separation allowed for the creation of a stereo image, which, when viewed properly, can give an object vivid three-dimensional form. "So I processed those pictures, and shot negatives of them, and brought them home—that was late on a Friday," he told me. "I had a darkroom at home, and later that night I made eight-by-tens of these two, and I had pinched a stereoscope from work. I popped in these two wonderful eight-by-tens and became the first human being to see a stereo image of an asteroid at high resolution!" Geissler chuckled. "That entire weekend, anyone who came close to my door was dragged over—'Look at this!' You know, the mailman, the babysitter. That was really a thrill."

*   *   *

FOR DECADES, SCIENTISTS HAVE KNOWN that three of Jupiter's four large moons have high concentrations of frozen water. But only the hardiest optimists among them dared to speculate that liquid water could exist that far from the Sun. Europa's average surface temperature is estimated to be two hundred and sixty degrees below zero.

In 1979, the twin *Voyager* space probes flew past Jupiter at approximately ten times the speed of a rifle bullet. The closest they got to Europa was about a hundred thousand miles; *Galileo* has veered to within a hundred and twenty-four miles of the moon. Despite being so far away, the *Voyager* probes compiled a photographic record suggesting—indirectly—that Europa might be warmer below its icy surface. The most obvious clue was to be found on images of Io, Jupiter's innermost large moon. Firmly gripped by the tidal pull of its parent planet's gravity, yet yanked the other way by the shifting gravitational fields of two of its three sister moons, Io produces seemingly endless chains of active volcanoes. At three thousand degrees, they are far hotter at their source than any volcano on Earth. Io is the most volcanic object in the solar system; the mere proximity of such an excitable object to Europa suddenly rendered the idea of subsurface water more imaginable. If such active volcanism was present on Io, why couldn't there be similar eruptions on Europa's seabed?

The other *Voyager*-era clue was more subtle and mysterious. Long, looping chains of scalloped cracks snake across large spans of Europa's surface. These unusual patterns, which extend for hundreds of miles across the crystalline topography encircling the moon's poles, were already clearly visible in the *Voyager* images. In 1996, *Galileo* began taking highly detailed photographs of Europa. Scientists concluded with excitement that the fissures on Europa—which were dubbed "arcuate ridges"—were unique in the solar system.

Meanwhile, a handful of planetary geologists struggled to sort out what the curved lines on Europa's surface signified. One of them was Randy Tufts, a geologist at the University of Arizona. Tufts had been fascinated by those eerie ridges even before *Galileo* reached Jupiter. In a conversation I had with him a few years ago, he recalled that in the early nineties he had printed multiple copies of the low-resolution *Voyager* pictures and handed them out to his nonscientist friends—hoping that one of them might miraculously intuit the cause of the surface cracks. He had even taken the pictures to a glass-blowing studio in downtown Tucson and asked the workers there if they had ever seen similar patterns. (They hadn't.) "I was just casting about for any kind of analogue," he told me.

In 1998, Tufts discovered an immense, gently curved fault line in the southern hemisphere of Europa. *Galileo* photographs revealed that the crack, which was subsequently named the Astypalaea Linea, extends about six hundred miles, which is comparable to the San Andreas Fault. This feature offered clear evidence that parts of Europa's crust were slowly moving—perhaps even floating.

That summer, it occurred to Tufts that the curvature exhibited by both the Astypalaea Linea and the arcuate ridges could be caused by the immense gravitational pull of Jupiter, which has three hundred times the mass of Earth. The linked curves of the arcuate ridges, he realized, could be explained by the fact that Jupiter does not exert a consistent amount of force on Europa. The planet pulls more strongly on the moon when the two bodies happen to be closer together. "Since Europa's elliptical orbit sometimes takes it farther away from Jupiter, the amount of stretching it undergoes kind of relaxes a little bit," he explained. Cracks start propagating—but then, as Europa recedes from Jupiter, they stop. Because Europa's Jupiter-facing hemisphere rocks back and forth during each orbit, by the time the gravitational stresses pick up again they're oriented in a slightly different direction.

With the help of Greg Hoppa, an orbital-dynamics specialist, Tufts plotted the effect of these fluctuating force levels; he ended up with looping cracks that look just like the ones on Europa. That was quite a breakthrough, but the team's next insight was even more significant: the whole process couldn't happen without the existence of a large body of subsurface water to exert tidal pressure from below. Ice crusted on solid rock could never be affected so much. The tides on Europa are much higher than those on Earth, reaching almost a hundred feet; when Jupiter pulls these enormous subsurface bulges of water in its direction, Tufts concluded, the ice on the surface begins to crack.

In the end, Tufts's insight is appealingly straightforward. By studying the elegant shapes on Europa's surface, he divined what lay beneath. "Later, I found myself sort of apologizing for its simplicity," he said. "And people said, 'Well, you know, some of the best ideas in science are very simple ones.' They're often so simple that everyone sees right through them." Tufts was excited by the idea that life might exist on Europa. "It always seemed to me that if we found life someplace else it would give us a vastly new perspective on existence," he told me. "And we would probably realize that we weren't quite so important as we thought we were." He frowned thoughtfully. "I mean, it might take us down a peg, which always could be useful."

Randy Tufts died last year, at the age of fifty-three, from a bone-marrow disorder. Not long before his death, he was working with scientists on plans for an orbiter that would investigate Europa's ocean more closely. In 2002, the project was cancelled, owing to budget cuts.

IN LATE JULY, I CALLED Arthur C. Clarke at his home in Colombo, Sri Lanka, and asked him to comment on *Galileo*'s impending death. Clarke has long been fascinated by Europa; it figures prominently in the sequels to *2001: A Space Odyssey.* In particular, I wondered if he shared NASA's concern that if *Galileo* were to crash into the distant moon it could transfer microbes from Earth to Europa's ocean. Clarke didn't answer directly, instead suggesting that I read an old tale of his, "Before Eden," written in 1961. "It's all about the danger that we might contaminate new worlds," he said.

The story is about a scouting expedition to the South Pole of

Venus, which is described as being "a hundred degrees hotter than Death Valley in midsummer." The expedition leaves behind a single human artifact—a bag of waste. It ends up contaminating a strange Venusian life-form that the expedition had discovered there, thus ending its evolution. I concluded that Clarke probably endorsed NASA's plan to destroy *Galileo*.

I spoke with Leslie Deutsch about his reaction to the decision, and he said he was initially angry, though he understood the rationale. Over the years, Deutsch admitted, he had become emotionally attached to the distant robot emissary, adding that this would be only the second time that NASA had deliberately destroyed a functioning spacecraft. When I asked Bill O'Neil, *Galileo*'s long-serving project director and one of the key architects of the effort to save the mission, what his reaction had been when he'd heard of the decision, he mulled it over for a few days, then sent me an e-mail. *Galileo*'s end would bring a personal sense of satisfaction at what had been achieved, he wrote. Still, he found it ironic that "Galileo Galilei only got house arrest by his sponsor the Roman Catholic Church for discovering things they didn't want to be true, whereas our Project Galileo gets a death sentence from NASA for its greatest discovery: the prospect of life on Europa."

WILLIAM LANGEWIESCHE

Columbia's *Last Flight*

FROM *THE ATLANTIC MONTHLY*

> On February 1, 2003, the space shuttle Columbia *broke apart*
> *catastrophically, just a few minutes before its scheduled touchdown*
> *at the Kennedy Space Center in Florida. William Langewiesche re-*
> *views the lapses, errors, and erroneous assumptions that led to this*
> *avoidable tragedy.*

SPACE FLIGHT IS KNOWN TO BE A RISKY BUSINESS, BUT during the minutes before dawn February 1, as the doomed shuttle *Columbia* began to descend into the upper atmosphere over the Pacific Ocean, only a handful of people—a few engineers deep inside of NASA—worried that the vehicle and its seven souls might actually come to grief. It was the responsibility of NASA's managers to hear those suspicions, and from top to bottom they failed. After the fact, that's easy to see. But in fairness to those whose reputations have now been sacrificed, seventeen years and eighty-nine shuttle flights had passed since the *Challenger* explosion, and within the agency a new generation had risen that was smart, perhaps, but also unwise—confined by NASA's walls and routines, and vulnerable to the self-satisfaction that inevitably had set in.

Moreover, this mission was a yawn—a low-priority "science" flight forced onto NASA by Congress and postponed for two years because of a more pressing schedule of construction deliveries to the International Space Station. The truth is, it had finally been launched as much to clear the books as to add to human knowledge, and it had gone nowhere except into low Earth orbit, around the globe every ninety minutes for sixteen days, carrying the first Israeli astronaut, and performing a string of experiments, many of which, like the shuttle program itself, seemed to suffer from something of a make-work character—the examination of dust in the Middle East (by the Israeli, of course); the ever popular ozone study; experiments designed by schoolchildren in six countries to observe the effect of weightlessness on spiders, silkworms, and other creatures; an exercise in "astroculture" involving the extraction of essential oils from rose and rice flowers, which was said to hold promise for new perfumes; and so forth. No doubt some good science was done too—particularly pertaining to space flight itself—though none of it was so urgent that it could not have been performed later, under better circumstances, in the under-booked International Space Station. The astronauts aboard the shuttle were smart and accomplished people, and they were deeply committed to human space flight and exploration. They were also team players, by intense selection, and nothing if not wise to the game. From orbit, one of them had radioed, "The science we're doing here is great, and it's fantastic. It's leading-edge." Others had dutifully reported that the planet seems beautiful, fragile, and borderless when seen from such altitudes, and they had expressed their hopes in English and Hebrew for world peace. It was Miracle Whip on Wonder Bread, standard NASA fare. On the ground so little attention was being paid that even the radars that could have been directed upward to track the *Columbia*'s reentry into the atmosphere—from Vandenberg Air Force Base, or White Sands Missile Range—were sleeping. As a result, no radar record of the breakup exists—only of the metal rain that drifted down over East Texas, and eventually came into the view of air-traffic control.

Along the route, however, stood small numbers of shuttle enthusiasts, who had gotten up early with their video cameras and had arrayed themselves on hills or away from city lights to record the spectacle of what promised to be a beautiful display. The shuttle came into view, on track and on schedule, just after 5:53 Pacific time, crossing the California coast at about 15,000 mph in the super-thin air 230,000 feet above the Russian River, northwest of San Francisco. It was first picked up on video by a Lockheed engineer in suburban Fairfield, who recorded a bright meteor passing almost directly overhead, not the shuttle itself but the sheath of hot gases around it, and the long, luminous tail of ionized air known as plasma. Only later, after the engineer heard about the accident on television, did he check his tape and realize that he had recorded what appeared to be two pieces coming off the Columbia in quick succession, like little flares in its wake. Those pieces were recorded by others as well, along with the third, fourth, and fifth "debris events" that are known to have occurred during the sixty seconds that it took the shuttle to cross California. From the top of Mount Hamilton, southeast of San Francisco, another engineer, the former president of the Peninsula Astronomical Society, caught all five events on tape but, again, did not realize it until afterward. He later said, "I'd seen four re-entries before this one. When we saw it, we did note that it was a little brighter and a little bit whiter in color than it normally is. It's normally a pink-magenta color. But you know, it wasn't so different that it really flagged us as something wrong. With the naked eye we didn't see the particles coming off."

One minute after the *Columbia* left California, as it neared southwestern Utah, the trouble was becoming more obvious to observers on the ground. There had been a bright flash earlier over Nevada, and now debris came off that was large enough to cause multiple secondary plasma trails. North of the Grand Canyon, in Saint George, Utah, a man and his grown son climbed onto a ridge above the county hospital, hoping for the sort of view they had seen several years before, of a fireball going by. It was a sight they remembered as "really neat." This time was different, though. The son, who was videotaping, started yelling, "Jesus, Dad, there's stuff falling off!" and the father saw it too, with his naked eyes.

The *Columbia* was flying on autopilot, as is usual, and though it continued to lay flares in its wake, the astronauts aboard remained blissfully unaware of the trouble they were in. They passed smoothly into dawn above the Arizona border, and sailed across the Navajo reservation and on over Albuquerque, before coming to the Texas Panhandle on a perfect descent profile, slowing through 13,400 mph at 210,000 feet five minutes after having crossed the California coastline. Nineteen seconds later, at 7:58:38 central time, they got the first sign of something being a little out of the ordinary: it was a cockpit indication of low tire pressures on the left main landing gear. This was not quite a trivial matter. A blown or deflated main tire would pose serious risks during the rollout after landing, including loss of lateral control and the possibility that the nose would slam down, conceivably leading to a catastrophic breakup on the ground. These scenarios were known, and had been simulated and debated in the inner world of NASA, leading some to believe that the best of the imperfect choices in such a case might be for the crew to bail out— an alternative available only below 30,000 feet and 220 mph of dynamic airspeed. Nonetheless, for *Columbia*'s pilots it was reasonable to assume for the moment that the indication of low pressure was due to a problem with the sensors rather than with the tires themselves, and that the teams of Mission Control engineers at NASA's Johnson Space Center, in Houston, would be able to sort through the mass of automatically transmitted data—the so-called telemetry, which was far more complete than what was available in the cockpit—and to draw the correct conclusion. The reverse side of failures in a machine as complex as the shuttle is that most of them can be worked around, or turn out to be small. In other words, there was no reason for alarm. After a short delay the *Columbia*'s commander, Rick Husband, calmly radioed to Mission Control, "And, ah, Houston . . ." Sheathed in hot atmospheric gases, the shuttle was slowing through 13,100 mph at 205,000 feet.

Houston did not clearly hear the call.

With the scheduled touchdown now only about fifteen minutes ahead, it was a busy time at Mission Control. Weather reports were coming in from the landing site at the Kennedy Space Center in Florida. Radar tracking of the shuttle, like the final accurate ground-based navigation, had not yet begun. Sitting at their specialized positions, and monitoring the numbers displayed on the consoles, a few of the flight controllers had begun to sense, just barely, that something was going seriously wrong. The worry was not quite coherent yet. One of the controllers later told me that it amounted to an inexplicable bad feeling in his gut. But it was undeniable nonetheless. For the previous few minutes, since about the time when the shuttle had passed from California to Nevada, Jeff Kling, an engineer who was working the mechanical-systems position known as MMACS (pronounced Macs), had witnessed a swarm of erratic indications and sensor failures. The pattern was disconcerting because of the lack of common circuitry that could easily explain the pattern of such failures—a single box that could be blamed.

Kling had been bantering good-naturedly on an intercom with one of his team, a technician sitting in one of the adjoining back rooms and monitoring the telemetry, when the technician noted a strange failure of temperature transducers on a hydraulic return line. The technician said, "We've had some hydraulic 'ducers go off-scale low."

Kling had seen the same indications. He said, "Well, I guess!"

The technician said, "What in the world?"

Kling said, "This is not funny. On the left side."

The technician confirmed, "On the left side . . ."

Now Kling got onto the main control-room intercom to the lead controller on duty, known as the flight director, a man named Leroy Cain. In the jargon-laced language of the control room Kling said, "Flight, Macs."

Cain said, "Go ahead, Macs."

"FYI, I've just lost four separate temperature transducers on the left side of the vehicle, hydraulic return temperatures. Two of them on system one, and one in each of systems two and three."

Cain said, "Four hyd return temps?"

Kling answered, "To the left outboard and left inboard elevon."

"Okay, is there anything common to them? DSC or MDM or anything? I mean, you're telling me you lost them all at exactly the same time?"

"No, not exactly. They were within probably four or five seconds of each other."

Cain struggled to assess the meaning. "Okay, where are those . . . where is that instrumentation located?"

Kling continued to hear from his back-room team. He said, "All four of them are located in the aft part of the left wing, right in front of the elevons . . . elevon actuators. And there is no commonality."

Cain repeated, "No commonality."

But all the failing instruments were in the left wing. The possible significance of this was not lost on Cain: during the launch a piece of solid foam had broken off from the shuttle's external fuel tank, and at high speed had smashed into the left wing; after minimal consideration the shuttle program managers (who stood above Mission Control in the NASA hierarchy) had dismissed the incident as essentially unthreatening. Like almost everyone else at NASA, Cain had taken the managers at their word—and he still did. Nonetheless, the strange cluster of left-wing failures was an ominous development. Kling had more specific reasons for concern. In a wonkish, engineering way he had discussed with his team the telemetry they might observe if a hole allowed hot gases into the wing during re-entry, and had come up with a profile eerily close to what was happening now. Still, he maintained the expected detachment.

Cain continued to worry the problem. He asked for reassurance from his "guidance, navigation, and control" man, Mike Sarafin. "Everything look good to you, control and rates and everything is normal, right?"

Sarafin said, "Control's been stable through the rolls that we've done so far, Flight. We have good trims. I don't see anything out of the ordinary."

Cain directed his attention back to Kling: "All other indications for your hydraulic systems indications are good?"

"They're all good. We've had good quantities all the way across."

Cain said, "And the other temps are normal?"

"The other temps are normal, yes, sir." He meant only those that the telemetry allowed him to see.

Cain said, "And when you say you lost these, are you saying they went to zero . . ."

"All four of them are off-scale low."

". . . or off-scale low?"

Kling said, "And they were all staggered. They were, like I said, within several seconds of each other."

Cain said, "Okay."

But it wasn't okay. Within seconds the *Columbia* had crossed into Texas and the left-tire-pressure indications were dropping, as observed also by the cockpit crew. Kling's informal model of catastrophe had predicted just such indications, whether from blown tires or wire breaks. The end was now coming very fast.

Kling said, "Flight, Macs."

Cain said, "Go."

"We just lost tire pressure on the left outboard and left inboard, both tires."

Cain said, "Copy."

At that moment, twenty-three seconds after 7:59 local time, the Mission Control consoles stopped receiving telemetry updates, for reasons unknown. The astronaut sitting beside Cain, and serving as the Mission Control communicator, radioed, "And *Columbia*, Houston, we see your tire-pressure messages, and we did not copy your last call."

At the same time, on the control-room intercom, Cain was talking again to Kling. He said, "Is it instrumentation, Macs? Gotta be."

Kling said, "Flight, Macs, those are also off-scale low."

From the speeding shuttle Rick Husband—Air Force test pilot, religious, good family man, always wanted to be an astronaut—began to answer the communicator. He said, "Roger, ah," and was cut off on a word that began with "buh . . ."

It turned out to be the *Columbia*'s last voice transmission. Brief communication breaks, however, are not abnormal during re-entries, and this one raised no immediate concern in Houston.

People on the ground in Dallas suddenly knew more than the flight controllers in Houston. Four seconds after eight they saw a large piece leave the orbiter and fall away. The shuttle was starting to come apart. It continued intermittently to send telemetry, which though not immediately displayed at Mission Control was captured by NASA computers and later discovered; the story it told was that multiple systems were failing. In quick succession two additional chunks fell off.

Down in the control room Cain said, "And there's no commonality between all these tire-pressure instrumentations and the hydraulic return instrumentations?"

High in the sky near Dallas the *Columbia*'s main body began to break up. It crackled and boomed, and made a loud rumble.

Kling said, "No, sir, there's not. We've also lost the nose-gear down talkback, and right-main-gear down talkback."

"Nose-gear and right-main-gear down talkbacks?"

"Yes, sir."

At Fort Hood, Texas, two Dutch military pilots who were training in an Apache attack helicopter locked on to the breakup with their optics and videotaped three bright objects—the main rocket engines—flying eastward in formation, among other, smaller pieces and their contrails.

Referring to the loss of communications, one minute after the main-body breakup, Laura Hoppe, the flight controller responsible for the communications systems, said to Cain, "I didn't expect, uh, this bad of a hit on comm."

Cain asked another controller about a planned switchover to a ground-based radio ahead, "How far are we from UHF? Is that two-minute clock good?"

Kling, also, was hanging on to hope. He said, "Flight, Macs."

Cain said, "Macs?"

Kling said, "On the tire pressures, we did see them go erratic for a little bit before they went away, so I do believe it's instrumentation."

"Okay."

At about that time the debris began to hit the ground. It fell in thousands of pieces along a swath ten miles wide and 300 miles long, across East Texas and into Louisiana. There were many stories later. Some of the debris whistled down through the leaves of trees and smacked into a pond where a man was fishing. Another piece went right through a backyard trampoline, evoking a mother's lament: "Those damned kids . . ." Still another piece hit the window of a moving car, startling the driver. The heaviest parts flew the farthest. An 800-pound piece of engine hit the ground in Fort Polk, Louisiana, doing 1,400 mph. A 600-pound piece landed nearby. Thousands of people began to call in, swamping the 911 dispatchers with reports of sonic booms and metal falling out of the sky. No one, however, was hit. This would be surprising were it not for the fact, so visible from above, that the world is still a sparsely populated place.

In Houston the controllers maintained discipline, and continued preparing for the landing, even as they received word that the Merritt Island radar, in Florida, which should by now have started tracking the inbound craft, was picking up only false targets. Shuttles arrive on time or they don't arrive at all. But, repeatedly, the communicator radioed, "*Columbia*, Houston, UHF comm. check," as if he might still hear a reply. Then, at thirteen minutes past the hour, precisely when the *Columbia* should have been passing overhead the runway before circling down for a landing at the Kennedy Space Center, a phone call came in from an off-duty controller who had just seen a video broadcast by a Dallas television station of multiple contrails in the sky. When Cain heard the news, he paused, and then put the contingency plan into effect. To the ground-control officer he said, "GC, Flight."

"Flight, GC."

"Lock the doors."

"Copy."

The controllers were stunned, but lacked the time to contemplate the horror of what had just happened. Under Cain's direction they set about collecting numbers, writing notes, and closing out their logs, for the investigation that was certain to follow. The mood in the room was somber and focused. Only the most basic facts were known: the *Columbia* had broken up at 200,000 feet doing 12,738 mph, and the crew could not possibly have survived. Ron Dittemore, the shuttle program manager, would be talking to reporters later that day, and he needed numbers and information. At some point sandwiches were brought in and consumed. Like the priests who harvest faith at the bedsides of the dying, grief counselors showed up too, but they were not much used.

Cain insisted on control-room discipline. He said, "No phone calls off site outside of this room. Our discussions are on these loops—the recorded DVIS loops only. No data, no phone calls, no transmissions anywhere, into or out."

Later this was taken by some critics to be a typical NASA reaction—insular, furtive, overcontrolling. And it may indeed have reflected certain aspects of what had become of the agency's culture. But it was also, more simply, a rulebook procedure meant to stabilize and preserve the crucial last data. The room was being frozen as a crime scene might be. Somewhere inside NASA something had obviously gone very wrong—and it made sense to start looking for the evidence here and now.

LESS THAN AN HOUR LATER, at 10:00 A.M. eastern time, a retired four-star admiral named Hal Gehman met his brother at a lawyer's office in Williamsburg, Virginia. At the age of sixty, Gehman was a tall, slim, silver-haired man with an unlined face and soft eyes. Dressed in civilian clothes, standing straight but not stiffly so, he had an accessible, unassuming manner that contrasted with the rank and power he had achieved. After an inauspicious start as a mediocre engineering student in the Penn State Naval ROTC program ("Top four fifths of the class," he liked to say), he had skippered a patrol boat through the thick of the Vietnam War and gone on to become an experienced sea captain, the commander of a carrier battle group, vice-chief of the Navy, and finally NATO Atlantic commander and head of the U.S. Joint Forces Command. Upon his retirement, in 2000, from the sixth-ranked position in the U.S. military, he had given all that up with apparent ease. He had enjoyed a good career in the Navy, but he enjoyed his civilian life now too. He was a rare sort of man—startlingly intelligent beneath his guileless exterior, personally satisfied, and quite genuinely untroubled. He lived in Norfolk in a pleasant house that he had recently remodeled; he loved his wife, his grown children, his mother and father, and all his siblings. He had an old Volkswagen bug convertible, robin's-egg blue, that he had bought from another admiral.

He had a modest thirty-four-foot sloop, which he enjoyed sailing in the Chesapeake, though its sails were worn out and he wanted to replace its icebox with a twelve-volt refrigeration unit. He was a patriot, of course, but not a reactionary. He called himself a fiscal conservative and a social moderate. His life as he described it was the product of convention. It was also the product of a strict personal code. He chose not to work with any company doing business with the Department of Defense. He liked power, but understood its limitations. He did not care to be famous or rich. He represented the American establishment at its best.

In the lawyer's office in Williamsburg his brother told him that the *Columbia* had been lost. Gehman had driven there with his radio off and so he had not heard. He asked a few questions, and absorbed the information without much reaction. He did not follow the space program and, like most Americans, had not been aware that a mission was under way. He spent an hour with the lawyer on routine family business. When he emerged, he saw that messages had been left on his cell phone, but because the coverage was poor, he could not retrieve them; only later, while driving home on the interstate, was he finally able to connect. To his surprise, among mundane messages he found an urgent request to call the deputy administrator of NASA, a man he had not heard of before, named Fred Gregory.

Like a good American, Gehman made the call while speeding down the highway. Gregory, a former shuttle commander, said, "Have you heard the news?"

Gehman said, "Only secondhand."

Gregory filled him in on what little was known, and explained that part of NASA's contingency plan, instituted after the *Challenger* disaster of 1986, was the activation of a standing "interagency" investigation board. By original design the board consisted of seven high-ranking civilian and military officials who were pre-selected mechanically on the basis of job titles—the institutional slots that they filled. For the *Columbia*, the names were now known: the board would consist of three Air Force generals, John Barry, Kenneth Hess, and Duane Deal; a Navy admiral, Stephen Turcotte; a NASA research director, G. Scott Hubbard; and two senior civil-aviation officials, James Hallock and Steven Wallace. Though only two of these men knew much about NASA or the space shuttle, in various ways each of them was familiar with the complexities of large-scale, high-risk activities. Most of them also had strong personalities. To be effective they would require even stronger management. Gregory said that it was NASA's administrator, Sean O'Keefe, who wanted Gehman to come in as chairman to lead the work. Gehman was not immune to the compliment, but he was cautious. He had met O'Keefe briefly years before, but did not know him. He wanted to make sure he wasn't being suckered into a NASA sideshow.

O'Keefe was an able member of Washington's revolving-door caste, a former congressional staffer and budget specialist—and a longtime protégé of Vice President Dick Cheney—who through the force of his competence and Republican connections had briefly landed the position of Secretary of the Navy in the early 1990s. He had suffered academic banishment through the Clinton era, but under the current administration had reemerged as a deputy at the Office of Management and Budget, where he had been assigned to tackle the difficult problem of NASA's cost overruns and lack of delivery, particularly in the Space Station program. It is hard to know what he thought when he was handed the treacherous position of

NASA administrator. Inside Washington, NASA's reputation had sunk so low that some of O'Keefe's former congressional colleagues snickered that Cheney was trying to kill his own man off. But O'Keefe was not a space crusader, as some earlier NASA administrators had been, and he was not about to pick up the fallen banners of the visionaries and try to lead the way forward; he was a tough, level-headed money man, grounded in the realities of Washington, DC, and sent in on a mission to bring discipline to NASA's budget and performance before moving on. NASA's true believers called him a carpetbagger and resented the schedule pressures that he brought to bear, but in fairness he was a professional manager, and NASA needed one.

O'Keefe had been at NASA for just over a year when the *Columbia* self-destructed. He was in Florida standing at the landing site beside one of his deputies, a former shuttle commander named William Readdy. At 9:05 eastern time, ten minutes before the scheduled landing, Readdy got word that communications with the shuttle, which had been lost, had not been reestablished; O'Keefe noticed that Readdy's face went blank. At 9:10 Readdy opened a book to check a time sequence. He said, "We should have heard the sonic booms by now. There's something really wrong." By 9:29 O'Keefe had activated the full-blown contingency plan. When word got to the White House, the executive staff ducked quickly into defensive positions: President Bush would grieve alongside the families and say the right things about carrying on, but rather than involving himself by appointing an independent residential commission, as Ronald Reagan had in response to the *Challenger* accident, he would keep his distance by expressing faith in NASA's ability to find the cause. In other words, this baby was going to be dropped squarely onto O'Keefe's lap. The White House approved Gehman's appointment to lead what would essentially be NASA's investigation—but O'Keefe could expect little further communication. There was a chance that the President would not even want to receive the final report directly but would ask that it be deposited more discreetly in the White House in-box. He had problems bigger than space on his mind.

Nonetheless, that morning in his car Gehman realized that even with a lukewarm White House endorsement, the position that NASA was offering, if handled correctly, would allow for a significant inquiry into the accident. Gregory made it clear that Gehman would have the full support of NASA's engineers and technical resources in unraveling the physical mysteries of the accident—what actually had happened to the *Columbia* out there in its sheath of fire at 200,000 feet. Moreover, Gehman was confident that if the investigation had to go further, into why this accident had occurred, he had the experience necessary to sort through the human complexities of NASA and emerge with useful answers that might result in reform. This may have been overconfident of him, and to some extent Utopian, but it was not entirely blind: he had been through big investigations before, most recently two years earlier, just after leaving the Navy, when he and a retired Army general named William Crouch had led an inquiry into the loss of seventeen sailors aboard the USS *Cole*, the destroyer that was attacked and nearly sunk by suicide terrorists in Yemen in October of 2000. Their report found fundamental errors in the functioning of the military command structure, and issued recommendations (largely classified) that are in effect today. The success of the *Cole* investigation was one of the arguments that Gregory used on him now. Gehman did not disagree, but he wanted to be very clear. He said, "I know you've got a piece of paper in front of you. Does it say that I'm not an aviator?"

Gregory said, "We don't need an aviator here. We need an investigator."

And so, driving down the highway to Norfolk, Gehman accepted the job. When he got home, he told his wife that he was a federal employee again and that there wouldn't be much sailing in the spring. That afternoon and evening, as the faxes and phone calls came in, he began to exercise control of the process, if only in his own mind, concluding that the board's charter as originally written by NASA would have to be strengthened and expanded, and that its name should immediately be changed from the absurd International Space Station and Space Shuttle Mishap Interagency Investigations

Board (the ISSSSMIIB) to the more workable *Columbia* Accident
Investigation Board, or CAIB, which could be pronounced in one
syllable, as Cabe.

NASA initially did not resist any of his suggestions. Gregory advised Gehman to head to Barksdale Air Force Base, in Shreveport,
Louisiana, where the wreckage was being collected. As Gehman
began to explore airline connections, word came that a NASA executive jet, a Gulfstream, would be dispatched to carry him, along with
several other board members, directly to Barksdale. The jet arrived
in Norfolk on Sunday afternoon, the day after the accident. One of
the members already aboard was Steven Wallace, the head of accident investigations for the FAA. Wallace is a second-generation pilot,
an athletic, tightly wound man with wide experience in government
and a skeptical view of the powerful. He later told me that when
Gehman got on the airplane, he was dressed in a business suit, and
that, having introduced himself, he explained that they might run into
the press, and if they did, he would handle things. This raised some
questions about Gehman's motivations (and indeed Gehman turned
out to enjoy the limelight), but as Wallace soon discovered, grand-
standing was not what Gehman was about. As the Gulfstream proceeded toward Louisiana, Gehman rolled up his sleeves and, sitting at
the table in the back of the airplane, began to ask for the thoughts and
perspectives of the board members there—not about what might have
happened to the *Columbia* but about how best to find out. It was the
start of what would become an intense seven-month relationship. It
was obvious that Gehman was truly listening to the ideas, and that he
was capable of integrating them quickly and productively into his own
thoughts. By the end of the flight even Wallace was growing impressed.

But Gehman was in some ways also naive, formed as he had been
by investigative experience within the military, in which much of the
work proceeds behind closed doors, and conflict of interest is not a
big concern. The *Columbia* investigation, he discovered, was going to
be a very different thing. Attacks against the CAIB began on the
second day, and by midweek, as the board moved from Shreveport to

Houston to set up shop, they showed no signs of easing. Congress in particular was thundering that Gehman was a captive investigator, that his report would be a whitewash, and that the White House should replace the CAIB with a *Challenger*-style presidential commission. This came as a surprise to Gehman, who had assumed that he could just go about his business but who now realized that he would have to accommodate these concerns if the final report was to have any credibility at all. Later he said to me, "I didn't go in thinking about it, but as I began to hear the independence thing—'You can't have a panel appointed by NASA investigating itself!'—I realized I'd better deal with Congress." He did this at first mainly by listening on the phone. "They told me what I had to do to build my credibility. I didn't invent it—they told me. They also said, 'We hate NASA. We don't trust them. Their culture is no good. And their cost accounting is no good.' And I said, 'Okay.'"

More than that, Gehman came to realize that it was the elected representatives in Congress—and neither O'Keefe nor NASA—who constituted the CAIB's real constituency, and that their concerns were legitimate. As a result of this, along with a growing understanding of the depth and complexity of the work at hand, he forced through a series of changes, establishing a congressional-liaison office, gaining an independent budget (ultimately of about $20 million), wresting the report from O'Keefe's control, rewriting the stated mission to include the finding of "root causes and circumstances," and hiring an additional five board members, all civilians of unimpeachable reputation: the retired Electric Boat boss Roger Tetrault, the former astronaut Sally Ride, the Nobel-laureate physicist Douglas Osheroff, the aerodynamicist and former Air Force Secretary Sheila Widnall, and the historian and space-policy expert John Logsdon. Afterward, the loudest criticism faded away. Still, Gehman's political judgment was not perfect. He allowed the new civilian members to be brought on through the NASA payroll (at prorated annual salaries of $134,000)—a strange lapse under the circumstances, and one that led to superficial accusations that the CAIB remained captive. The *Orlando Sentinel* ran a story about the lack of public access to the CAIB's interviews under the ambiguous head-line "BOARD PAID TO ENSURE SECRECY." The idea evoked laughter among some of the investigators, who knew the inquiry's direction. But unnecessary damage was done.

Equally unnecessary was Gehman's habit of referring to O'Keefe as "Sean," a clubbish mannerism that led people to conclude, errone-ously, that the two men were friends. In fact their relationship was strained, if polite. Gehman told me that he had never asked for the full story behind his selection on the morning of the accident—maybe because it would have been impossible to know the unvar-nished truth. Certainly, though, O'Keefe had had little opportunity to contemplate his choice. By quick view Gehman was a steady hand and a good establishment man who could lend the gravitas of his four stars to this occasion; he was also, of course, one of the men behind the *Cole* investigation. O'Keefe later told me that he had read the *Cole* report during his stint as a professor, but that he remem-bered it best as the subject of a case study presented by one of his academic colleagues as an example of a narrowly focused investiga-tion that, correctly, had not widened beyond its original mandate. This was true, but a poor predictor of Gehman as a man. His *Cole* investigation had not widened (for instance, into assigning individ-ual blame) for the simple reason that other investigations, by the Navy and the FBI, were already covering that ground. Instead, Gehman and Crouch had gone deep, and relentlessly so. The result was a document that bluntly questioned current American dogma, identified arrogance in the command structure, and critiqued U.S. military assumptions about the terrorist threat. The tone was frank. For example, while expressing understanding of the diplomatic util-ity of labeling terrorists as "criminals," the report warned against buying into that language, or into the parallel idea that these terror-ists were "cowards." When, later, I expressed my surprise at his free-dom of expression, Gehman did not deny that people have recently been decried as traitors for less. But freedom of expression was clearly his habit: he spoke to me just as openly about the failures of his cher-ished Navy, of Congress, and increasingly of NASA.

When I mentioned this character trait to one of the new board members, Sheila Widnall, she laughed and said she'd seen it before inside the Pentagon, and that people just didn't understand the highest level of the U.S. military. These officers are indeed the establishment, she said, but they are so convinced of the greatness of the American construct that they will willingly tear at its components in the belief that its failures can be squarely addressed. Almost all of the current generation of senior leaders have also been through the soul-searching that followed the defeat in Vietnam.

O'Keefe had his own understanding of the establishment, and it was probably sophisticated, but he clearly did not anticipate Gehman's rebellion. By the end of the second week, as Gehman established an independent relationship with Congress and began to break through the boundaries initially drawn by NASA, it became clear that O'Keefe was losing control. He maintained a brave front of wanting a thorough inquiry, but it was said that privately he was angry. The tensions came to the surface toward the end of February, at about the same time that Gehman insisted, over O'Keefe's resistance, that the full report ultimately be made available to the public. The CAIB was expanding to a staff of about 120 people, many of them professional accident investigators and technical experts who could support the core board members. They were working seven days a week out of temporary office space in the sprawling wasteland of South Houston, just off the property of the Johnson Space Center. One morning several of the board members came in to see Gehman, and warned him that the CAIB was headed for a "shipwreck."

Gehman knew what they meant. In the days following the accident O'Keefe had established an internal Mishap Investigation Team, whose job was to work closely with the CAIB, essentially as staff, and whose members—bizarrely—included some of the decision-makers most closely involved with the *Columbia*'s final flight. The team was led by Linda Ham, a razor-sharp manager in the shuttle program, whose actions during the flight would eventually be singled out as an egregious example of NASA's failings. Gehman did not know that yet, but it dawned on him that Ham was in a position to filter the inbound NASA reports, and he remembered a recent three-hour briefing that she had run with an iron hand, allowing little room for spontaneous exploration. He realized that she and the others would have to leave the CAIB, and he wrote a careful letter to O'Keefe in Washington, requesting their immediate removal. It is a measure of the insularity at the Johnson Space Center that NASA did not gracefully acquiesce. Ham and another manager, Ralph Roe, in particular reacted badly. In Gehman's office, alternately in anger and tears, they refused to leave, accusing Gehman of impugning their integrity and asking him how they were supposed to explain their dismissal to others. Gehman suggested to them what Congress had insisted to him—that people simply cannot investigate themselves. Civics 101. Once stated, it seems like an obvious principle.

O'Keefe had a master's degree in public administration, but he disagreed. It was odd. He had not been with the agency long enough to be infected by its insularity, and as he later promised Congress, he was willing—no, eager—to identify and punish any of his NASA subordinates who could be held responsible for the accident. Nonetheless, he decided to defy Gehman, and he announced that his people would remain in place. It was an ill-considered move. Gehman simply went public with his letter, posting it on the CAIB Web site. Gehman understood that O'Keefe felt betrayed—"stabbed in the back" was the word going around—but NASA had left him no choice. O'Keefe surrendered. Ham and the others were reassigned, and the Mishap Investigation Team was disbanded, replaced by NASA staffers who had not been involved in the *Columbia*'s flight and would be more likely to cooperate with the CAIB's investigators. The board was never able to overcome completely the whiff of collusion that had accompanied its birth, but Gehman had won a significant fight, even if it meant that he and "Sean" would not be friends.

THE SPACE SHUTTLE IS THE most audacious flying machine ever built, an engineering fantasy made real. Before each flight it stands vertically on the launch pad at the Kennedy Space Center, as the core component of a rocket assembly 184 feet tall. The shuttle itself, which is also known as the orbiter, is a winged vehicle roughly the size of a DC-9, with three main rocket engines in the tail, a large unpressurized cargo bay in the midsection, and a cramped two-level crew compartment in the nose. It is attached to a huge external tank containing liquid fuel for the three main engines. That tank in turn is attached to two solid-fuel rockets, known as boosters, which flank the assembly and bear its full weight on the launch pad. Just before the launch, the weight is about 4.5 million pounds, 90 percent of which is fuel. It is a dramatic time, ripe with anticipation; the shuttle vents vapors like a breathing thing; the ground crews pull away until finally no one is left; the air seems unusually quiet.

Typically there are seven astronauts aboard. Four of them sit in the cockpit, and three on the lower level, in the living quarters known as the mid-deck. Because of the shuttle's vertical position, their seats are effectively rotated backward 90 degrees, so they are sitting on their backs, feeling their own weight in a way that tends to emphasize gravity's pull. At the front of the cockpit, positioned closer to the instrument panel than is necessary for the typical astronaut's six-foot frame, the commander and the pilot can look straight ahead into space. They are highly trained. They know exactly what they are getting into. Sometimes they have waited years for this moment to arrive.

The launch window may be just a few minutes wide. It is ruled by orbital mechanics, and defined by the track and position of the destination—usually now the unfinished International Space Station. Six seconds before liftoff the three main engines are ignited and throttled up to 100 percent power, producing more than a million pounds of thrust. The shuttle responds with what is known as "the twang," swaying several feet in the direction of the external tank and then swaying back. This is felt in the cockpit. The noise inside is not very loud. If the computers show that the main engines are operating correctly, the solid rocket boosters ignite. The boosters are ferocious devices—the same sort of monsters that upon failure blew the *Challenger* apart. Each of them produces three million pounds of thrust. Once ignited, they cannot be shut off or throttled back. The shuttle lifts off. It accelerates fast enough to clear the launch tower doing about 100 mph, though it is so large that seen from the outside, it appears to be climbing slowly.

The flying is done entirely by autopilot unless something goes wrong. Within seconds the assembly rotates and aims on course, tilting slightly off the vertical and rolling so that the orbiter is inverted beneath the external tank. Although the vibrations are heavy enough to blur the instruments, the acceleration amounts to only about 2.5 Gs—a mild sensation of heaviness pressing the astronauts back into their seats. After about forty seconds the shuttle accelerates through Mach 1, 760 mph, at about 17,000 feet, climbing nearly straight up. Eighty seconds later, with the shuttle doing about 3,400 mph and approaching 150,000 feet, the crew can feel the thrust from the solid rocket boosters begin to tail off. Just afterward, with a bright flash and a loud explosion heard inside the orbiter, the rocket boosters separate from the main tank; they continue to travel upward on a ballistic path to 220,000 feet before falling back and parachuting into the sea. Now powered by the main engines alone, the ride turns smooth, and the forces settle down to about 1 G.

One pilot described the sensations to me on the simplest level. He said, "First it's like, 'Hey, this is a rough ride!' and then, 'Hey, I'm on an electric train!' and then, 'Hey, this train's starting to go pretty darned fast!'" Speed is the ultimate goal of the launch sequence. Having climbed steeply into ultrathin air, the shuttle gently pitches over until it is flying nearly parallel to Earth, inverted under the external tank, and thrusting at full power. Six minutes after launch, at about 356,000 feet, the shuttle is doing around 9,200 mph, which is fast, but only about half the speed required to sustain an orbit. It therefore begins a shallow dive, during which it gains speed at the rate of 1,000 mph every twenty seconds—an acceleration so fast that it presses the shuttle against its 3 G limit, and the engines have to be briefly throttled back. At 10,300 mph the shuttle rolls to a head-up position. Passing through 15,000 mph, it begins to climb again, still accelerating at 3 Gs, until, seconds later, in the near vacuum of space, it achieves orbital velocity, or 17,500 mph. The plumes from the main engines wrap forward and dance across the cockpit windows, making light at night like that of Saint Elmo's fire. Only eight and a half minutes have passed since the launch. The main engines are extinguished, and the external tank is jettisoned. The shuttle is in orbit. After further maneuvering it assumes its standard attitude, flying inverted in relation to Earth and tail first as it proceeds around the globe.

For the astronauts aboard, the uphill flight would amount to little more than an interesting ride were it not for the possibility of failures. That possibility, however, is very real, and as a result the launch is a critical and complicated operation, demanding close teamwork, tight coordination with Mission Control, and above all extreme concentration—a quality often confused with coolness under fire. I was given a taste of this by an active shuttle commander named Michael Bloomfield, who had me strap in beside him in NASA's full-motion simulator in Houston, and take a realistic run from the launch pad into space. Bloomfield is a former Air Force test pilot who has flown three shuttle missions. He had been assigned to assist the CAIB, and had been watching the investigation with mixed emotions—hopeful that some effects might be positive, but concerned as well that the inquiry might veer into formalism without sufficiently taking into account the radical nature of space flight, or the basic truth that every layer of procedure and equipment comes at a cost, often unpredictable. Bloomfield called this the "risk versus risk" tradeoff, and made it real not by defending NASA against specific criticisms but by immersing me, a pilot myself, in the challenges of normal operations.

Much of what he showed me was of the what-if variety, the essence not only of simulator work but also of the crew's real-world thinking. For instance, during the launch, as the shuttle rockets upward on autopilot, the pilots and flight controllers pass through a succession of mental gates, related to various combinations of main-engine failures, at various altitudes and speeds. The options and resulting maneuvers are complicated, ranging from a quick return to the launch site, to a series of tight arrivals at select runways up the eastern seaboard, to transatlantic glides, and finally even an "abort into orbit"—an escape route used by a *Challenger* crew in 1985 after a single main-engine failure. Such failures allow little time to make the right decision. As Bloomfield and I climbed away from Earth, tilted onto our backs, he occasionally asked the operators to freeze the simulation so that he could unfold his thoughts to me. Though the choices were clear, the relative risks were rarely so obvious. It was a deep view into the most intense sort of flying.

After we arrived in space, we continued to talk. One of the gates for engine failure during the climb to the Space Station stands at Mach 21.8 (14,900 mph), the last point allowed for a "high energy" arrival into Gander, Newfoundland, and the start of the emergency transatlantic track for Shannon, Ireland. An abort at that point provides no easy solution. The problem with Gander is how to bleed off excess energy before the landing (Bloomfield called this "a take-all-your-brain-cells type of flying"), whereas the problem with Shannon is just the opposite—how to stretch the glide. Bloomfield told me that immediately before his last space flight, in the spring of 2002, his crew and a Mission Control team had gone through a full-dress simulation during which the orbiter had lost all three engines by Mach 21.7 (less than 100 mph from the decision speed). Confident in his ability to fly the more difficult Canadian arrival, Bloomfield, from the cockpit of the simulator, radioed, "We're going high-energy into Gander."

Mission Control answered, "Negative," and called for Shannon instead. Bloomfield looked over at his right-seat pilot and said, "I think we oughta go to Gander. What do you think?"

"Yeah."

Bloomfield radioed back: "No, we think we oughta go to Gander."

Mission Control was emphatic. "Negative. We see you having enough energy to make Shannon."

As commander, Bloomfield had formal authority for the decision, but Mission Control, with its expert teams and wealth of data, was expressing a strong opinion, so he acquiesced. Acquiescence is standard in such cases, and usually it works out for the best. Bloomfield had enormous respect for the expertise and competence of Mission Control. He was also well aware of errors he had made in the past, despite superior advice or instructions from the flight controllers. This time, however, it turned out that two of the flight controllers had not communicated correctly with each other, and that the judgment of Mission Control therefore was wrong. Lacking the energy to reach Shannon, the simulator went into the ocean well short of the airport. The incident caused a disturbance inside the Johnson Space Center, particularly because of the longstanding struggle for the possession of data (and ultimately control) between the pilots in flight and the engineers at their consoles. Nevertheless, the two groups worked together, hammered out the problems, and the next day flew the same simulator profile successfully. But that was not the point of Bloomfield's story. Rather, it was that these calls are hard to make, and that mistakes—whether his or the controllers'—may become obvious only after it is too late.

For all its realism, the simulator cannot duplicate the gravity load of the climb, or the lack of it at the top. The transition to weightlessness is abrupt, and all the more dramatic because it occurs at the end of the 3 G acceleration: when the main engines cut off, the crew gets the impression of going over an edge and suddenly dropping into a free fall. That impression is completely accurate. In fact the term zero gravity (0 G), which is loosely used to describe the orbital environment, refers to physical acceleration, and does not mean that Earth's gravitational pull has somehow gone away. Far from it: the diminution of gravitational pull that comes with distance is small at these low-orbit altitudes (perhaps 200 miles above the surface), and the shuttle is indeed now falling—about like a stone dropped off a cliff. The fall does not, of course, diminish the shuttle's mass (if it bumps the Space Station, it does so with tremendous force), but it does make the vehicle and everything inside it very nearly weightless. The orbital part of the trick is that though the shuttle is dropping like a stone, it is also progressing across Earth's surface so fast

(17,500 mph) that its path matches (roughly) the curvature of the globe. In other words, as it plummets toward the ground, the ground keeps getting out of its way. Like the orbits of all other satellites, and of the Space Station, and of the Moon as well, its flight is nothing but an unrestricted free fall around and around the world.

To help the astronauts adapt to weightlessness, the quarters are designed with a conventional floor-down orientation. This isn't quite so obvious as it might seem, since the shuttle flies inverted in orbit. "Down" therefore is toward outer space—and the view from the cockpit windows just happens to be of Earth sliding by from behind and overhead. The crews are encouraged to live and work with their heads "up" nonetheless. It is even recommended that they use the ladder while passing through the hatch between the two levels, and that they "descend" from the cockpit to the mid-deck feet first. Those sorts of cautions rarely prevail against the temptations of weightlessness. After Bloomfield's last flight one of his crew commented that they had all been swimming around "like eels in a can." Or like superhumans, as the case may be. It's true that there are frustrations: if you try to throw a switch without first anchoring your body, the switch will throw you. On the other hand, once you are anchored, you can shift multi-ton masses with your fingertips. You can also fly without wings, perform unlimited flips, or simply float for a while, resting in midair. Weightlessness is bad for the bones, but good for the soul. I asked Bloomfield how it had felt to experience gravity again. He said he remembered the first time, after coming to a stop on the runway in Florida, when he picked up a small plastic checklist in the cockpit and thought, "Man, this is so heavy!" He looked at me and said, "Gravity sucks."

And orbital flight clearly does not. The ride is smooth. When the cabin ventilation is turned off, as it must be once a day to exchange the carbon dioxide scrubbers, the silence is absolute. The smell inside the shuttle is distinctly metallic, unless someone has just come in from a spacewalk, after which the quarters are permeated for a while with "the smell of space," a pungent burned odor that some compare to that of seared meat, and that Bloomfield describes as closer to the smell of a torch on steel. The dominant sensation, other than weight-lessness, is of the speed across the ground. Bloomfield said, "From California to New York in ten minutes, around the world once in ninety minutes—I mean, we're moving." He told me that he took to loitering in the cockpit at the end of the workdays, just for the view. By floating forward above the instrument panel and wrapping his legs around one of the pilot seats, he could position his face so close to the front windshield that the structure of the shuttle would seem to disappear.

The view from there was etched into his memory as a continuous loop. In brief, he said: It's night and you're coming up on California, with that clearly defined coastline, and you can see all the lights all the way from Tijuana to San Francisco, and then it's behind you, and you spot Las Vegas and its neon-lit Strip, which you barely have time to identify before you move across the Rockies, with their helter-skelter of towns, and then across the Plains, with its monotony of look-alike wheels and spokes of light, until you come to Chicago and its lakefront, from which point you can see past Detroit and Cleveland all the way to New York. These are big cities, you think. And because you grew up on a farm in Michigan, played football there in high school, and still know it like a home, you pick out Ann Arbor and Flint, and the place where I-75 joins U.S. Highway 23, and you get down to within a couple of miles of your house before zip, you're gone. Zip goes Cleveland, and zip New York, and then you're out over the Atlantic beyond Maine, looking back down the eastern sea-board all the way past Washington, DC. Ten minutes later you come up on Europe, and you hardly have time to think that London is a sprawl, France is an orderly display, the Alps are the Rockies again, and Italy is indeed a boot. Over Sicily you peer down into Etna's crater, into the glow of molten rock on Earth's inside, and then you are crossing Africa, where the few lights you see are not yellow but orange, like open flames. Past the Equator and beyond Madagascar you come to a zone of gray between the blackness of the night and the bright blue of the day. At the center of that zone is a narrow pink slice, which is the atmospheric dawn as seen from above. Daylight is for the oceans—first the Indian and then the Pacific, which is very, very large. Atolls appear with coral reefs and turquoise lagoons, but mostly what you see is cloud and open water.

Then the pink slice of sunset passes below, and the night, and soon afterward you come again to California, though at another point on the coast, because ninety minutes have passed since you were last here, and during that time the world has revolved beneath you.

Ultimately the shuttle must return to Earth and land. The problem then is what to do with the vast amount of physical energy that has been invested in it—almost all the calories once contained in the nearly four million pounds of rocket fuel that was used to shove the shuttle into orbit. Some of that energy now resides in the vehicle's altitude, but most resides in its speed. The re-entry is a descent to a landing, yes, but primarily it is a giant deceleration, during which atmospheric resistance is used to convert velocity into heat, and to slow the shuttle by roughly 17,000 mph, so that it finally passes overhead the runway in Florida at airline speeds, and circles down to touch the ground at a well tamed 224 mph or less. Once the shuttle is on the runway, the drag chute and brakes take care of the rest.

The re-entry is a one-way ride that cannot be stopped once it has begun. The opening move occurs while the shuttle is still proceeding tail first and inverted, halfway around the world from the runway, high above the Indian Ocean. It is a simple thing, a brief burn by the twin orbital maneuvering rockets against the direction of flight, which slows the shuttle by perhaps 200 mph. That reduction is enough. The shuttle continues to free-fall as it has in orbit, but it now lacks the speed to match the curvature of Earth, so the ground no longer gets out of its way. By the time it reaches the start of the atmosphere, the "entry interface" at 400,000 feet, it has gently flipped itself around so that it is right-side up and pointed for Florida, but with its nose held 40 degrees higher than the angle of the descent path. The effect of this so-called angle of attack (which technically refers to the wings, not the nose) is to create drag, and to shield the shuttle's internal structures from the intense re-entry heat by cocking the vehicle up to greet the atmosphere with leading edges made of heat-resistant carbon-composite panels, and with 24,305 insulating surface tiles, each one unique, which are glued primarily to the vehicle's underside. To regulate the sink and drag (and to control the heating), the shuttle goes through a program of sweeping S-turns, banking as steeply as 80 degrees to one side and then the other, tilting its lift vector and digging into the atmosphere. The thinking is done by redundant computers, which use onboard inertial sensing systems to gauge the shuttle's position, altitude, descent rate, and speed. The flying is done by autopilot. The cockpit crews and mission controllers play the role of observers, albeit extremely interested ones who are ready to intervene should something go wrong. In a basic sense, therefore, the re-entry is a mirror image of the launch and climb, decompressed to forty-five minutes instead of eight, but with the added complication that it will finish with the need for a landing.

Bloomfield took me through it in simulation, the two of us sitting in the cockpit to watch while an experienced flight crew and full Mission Control team brought the shuttle in from the de-orbit burn to the touchdown, dealing with a complexity of cascading system failures. Of course, in reality the automation usually performs faultlessly, and the shuttle proceeds to Florida right on track, and down the center of the desired descent profile. Bloomfield expressed surprise at how well the magic had worked on his own flights. Because he had launched on high-inclination orbits to the Russian station *Mir* and the International Space Station, he had not flown a *Columbia*-style re-entry over the United States, but had descended across Central America instead. He said, "You look down over Central America, and you're so low that you can see the forests! You think, 'There's no way we're going to make it to Florida!' Then you cross the west coast of Florida, and you look inside, and you're still doing Mach 5, and you think, 'There's no way we're going to slow in time!'" But you do. Mach 5 is 3,500 mph. At that point the shuttle is at 117,000 feet, about 140 miles out. At Mach 2.5, or 1,650 mph, it is at 81,000 feet, about sixty miles out. At that point the crew activates the head-up displays, which project see-through flight guidance into the field of vision through the windshield. When the shuttle slows below the speed of sound, it shudders as the shock waves shift. By tradition if not necessity, the commander then takes over from the autopilot, and flies the rest of the arrival manually, using the control stick.

Bloomfield invited me to fly some simulated arrivals myself, and prompted me while I staggered around for a few landings—overhead the Kennedy Space Center at 30,000 feet with the runway and the coastal estuaries in sight below, banking left into a tight, plunging energy-management turn, rolling out onto final approach at 11,000 feet, following an extraordinarily steep, 18-degree glide slope at 345 mph, speed brakes on, pitching up through a "pre-flare" at 2,000 feet to flatten the descent, landing gear out at 300 feet, touching down on the main wheels with some skips and bumps, then drag chute out, nose gear gently down, and brakes on. My efforts were crude, and greatly assisted by Bloomfield, but they gave me an impression of the shuttle as a solid, beautifully balanced flying machine that in thick air, at the end, is responsive and not difficult to handle—if everything goes just right. Bloomfield agreed. Moreover, years have passed in which everything did go just right—leaving the pilots to work on the finesse of their touchdowns, whether they were two knots fast, or 100 feet long. Bloomfield said, "When you come back and you land, the engineers will pull out their charts and they'll say things like 'The boundary layer tripped on the left wing before the right one. Did you feel anything?' And the answer is always 'Well . . . no. It was an incredibly smooth ride all the way down.'" But then, on the morning of February 1, something went really wrong—something too radical for simulation, that offered the pilots no chance to fly— and the *Columbia* lay scattered for 300 miles across the ground.

The foam did it. That much was suspected from the start, and all the evidence converged on it as the CAIB's investigation proceeded through the months that followed. The foam was dense and dry; it was the brownish-orange coating applied to the outside of the shuttle's large external tank to insulate the extreme cold of the rocket fuels inside from the warmth and moisture of the air. Eighty-two seconds after liftoff, as the *Columbia* was accelerating through 1,500 mph, a piece of that foam—about nineteen inches long by eleven inches wide, weighing about 1.7 pounds—broke off from the external tank and collided with the left wing at about 545 mph. Cameras near the launch site recorded the event—though the images when viewed the following day provided insufficient detail to know the exact impact point, or the consequences. The CAIB's investigation ultimately found that a gaping hole about ten inches across had been punched into the wing's leading edge, and that sixteen days later the hole allowed the hot gases of the re-entry to penetrate the wing and consume it from the inside. Through enormous effort this would be discovered and verified beyond doubt. It was important nonetheless to explore the alternatives. In an effort closely supervised by the CAIB, groups of NASA engineers created several thousand flow charts, one for each scenario that could conceivably have led to the re-entry breakup. The thinking was rigorous. For a scenario to be "closed," meaning set aside, absolute proof had to be found (usually physical or mathematical) that this particular explanation did not apply: there was no cockpit fire, no flight-control malfunction, no act of terrorism or sabotage that had taken the shuttle down. Unexpected vulnerabilities were found during this process, and even after the investigation was formally concluded, in late August, more than a hundred scenarios remained technically open, because they could not positively be closed. For lack of evidence to the contrary, for instance, neither bird strikes nor micrometeorite impacts could be completely ruled out.

But for all their willingness to explore less likely alternatives, many of NASA's managers remained stubbornly closed-minded on the subject of foam. From the earliest telemetric data it was known that intense heat inside the left wing had destroyed the *Columbia*, and that such heat could have gotten there only through a hole. The connection between the hole and the foam strike was loosely circumstantial at first, but it required serious consideration nonetheless. NASA balked at going down that road. Its reasons were not rational and scientific but, rather, complex and cultural, and they turned out to be closely related to the errors that had led to the accident in the first place: simply put, it had become a matter of faith within NASA that foam strikes—which were a known problem— could not cause mortal damage to the shuttle. Sean O'Keefe, who was badly advised by his NASA lieutenants, made unwise public statements deriding the "foamologists"; and even Ron Dittemore, NASA's technically expert shuttle program manager, joined in with categorical denials.

At the CAIB, Gehman, who was not unsympathetic to NASA, watched these reactions with growing skepticism and a sense of déjà vu. Over his years in the Navy, and as a result of the *Cole* inquiry, he had become something of a student of large organizations under stress. To me he said, "It has been scorched into my mind that bureaucracies will do anything to defend themselves. It's not evil—it's just a natural reaction of bureaucracies, and since NASA is a bureaucracy, I expect the same out of them. As we go through the investigation, I've been looking for signs where the system is trying to defend itself." Of those signs the most obvious was this display of blind faith by an organization dependent on its engineering cool; NASA, in its absolute certainty, was unintentionally signaling the very problem that it had. Gehman had seen such certainty proved wrong too many times, and he told me that he was not about to get "rolled by the system," as he had been rolled before. He said, "Now when I hear NASA telling me things like 'Gotta be true!' or 'We know this to be true!' all my alarm bells go off. . . . Without hurting anybody's feelings, or squashing people's egos, we're having to say, 'We're sorry, but we're not accepting that answer.'"

That was the form that the physical investigation took on, with hundreds of NASA engineers and technicians doing most of the detailed work, and the CAIB watching closely and increasingly stepping in. Despite what Gehman said, it was inevitable that feelings got hurt and egos squashed—and indeed that serious damage to people's lives and careers was inflicted. At the NASA facilities dedicated to shuttle operations (Alabama for rockets, Florida for launch and landing, Texas for management and mission control) the CAIB investigators were seen as invaders of sorts, unwelcome strangers arriving to pass judgment on people's good-faith efforts. On the ground level, where the detailed analysis was being done, there was active resistance at first, with some NASA engineers openly refusing to cooperate, or to allow access to records and technical documents that had not been pre-approved for release. Gehman had to intervene. One of the toughest and most experienced of the CAIB investigators later told me he had a gut sense that NASA continued to hide relevant information, and that it does so to this day. But cooperation between the two groups gradually improved as friendships were made, and the intellectual challenges posed by the inquiry began to predominate over fears about what had happened or what might follow. As so often occurs, it was on an informal basis that information flowed best, and that much of the truth was discovered.

Board member Steven Wallace described the investigation not as a linear path but as a picture that gradually filled in. Or as a jigsaw puzzle. The search for debris began the first day, and soon swelled to include more than 25,000 people, at a cost of well over $300 million. NASA received 1,459 debris reports, including some from nearly every state in the union, and also from Canada, Jamaica, and the Bahamas. Discounting the geographic extremes, there was still a lot to follow up on. Though the amateur videos showed pieces separating from the shuttle along the entire path over the United States, and though search parties backtracked all the way to the Pacific coast in the hope of finding evidence of the breakup's triggering mechanism, the westernmost piece found on the ground was a left-wing tile that landed near a town called Littlefield, in the Texas Panhandle. Not surprisingly, the bulk of the wreckage lay under the main breakup, from south of Dallas eastward across the rugged, snake-infested brushland of East Texas and into Louisiana; and that is where most of the search took place. The best work was done on foot, by tough and dedicated crews who walked in tight lines across several thousand square miles. Their effort became something of a close sampling of the American landscape, turning up all sorts of odds and ends, including a few apparent murder victims, plenty of junked cars, and the occasional clandestine meth lab. More to the point, it also turned up crew remains and more than 84,000 pieces of the *Columbia*, which, at 84,900 pounds, accounted for 38 percent of the vehicle's dry weight. Certain pieces that had splashed into the murky waters of lakes and reservoirs were never found. It was presumed that most if not all the remaining pieces had been vaporized by the heat of re-entry, either before or after the breakup.

Some of the shuttle's contents survived intact. For instance, a vacuum cleaner still worked, as did some computers and printers and a Medtronic Tono-Pen, used to measure ocular pressure. A group of worms from one of the science experiments not only survived but continued to multiply. Most of the debris, however, was a twisted mess. The recovered pieces were meticulously plotted and tagged, and transported to a hangar at the Kennedy Space Center, where the wing remnants were laid out in correct position on the floor, and what had been found of the left wing's reinforced carbon-carbon (RCC) leading edge was reconstructed in a transparent Plexiglas mold—though with large gaps where pieces were missing. The hangar was a quiet, poignant, intensely focused place, with many of the same NASA technicians who had prepared the *Columbia* for flight now involved in the sad task of handling its ruins. The assembly and analysis went on through the spring. One of the principal CAIB agents there was an affable Air Force pilot named Patrick Goodman, an experienced accident investigator who had made both friends and enemies at NASA for the directness of his approach. When I first met him, outside the hangar on a typically warm and sunny Florida day, he explained some of the details that I had just seen on the inside—heat-eroded tiles, burned skin and structure, and aluminum slag that had emerged in molten form from inside the left wing, and had been deposited onto the aft rocket pods. The evidence was complicated because it resulted from combinations of heat, physical forces, and wildly varying airflows that had occurred before, during, and after the main-body breakup, but for Goodman it was beginning to read like a map. He had faith. He said, "We know what we have on the ground. It's the truth. The debris is the truth, if we can only figure out what it's saying. It's not a theoretical model. It exists." Equally important was the debris that did not exist, most significantly large parts of the left wing, including the lower part of a section of the RCC leading edge, a point known as Panel Eight, which was approximately where the launch cameras showed that the foam had hit. Goodman said, "We look at what we don't have. What we do have. What's on what we have. We start from there, and try to work backwards up the timeline, always trying to see the previous significant event." He called this "looking uphill." It was like a movie run in reverse, with the found pieces springing off the ground and flying upward to a point of reassembly above Dallas, and then the *Columbia*, looking nearly whole, flying tail-first toward California, picking up the Littlefield tile as it goes, and then higher again, through entry interface over the Pacific, through orbits flown in reverse, inverted but nose first, and then back down toward Earth, picking up the external tank and the solid rocket boosters during the descent, and settling tail-first with rockets roaring, until just before a vertical touchdown a spray of pulverized foam appears below, pulls together at the left-wing leading edge, and rises to lodge itself firmly on the side of the external tank.

The foam did it.

There was plenty of other evidence, too. After the accident the Air Force dug up routine radar surveillance tapes that upon close inspection showed a small object floating alongside the *Columbia* on the second day of its mission. The object slowly drifted away and disappeared from view. Subsequent testing of radar profiles and ballistic coefficients for a multitude of objects found a match for only one—a fragment of RCC panel of at least 140 square inches. The match never quite passed muster as proof, but investigators presumed that the object was a piece of the leading edge, that it had been shoved into the inside of the wing by the impact of the foam, and that during maneuvering in orbit it had floated free. The picture by now was rapidly filling in.

But the best evidence was numerical. It so happened that because the *Columbia* was the first of the operational shuttles, it was equipped with hundreds of additional engineering sensors that fed into an onboard data-collection device, a box known as a modular auxiliary data system, or MADS recorder, that was normally used for post-flight analysis of the vehicle's performance. During the initial debris search this box was not found, but such was its potential importance that after careful calculation of its likely ballistic path, another search was mounted, and on March 19 it was discovered—lying in full view on ground that had been gone over before. The really surprising thing was its condition. Though the recorder was not designed to be crashproof, and used Mylar tape that was vulnerable to heat, it had survived the breakup and fall completely intact, as had the data that it contained, the most interesting of which pertained to heat rises and sequential sensor failures inside the left wing. When combined with the telemetric data that already existed, and with calculations of the size and location of the sort of hole that might have been punched through the leading edge by the foam, the new data allowed for a good fit with computational models of the theoretical airflow and heat propagation inside the left wing, and it steered the investigation to an inevitable conclusion that the breach must have been in the RCC at Panel Eight.

By early summer the picture was clear. Though strictly speaking the case was circumstantial, the evidence against the foam was so persuasive that there remained no reasonable doubt about the physical cause of the accident. As a result, Gehman gave serious consideration to NASA's request to call off a planned test of the launch incident, during which a piece of foam would be carefully fired at a fully rigged RCC Panel Eight. NASA's argument against the test had some merit: the leading-edge panels (forty-four per shuttle) are custom-made, $700,000 components, each one different from the others, and the testing would require the use of the last spare Panel Eight in the entire fleet. NASA said that it couldn't afford the waste, and Gehman was inclined to agree, precisely because he felt that breaking the panel would prove nothing that hadn't already been amply proved. By a twist of fate it was the sole NASA member of the CAIB, the quiet, cerebral, earnestly scientific Scott Hubbard, who insisted that the test proceed. Hubbard was one of the original seven board members. At the time of the accident he had just become the director of NASA's Ames Research Center, in California. Months later now, in the wake of Gehman's rebellion, and with the CAIB aggressively moving beyond the physical causes and into the organizational ones, he found himself in the tricky position of collaborating with a group that many of his own people at NASA saw as the enemy. Hubbard, however, had an almost childlike belief in doing the right thing, and having been given this unfortunate job, he was determined to see it through correctly. Owing to the closeness of his ties to NASA, he understood an aspect of the situation that others might have overlooked: despite overwhelming evidence to the contrary, many people at NASA continued stubbornly to believe that the foam strike on launch could not have caused the *Columbia*'s destruction. Hubbard argued that if NASA was to have any chance of self-reform, these people would have to be confronted with reality, not in abstraction but in the most tangible way possible. Gehman found the argument convincing, and so the foam shot proceeded.

The work was done in San Antonio, using a compressed-nitrogen gun with a thirty-five-foot barrel, normally used to fire dead chickens—real and artificial—against aircraft structures in bird-strike certification tests. NASA approached the test kicking and screaming all the way, insisting, for instance, that the shot be used primarily to validate an earlier debris-strike model (the so-called Crater model of strikes against the underside tiles) that had been used for decision-making during the flight, and was now known to be irrelevant. Indeed, it was because of NASA obstructionism—and specifically the illogical insistence by some of the NASA rocket engineers that the chunk of foam that had hit the wing was significantly smaller (and therefore lighter) than the video and film record showed it to be—that the CAIB and Scott Hubbard finally took direct control of the testing. There was in fact a series of foam shots, increasingly realistic according to the evolving analysis of the actual strike, that raised the stakes from a glancing blow against the underside tiles to steeper-angle hits directly against leading-edge panels. The second to last shot was a 22-degree hit against the bottom of Panel Six: it produced some cracks and other damage deemed too small to explain the shuttle's loss. Afterward there was some smugness at NASA, and even Sean O'Keefe, who again was badly advised, weighed in on the matter, belittling the damage. But the shot against Panel Six was not yet the real thing. That was saved for the precious Panel Eight, in a test that was painstakingly designed to duplicate (conservatively) the actual impact against the *Columbia*'s left wing, assuming a rotational "clocking angle" 30 degrees off vertical for the piece of foam. Among the engineers who gathered to watch were many of those still living in denial. The gun fired, and the foam hit the panel at a 25-degree relative angle at about 500 mph. Immediately afterward an audible gasp went through the crowd. The foam had knocked a hole in the RCC large enough to allow people to put their heads through. Hubbard told me that some of the NASA people were close to tears. Gehman had stayed away in order to avoid the appearance of gloating. He could not keep the satisfaction out of his voice, however, when later he said to me, "Their whole house of cards came falling down."

NASA's house was by then what this investigation was really all about. The CAIB discovered that on the morning of January 17, the day after the launch, the low-level engineers at the Kennedy Space Center whose job was to review the launch videos and film were immediately concerned by the size and speed of the foam that had struck the shuttle. As expected of them, they compiled the imagery and disseminated it by e-mail to various shuttle engineers and managers—most significantly those in charge of the shuttle program at the Johnson Space Center. Realizing that their blurred or otherwise inadequate pictures showed nothing of the damage that might have been inflicted, and anticipating the need for such information by others, the engineers at Kennedy then went outside normal channels and on their own initiative approached the Department of Defense with a request that secret military satellites or ground-based high-resolution cameras be used to photograph the shuttle in orbit. After a delay of several days for the back-channel request to get through, the Air Force proved glad to oblige, and made the first moves to honor the request. Such images would probably have shown a large hole in the left wing—but they were never taken.

When news of the foam strike arrived in Houston, it did not seem to be crucially important. Though foam was not supposed to shed from the external tank, and the shuttle was not designed to withstand its impacts, falling foam had plagued the shuttle from the start, and indeed had caused damage on most missions. The falling foam was usually popcorn sized, too small to cause more than superficial dents in the thermal protection tiles. The CAIB, however, discovered a history of more-serious cases. For example, in 1988 the shuttle *Atlantis* took a heavy hit, seen by the launch cameras eighty-five seconds into the climb, nearly the same point at which the *Columbia* strike occurred. On the second day of the *Atlantis* flight Houston asked the crew to inspect the vehicle's underside with a video camera on a robotic arm (which the *Columbia* did not have). The commander, Robert "Hoot" Gibson, told the CAIB that the belly looked as if it had been blasted with shotgun fire. The *Atlantis* returned safely anyway, but afterward was found to have lost an entire tile, exposing its bare metal belly to the re-entry heat. It was lucky that the damage had happened in a place where a heavy aluminum plate covered the skin, Gibson said, because otherwise the belly might have been burned through.

Nonetheless, over the years foam strikes had come to be seen within NASA as an "in-family" problem, so familiar that even the most serious episodes seemed unthreatening and mundane. Douglas Osheroff, a normally good-humored Stanford physicist and Nobel laureate who joined the CAIB late, went around for months in a state of incredulity and dismay at what he was learning about NASA's operational logic. He told me that the shuttle managers acted as if they thought the frequency of the foam strikes had somehow reduced the danger that the impacts posed. His point was not that the managers really believed this but that after more than a hundred successful flights they had come blithely to accept the risk. He said, "The excitement that only exists when there is danger was kind of gone—even though the danger was not gone." And frankly, organizational and bureaucratic concerns weighed more heavily on the managers' minds. The most pressing of those concerns were the new performance goals imposed by Sean O'Keefe, and a tight sequence of flights leading up to a drop-dead date of February 19, 2004, for the completion of the International Space Station's "core." O'Keefe had made it clear that meeting this deadline was a test, and that the very future of NASA's human spaceflight program was on the line.

From Osheroff 's scientific perspective, deadlines based on completion of the International Space Station were inherently absurd. To me he said, "And what would the next goal be after that? Maybe we should bring our pets up there! 'I wonder how a Saint Bernard urinates in zero gravity!' NASA sold the International Space Station to Congress as a great science center—but most scientists just don't agree with that. We're thirty years from being able to go to Mars. Meanwhile, the only reason to have man in space is to study man in space. You can do that stuff—okay—and there are also some biology experiments that are kind of fun. I think we are learning things. But I would question any statement that you can come up with better drugs in orbit than you can on the ground, or that sort of thing. The truth is, the International Space Station has become a huge liability for NASA"—expensive to build, expensive to fly, expensive to resupply. "Now members of Congress are talking about letting its orbit decay—just letting it fall into the ocean. And it does turn out that orbital decay is a very good thing, because it means that near space is a self-cleaning place. I mean, garbage does not stay up there forever."

In other words, completion of the Space Station could provide a measure of NASA's performance only in the most immediate and superficial manner, and it was therefore an inherently poor reason for shuttle managers to be ignoring the foam strikes and proceeding at full speed. It was here that you could see the limitations of leadership without vision, and the consequences of putting an executive like

O'Keefe in charge of an organization that needed more than mere discipline. This, however, was hardly an argument that the managers could use, or even in private allow themselves to articulate. If the Space Station was unimportant—and perhaps even a mistake—then one had to question the reason for the shuttle's existence in the first place. Like O'Keefe and the astronauts and NASA itself, the managers were trapped by a circular space policy thirty years in the making, and they had no choice but to strive to meet the timelines directly ahead. As a result, after the most recent *Atlantis* launch, in October of 2002, during which a chunk of foam from a particularly troublesome part of the external tank, known as the "bipod ramp," had dented one of the solid rocket boosters, shuttle managers formally decided during the post-flight review not to classify the incident as an "in-flight anomaly." This was the first time that a serious bipod-ramp incident had escaped such a classification. The decision allowed the following two launches to proceed on schedule. The second of those launches was the *Columbia*'s, on January 16.

The videos of the foam strike reached Houston the next day, January 17. They made it clear that again the offending material had come from the area of the bipod ramp, that this time the foam was larger than ever before, that the impact had occurred later in the climb (meaning at higher speed), and that the wing had been hit, though exactly where was not clear. The astronauts were happily in orbit now, and had apparently not felt the impact, or been able to distinguish it from the heavy vibrations of the solid rocket boosters. In other words, they were unaware of any trouble. Responsibility for disposing of the incident lay with engineers on the ground, and specifically with the Mission Management Team, or MMT, whose purpose was to make decisions about the problems and unscripted events that inevitably arose during any flight. The MMT was a high-level group. In the Houston hierarchy it operated above the flight controllers in the Mission Control room, and just below the shuttle program manager, Ron Dittemore. Dittemore was traveling at the time, and has since retired. The MMT meetings were chaired by his protégée, the once rising Linda Ham, who has come to embody

NASA's arrogance and insularity in many observers' minds. Ham is the same hard-charging manager who, with a colleague, later had to be forcefully separated from the CAIB's investigation. Within the strangely neutered engineering world of the Johnson Space Center, she was an intimidating figure, a youngish, attractive woman given to wearing revealing clothes, yet also known for a tough and domineering management style. Among the lower ranks she had a reputation for brooking no nonsense and being a little hard to talk to. She was not smooth. She was a woman struggling upward in a man's world. She was said to have a difficult personality.

As the head of the MMT, Ham responded to news of the foam strike as if it were just another item to be efficiently handled and then checked off the list: a water leak in the science lab, a radio communication failure, a foam strike on the left wing, okay, no safety-of-flight issues here—right? What's next? There was a trace of vanity in the way she ran her shows. She seemed to revel in her own briskness, in her knowledge of the shuttle systems, in her use of acronyms and the strange, stilted syntax of aerospace engineers. She was decisive, and very sure of her sense for what was important and what was not. Her style got the best of her on day six of the mission, January 21, when at a recorded MMT meeting she spoke just a few words too many, much to her later regret.

It was at the end of a report given by a mid-ranking engineer named Don McCormack, who summarized the progress of an ad hoc engineering group, called the Debris Assessment Team, that had been formed at a still lower level to analyze the foam strike. The analysis was being done primarily by Boeing engineers, who had dusted off the soon to be notorious Crater model, primarily to predict damage to the underwing tile. McCormack reported that little was yet resolved, that the quality of the Crater as a predictor was being judged against the known damage on earlier flights, and that some work was being done to explore the options should the analysis conclude that the *Columbia* had been badly wounded. After a brief exchange Ham cut him short, saying, "And I'm really . . . I don't think there is much we can do, so it's not really a factor during the flight, since there is not much we can do about it." She was making assumptions, of course, and they were later proved to be completely wrong, but primarily she was just being efficient, and moving the meeting along. After the accident, when the transcript and audio-tapes emerged, those words were taken out of context, and used to portray Ham as a villainous and almost inhumanly callous person, which she certainly was not. In fact, she was married to an astronaut, and was as concerned as anyone about the safety of the shuttle crews. This was a dangerous business, and she knew it all too well. But like her boss, Ron Dittemore, with whom she discussed the *Columbia* foam strike several times, she was so immersed in the closed world of shuttle management that she simply did not elevate the event—this "in-family" thing—to the level of concerns requiring action. She was intellectually arrogant, perhaps, and as a manager she failed abysmally. But neither she nor the others of her rank had the slightest suspicion that the *Columbia* might actually go down.

The frustration is that some people on lower levels were actively worried about that possibility, and they understood clearly that not enough was known about the effects of the foam strike on the wing, but they expressed their concerns mostly to one another, and for good reason, because on the few occasions when they tried to alert the decision-makers, NASA's management system overwhelmed them and allowed none of them to be heard. The question now, of course, is why.

The CAIB's search for answers began long before the technical details were resolved, and it ultimately involved hundreds of interviews and 50,000 pages of transcripts. The manner in which those interviews were conducted became a contentious issue, and it was arguably Gehman's biggest mistake. As a military man, advised by military men on the board, he decided to conduct the interviews according to a military model of safety probes, in which individual fault is not formally assigned, and the interviews themselves are "privileged," meaning forever sealed off from public view. It was understood that identities and deeds would not be protected from view, only individual testimonies to the CAIB, but serious critics cried foul nonetheless, and pointed out correctly that Gehman was using loopholes to escape sunshine laws that otherwise would have applied. Gehman believed that treating the testimony as privileged was necessary to encourage witnesses to talk, and to get to the bottom of the story, but the long-term effect of the investigation will be diminished as a result (for instance, by lack of access to the raw material by outside analysts), and there was widespread consensus among the experienced (largely civilian) investigators actually conducting the interviews that the promise of privacy was having little effect on what people were willing to say. These were not criminals they were talking to, or careful lawyers. For the most part they were sincere engineering types who were concerned about what had gone wrong, and would have been willing even without privacy to speak their minds. The truth, in other words, would have come out even in the brightest of sunshine.

The story that emerged was a sad and unnecessary one, involving arrogance, insularity, and bad luck allowed to run unchecked. On the seventh day of the flight, January 22, just as the Air Force began to move on the Kennedy engineers' back-channel request for photographs, Linda Ham heard to her surprise that this approach (which according to front-channel procedures would have required her approval) had been made. She immediately telephoned other high-level managers in Houston to see if any of them wanted to issue a formal "requirement" for imagery, and when they informed her that they did not, rather than exploring the question with the Kennedy engineers she simply terminated their request with the Department of Defense. This appears to have been a purely bureaucratic reaction. A NASA liaison officer then e-mailed an apology to Air Force personnel, assuring them that the shuttle was in "excellent shape," and explaining that a foam strike was "something that has happened before and is not considered to be a major problem." The officer continued, "The one problem that this has identified is the need for some additional coordination within NASA to assure that when a request is made it is done through the official channels." Months later one of the CAIB investigators who had followed this trail was still seething with anger at what had occurred. He said, "Because the problem was not identified in the traditional way—'Houston, we have a problem!'—well, then, 'Houston, we don't have a problem!' Because Houston didn't identify the problem."

But another part of Houston was doing just that. Unbeknownst to Ham and the shuttle management, the low-level engineers of the Debris Assessment Team had concluded that the launch films were not clear enough to indicate where the foam had hit, and particularly whether it had hit the underside tile or a leading-edge RCC panel. Rather than trying to run their calculations in the blind, they had decided that they should do the simple thing and have someone take a look for damage. They had already e-mailed one query to the engineering department, about the possibility of getting the astronauts themselves to take a short spacewalk and inspect the wing. It later turned out that this would have been safe and easy to do. That e-mail, however, was never answered. This time the Debris Assessment engineers decided on a still simpler solution—to ask the Department of Defense to take some high-resolution pictures. Ignorant of the fact that the Kennedy group had already made such a request, and that it had just been peevishly canceled, they sent out two requests of their own, directed, appropriately, to Ron Dittemore and Linda Ham, but through channels that were a little off-center, and happened to fail. Those channels were ones they had used in their regular work as engineers, outside the formal shuttle-management structure. By unfortunate circumstance, the request that came closest to getting through was intercepted by a mid-level employee (the assistant to an intended recipient, who was on vacation) who responded by informing the Debris Assessment engineers, more or less correctly, that Linda Ham had decided against Air Force imagery.

The confusion was now total, yet also nearly invisible—and within the suppressive culture of the human spaceflight program, it had very little chance of making itself known. At the top of the tangle, neither Ron Dittemore nor Linda Ham ever learned that the Debris Assessment Team wanted pictures; at the bottom, the Debris Assessment engineers heard the "no" without suspecting that it was not an answer to their request. They were told to go back to the Crater model and numerical analysis, and as earnest, hardworking engineers (hardly rebels, these), they dutifully complied, all the while regretting the blind assumptions that they would have to make. Given the obvious potential for a catastrophe, one might expect that they would have gone directly to Linda Ham, on foot if necessary, to make the argument in person for a spacewalk or high-resolution photos. However, such were the constraints within the Johnson Space Center that they never dared. They later said that had they made a fuss about the shuttle, they might have been singled out for ridicule. They feared for their standing, and their careers.

The CAIB investigator who asked the engineers what conclusion they had drawn at the time from management's refusal later said to me, "They all thought, 'Well, none of us have a security clearance high enough to view any of this imagery.' They talked about this openly among themselves, and they figured one of three things:

" 'One: The "no" means that management's already got photos, and the damage isn't too bad. They can't show us the photos, because we don't have the security clearance, and they can't tell us they have the photos, or tell us the damage isn't bad, because that tells us how accurate the photos are—and we don't have the security clearance. But wait a minute, if that's the case, then what're we doing here? Why are we doing the analysis? So no, that can't be right.

" 'Okay, then, two: They already took the photos, and the damage is so severe that there's no hope for recovery. Well . . . that can't be right either, because in that case, why are we doing the analysis?

" 'Okay, then, three: They took the photos. They can't tell us they took the photos, and the photos don't give us clear definition. So we need to do the analysis. That's gotta be it!' "

What the Debris Assessment engineers could not imagine is that no photos had been taken, or ever would be—and essentially for lack of curiosity by NASA's imperious, self-convinced managers. What those managers in turn could not imagine was that people in their own house might really be concerned. The communication gap had nothing to do with security clearances, and it was complete.

Gehman explained the underlying realities to me. He said, "They claim that the culture in Houston is a 'badgeless society,' meaning it doesn't matter what you have on your badge—you're concerned about shuttle safety together. Well, that's all nice, but the truth is that it does matter what badge you're wearing. Look, if you really do have an organization that has free communication and open doors and all that kind of stuff, it takes a special kind of management to make it work. And we just don't see that management here. Oh, they say all the right things. 'We have open doors and e-mails, and anybody who sees a problem can raise his hand, blow a whistle, and stop the whole process.' But then when you look at how it really works, it's an incestuous, hierarchical system, with invisible rankings and a very strict informal chain of command. They all know that. So even though they've got all the trappings of communication, you don't actually find communication. It's very complex. But if a person brings an issue up, what caste he's in makes all the difference. Now, again, NASA will deny this, but if you talk to people, if you really listen to people, all the time you hear 'Well, I was afraid to speak up.' Boy, it comes across loud and clear. You listen to the meetings: 'Anybody got anything to say?' There are thirty people in the room, and slam! There's nothing. We have plenty of witness statements saying, 'If I had spoken up, it would have been at the cost of my job.' And if you're in the engineering department, you're a nobody."

One of the CAIB investigators told me that he asked Linda Ham, "As a manager, how do you seek out dissenting opinions?"

According to him, she answered, "Well, when I hear about them . . ."

He interrupted. "Linda, by their very nature you may not hear about them."

"Well, when somebody comes forward and tells me about them."

"But Linda, what techniques do you use to get them?"

He told me she had no answer.

This was certainly not the sort of risk-versus-risk decision-making that Michael Bloomfield had in mind when he described the thinking behind his own shuttle flights.

* * *

AT 7:00 A.M. ON THE ninth day, January 24, which was one week before the *Columbia*'s scheduled re-entry, the engineers from the Debris Assessment Team formally presented the results of their numerical analysis to Linda Ham's intermediary, Don McCormack. The room was so crowded with concerned observers that some people stood in the hall, peering in. The fundamental purpose of the meeting would have been better served had the engineers been able to project a photograph of a damaged wing onto the screen, but, tragically, that was not to be. Instead they projected a typically crude PowerPoint summary, based on the results from the Crater model, with which they attempted to explain a nuanced position: first, that if the tile had been damaged, it had probably endured well enough to allow the *Columbia* to come home; and second, that for lack of information, they had needed to make assumptions to reach that conclusion, and that troubling unknowns therefore limited the meaning of the results. The latter message seems to have been lost. Indeed, this particular PowerPoint presentation became a case study for Edward Tufte, the brilliant communications specialist from Yale, who in a subsequent booklet, "The Cognitive Style of PowerPoint," tore into it for its dampening effect on clear expression and thought. The CAIB later joined in, describing the widespread use of PowerPoint within NASA as one of the obstacles to internal communication, and criticizing the Debris Assessment presentation for mechanically underplaying the uncertainties that remained.

Had the uncertainties been more strongly expressed as the central factor in question, the need to inspect the wing by spacewalk or photograph might have become obvious even to the shuttle managers. Still, the Mission Management Team seemed unprepared to hear nuance. Fixated on potential tile damage as the relevant question, assuming without good evidence that the RCC panels were strong enough to withstand a foam strike, subtly skewing the discussion away from catastrophic burn-through and toward the potential effects on turnaround times on the ground and how that might affect the all-important launch schedule, the shuttle managers were convinced that they had the situation as they defined it firmly under control.

At a regularly scheduled MMT meeting later that morning McCormack summarized the PowerPoint presentation for Linda Ham. He said, "The analysis is not complete. There is one case yet that they wish to run, but kind of just jumping to the conclusion of all that, they do show that [there is], obviously, a potential for significant tile damage here, but thermal analysis does not indicate that there is potential for a burn-through. I mean, there could be localized heating damage. There is . . . obviously there is a lot of uncertainty in all this in terms of the size of the debris and where it hit and the angle of incidence."

Ham answered, "No burn-through means no catastrophic damage. And the localized heating damage would mean a tile replacement?"

"Right, it would mean possible impacts to turnaround repairs and that sort of thing, but we do not see any kind of safety-of-flight issue here yet in anything that we've looked at."

This was all too accurate in itself. Ham said, "And no safety of flight, no issue for this mission, nothing that we're going to do different. There may be a turnaround [delay]."

McCormack said, "Right. It could potentially [have] hit the RCC. . . . We don't see any issue if it hit the RCC . . ."

The discussion returned to the tiles. Ham consulted with a tile specialist named Calvin Schomburg, who for days had been energetically making a case independent of the Debris Assessment analysis that a damaged tile would endure re-entry—and thereby adding, unintentionally, to the distractions and false assumptions of the management team. After a brief exchange Ham cut off further discussion with a quick summary for some people participating in the meeting by conference call, who were having trouble hearing the speakerphone. She said, "So, no safety-of-flight kind of issue. It's more of a turnaround issue similar to what we've had on other flights. That's it? All right, any questions on that?"

And there were not.

For reasons unexplained, when the official minutes of the meeting were written up and distributed (having been signed off on by Ham), all mention of the foam strike was omitted. This was days before the *Columbia*'s re-entry, and seems to indicate sheer lack of attention to this subject, rather than any sort of cover-up.

The truth is that Linda Ham was as much a victim of NASA as were *Columbia*'s astronauts, who were still doing their science experiments then, and freefalling in splendor around the planet. Her predicament had roots that went way back, nearly to the time of Ham's birth, and it involved not only the culture of the human space-flight program but also the White House, Congress, and NASA leadership over the past thirty years. Gehman understood this fully, and as the investigation drew to a close, he vowed to avoid merely going after the people who had been standing close to the accident when it occurred. The person standing closest was, of course, Linda Ham, and she will bear a burden for her mismanagement. But by the time spring turned to summer, and the CAIB moved its operation from Houston to Washington, DC, Gehman had taken to saying, "Complex systems fail in complex ways," and he was determined that the CAIB's report would document the full range of NASA's mistakes. It did, and in clean, frank prose, using linked sentences and no PowerPoint displays.

As the report was released, on August 26, Mars came closer to Earth than it had in 60,000 years. Gehman told me that he continued to believe in the importance of America's human space-flight effort, and even of the return of the shuttle to flight—at least until a replacement with a clearer mission can be built and put into service. It was a quiet day in Washington, with Congress in recess and the President on vacation. Aides were coming from Capitol Hill to pick up several hundred copies of the report and begin planning hearings for the fall. The White House was receiving the report too, though keeping a cautious distance, as had been expected; it was said that the President might read an executive summary. Down in Houston, board members were handing copies to the astronauts, the managers, and the families of the dead.

Gehman was dressed in a suit, as he had been at the start of all this, seven months before. It was up to him now to drive over to NASA headquarters, in the southwest corner of the city, and deliver the report personally to Sean O'Keefe. I went along for the ride, as did the board member Sheila Widnall, who was there to lend Gehman some moral support. The car was driven by a Navy officer in whites. At no point since the accident had anyone at NASA stepped forward to accept personal responsibility for contributing to this accident— not Linda Ham, not Ron Dittemore, and certainly not Sean O'Keefe.

However, the report in Gehman's hands (248 pages, full color, well bound) made responsibility very clear. This was not going to be a social visit. Indeed, it turned out to be extraordinarily tense. Gehman and Widnall strode up the carpeted hallways in a phalanx of anxious, dark-suited NASA staffers, who swung open the doors in advance and followed close on their heels. O'Keefe's office suite was practically imperial in its expense and splendor. High officials stood in small, nervous groups, murmuring. After a short delay O'Keefe appeared—a tall, balding, gray-haired man with stooped shoulders. He shook hands and ushered Gehman and Widnall into the privacy of his inner office. Ten minutes later they emerged. There was a short ceremony for NASA cameras, during which O'Keefe thanked Gehman for his important contribution, and then it was time to leave. As we drove away, I asked Gehman how it had been in there with O'Keefe.

He said "Stiff. Very stiff."

We talked about the future. The report had made a series of recommendations for getting the shuttle back into flight, and beyond that for beginning NASA's long and necessary process of reform. I knew that Gehman, along with much of the board, had volunteered to Congress to return in a year, to peer in deeply again, and to try to judge if progress had been made. I asked him how genuine he thought such progress could be, and he managed somehow to express hope, though skeptically.

* * *

By January 23, the *Columbia*'s eighth day in orbit, the crew had solved a couple of minor system problems, and after a half day off, during which no doubt some of the astronauts took the opportunity for some global sightseeing, they were proceeding on schedule with their laboratory duties, and were in good spirits and health. They had been told nothing of the foam strike. Down in Houston, the flight controllers at Mission Control were aware of it, and they knew that the previous day Linda Ham had canceled the request for Air Force photographs. Confident that the issue would be satisfactorily resolved by the shuttle managers, they decided nonetheless to inform the flight crew by e-mail—if only because certain reporters at the Florida launch site had heard of it, and might ask questions at an upcoming press conference, a Public Affairs Office, or PAO, event. The e-mail was written by one of the lead flight controllers, in the standard, overly upbeat style. It was addressed to the pilots, Rick Husband and William McCool.

Under the subject line "INFO: Possible PAO Event Question," it read,

> Rick and Willie,
>
> You guys are doing a fantastic job staying on the timeline and accomplishing great science.
>
> Keep up the good work and let us know if there is anything that we can do better from an MCC/POCC standpoint.
>
> There is one item that I would like to make you aware of for the upcoming PAO event. . . . This item is not even worth mentioning other than wanting to make sure that you are not surprised by it in a question from a reporter.

The e-mail then briefly explained what the launch pictures had shown—a hit from the bipod-ramp foam. A video clip was attached. The e-mail concluded,

Experts have reviewed the high speed photography and there is no concern for RCC or tile damage. We have seen this same phenomenon on several other flights and there is absolutely no concern for entry. That is all for now. It's a pleasure working with you every day.

The e-mail's content honestly reflected what was believed on the ground, though in a repackaged and highly simplified form. There was no mention of the inadequate quality of the pictures, of the large size of the foam, of the ongoing analysis, or of Linda Ham's decision against Air Force imagery. This was typical for Mission Control communications, a small example of a longstanding pattern of something like information-hoarding that was instinctive and a matter as much of style as of intent: the astronauts had been told of the strike, but almost as if they were children who didn't need to be involved in the grown-up conversation. Two days later, when Rick Husband answered the e-mail, he wrote, "Thanks a million!" and "Thanks for the great work!" and after making a little joke, that "Main Wing" could sound like a Chinese name, he signed off with an e-mail smile —:). He made no mention of the foam strike at all. And with that, as we now know, the crew's last chance for survival faded away.

Linda Ham was wrong. Had the hole in the leading edge been seen, actions could have been taken to try to save the astronauts' lives. The first would have been simply to buy some time. Assuming a starting point on the fifth day of the flight, NASA engineers subsequently calculated that by requiring the crew to rest and sleep, the mission could have been extended to a full month, to February 15. During that time the *Atlantis*, which was already being prepared for a scheduled March 1 launch, could have been processed more quickly by ground crews working around the clock, and made ready to go by February 10. If all had proceeded perfectly, there would have been a five-day window in which to blast off, join up with the *Columbia*, and transfer the stranded astronauts one by one to safety, by means of tethered spacewalks. Such a rescue would not have been easy, and it would have involved the possibility of another fatal foam strike and the loss of two shuttles instead of one; but in the risk-versus-risk world of space flight, veterans like Mike Bloomfield would immediately have volunteered, and NASA would have bet the farm.

The fallback would have been a desperate measure—a jury-rigged repair performed by the *Columbia* astronauts themselves. It would have required two spacewalkers to fill the hole with a combination of heavy tools and metal scraps scavenged from the crew compartment, and to supplement that mass with an ice bag shaped to the wing's leading edge. In theory, if much of the payload had been jettisoned, and luck was with the crew, such a repair might perhaps have endured a modified re-entry and allowed the astronauts to bail out at the standard 30,000 feet. The engineers who came up with this plan realized that in reality it would have been extremely dangerous, and might well have led to a high-speed burn-through and the loss of the crew. But anything would have been better than attempting a normal re-entry as it was actually flown.

The blessing, if one can be found, is that the astronauts remained unaware until nearly the end. A home video shot on board and found in the wreckage documented the relaxed mood in the cockpit as the shuttle descended through the entry interface at 400,000 feet, at 7:44:09 Houston time, northwest of Hawaii. The astronauts were drinking water in anticipation of gravity's redistributive effect on their bodies. The *Columbia* was flying at the standard 40-degree nose-up angle, with its wings level, and still doing nearly 17,000 mph; outside, though the air was ultrathin and dynamic pressures were very low, the aerodynamic surfaces were beginning to move in conjunction with the array of control jets, which were doing the main work of maintaining the shuttle's attitude, and would throughout the re-entry. The astronauts commented like sightseers as sheets of fiery plasma began to pass by the windows.

The pilot, McCool, said, "Do you see it over my shoulder now, Laurel?"

Sitting behind him, the mission specialist Laurel Clark said, "I was filming. It doesn't show up nearly as much as the back."

McCool said to the Israeli payload specialist, Ilan Ramon, "It's going pretty good now. Ilan, it's really neat—it's a bright orange-yellow out over the nose, all around the nose."

The commander, Husband, said, "Wait until you start seeing the swirl patterns out your left or right windows."

McCool said, "Wow."

Husband said, "Looks like a blast furnace."

A few seconds later they began to feel gravity. Husband said, "Let's see here . . . look at that."

McCool answered, "Yup, we're getting some Cs." As if it were unusual, he said, "I let go of the card, and it falls." Their instruments showed that they were experiencing one hundredth of a G. McCool looked out the window again. He said, "This is amazing. It's really getting, uh, fairly bright out there."

Husband said, "Yup. Yeah, you definitely don't want to be outside now."

The flight engineer, Kalpana Chawla, answered sardonically, "What—like we did before?" The crew laughed.

Outside, the situation was worse than they imagined. Normally, as a shuttle streaks through the upper atmosphere it heats the air immediately around it to temperatures as high as 10,000°, but largely because of the boundary layer—a sort of air cushion created by the leading edges—the actual surface temperatures are significantly lower, generally around 3,000°, which the vehicle is designed to withstand, if barely. The hole in the *Columbia*'s leading edge, however, had locally undermined the boundary layer, and was now letting in a plume of superheated air that was cutting through insulation and working its way toward the inner recesses of the left wing. It is estimated that the plume may have been as hot as 8,000° near the RCC breach. The aluminum support structures inside the wing had a melting point of 1,200°, and they began to burn and give way.

The details of the left wing's failure are complex and technical, but the essentials are not difficult to understand. The wing was attacked by a snaking plume of hot gas, and eaten up from the inside. The consumption began when the shuttle was over the Pacific, and it grew worse over the United States. It included wire bundles leading from the sensors, which caused the data going into the MADS recorder and the telemetry going to Houston to fail in ways that only later made sense. At some point the plume blew right through the top of the left wing, and began to throw molten metal from the insides all over the aft rocket pods. At some point it burned its way into the left main gear well, but it did not explode the tires.

As drag increased on the left wing, the autopilot and combined flight-control systems at first easily compensated for the resulting tendency to roll and yaw to the left. By external appearance, therefore, the shuttle was doing its normal thing, banking first to the right and then to the left for the scheduled energy-management turns, and tracking perfectly down the descent profile for Florida. The speeds were good, the altitudes were good, and all systems were functioning correctly. From within the cockpit the ride appeared to be right.

By the time it got to Texas the *Columbia* had already proved itself a heroic flying machine, having endured for so long at hypersonic speeds with little left of the midsection inside its left wing, and the plume of hot gas still in there, alive, and eating it away. By now, however, the flight-control systems were nearing their limits. The breakup was associated with that. At 7:59:15 Mission Control noticed the sudden loss of tire pressure on the left gear as the damage rapidly progressed. This was followed by Houston's call "And *Columbia*, Houston, we see your tire-pressure messages, and we did not copy your last call," and at 7:59:32 by *Columbia*'s final transmission, "Roger, ah, buh . . ."

The *Columbia* was traveling at 12,738 mph, at 200,000 feet, and the dynamic pressures were building, with the wings "feeling" the air at about 170 mph. Now, suddenly, the bottom surface of the left wing began to cave upward into the interior void of melted and burned-through bracing and structure. As the curvature of the wing changed, the lift increased, causing the *Columbia* to want to roll violently to the right; at the same time, because of an increase in asymmetrical drag, it yawed violently to the left. The control systems went to their limits to maintain order, and all four right yaw jets on the tail fired simultaneously, but to no avail. At 8:00:19 the *Columbia* rolled over the top and went out of control.

The gyrations it followed were complex combinations of roll, yaw, and pitch, and looked something like an oscillating flat spin. They seem to have resulted in the vehicle's flying backwards. At one point the autopilot appears to have been switched off and then switched on again, as if Husband, an experienced test pilot, was trying to sort things out. The breakup lasted more than a minute. Not surprisingly, the left wing separated first. Afterward the tail, the right wing, and the main body came apart in what investigators later called a controlled sequence "right down the track." As had happened with the *Challenger* in 1986, the crew cabin broke off intact. It assumed a stable flying position, apparently nose high, and later disintegrated like a falling star across the East Texas sky.

2005

Editor: ALAN LIGHTMAN

ROBIN MARANTZ HENIG

The Genome in Black and White (and Gray)

FROM *THE NEW YORK TIMES MAGAZINE*

Are there differences in race, beyond superficial features, that are rooted in our genes? As Robin Marantz Henig writes, it is a question that has major researchers divided, as new medications, designed especially to treat particular populations, return the issue, uncomfortably, to the forefront of scientific debate.

IMAGINE THAT YOU HAVE HEART FAILURE. WHAT CAN medicine do for you? It depends: are you white or black? If you're white, your doctor may prescribe one of the drugs that seem to ease the symptoms, maybe a beta-blocker or an ACE inhibitor. And if you're black, your doctor may still prescribe those drugs, but they might not really help.

That's about to change. In the not-too-distant future, if you're black and have heart failure, drug-company researchers predict you'll be able to go to the doctor and walk out with a prescription tailor-made for you. Well, not tailor-made, exactly, but something that seems to work in people a lot like you. Well, not a lot like you, exactly, except that they're black too. In this not-too-distant future, if you're black, your doctor will be able to prescribe BiDil, the first drug in America that's being niche-marketed to people of a particular race—our first ethnic medicine.

BiDil, expected to be approved in early 2005 by the Food and Drug Administration, is on the leading edge of the emerging field of race-based pharmacogenomics. It signals a shift in perception, a new approach to medicine that has at its core an idea at once familiar and incendiary: the assumption that there are biological differences among the races.

BiDil is also a feat of creative repackaging. In 1999 the FDA rejected it for use in the general population because it was found to be ineffective in the treatment of heart failure, a common complication of cardiovascular disease that affects some five million Americans and leads to three hundred thousand deaths a year. But in 2001 the manufacturer, NitroMed, asked permission to test BiDil exclusively in blacks, whose heart failure tends to be more severe and harder to treat. The company reasoned that the drug's effect on nitric-oxide deficiency, more common in black heart-failure patients than in nonblacks, might make it especially suited to them. With the collaboration of the Association of Black Cardiologists, NitroMed embarked on a large clinical trial involving more than four hundred black women and six hundred black men, all of whom had heart failure.

Last summer, investigators called an early end to the study because they thought BiDil was so effective that it would be unethical to continue to deny it to people in the control group. Thus, a drug that had been deemed ineffective in the population at large seemed to work so well in one racial subgroup that the scientists thought everyone in that subgroup should get it.

Pharmacogenomics has for years been touted as the ultimate benefit of the genomics revolution. But to many, this revolution has a troubling side. For race-based niche marketing to work, drug developers first will have to explore the ways that blacks, whites, Asians, and Native Americans are biologically different. And the more they explore and describe such differences, critics say, the more they play into the hands of racists. Even the broad-minded might inadvertently use such information to stigmatize, isolate, or categorize the races. Could it be that this terrain is too dangerous to let anyone, no matter how well meaning, try to navigate it?

In the fall of 2004 a major scientific journal, *Nature Genetics*, published a special issue on the genetics of race. This came on the heels of several conferences on the subject, as well as editorials in the science press, including one in the *Journal of the American Medical Association* that appeared just weeks before the *Nature Genetics* special issue. All of these forums pose some thorny questions: Can genes tell us anything meaningful about race, beyond the obvious connection to things like skin color? Do the races differ biologically in terms of drug response or disease susceptibility? Can genes say anything about how "race"—which is itself all but impossible to define—is related to complex traits like behavior and intelligence?

Looking for biological determinants of race is nothing new. It has a potent history, with poisonous associations dating back to the early days of eugenics. But contemporary science has given these efforts a new respectability. In the wake of the completion of the Human Genome Project, geneticists are trying to arrange pieces of the genome like a Rubik's Cube, searching for patterns of variation that align into some useful matrix. Their goal is to generate information that will help prevent and treat common diseases. But in the process, they're generating information that might also lead to declarations about the biological meaning of race.

The new interest in racial genetics comes at a time when the softer sciences, like anthropology and sociology, have declared that race is a cultural construct, without any biological significance. The social designations go back at least to the nineteenth century, when humans were generally divided into five races that were loosely tied to skin color; this has lingered as the basic grammar of race even into the twenty-first century. But in a 1998 position paper, the American Anthropological Association called race a social invention, with a variety of pernicious consequences ranging from day-to-day bigotry to the Holocaust. Racial beliefs are myths, the anthropologists wrote, and the myths fuse "behavior and physical features together in the public mind, impeding our comprehension of both biological variations and cultural behavior, implying that both are genetically determined."

Genetiscists, too, have gone on record as saying that race has no biological significance. "The concept of race has no genetic or scientific basis," said J. Craig Venter in 2000, standing beside President Bill Clinton to announce the completion of the first draft of the human genome sequence. Venter was at the time the president of Celera, the private company that competed with the National Human Genome Research Institute, a publicly financed international team, to sequence the genome. (It was declared a tie.)

Venter's scientific rival, Francis S. Collins, the head of the genome institute, stood at the podium that day on Clinton's other side—two male, middle-aged white scientists saying we're all brothers and sisters under the skin. Collins made much of the fact that humans share 99.9 percent of their genome with one another—and that the remaining 0.1 percent probably codes for variations, like skin color, that are for the most part biologically insignificant. In fact, there is more variation within races than between them. A few months later he made the point more informally, playing his electric guitar and regaling his coworkers with a musical ditty he had written to the tune of Woody Guthrie's "This Land Is Your Land":

> We only do this once, it's our inheritance,
> Joined by this common thread—black, yellow, white or
> red,
> It is our family bond, and now its day has dawned.
> This draft was made for you and me.

Today, the two men have parted company on this narrow strip of common ground. Venter says he still believes the genome is color-blind. "I don't see that there's any fundamental need to classify people by race," he says. "What's the goal of that, other than discrimination?"

But Collins sees the matter differently now. Maybe in that 0.1 percent of the genome there are some variations with relevance to medicine, he says. And maybe identifying them could help reduce health disparities among the races. He is using his bully pulpit at the genome institute to urge scientists to study whether these variations can, or should, be categorized according to racial groupings.

"It's always better to face up to a controversial scientific issue, to tackle the issue head-on and not run away from it," Collins says. "And if we don't do it, someone else will—and probably not as well."

ONE REASON TO FOCUS ON the genetics of race is to try to make a dent in health disparities: the frustrating gap in the health status of different racial groups that stubbornly refuses to close or even to be adequately explained. In terms of national measures of physical well-being—life expectancy, infant mortality, some chronic diseases—blacks tend to do worse than whites. Many factors account for this health gap, including the fact that minorities suffer disproportionately the effects of low income, lack of health insurance, poor diet, exposure to environmental toxins, discrimination, and stress. But some geneticists think that at least some part of health disparities can be explained by genes. Social scientists think genetic explanations might obscure the all-too-real social and economic causes.

Take hypertension, which affects black Americans at a higher rate than white Americans. Geneticists try to explain this difference in terms of genes: genes for salt retention, genes for low levels of renin in the kidneys. But a classic study found that one thing that correlated most strongly with level of blood pressure was, surprisingly, skin color. Among black subjects of low socioeconomic status, the darker the skin, the higher the blood pressure. Social scientists' explanation is that people with darker skin are subject to greater discrimination, and therefore to greater stress.

"If you follow me around Nordstrom's, and put me in jail at nine times the rate of whites, and refuse to give me a bank loan, I might get hypertensive," says Troy Duster, a professor of sociology at New York University and at the University of California, Berkeley. "What's generating my increased blood pressure are the social forces at play, not my DNA."

But pharmacogenomics researchers presume that health disparities can be addressed, at least in part, by exploiting tiny group differences in DNA. If the BiDil experience pans out, other companies are likely to try their own versions of race-based drug development. Some candidates already exist. People known as slow acetylators, for instance, take a longer time than fast acetylators to clear certain drugs from the liver. This means they're more likely to build up toxic levels of some common drugs. The proportion of slow acetylators in different racial groups ranges from a low of 14 percent among East Asians to a high of 54 percent among whites. Some whites, therefore, might benefit from a different version of medications that are cleared through the liver.

The ultimate goal of pharmacogenomics would be for everyone's genome to be analyzed individually, so that doctors could gauge how much of a medication, and which type, is most likely to work for a specific patient. Even the BiDil investigators are moving in that direction. Michael D. Loberg, the president of NitroMed, says that the company asked each participant in the BiDil trial for permission to take a DNA sample and that he hopes to get a total of at least four hundred such samples. These will be sequenced, he says, "to see if there's some genetic marker that predicts which of the trial patients responded to BiDil favorably and which didn't."

But at this point, geneticists cannot sequence individual genomes in a cost-effective way. Until they can, they may view race as a handy shortcut, a way to make some useful generalizations about how an individual patient will fare with a particular drug. But while using race this way might increase the odds of finding the right medication, it is an imprecise method, a kind of roulette in which the physician is making educated guesses based on probabilities.

The temptation of race-based medication is clear: it's convenient for the investigator, and it suits the way drug companies' products are sold. "The mantra of pharmacogenomics is that drugs will be fine-tuned for the individual," Duster says. "But individuals are not a market. Groups are a market." And one typical way to identify markets, in a country where skin color seems to count for so much, is race.

In terms of our genes, we humans are all the same—except for the ways in which we're different. The human genome comprises three billion nucleotides, strung together in a specific order along the chromosomes. About 99.9 percent are identical from one person to another, no matter what the person's race, ethnicity, continent of origin, or bank account.

Among our three billion nucleotides, an estimated ten million are locations of common variations. Where most people will have a nucleotide represented by the letter A, for instance, a big group of people might have a T instead. Elucidating where those spots are, and whether replacing a T with an A has any clinical significance, are what occupies today's geneticists.

The most common type of variants are called single nucleotide polymorphisms, or SNPs (pronounced "snips"). Usually they occur in regions where the nucleotides seem to be doing nothing. This means the SNPs don't have any function, either, or at least none that has been discovered yet; they're just there.

Still, SNPs tend to occur in different patterns in different populations. Say there's a SNP on Chromosome 12 in which a person might have either an A or a T. At this hypothetical SNP, 20 percent of Africans might have an A, and 80 percent a T. At the same spot, the frequency might be flipped in Europeans: 80 percent might have an A, while only 20 percent have a T.

So while SNP patterns don't reveal anything about the function of the genes, they can say something about an individual's continent of ancestry—and, by extension, something about migration pathways through human history. SNPs tend to be inherited in clusters, called haplotype blocks. Like SNPs, varieties of haplotype blocks occur at different frequencies in different regions of the world—and that's how population geneticists have managed to reconstruct the story of human migration.

The biggest variety of haplotype blocks occurs in Africa, because modern humans arose there more than 150,000 years ago, and variations have had the longest chance to accrue simply because of random mutations. About 55,000 years ago, a small group of modern humans, who carried in their genomes a subset of the original haplotype varieties, traveled to Australia; later, in sequence and timing that are still a source of controversy among paleoanthropologists, other small groups migrated to parts of Europe, Asia, and the Middle East.

As time went on, there were some evolutionary changes in response to the new environments. In Northern Europe, for instance, people carrying mutations for lighter skin color thrived, probably because the scarcity of sunlight made dark-skinned people especially susceptible to Vitamin D deficiency and rickets. But most of the variations occurred in the nonfunctional regions of the genome, with no effect on an individual's appearance or health. All that the variations did was allow geneticists, some two thousand generations later, to assign a continent of origin to the descendants of these original travelers based on the descendants' DNA.

To the dismay of Troy Duster, several private companies are now taking these findings about SNPs to a new level: scanning the genome for variations that can say something about an individual's race. Last year, a company called DNAPrint Genomics made headlines by telling law-enforcement officials in Louisiana that they'd been looking for a serial killer of the wrong race. Eyewitnesses had offered different accounts of the race of the suspect—some thought he was black, others white—and authorities had focused their search on white males between the ages of twenty-five and thirty-five based in part on an FBI psychological profile. But based on crime-scene specimens, DNAPrint said the murderer was probably black—in fact, the company said it could detect 85 percent sub-Saharan African ancestry and 15 percent Native American—and even gave an assessment of his skin tone. When a black male was apprehended, his DNA was found to match that at one of the crime scenes. He was convicted of second-degree murder in August.

For some, this would be a story of science advancing police work. But for people like Duster, the forensic use of genetic markers raises troubling questions. Can a DNA screen of a person's blood or hair really tell you anything more than where his ancestors probably came from? Would it lead to witch hunts based on some uncertain appraisal of skin color? Would it be used, wrongly, to give a patina of scientific authority to group prejudices?

Worried, Duster approached his friend and colleague, Francis Collins, to suggest that Collins might want to use his position at the genome institute to mount an investigation into the genetics of race—before the drug manufacturers and genomics companies set the tone for the public debate.

Collins says he was already thinking the same thing. The two men approach the venture from different perspectives, less because Collins is white and Duster is black than because one is a geneticist and the other a sociologist. As Duster sees it, race is a relationship, largely dependent on social context. Take a Tutsi and a Hutu and set them down in Los Angeles, he says, and they're both the same race, both black. But put them back in Rwanda, and they're two different races, different enough to slaughter each other.

There may be biological dimensions to race, Duster says, but that doesn't take away from his belief that race should be understood as a social construction. "The myth is that somehow the biology is real and the social forces are unreal," he says. "In fact, the social forces can feed the biological forces."

Collins, for his part, recognizes that social forces explain many of the observed differences among the races—but says he thinks something else might be involved as well. "We need to try to understand what there is about genetic variation that is associated with disease risk," he says, "and how that correlates, in some very imperfect way, with self-identified race, and how we can use that correlation to reduce the risk of people getting sick."

Taking up Duster's challenge, Collins knew, meant walking into a quagmire. A decade earlier, another top government scientist lost his job by discussing the genetics of urban violence (though his case was egregious: he compared young black men with male monkeys). But Collins said he believed the idea, risky as it was, was worth pursuing because it offered the best chance of converting new genomic information into something of medical significance.

The genome institute, part of the National Institutes of Health in Bethesda, Maryland, currently spends some $31 million for studies into human genetic variation. The institute is also a major contributor to the Hap Map project, a $110 million international collaboration that by late 2005 will have put together a coherent almanac of human variation using haplotype blocks. The Hap Map is meant to help scientists in their search for common disease-causing genes, but in the process it will also generate new information about the specific ways in which populations from the places being studied—China, Japan, Nigeria, and, in the United States, Utah—differ from one another genetically.

Collins is clean-cut and homespun, emphatically tall, with a fringe of sandy hair that makes him look younger than his fifty-four years. He exudes an aw-shucks earnestness when he talks about his favorite topics, which include his rebirth as a Christian during his medical training. Each time he makes a scientific discovery, he says, he gets a glimmer of insight into the workings of the mind of God.

But for all his personal sincerity, Collins is finding that some of his allies are wary of this newest undertaking. They know that even a man with the best intentions can muck it up when it comes to race.

WHILE WRITING THIS ARTICLE, I took a trip to the Holocaust Memorial Museum in Washington. I wanted to see the museum's exhibit about eugenics, the scientific movement of the early twentieth century that looked for evidence of biological racial differences to promote creation of a "fitter" species. In a very short time, eugenic ideas were subverted to support Nazi policies of ethnic cleansing and racial extermination. Since the spring of 2004, when Collins called to suggest that I might be interested in his institute's plan to investigate the genetics of race, I had talked to more than two dozen scientists about the issue. Uncomfortable questions about where such inquiries could lead underscored a number of those conversations— the sort of questions that, as a white person in America today, I don't usually have to confront. I went to the Holocaust museum looking for resonances.

How disturbing it was to see that the activities of the early eugenicists resembled, from a certain perspective, the activities of specimen collectors of the early days of zoology—as well as those of genomics researchers today, going around collecting specimens of human variation. The eugenicists engaged in some straightforward scientific studies that can seem almost harmless, even ordinary. And that's what makes it so troubling to look back.

With rulers, calipers, charts of eye shapes, and elaborate reconstructions of family trees, eugenicists of the 1920s and 1930s took great care to describe physical characteristics of different racial groups. They photographed subjects, measured their noses and mouths, made plaster casts of their faces and documented variations in facial features and head proportions. It is possible that the difference between then and now is that the tools have changed—that instead of using calipers and scales, scientists now use DNA-sequencing machines?

Connecting contemporary genomic studies to the Holocaust is too glib, of course, and it obscures one crucial point: that the anthropometrics of the early eugenics movement turned ugly once fanatics perverted the information. But the exhibit is a sobering reminder of how easy it would be to travel down that path. "I think our best protection against that—because this work is going to be done by somebody—is to have it done by the best and brightest and hopefully most well attuned to the risk of abuse," Collins says. "That's why I think this has to be a mainstream activity of genomics, and not something we avoid and then watch burst out somewhere from some sort of goofy fringe."

Collins doesn't quote the Bible often—he tends to neither hide nor flaunt his religious faith—but he quotes it now. He chooses a line from the New Testament's Book of John, in which Jesus says to his disciples, "And you shall know the truth, and the truth shall set you free."

Reducing health disparities and catching criminals are serious reasons for pursuing the genetics of race, but there's also a small but growing trend toward something its practitioners call "recreational genomics." To satisfy curiosity about their heritage, more and more people are experiencing race-based genomics as a mail-test, for which they pay up to four hundred dollars, that will tell them how much of their genome is black, white, American Indian, or Asian. These companies go beyond old-fashioned genealogical services, the kind that involve scouring archives and huddling over microfiche machines, and trace genetic linkages back many generations to a particular geographic location. Critics say that what these companies are doing sanctifies the genetic distinctions among racial groups, as if the question of whether race has a biological basis has been settled.

The services, with names like GeoGene, AncestryByDNA, and Roots for Real, begin by asking clients to mail in a cheek swab to get some stray skin cells from which DNA can be extracted. Though the process may feel like a parlor game, the results can be deeply affecting. One of those who traced his genetic lineage through a company called African Ancestry is Andrew Young, former United States ambassador to the United Nations and now chairman of an organization called Good Works International.

Young was looking for information about his maternal lineage only; he assumed, he told me, that his paternal lineage would be "contaminated" with white DNA, a bitter memento of slave rape that he didn't feel ready to confront. (According to Rick Kittles, a co-founder of African Ancestry and a geneticist at Ohio State University, about one-third of blacks who do a paternal lineage analysis, himself included, find that there is European DNA somewhere in their past.)

When a black client discovers that there's white in his genome, the results can be shattering. In 2003 the ABC News program *Nightline* profiled a fifty-year-old California man who had assumed his whole life that he was black. But a recreational genomics analysis by DNAPrint Genomics indicated that his genome was 57 percent of what the company called Indo-European, 39 percent Native American, 4 percent East Asian—and zero percent African. So what is this man: the race he has always thought himself to be, or the race his genome says he is?

Young's reaction to his African Ancestry report is an indication of how much weight we ascribe to genes, how much we believe our DNA reflects not only our racial identity but our individual identity too. When Young heard that the company had traced his DNA back to what is now Sierra Leone, he was disappointed because he considered Sierra Leone to have a "snobbish" middle class. But the report got much more specific: the people whose SNP pattern most resembled Young's, it said, were from the Mende tribe. Whether a few SNP matches can allow such precision is a matter of debate, but it fit happily into Young's self-image. Young, who got his start in the civil rights movement, was raised on tales about the *Amistad* slave-ship rebellion of 1839, for which the Mende were responsible. "I always had a spiritual connection to these stories," he says. "Now I have a genetic connection."

So is there such a thing as race? It depends on whether you're defining it in terms of culture or biology. Culturally, there is no denying it. In the United States, with its race-stained legacy dating back to slavery, the government has tried for centuries to define a person's race. The Census Bureau has been asking about race on its forms since the very first census in 1790, most recently giving individuals the opportunity to check off more than one race if they so desire.

But the more vexing question is whether there's such a thing as race in terms of biology. Genetic variations do seem to cluster differently for people with different continents of origin, but is this race? And what does it mean if it is—or if it isn't? Do we need to agree on whether race is a biological entity, since we can so readily agree that it's a social one?

"Race is a reality in this country, no matter what the genome tells us," says Vanessa Northington Gamble, director of the National Center for Bioethics in Research and Health Care at Tuskegee University. "If I can't get a cab in New York, it's because my skin is black. And I can't hold up my DNA and say: 'Wait a minute! I'm just the same as you!' "

Some critics worry that the more we find out about genetic differences among people of different racial groups, the more such information will be misinterpreted or abused. Already there are fears that the biological measures of racial differences might lead to pronouncements about inherent differences in such complex traits as intelligence, athletic ability, aggressiveness, or susceptibility to addiction. Once such measures are given the imprimatur of science, especially genomic science, loathsome racist stereotypes can take on the sheen of received wisdom.

Looking for racial genetic markers does indeed risk creating categories that can get us in trouble. It bears remembering, however, that the "slippery slope" argument is itself a danger. Rather than abort a whole field of research because it might bolster cranks and demagogues, maybe one solution to our national angst over race is to let scientists hunt down the facts—facts that will no doubt affirm, one way or another, that the human genome is indeed our common thread.

DAVID QUAMMEN

Darwin or Not

FROM *NATIONAL GEOGRAPHIC*

> It may seem startling that a major magazine today would need to
> defend the validity of evolutionary theory. But given that nearly half
> of Americans disavow evolution, it's no wonder that the editors of
> National Geographic *commissioned nature writer David Quam-*
> men to utter a hearty "No" to the question "Was Darwin wrong?"

EVOLUTION BY NATURAL SELECTION, THE CENTRAL
concept of the life's work of Charles Darwin, is a theory. It's a
theory about the origin of adaptation, complexity, and diversity among Earth's living creatures. If you are skeptical by nature,
unfamiliar with the terminology of science, and unaware of the
overwhelming evidence, you might even be tempted to say that it's
"just" a theory. In the same sense, relativity as described by Albert
Einstein is "just" a theory. The notion that Earth orbits around the
Sun rather than vice versa, offered by Copernicus in 1543, is a theory.
Continental drift is a theory. The existence, structure, and dynamics
of atoms? Atomic theory. Even electricity is a theoretical construct,

involving electrons, which are tiny units of charged mass that no one has ever seen. Each of these theories is an explanation that has been confirmed to such a degree, by observation and experiment, that knowledgeable experts accept it as fact. That's what scientists mean when they talk about a theory: not a dreamy and unreliable speculation, but an explanatory statement that fits the evidence. They embrace such an explanation confidently but provisionally—taking it as their best available view of reality, at least until some severely conflicting data or some better explanation might come along.

The rest of us generally agree. We plug our televisions into little wall sockets, measure a year by the length of Earth's orbit, and in many other ways live our lives based on the trusted reality of those theories.

Evolutionary theory, though, is a bit different. It's such a dangerously wonderful and far-reaching view of life that some people find it unacceptable, despite the vast body of supporting evidence. As applied to our own species, *Homo sapiens*, it can seem more threatening still. Many fundamentalist Christians and ultra-orthodox Jews take alarm at the thought that human descent from earlier primates contradicts a strict reading of the Book of Genesis. Their discomfort is paralleled by Islamic creationists such as Harun Yahya, author of a recent volume titled *The Evolutionary Deceit*, who points to the six-day creation story in the Koran as literal truth and calls the theory of evolution "nothing but a deception imposed on us by the dominators of the world system." The late Srila Prabhupada, of the Hare Krishna movement, explained that God created "the 8,400,000 species of life from the very beginning," in order to establish tiers of reincarnation for rising souls. Although souls ascend, the species themselves don't change, he insisted, dismissing "Darwin's nonsensical theory."

Other people too, not just scriptural literalists, remain unpersuaded about evolution. According to a Gallup poll drawn from more than a thousand telephone interviews conducted in February 2001, no less than 45 percent of responding U.S. adults agreed that "God created human beings pretty much in their present form at one time within the last ten thousand years or so." Evolution, by their lights, played no role in shaping us.

Only 37 percent of the polled Americans were satisfied with allowing room for both God and Darwin—that is, divine initiative to get things started, evolution as the creative means. (This view, according to more than one papal pronouncement, is compatible with Roman Catholic dogma.) Still fewer Americans, only 12 percent, believed that humans evolved from other life-forms without any involvement of a god.

The most startling thing about these poll numbers is not that so many Americans reject evolution, but that the statistical breakdown hasn't changed much in two decades. Gallup interviewers posed exactly the same choices in 1982, 1993, 1997, and 1999. The creationist conviction—that God alone, and not evolution, produced humans— has never drawn less than 44 percent. In other words, nearly half the American populace prefers to believe that Charles Darwin was wrong where it mattered most.

Why are there so many antievolutionists? Scriptural literalism can only be part of the answer. The American public certainly includes a large segment of scriptural literalists—but not *that* large, not 44 percent. Creationist proselytizers and political activists, working hard to interfere with the teaching of evolutionary biology in public schools, are another part. Honest confusion and ignorance, among millions of adult Americans, must be still another. Many people have never taken a biology course that dealt with evolution nor read a book in which the theory was lucidly explained. Sure, we've all heard of Charles Darwin, and of a vague, somber notion about struggle and survival that sometimes goes by the catchall label "Darwinism." But the main sources of information from which most Americans have drawn their awareness of this subject, it seems, are haphazard ones at best: cultural osmosis, newspaper and magazine references, half-baked nature documentaries on the tube, and hearsay.

Evolution is both a beautiful concept and an important one, more crucial nowadays to human welfare, to medical science, and to our understanding of the world than ever before. It's also deeply persuasive—a theory you can take to the bank. The essential points are slightly more complicated than most people assume, but not so complicated that they can't be comprehended by any attentive person.

Furthermore, the supporting evidence is abundant, various, ever increasing, solidly interconnected, and easily available in museums, popular books, textbooks, and a mountainous accumulation of peer-reviewed scientific studies. No one needs to, and no one should, accept evolution merely as a matter of faith.

TWO BIG IDEAS, NOT JUST one, are at issue: the evolution of all species, as a historical phenomenon, and natural selection, as the main mechanism causing that phenomenon. The first is a question of what happened. The second is a question of how. The idea that all species are descended from common ancestors had been suggested by other thinkers, including Jean-Baptiste Lamarck, long before Darwin published *The Origin of Species* in 1859. What made Darwin's book so remarkable when it appeared, and so influential in the long run, was that it offered a rational explanation of how evolution must occur. The same insight came independently to Alfred Russel Wallace, a young naturalist doing fieldwork in the Malay Archipelago during the late 1850s. In historical annals, if not in the popular awareness, Wallace and Darwin share the kudos for having discovered natural selection.

The gist of the concept is that small, random, heritable differences among individuals result in different chances of survival and reproduction—success for some, death without offspring for others—and that this natural culling leads to significant changes in shape, size, strength, armament, color, biochemistry, and behavior among the descendants. Excess population growth drives the competitive struggle. Because less successful competitors produce fewer surviving offspring, the useless or negative variations tend to disappear, whereas the useful variations tend to be perpetuated and gradually magnified throughout a population.

So much for one part of the evolutionary process, known as anagenesis, during which a single species is transformed. But there's also a second part, known as speciation. Genetic changes sometimes accumulate within an isolated segment of a species, but not throughout the whole, as that isolated population adapts to its local conditions. Gradually it goes its own way, seizing a new ecological niche. At a certain point it becomes irreversibly distinct—that is, so different that its members can't interbreed with the rest. Two species now exist where formerly there was one. Darwin called that splitting-and-specializing phenomenon the "principle of divergence." It was an important part of his theory, explaining the overall diversity of life as well as the adaptation of individual species.

This thrilling and radical assemblage of concepts came from an unlikely source. Charles Darwin was shy and meticulous, a wealthy landowner with close friends among the Anglican clergy. He had a gentle, unassuming manner, a strong need for privacy, and an extraordinary commitment to intellectual honestly. As an undergraduate at Cambridge, he had studied halfheartedly toward becoming a clergyman himself, before he discovered his real vocation as a scientist. Later, having established a good but conventional reputation in natural history, he spent twenty-two years secretly gathering evidence and pondering arguments—both for and against his theory—because he didn't want to flame out in a burst of unpersuasive notoriety. He may have delayed, too, because of his anxiety about announcing a theory that seemed to challenge conventional religious beliefs—in particular, the Christian beliefs of his wife, Emma. Darwin himself quietly renounced Christianity during his middle age, and later described himself as an agnostic. He continued to believe in a distant, impersonal deity of some sort, a greater entity that had set the universe and its laws into motion, but not in a personal God who had chosen humanity as a specially favored species. Darwin avoided flaunting his lack of religious faith, at least partly in deference to Emma. And she prayed for his soul.

In 1859 he finally delivered his revolutionary book. Although it was hefty and substantive at 490 pages, he considered *The Origin of Species* just a quick-and-dirty "abstract" of the huge volume he had been working on until interrupted by an alarming event. (In fact, he'd wanted to title it *An Abstract of an Essay on the Origin of Species and Varieties Through Natural Selection*, but his publisher found that insufficiently catchy.) The alarming event was his receiving a letter and an enclosed manuscript from Alfred Wallace, whom he knew only as a distant pen pal. Wallace's manuscript sketched out the same great idea—evolution by natural selection—that Darwin considered his own. Wallace had scribbled this paper and (unaware of Darwin's own evolutionary thinking, which so far had been kept private) mailed it to him from the Malay Archipelago, along with a request for reaction and help. Darwin was horrified. After two decades of painstaking effort, now he'd be scooped. Or maybe not quite. He forwarded Wallace's paper toward publication, though managing also to assert his own prior claim by releasing two excerpts from his unpublished work. Then he dashed off *The Origin*, his "abstract" on the subject. Unlike Wallace, who was younger and less meticulous, Darwin recognized the importance of providing an edifice of supporting evidence and logic.

The evidence, as he presented it, mostly fell within four categories: biogeography, paleontology, embryology, and morphology. Biogeography is the study of the geographical distribution of living creatures—that is, which species inhabit which parts of the planet and why. Paleontology investigates extinct life-forms, as revealed in the fossil record. Embryology examines the revealing stages of development (echoing earlier stages of evolutionary history) that embryos pass through before birth or hatching; at a stretch, embryology also concerns the immature forms of animals that metamorphose, such as the larvae of insects. Morphology is the science of anatomical shape and design. Darwin devoted sizable sections of *The Origin of Species* to these categories.

Biogeography, for instance, offered a great pageant of peculiar facts and patterns. Anyone who considers the biogeographical data, Darwin wrote, must be struck by the mysterious clustering pattern among what he called "closely allied" species—that is, similar creatures sharing roughly the same body plan. Such closely allied species tend to be found on the same continent (several species of zebras in Africa) or within the same group of oceanic islands (dozens of species of honeycreepers in Hawaii, thirteen species of Galápagos finch), despite their species-by-species preferences for different habitats, food sources, or conditions of climate. Adjacent areas of South America, Darwin noted, are occupied by two similar species of large, flightless birds (the rheas, *Rhea americana* and *Pterocnemia pennata*), not by ostriches as in Africa or emus as in Australia. South America also has agoutis and viscachas (small rodents) in terrestrial habitats, plus coypus and capybaras in the wetlands, not—as Darwin wrote—hares and rabbits in terrestrial habitats or beavers and muskrats in the wetlands. During his own youthful visit to the Galápagos, aboard the survey ship *Beagle*, Darwin himself had discovered three very similar forms of mockingbird, each on a different island.

Why should "closely allied" species inhabit neighboring patches of habitat? And why should similar habitat on different continents be occupied by species that aren't so closely allied? "We see in these facts some deep organic bond, prevailing throughout space and time," Darwin wrote. "This bond, on my theory, is simply inheritance." Similar species occur nearby in space because they have descended from common ancestors.

Paleontology reveals a similar clustering pattern in the dimension of time. The vertical column of geologic strata, laid down by sedimentary processes over the eons, lightly peppered with fossils, represents a tangible record showing which species lived when. Less ancient layers of rock lie atop more ancient ones (except where geologic forces have tipped or shuffled them), and likewise with the animal and plant fossils that the strata contain. What Darwin noticed about this record is that closely allied species tend to be found adjacent to one another in successive strata. One species endures for millions of years and then makes its last appearance in, say, the middle Eocene epoch; just above, a similar but not identical species replaces it. In North America, for example, a vaguely horselike creature known as *Hyracotherium* was succeeded by *Orohippus*, then *Epihippus*, then *Mesohippus*, which in turn were succeeded by a variety of horsey American critters. Some of them even galloped across the Bering land bridge into Asia, then onward to Europe and Africa. By five million years ago they had nearly all disappeared, leaving behind *Dinohippus*, which was succeeded by *Equus*, the modern genus of horse. Not all these fossil links had been unearthed in Darwin's day, but he captured the essence of the matter anyway. Again, were such sequences just coincidental? No, Darwin argued. Closely allied species succeed one another in time, as well as living nearby in space, because they're related through evolutionary descent.

Embryology too involved patterns that couldn't be explained by coincidence. Why does the embryo of a mammal pass through stages resembling stages of the embryo of a reptile? Why is one of the larval forms of a barnacle, before metamorphosis, so similar to the larval form of a shrimp? Why do the larvae of moths, flies, and beetles resemble one another more than any of them resemble their respective adults? Because, Darwin wrote, "the embryo is the animal in its less modified state" and that state "reveals the structure of its progenitor."

MORPHOLOGY, HIS FOURTH CATEGORY OF evidence, was the "very soul" of natural history, according to Darwin. Even today it's on display in the layout and organization of any zoo. Here are the monkeys, there are the big cats, and in that building are the alligators and crocodiles. Birds in the aviary, fish in the aquarium. Living creatures can be easily sorted into a hierarchy of categories—not just species but genera, families, orders, whole kingdoms—based on which anatomical characters they share and which they don't.

All vertebrate animals have backbones. Among vertebrates, birds have feathers, whereas reptiles have scales. Mammals have fur and mammary glands, not feathers or scales. Among mammals, some have pouches in which they nurse their tiny young. Among these species, the marsupials, some have huge rear legs and strong tails by which they go hopping across miles of arid outback; we call them kangaroos. Bring in modern microscopic and molecular evidence, and you can trace the similarities still further back. All plants and fungi, as well as animals, have nuclei within their cells. All living organisms contain DNA and RNA (except some viruses with RNA only), two related forms of information-coding molecules.

Such a pattern of tiered resemblances—groups of similar species nested within broader groupings, and all descending from a single source—isn't naturally present among other collections of items. You won't find anything equivalent if you try to categorize rocks, or musical instruments, or jewelry. Why not? Because rock types and styles of jewelry don't reflect unbroken descent from common ancestors. Biological diversity does. The number of shared characteristics between any one species and another indicates how recently those two species have diverged from a shared lineage.

That insight gave new meaning to the task of taxonomic classification, which had been founded in its modern form back in 1735 by the Swedish naturalist Carolus Linnaeus. Linnaeus showed how species could be systematically classified, according to their shared similarities, but he worked from creationist assumptions that offered no material explanation for the nested pattern he found. In the early and middle nineteenth century, morphologists such as George Cuvier and Étienne Geoffroy Saint-Hilaire in France and Richard Owen in England improved classification with their meticulous studies of internal as well as external anatomies, and tried to make sense of what the ultimate source of these patterned similarities could be. Not even Owen, a contemporary and onetime friend of Darwin's (later in life they had a bitter falling-out), took the full step to an evolutionary vision before *The Origin of Species* was published. Owen made a major contribution, though, by advancing the concept of homologues— that is, superficially different but fundamentally similar versions of a single organ or trait, shared by dissimilar species.

For instance, the five-digit skeletal structure of the vertebrae hand appears not just in humans and apes and raccoons and bears but also, variously modified, in cats and bats and porpoises and lizards and turtles. The paired bones of our lower leg, the tibia and the fibula, are also represented by homologous bones in other mammals and in reptiles, and even in the long-extinct bird-reptile *Archaeopteryx*. What's the reason behind such varied recurrence of a few basic designs? Darwin, with a nod to Owen's "most interesting work," supplied the answer: common descent, as shaped by natural selection, modifying the inherited basics for different circumstances.

Vestigial characteristics are still another form of morphological evidence, illuminating to contemplate because they show that the living world is full of small, tolerable imperfections. Why do male mammals (including human males) have nipples? Why do some snakes (notably boa constrictors) carry the rudiments of a pelvis and tiny legs buried inside their sleek profiles? Why do certain species of flightless beetle have wings, sealed beneath wing covers that never open? Darwin raised all these questions, and answered them, in *The Origin of Species*. Vestigial structures stand as remnants of the evolutionary history of lineage.

Today the same four branches of biological science from which Darwin drew—biogeography, paleontology, embryology, morphology—embrace an ever growing body of supporting data. In addition to those categories we now have others: population genetics, biochemistry, molecular biology, and, most recently, the whiz-bang field of machine-driven genetic sequencing known as genomics. These new forms of knowledge overlap one another seamlessly and intersect with the older forms, strengthening the whole edifice, contributing further to the certainty that Darwin was right.

He was right about evolution, that is. He wasn't right about *everything*. Being a restless explainer, Darwin floated a number of theoretical notions during his long working life, some of which were mistaken and illusory. He was wrong about what causes variation within a species. He was wrong about what causes variation within a species. He was wrong about a famous geologic mystery, the parallel shelves along a Scottish valley called Glen Roy. Most notably, his theory of inheritance—which he labeled pangenesis—turned out to be dead wrong. Fortunately for Darwin, the correctness of his most famous good idea stood independent of that particular bad idea. Evolution by natural selection represented Darwin at his best—which is to say, scientific observation and careful thinking at its best.

DOUGLAS FUTUYMA IS A HIGHLY respected evolutionary biologist, author of textbooks as well as influential research papers. His office, at the University of Michigan, is a long narrow room in the natural sciences building, well stocked with journals and books, including volumes about the conflict between creationism and evolution. I arrived carrying a well-thumbed copy of his own book on that subject, *Science on Trial: The Case for Evolution.* Killing time in the corridor before our appointment, I noticed a blue flyer on a departmental bulletin board, seeming oddly placed there amid the announcements of career opportunities for graduate students. "CREATION VS. EVOLUTION," it said. "A series of messages challenging popular thought with Biblical truth and scientific evidences." A traveling lecturer from something called the Origins Research Association would deliver these messages at a local Baptist church. Beside the lecturer's photo was a drawing of a dinosaur. "Free pizza following the evening service," said a small line at the bottom. Dinosaurs, biblical truth, and pizza: something for everybody.

In response to my questions about evidence, Dr. Futuyma moved quickly through the traditional categories—paleontology, biogeography—and talked mostly about modern genetics. He pulled out his heavily marked copy of the journal *Nature* for February 15, 2001, a historic issue, fat with articles reporting and analyzing the results of the Human Genome Project. Beside it he slapped down a more recent issue of *Nature*, this one devoted to the sequenced genome of the house mouse, *Mus musculus*. The headline of the lead editorial announced: "Human Biology by Proxy." The mouse genome effort, according to *Nature*'s editors, had revealed "about thirty thousand genes, with 99 percent having direct counterparts in humans."

The resemblance between our thirty thousand human genes and those thirty thousand mousy counterparts, Futuyma explained, represents another form of homology, like the resemblance between a five-fingered hand and a five-toed paw. Such genetic homology is what gives meaning to biomedical research using mice and other animals, including chimpanzees, which (to their sad misfortune) are our closest living relatives.

No aspect of biomedical research seems more urgent today than the study of microbial diseases. And the dynamics of those microbes within human bodies, within human populations, can only be understood in terms of evolution.

Nightmarish illnesses caused by microbes include both the infectious sort (AIDS, Ebola, SARS) that spread directly from person to person and the sort (malaria, West Nile fever) delivered to us by biting insects or other intermediaries. The capacity for quick change among disease-causing microbes is what makes them so dangerous to large numbers of people and so difficult and expensive to treat. They leap from wildlife or domestic animals into humans, adapting to new circumstances as they go. Their inherent variability allows them to find new ways of evading and defeating human immune systems. By natural selection they acquire resistance to drugs that should kill them. They evolve. There's no better or more immediate evidence supporting the Darwinian theory that this process of forced transformation among our inimical germs.

Take the common bacterium *Staphylococcus aureus*, which lurks in hospitals and causes serious infections, especially among surgery patients. Penicillin, becoming available in 1943, proved almost miraculously effective in fighting staphylococcus infections. Its deployment marked a new phase in the old war between humans and disease microbes, a phase in which humans invent new killer drugs and microbes find new ways to be unkillable. The supreme potency of penicillin didn't last long. The first resistant strains of *Staphylococcus aureus* were reported in 1947. A newer staph-killing drug, methicillin, came into use during the 1960s, but methicillin-resistant strains appeared soon, and by the 1980s those strains were widespread. Vancomycin became the next great weapon against staph, and the first vancomycin-resistant strain emerged in 2002. These antibiotic-resistant strains represent an evolutionary series, not much different in principle from the fossil series tracing horse evolution from *Hyracotherium* to *Equus*. They make evolution a very practical problem by adding expense, as well as misery and danger, to the challenge of coping with staph.

The biologist Stephen Palumbi has calculated the cost of treating penicillin-resistant and methicillin-resistant staph infections, just in the United States, at $30 billion a year. "Antibiotics exert a powerful evolutionary force," he wrote last year, "driving infectious bacteria to evolve powerful defenses against all but the most recently invented drugs." As reflected in their DNA, which uses the same genetic code found in humans and horses and hagfish and honeysuckle, bacteria are part of the continuum of life, all shaped and diversified by evolutionary forces.

Even viruses belong to that continuum. Some viruses evolve quickly, some slowly. Among the fastest is HIV, because its method of replicating itself involves a high rate of mutation, and those mutations allow the virus to assume new forms. After just a few years of infection and drug treatment, each HIV patient carries a unique version of the virus. Isolation within one infected person, plus differing conditions and the struggle to survive, forces each version of HIV to evolve independently. It's nothing but a speeded up and microscopic case of what Darwin saw in the Galápagos—except that each human body is an island, and the newly evolved forms aren't so charming as finches or mockingbirds.

Understanding how quickly HIV acquires resistance to antiviral drugs, such as AZT, has been crucial to improving treatment by way of multiple-drug cocktails. "This approach has reduced deaths due to HIV by severalfold since 1996," according to Palumbi, "and it has greatly slowed the evolution of this disease within patients."

Insects and weeds acquire resistance to our insecticides and herbicides through the same process. As we humans try to poison them, evolution by natural selection transforms the population of a mosquito or thistle into a new sort of creature, less vulnerable to that particular poison. So we invent another poison, then another. It's a futile effort. Even DDT, with its ferocious and long-lasting effects throughout ecosystems, produced resistant house flies within a decade of its discovery in 1939. By 1990 more than 500 species (including 114 kinds of mosquitoes) had acquired resistance to at least one pesticide. Based on these undesired results, Stephen Palumbi has commented glumly, "humans may be the world's dominant evolutionary force."

Among most forms of living creatures, evolution proceeds slowly—

too slowly to be observed by a single scientist within a research lifetime. But science functions by interference, not just by direct observation, and the inferential sorts of evidence such as paleontology and biogeography are no less cogent simply because they're indirect. Still, skeptics of evolutionary theory ask: Can we see evolution in action? Can it be observed in the wild? Can it be measured in the laboratory?

The answer is yes. Peter and Rosemary Grant, two British-born researchers who have spent decades where Charles Darwin spent weeks, have captured a glimpse of evolution with their long-term studies of beak size among Galápagos finches. William R. Rice and George W. Salt achieved something similar in their lab, through an experiment involving thirty-five generations of the fruit fly *Drosophila melanogaster*. Richard E. Lenski and his colleagues at Michigan State University have done it too, tracking twenty thousand generations of evolution in the bacterium *Escherichia coli*. Such field studies and lab experiments document anagenesis—that is, slow evolutionary change within a single, unsplit lineage. With patience it can be seen, like the movement of a minute hand on a clock.

Speciation, when a lineage splits into two species, is the other major phase of evolutionary change, making possible the divergence between lineages about which Darwin wrote. It's rarer and more elusive even than anagenesis. Many individual mutations must accumulate (in most cases, anyway, with certain exceptions among plants) before two populations become irrevocably separated. The process is spread across thousands of generations, yet it may finish abruptly—like a door going *slam!*—when the last critical changes occur. Therefore it's much harder to witness. Despite the difficulties, Rice and Salt seem to have recorded a speciation event, or very nearly so, in their extended experiment on fruit flies. From a small stock of mated females they eventually produced two distinct fly populations adapted to different habitat conditions, which the researchers judged "incipient species."

AFTER MY VISIT WITH DOUGLAS FUTUYMA in Ann Arbor, I spent two hours at the university museum there with Philip D. Gingerich, a paleontologist well-known for his work on the ancestry of whales. As we talked, Gingerich guided me through an exhibit of ancient cetaceans on the museum's second floor. Amid weird skeletal shapes that seemed almost chimerical (some hanging overhead, some in glass cases) he pointed out significant features and described the progress of thinking about whale evolution. A burly man with a broad open face and the gentle manner of a scoutmaster, Gingerich combines intellectual passion and solid expertise with one other trait that's valuable in a scientist: a willingness to admit when he's wrong.

Since the late 1970s Gingerich has collected fossil specimens of early whales from remote digs in Egypt and Pakistan. Working with Pakistani colleagues, he discovered *Pakicetus*, a terrestrial mammal dating from fifty million years ago, whose ear bones reflect its membership in the whale lineage but whose skull looks almost doglike. A former student of Gingerich's, Hans Thewissen, found a slightly more recent form with webbed feet, legs suitable for either walking or swimming, and a long toothy snout. Thewissen called it *Ambulocetus natans*, or the "walking-and-swimming whale." Gingerich and his team turned up several more, including *Rodhocetus balochistanensis*, which was fully a sea creature, its legs more like flippers, its nostrils shifted backward on the snout, halfway to the blowhole position on a modern whale. The sequence of known forms was becoming more and more complete. And all along, Gingerich told me, he leaned toward believing that whales had descended from a group of carnivorous Eocene mammals known as mesonychids, with cheek teeth useful for chewing meat and bone. Just a bit more evidence, he thought, would confirm that relationship. By the end of the 1990s most paleontologists agreed.

Meanwhile, molecular biologists had explored the same question and arrived at a different answer. No, the match to those Eocene carnivores might be close, but not close enough. DNA hybridization and other tests suggested that whales had descended from artiodactyls (that is, even-toed herbivores, such as antelopes and hippos), not from meat-eating mesonychids.

In the year 2000 Gingerich chose a new field site in Pakistan, where one of his students found a single piece of fossil that changed the prevailing view in paleontology. It was half of a pulley-shaped anklebone, known as an astragalus, belonging to another new species of whale. A Pakistani colleague found the fragment's other half. When Gingerich fitted the two pieces together, he had a moment of humbling recognition: The molecular biologists were right. Here was an anklebone, from a four-legged whale dating back forty-seven million years, that closely resembled the homologous anklebone in an artiodactyl. Suddenly he realized how closely whales are related to antelopes.

This is how science is supposed to work. Ideas come and go, but the fittest survive. Downstairs in his office Phil Gingerich opened a specimen drawer, showing me some of the actual fossils from which the display skeletons upstairs were modeled. He put a small lump of petrified bone, no larger than a lug nut, into my hand. It was the famous astragalus, from the species he had eventually named *Artiocetus clavis*. It felt solid and heavy as truth.

Seeing me to the door, Gingerich volunteered something personal: "I grew up in a conservative church in the Midwest and was not taught anything about evolution. The subject was clearly skirted. That helps me understand the people who are skeptical about it. Because I come from that tradition myself." He shares the same skeptical instinct. Tell him that there's an ancestral connection between land animals and whales, and his reaction is: Fine, maybe, but show me the intermediate stages. Like Charles Darwin, the onetime divinity student, who joined that round-the-world voyage aboard the *Beagle* instead of becoming a country parson, and whose grand view of life on Earth was shaped by close attention to small facts, Phil Gingerich is a reverent empiricist. He's not satisfied until he sees solid data. That's what excites him so much about pulling whale fossils out of the ground. In thirty years he has seen enough to be satisfied. For him, Gingerich said, it's "a spiritual experience."

"The evidence is there," he added. "It's buried in the rocks of ages."

2006

Editor: ATUL GAWANDE

JACK HITT

Mighty White of You

FROM *HARPER'S*

> *Who were the first Americans? Were they people from Asia who crossed a land bridge between Siberia and Alaska twelve thousand years ago and then moved their way down the continent? Recently there have been challenges to this account—with some hypothesizing a pre-Amerindian settlement by Europeans. Jack Hitt finds that these new theories have less to do with science than with a distressing and not-so-subtle racism.*

I. CHARLEMAGNE'S HEIR

I was seventeen years old when I discovered that I was the great-great (and forty-six more of those) grandson of Charlemagne—king of the Franks and Holy Roman Emperor. Where I grew up, it's not unusual to find out such things. The culture of Charleston, South Carolina, is built around the pride associated with a handful of family histories. Like most of my friends downtown, I spent my youth in an unconscious state of genealogical questing. Might I be the descendant of a signer of the Declaration? Robert E. Lee's messenger? I bugged my mom and aunts and uncles. Who am I really? Might my childhood friends turn out to be third cousins? In Charleston, that one's almost too easy.

My mother grew exhausted with my pestering and sent me to see Mary Pringle, a cousin who was said to spend her days studying the family genealogy. Primed with curiosity, I arrived at Cousin Mary's elegant antebellum home on a hot summer day. After some iced tea and pleasantries, I was presented with a large, unwieldy sheet of paper bearing a set of concentric circles. In the center, Mary wrote my name, and in the next circle, divided in half, she wrote the names of my parents. In the next circle, divided now into fourths, she wrote the names of my four grandparents. We filled it out as far as we could in every direction, and in that area where her family and mine converged—her life's work—a seemingly unbounded wedge flew backward to Scotland and England, until my ancestors were hobnobbing with William Shakespeare and Mary, Queen of Scots. *This line*, she said, pointing to one of the ancient British earls we could claim, *leads in a direct line all the way to Charlemagne.*

This was almost too much past to absorb and too much pride to possess. I wanted to ask her what the Holy Roman Emperor had left me in the will. But Mary's tone was solemn, nearly religious: *You are the direct descendant of King Charlemagne.*

The room felt still as the rest of the universe slowly turned on its gyre about me, just as it did on the paper.

I left Mary Pringle's house feeling pretty, well, rooted. It's an important feeling for most people—knowing where they come from. And being heir to Charlemagne would serve me just fine on the gentlemen's party circuit. Over the next few years, I became as cunning at hefting this lumbering chunk of self-esteem into passing conversation as a Harvard grad is at alluding to his alma mater.

Roots are crucial to us—us being all Americans—because they are the source of so much of our national anxiety about not quite belonging. Has any passenger manifest been more fretted over than the *Mayflower*'s? One of the few Internet uses that seems able to compete with porn is genealogy. The most significant television miniseries—*Roots*—spawned a wave of pride among African Americans (and, arguably, even that compound name) and is partly responsible for the ongoing effort to drain the word "white" of its racist intimations by redefining it as "Irish American," "Scottish American," "Italian American," and the like. For everyone—including Native Americans, who itchily remind the rest of us that they might also be called First Americans—there is a deep anxiety about rootedness and its claims.

After Bill Frist was elevated to majority leader of the Senate, he self-published a book. Its title cries out as much with this anxiety as it does with pride: *Good People Beget Good People*: *A Genealogy of the Frist Family.*

And the truth is, this anxiety can never quite be quelled. About three years after I had tea with Mary Pringle, I was in a college calculus class when the teacher made a point about factoring large numbers. He dramatized it by giving an example from the real world, explaining how redundancy affected genealogy. He noted that if you run your line back to AD 800, the number of direct ancestors you would have is preposterously large (today, it would be 281,474,976,710,656, or a quarter quadrillion). Since the total human population for all time is estimated at a sparse 106 billion, the huge number makes no sense unless there is massive redundancy far back in time.

The upshot, the teacher explained, is that nearly everyone currently living anywhere on the planet can claim (and he paused for emphasis) . . . *to be the direct descendant of Charlemagne.*

The room felt still, as the rest of the universe slowly turned on its gyre about me, laughing.

Not long afterward, I learned from Alex Shoumatoff 's book *The Mountain of Names* that this paradox has a name, "pedigree collapse," which explains how the old practice of cousins marrying creates super-redundancy in the deep past (and why the planet's total population of 268,435,456 in AD 1300 roughly equals the number of ancestors you would have had at that time). A while back, my aunt

Mary died, but her dream lives as one of Amazon's favorite genealogy books: *The Everything Online Genealogy Book: Use the Web to
Discover Long-Lost Relations, Trace Your Family Tree Back to Royalty,
and Share Your History with Far-Flung Cousins.*

Recognizing the delusional fiction of it all, I swore off distant genealogy forever. That is, until recently, when I learned that new technologies and laboratory breakthroughs have revealed that my
great-great (and 638 more of them) grandfather was the first man to
set foot on the continent of North America, some sixteen thousand
years ago.

II. THE ALLEGORY OF THE CAVE

On a cool leafy hillside above a trickling Cross Creek in remote
Pennsylvania, the sun creeps through the trees, primordial. Nestled
into the slope above, an open rock-shelter seems just the place where
any self-respecting *Homo sapiens* might set down his basketry and
spear and light a fire.

Today there's a parking lot at the hill's base and a set of sturdy
stairs that lead to a wooden enclosure built by James Adovasio. He's
the Mercyhurst College archaeologist who's been excavating this
controversial site since the mid-1970s. Adovasio is guiding a rare
tour for a dozen or so amateurs, myself included. He arrives in full
archaeological drag: sleeveless flak jacket, boots, work pants, mysti-
cal belt buckle. His broad scowling face gives him the look of Martin
Scorsese and George Lucas's love child.

Inside the shelter, there's an office, electricity, good lighting, and a
suspended boardwalk so that visitors and workers don't stomp over
all the evidence. Enormous squared-out holes plunge down into the
dense earth, where tiny round markers dangle like pinned earrings
in the stone.

It was here that Adovasio found his controversial evidence, stone
tools that carbon-date to 16,000 ± 150 years BC.

This makes them at least four millennia older than the last ice
age, after which the first humans were traditionally believed to have

arrived in North America. Adovasio asks us to notice a pencil-thin black line in the stone. No one can really see it. So Adovasio splashes water on it and the line darkens into little more than a pencil swipe across the rock.

"This is a fire pit," he declares. All of us move closer to the rail to squint and then decide, as with so much of prehistoric archaeology, that we'll just take his word for it. He describes the scene that once occurred here. Folks sat around the fire and cooked deer and squirrel while snacking on hackberries and nuts. Maybe they battered some rocks into spear points or wove some grasses into primitive baskets. In the chilly rock-shelter, it is easy to look around and imagine this ancient gathering. Typically, the prehistoric picture show that plays on the cave wall of our minds involves bandy-legged men with spears pursuing mastodons. Here we are in the kitchen, where people sat around the fire, eating and talking. Away from the picturesque hunt. Quiet time, culture time, story time.

Now, 16,000 ± 150 years later, we are once again gathered here for story time. But Adovasio is not alone in trying to tell this story. Helping him, sort of, is the fat guy in front of me. He's just one of the crowd, like me, but he has spent much of the tour loudly explaining—allegedly to his long-suffering girlfriend but really to the confederacy of dunces that is the rest of us—just how much he knows about this place. He's wearing a fanny pack the size of a car tire cinched above pastel shorts, robin's-egg-blue socks, and black tennis shoes. His XXL T-shirt declares, KLINGON ASSAULT GROUP.

He has already sneeringly uttered the phrase "politically incorrect" several times to signal that he is not a victim of conventional wisdom but a man of daring opinions. He has let everyone in the place know that he very well intends to ask Adovasio the tough questions. And now the time has come: "Professor Adovasio, does working here in the rock-shelter in western Pennsylvania keep you safe from resentments with Native Americans?" He makes an interrogative honking noise.

"No," Adovasio insists. "Native Americans have an intense interest in this site." Adovasio segues quickly into a shaggy-dog story about a certain Indian who was nothing but supportive. I look at the dozen or so of us, all white folks in their forties and fifties, and none of us seems a bit mystified about why Native Americans might be resentful. Perhaps that is why Adovasio doesn't feel it necessary to address this issue. His work, after all, implies that the Native Americans were latecomers, that before Asians crossed the Bering Strait and began settling North America around the commonly agreed time of thirteen thousand years ago, there was already somebody here. He also knows that other scientists claim to have fresh evidence suggesting that these earliest people, and hence the true First Americans, were, in the scientific jargon, "Caucasoid." That is, white people who looked just like the Klingon ± two hundred pounds.

III. AMERICAN GENESIS

Our continent's creation story about the Asian hunter/gatherer crossing the Bering Strait is only about a century old and owes its origin to a black cowboy named George McJunkin. A former slave, McJunkin went out West, taught himself book learning, and herded cattle while pondering the world around him. He was said to ride a horse fixed with a big rifle holster that toted his telescope.

McJunkin was studied-up enough to know that some old bones he found near Clovis, New Mexico, in 1908 belonged to extinct animals. Twenty-five years later, experts investigating McJunkin's discovery found embedded in some of these ancient bison bones a flat, rounded arrowhead with a bit of fluting at the base to assist its fastening to a spear. It would eventually become known as the Clovis point—the oldest spearhead type ever found on the continent.

What makes the Clovis point so special is that it is found in massive numbers all across the continent and reliably enough at a level where organic material generally carbon-dates to roughly twelve thousand years ago. How massive? Take Bell County, Texas. The area north of Austin—known as the Gault site—must have been a well-known pit stop among the Clovis tribes. The place has yielded more than half a million stone artifacts from the Clovis era.

"The whole idea of archaeology is that there must be enough re-dundancy in the record," said Richard Burger, a professor of anthro-pology at Yale. Why? Because there is no other way to prove the case in archaeology, no other path to certainty.

"Archaeologists can't do experiments," Burger said. "Unlike lab science, we can't mix carbon and sulfur and conclude that such and such happens. So we have something else approaching that. We take advantage of redundancy, so that the evidence repeats itself in broad patterns. With Clovis, this happens with confidence."

In the last two decades, though, the confident tellers of Clovis Man's tale have been challenged by academic renegades devoted to identifying a new "First American." There are at least four major sites (and some minor ones) in the Americas that claim to have found man-made objects dating to tens of thousands of years before Clovis time. These theorists argue that although Clovis Man might still have crossed the Bering Strait thirteen thousand years ago, there is evidence that somebody else was already here. Given their natural caution, academics generally stop right there.

In the meantime, though, other theorists have stepped forward to identify the pre-Clovis somebody. This process has happened not on the front page of the newspapers but in the rumor mill at the edge of archaeology and anthropology and in the pages of popular-science magazines. The new theory holds that Caucasians from Europe set-tled this continent first and that Native Americans are just another crowd of later visitors, like Leif Ericson's Vikings and Christopher Columbus's Spaniards. Most important, the way this theory has seeped out of cautious academia and into the pop culture as slightly naughty fact suggests that America's neurosis about race has taken up a new and potentially toxic location—deep in the heart of our continent's creation myth.

IV. Sesquipedalianismo

For any new story to get told, there has to be an opening, a sudden tectonic jarring of a discipline's conventional wisdom. Thomas Kuhn described this critical moment with the now much weathered phrase "paradigm shift." It's the precise moment of the tilt between an old worldview and a new one. And that's where we are now in the subdiscipline of ancient-American archaeology, poised between those views held (as always) by mossbacked conservative traditionalists on the one side and young agitated revolutionaries on the other.

The voice of skepticism and orthodoxy is best embodied by Professor C. Vance Haynes of the University of Arizona. He comes by his skepticism honestly. He once bought into a claim quite similar to Adovasio's, back in the 1960s, at a site called Tule Springs in Nevada. He, too, thought the Clovis line had been breached. He was convinced by extensive evidence of "hearths" filled with charcoal and animal bones, revealing a human encampment dating back twenty-eight thousand years. But later, when Haynes conducted precise tests of the charcoal, he realized that it was merely very old wood turning into coal. All of it was wrong. "You begin to see how easy it is to misinterpret things," Haynes said.

When you look at the evidence and the fights around it, you can understand why. First, arrowheads are cool things. Every little kid who has ever dug one up knows this. To hold in your hand a weapon that is five hundred, a thousand, five thousand years old is humbling and, just, neato. Arrowheads are symmetrical and beautiful objects. Their flutes, their chipped edges, their flared tails have all been studied, categorized, and given handsome names, dozens of them. The Madison point dates from AD 1400, the Whitlock point from 400 BC, further back to the Haywood point at 5000 BC, deeper still to the Cascade point at 8000 BC (or so), and finally to the oldest, the Clovis point.

With each older style, the artifacts become less *arrowheady*. Instead of having tooled edges, they are clearly flintnapped—i.e., beat at with another stone. A beveled edge might be replaced by a straight blade. Those graceful fishtails disappear, and then you get a simple stone point with a groove banged out at the bottom, the telltale primitivity signifying Clovis time. Beyond that, it is hard to tell whether the evidence is, in fact, man-made. Archaeology has a term for naturally occurring objects that appear to be artifacts: geofacts.

The archaeology establishment believes that the entire array of pre-Clovis evidence is a pile of geofacts. And not all that big a pile either. Whereas all the evidence of Clovis Man would crowd a boxcar, all the good physical evidence of pre-Clovis Man could probably fit in your bureau drawer. And when you look at the individual artifacts themselves, the evidence can be pretty underwhelming. There are no broad patterns, there are no similarities, and there is no redundancy.

The dates are a mixed bag, ranging as far back as fifty thousand years ago to more recent sixteen-thousand-year dates. And obtaining those dates is a messy business. Rocks cannot be carbon-dated. Only the organic material they are found nested in can be, and that material is easily contaminated by rain, by burrowing animals, by time. And carbon dating may sound precise, but the idea of it—that carbon 14 molecules throw off electrons at a metronomically consistent geological pace—is more exact than the reality. Almost since the discovery of carbon dating, scientists have been noting phenomena that cause variations with the regularity of carbon's internal clock—sunspots, stray comets, atomic bombs—such that it requires applying a "correction factor." Thus, for any ancient evidence to be confirmed, the punk rockers of archaeology have to look for affirmation from their elders, the Lawrence Welk orchestra. Worse, the old fogies, like Vance Haynes and others, are essentially being asked to confirm a theory that overturns their entire life's work. This combination of murky evidence and professional oedipalism can mean only one thing: academic food fight.

In prehistoric archaeology there's a lot of dialogue between the conservative traditionalists and the rebel theorists that, boiled down, typically goes like this:

Upstart Archaeologist: "This is a primitive stone tool that's sixteen thousand years old."

Eminence Grise: "No, it's not."

Upstart Archaeologist: "Fuck you."

Actually, that's not much of an exaggeration. In Adovasio's book,

The First Americans, he quotes a friend who said, "'If they don't be-lieve the evidence, fuck 'em'—definitely not scientific discourse but not ill considered, either!"

From its opening line—"'Damn,' I said."—Adovasio's book quiv-ers with the fury of a scolded teenager. His own site, the Meadow-croft Rock-shelter I visited in southwest Pennsylvania, has been roundly dismissed by elders who note the existence of nearby "coal seams" (yet another factor that throws off carbon dating) and ground-water seepage. C. Vance Haynes is among those who have wrinkled their noses at Meadowcroft. In his book, Adovasio dis-misses Haynes as the "grinch of North American archaeology." In fact, anyone who has questioned Adovasio's site at Meadowcroft is generally referred to as a "gnat."

And no love is lost among the rebels themselves. When a Parisian archaeologist discovered an amazing site called Pedra Furada in Brazil, the initial reports were breathtaking. Besides numerous pieces of pre-Clovis evidence, there were cave paintings said to be even older than the images at Lascaux in France or at Altamira in Spain. Some of the Pedra Furada drawings are said to depict hot Pleistocene-era group sex. Brazil's government developed plans to capitalize on the site as a tourist attraction. Adovasio himself was part of the expert panel that, sorrowfully, declared it all wrong. Adovasio wrote that he saw nothing but "almost surely broken rocks that had fallen into the rockshelter." He dismissed the find of "ancient fireplaces" as "nothing more than material blown in from nearby forest fires."

Of course, the language of this brawl is usually academic and Latinate, mostly fought with the manly sesquipedalianisms of sci-ence jargon. Here, tree rings are "dendrochronological samples." A rock is a "lithic," and a rock that's clearly been flaked by human hands is "an indubitable lithic artifact." Bits of stone chipped off to make a tool are "percussion flakes."

These are the lyrics of the trade, played in the key of high-science formality. And it's with such swaggering sesquipedalianismo that an entire career of work can be cattily dismissed: "My review has raised doubts about the provenience of virtually every 'compelling,' unambiguous artifact ... ," wrote the archaeologist Stuart Fiedel in 1999 of the most promising pre-Clovis site ever.

The archaeologist whose work is being trashed here is Tom Dillehay of the University of Kentucky. He had claimed to find—at a Chilean site called Monte Verde—fantastic evidence of a pre-Clovis community: a series of huts, one of which might have been some kind of primitive drugstore, as it contained traces of pharmaceutical herbs. He found a tent post still staked in the ground with knotted twine from a Juncus tree, or, in the jargon, "the indisputably anthropogenic knotted Juncus."

In 1997 a team of specialists, including C. Vance Haynes, visited the site, examined all of Dillehay's cool evidence, and unanimously approved it. The pre-Clovis line was officially breached. Tom Dillehay was the man, though not for long. Haynes began to waver. Then Fiedel, a private-sector archaeologist, wrote a withering dismissal of every single piece of evidence presented.

In his book, Adovasio (who sided with Dillehay on this one) suggested that Fiedel "reserve some space in the State Home for the Terminally Bewildered." Adovasio whacked Fiedel as "a previously little known archaeologist now working for a private salvage archaeology firm" who "has no field experience in Paleo-Indian sites or complex late Pleistocene or Holocene sites" and "has published one rarely used prehistory textbook but otherwise has no apparent credentials."*

Archaeology's caste system is another facet of the discipline that makes it more amateurish a science than, say, particle physics. How many weekend astrophysicists could write up a report challenging Stephen Hawking that would be widely accepted as truth? When

---

*Professional archaeology is a sort of caste system. The Brahmins are the credentialed, tenured professors at known colleges. They publish in peer-review journals. Beneath them are private-sector archaeologists, also known as salvage archaeologists. They might publish in popular journals such as *National Geographic*, but their day work is something different altogether. They determine for, say, a mall developer whether there are any "significant" remains on a piece of real estate slated to become a food court. Below the salvagers are the rank amateurs and hobbyists who often spend a weekend out at some site hoping to find a Clovis point or two to sell on eBay or to keep in their special cigar box back home.

new evidence in, say, particle physics opens up a Kuhnian melee, the folks who rush in to the breach tend to be, well, particle physicists. But in prehistoric archaeology, with its rather elastic sense of membership ranging from well-credentialed academics like Adovasio to salvage archaeologists to slightly bonkers theorists to ranting neo-Nazis, all of them can rush right in. And do.

What underlies the mudslinging use of bloated Latinisms as well as the compulsion to make a show of tidy whisk brooms and Euclidean grids is the sense, maybe even fear, that archaeology is not a science at all. There's a lot of play in the carbon dating, all the evidence is in dispute, and, sure, maybe the elders' caution can easily be dismissed as a Freudian conflict of interest. All of this means that the pre-Clovis evidence requires a lot of interpretation, a fact that makes it very easy for personal desire and anxiety to leach like groundwater into that drawerful of cobbles and lithics. As one defender of Dillehay confessed in his own report, "I wondered if, by being too close to these stones for too long, I was building an interpretive sandcastle."

But the sandcastle's been built, and some have begun to tell a new creation story—about just who pre-Clovis Man was, where he came from, how he lived and died. The sudden appearance of this yarn explains why prehistoric archaeology really isn't as much a science as it is a form of tribal narrative. These stories have less to do with what's obvious from the evidence than with what some deeply long to hear. It's time to look closely at the story that's getting told right now about the earliest inhabitants of this continent. I have a little experience in this field. I know how to jury-rig a narrative using only a couple of wayward factoids to make it sound just right. It's something I was born to do. I am the direct descendant of Charlemagne.

V. LADIES AND GENTLEMEN, KENNEWICK MAN

For most of the 1990s, the sotto-voce chatter about pre-Clovis Man and his possible identity was little more than politically mischievous buzz out on the edge of archaeology. Insiders talked about spear-points and some disputed bones, DNA, and cordage, but it wasn't a story so much as it was narrative tinder, very dry, waiting for a spark.

That spark finally flew one hot summer afternoon in 1996, on the banks of the Columbia River. Some college students were trying to sneak into a hydroplane race, and as they stomped through the muck of a bank, one of them saw a few bones and then pieces of a skull.

The find eventually was passed on to a local forensic expert, a salvage archaeologist who worked out of a converted rec room in his house. He would become the rhapsode for these bones. Divinely, his name was James Chatters.

Chatters released the carbon dating that put the bones as far back as 7,600 BC. He also described a Cascade point embedded in the hip. This style of Paleo-Indian arrowhead is a long, thin design that would fit right in with the skeleton's age. But Chatters also said that he didn't believe this skeleton belonged to a Paleo-Indian but rather to "a trapper/explorer who'd had difficulties with 'stone-age' peoples during his travels."

In other words, this skeleton represented a crime scene, and the victim was not Paleo-Indian. Immediately, several Indian tribes, such as the Umatilla, demanded the bones, charging that they had to be of Native-American heritage. Over the next few years, what was at first a strange political dustup grew into an even more bizarre legal battle. The scientists held to simple principles of open inquiry: all we want to do is examine the skeleton more closely. The Native Americans suspected a ruse to get around new laws protecting the burial of ancient bones.

In 1990 President George H.W. Bush signed the Native American Graves Protection and Repatriation Act (NAGPRA), which sought to make amends for the grave robbing and bizarre antics of the previous decades. In the nineteenth century, the Smithsonian Institution wanted Indians' skulls to mount on display. So quite often after a battle, Indian corpses were decapitated, the heads packed in boxes and shipped back to Washington to be "studied." The money was good enough that often violence broke out when Indians saw white men—the emissaries of European civilization—loitering around a burial ground, since the suspicion was that they were waiting around in order to dig up grandma and cut off her head. A few centuries' worth of desecration of the Indian body is something mainstream history still avoids. It's hard for non-Native Americans today to understand all the lingering resentment. Try this on: toward the end of the Civil War, in Denver, a group of marauding white men provided theatergoers with a mid-show display of fresh Indian scalps—not merely from heads but from women's vaginas as well. The audience whooped with approval.

Some estimates put the number of Indian skeletons held in museums at two hundred thousand. NAGPRA was an attempt to return those and make sure it didn't happen again. It decreed that all Native-American remains that could be culturally identified were to be returned to the appropriate tribe.

In the past, a number of skeletons that fed the pre-Clovis rumor mill had in fact been seized and reburied. In the back alley of amateur American archaeology, these are notorious: the 10,800-year-old Buhl Woman found in Idaho in 1989, the 7,800-year-old Hourglass Cave skeleton found in Colorado, the 7,800-year-old Pelican Rapids Woman skull, and the 8,900-year-old Browns Valley Man, both found in Minnesota—all reburied.

The Native Americans in Washington State immediately assumed that this talk of Kennewick not being a Paleo-Indian was little more than a scientific tactic to get around the requirements of NAGPRA. Whatever the merits of the case, the issue quickly got caught up in contemporary politics. At the time of the discovery, the Umatilla Indians were working with the Clinton administration to dispose of some chemical weapons (WMD, as we say nowadays). The federal government desperately wanted tribal support on this difficult matter. By the late 1990s, the Umatilla had a casino, which meant they had political and financial clout and couldn't easily be kicked around. When they screamed for the bones, the Clinton administration jumped. Bruce Babbitt, the then secretary of the interior, ordered that the U.S. Army Corps of Engineers take control of the bones. Then, to "stabilize" the site where the bones were found, the army choppered in five hundred tons of riprap and buried the bank. The archaeological site was protected by being destroyed.

Chatters and the group of scientists who had gathered around him, calling for an open inquiry into the skeleton, were stunned. This wasn't just politics; it was medieval obscurantism. To the scientists, this was the equivalent of locking Galileo in his room and demanding that he recant. And there the story might have ended, but for one word that totally changed the nature of the debate in the pop culture outside the courtroom. When Chatters first examined Kennewick in his rec room, he looked at the skull and then described what he saw as "Caucasoid-like."

The narrative tinder of decades suddenly exploded in flames, and from the fire, like a phoenix, arose a new and wild story: A Caucasoid man, who was among the First Americans, was murdered by genocidal newcomers, Mongoloid invaders coming across Berengia after the last ice age.*

To color the fight with the absurdity peculiar to all truly American events, the Asatru Folk Assembly—a neo-Norse movement that claims to represent the "native European" religion—asserted its rights to Kennewick's bones. The neo-Norsemen argued that they were the nearest tribe related to Kennewick Man and that under NAGPRA they should be given the bones for reburial. The federal courts did not give them Kennewick but did allow them to perform funeral rites over the bones. And so a year after that hydroplane race, big hairy blond men wearing horns and garish furs performed the Norse burial ceremony in Washington State for their mourned errant ancestor.

---

*Throughout the theories and quarrels surrounding this prehistory, there is a strange kind of recapitulation going on. Every theory propagated about the European conquest of the Indians after Columbus seems to have its Doppelgänger in the pre-Clovis era. Just as American Indians were the victims of genocide in the colonial period, so it seems were the early Caucasoids at the hands of Paleo-Indians. Some theories say that the early Caucasoids were wiped out by germs, a recapitulation of the account of smallpox-infected blankets that has become a near parable in American history. In this way, the Indians' attempt to claim the Kennewick skeleton is simply the evil twin of nineteenth-century grave robbing.

VI. A Brief History of Caucasians

Does race exist? Of course it does. We see it every day. Guy steals a purse, the cop asks, What did he look like? You say, He was a six-foot-tall black guy, or a five-and-a-half-foot-tall Asian man, or a white guy with long red hair. As a set of broad descriptions of how people look, race exists.

If you were to look at me, you would easily categorize me as Caucasian. I'm the ruddy sort that burns quickly, with reddish hair now shading into white. Most people hazarding a guess might say Scottish, which is what I have always said. Just to be sure, I recently submitted my DNA to see what the incontrovertible scientific evidence might show. The result was surprising (though in some ways not surprising): I carry the DNA marker found in great abundance among the Fulbe tribe of contemporary Nigeria.

Sure, maybe the marker is about as significant as my Charlemagne genes. On the other hand, that very Nigerian coast is the tribal location where many slaves were captured and held in the notorious slave castles until traders' galleys could transport them to American ports. The main harbor that received more slaves than any other on the eastern seaboard was Charleston, South Carolina. My mother's family has lived there nearly three hundred years. Maybe I have a Thomas Jefferson problem. Whenever it was that a black woman* entered my bloodline (and my white ancestor entered hers), it's no longer apparent in the way I now look. I am Caucasian as surely as my Fulbe cousins are black, because race is a set of visual cues we all recognize—skin shade, nose shape, eyelid folds, cheekbone prominence, etc. We hold these vague blueprints of race in our heads because, as primates, one of the great tools of consciousness we possess is the ability to observe patterns in nature. It's no surprise that we'd train this talent on ourselves

Here's another example, a little closer in time. My grandmother

---

*I trust that I don't need to explain why I make this assumption.

was Weinona Strom. Her first cousin was Strom Thurmond, which makes the late senator my first cousin, twice removed. It also makes his half-black daughter, Essie Mae Washington-Williams, my second cousin once removed.

For those of us who have had to contend with Strummy-boo all our lives,* looking at Essie Mae and seeing the senator's face gazing out from her own is a kind of thrilling shock. But what's far more interesting is Essie Mae's daughter. Because Essie Mae married a man our pattern-seeking brains would recognize as black, the evidence of Strummy's whiteness is practically gone only one generation later. I suspect that among the great grandchildren, Strummy's presence in the Washington-Williams family will be as washed away as the Fulbe tribe is in me.

Yet the notion of race as an unchanging constant through time is as old as the Bible. When Noah's Flood receded, the three boys Japheth, Shem, and Ham went out into the world to engender white people, Semites, and all others, respectively. This doesn't quite shake out into the later notions of white, black, and yellow, but you get the idea. The boys are still with us. The early word "Shemitic" settled down to become "semitic." And among amateur chroniclers writing in the ponderous style of the town historian, it's not hard to find references to the "Hamitic race" as a way of saying "black folks." Japheth never became a common adjective, perhaps because of that thicket of consonants. More likely, though, it's because whites appointed themselves the Adamic task of naming the other races. It was not until the Age of Reason that scientists tried to figure out empirically what race meant and how it came to be. The signal year was 1776, with the publication of a book called *On the Natural Varieties of Mankind* by German biologist Johann Friedrich Blumenbach.

At the time, Blumenbach's theory had a certain symmetry that made it the very model of good science. These days, his theory seems

---

*That's really what we called him.

260 I JACK HITT

insane. He argued that Native American Indians were the transitional race that eventually led to Asians. (Don't try to work out the geography of this: it will make your head explode.) And another group—which Blumenbach simply conjured from a far-away people, the "Malayans"—evolved over time to become Africans. (Again, if you're puzzling out the geography, watch your head.)

At the center of all this change was the white race, which was constant. Blumenbach believed darkness was a sign of change from the original. All of mankind had fallen from perfection, but the darker you were, the farther you had fallen. As a result, the best way to locate the original Garden of Eden, according to Blumenbach, was to follow the trail of human . . . *beauty.* The hotter the women, the hunkier the men, the closer you were to what was left of God's first Paradise. Here is Blumenbach explaining the etymology of the new word he hoped to coin:

> I have taken the name of this variety from Mount Caucasus, both because its neighborhood, and especially its southern slope, produces the most beautiful race of men, I mean the Georgian . . .

Blumenbach's theory is totally forgotten today by everybody (except maybe Georgian men). All that remains is a single relic, the word he coined for God's most gorgeous creation—"Caucasian."

The word itself is lovely. Say it: Caucasian. The word flows off the tongue like a stream trickling out of Eden. Its soothing and genteel murmur poses quite a patrician contrast to the field-labor grunts of the hard *g*'s in "Negroid" and "Mongoloid." Caucasian. The exotic isolation of those mountains intimates a biblical narrative. You can almost see it when you say it: the early white forebears walking away from Paradise to trek to Europe and begin the difficult task of creating Western Civilization.

Ever since Blumenbach launched this word two and a half centuries ago, the effort to pin down the exact and scientific meaning of race has never ceased. Even today, the U.S. Census is little more than an explosion of ethnic agony that arrives every ten years like constitutional clockwork. The number of races has expanded and contracted wildly between Blumenbach and now, depending on the mood of the culture. The basic three have gone through scores of revisions, growing as high as Ernst Haeckel's thirty-four different races in 1879 or Paul Topinard's nineteen in 1885 or Stanley Garn's nine in 1971. Today, we nervously ask if you're white, African American, Native American, Asian, or of Hawaiian or Pacific Islander descent.

But it wasn't that long ago that the question would have turned upon races only our great-grandfathers would recognize. Let us mourn their passing: the Armenoids, the Assyroids, the Veddoids, the Orientalids, the Australoids, the Dalo-Nordic, the Fälish, the Alpines, the Dinarics, the Fenno-Nordic, the Osteuropids, the Lapponoids, the Osterdals, the Cappadocians, the Danubians, the Ladogans, the Trondelagens, and the Pile Dwellers.

In the meantime, science has made its discoveries. The mystery of race has been solved. For the longest time, scientists were stymied by a contradiction. Surely skin tone had something to do with colder climates creating paler shades, but then why weren't Siberians as pale as Swedes, and why were Eskimos as dark as equatorial islanders? The answer was announced in 2000, but it's so tedious hardly anyone noticed.

Skin pigmentation changed long ago not only to protect skin from different levels of sun exposure—that's obvious—but also in order to regulate the amount of vitamin D3 manufactured by the sun just under the skin. This is the theory of Professor Nina Jablonski, a paleoanthropologist with the California Academy of Sciences. So when the first swarthy inhabitants of modern Scandinavia confronted a lack of ultraviolet light, their kind quickly selected out for paler children whose skin would manufacture enough vitamin D3 to keep them healthy. Meanwhile, Eskimos arrived in the Arctic darkskinned. The local cuisine of seal and whale is rich in vitamin D3, so the skin was never summoned into action. Evolution has one big rule. If there's no pressure on the system to change, then it doesn't bother. So Eskimos remained dark.

When we look at the different races, according to Jablonski's theory, what we're actually seeing is not "superiority" or "good people" or "race." All that we are seeing, the *only* thing we are seeing when we look at skin color, is a meandering trail of vitamin D3 adaptation rates.

VII. The Mounting Evidence

Science prefers to confirm its newest findings with the newest tools. Just as fingerprinting is no longer the gold standard of guilt or innocence now that DNA testing is the rage, archaeologists have a few new tricks. These cutting-edge techniques come with gleaming names—Optically Stimulated Luminescence, Electron Spin Resonance Dating, and Accelerator Mass Spectrometry—and they are confirming pre-Clovis dates in ways that make carbon dating look like counting tree rings. By the time we figure out how these techniques are flawed, of course, our prejudices will be so well muddled among the tentative facts that they will be as inextricable as ink from milk.

According to the revolutionaries heralding pre-Clovis Man, that hardly matters, since so much other corroborative evidence is appearing. Some lab tests reveal that Native American Indians apparently have a signature strand of DNA known as Haplogroup X. The only other large population on the earth carrying this genetic marker is Europeans. The suggestion is that there must have been intermarriage in North America before Columbus, possibly before the last ice age. Moreover, now that the Iron Curtain has fallen, archaeologists have been able to do more digging in Siberia, where they expected to find Clovis points or something like them. They haven't. This absence, as well as the presence of Haplogroup X, has led some people to theorize that although Clovis Man might have crossed over to North America thirteen thousand years ago at the end of the last ice age, he would have encountered people already here—people possessed of the X gene as well as the Clovis tool kit.

Who might these people have been, and where might they have come from? One prominent theorist with an answer is America's chief archaeologist at the Smithsonian. A big, bearded bear of a man, Dennis Stanford could pass for a Norse king in some other time. Stanford has struggled with the mystery of why Clovis points *don't* show up in Siberia. He notes that they resemble the early work of Solutrean culture. The Solutreans were prehistoric people who lived in modern-day France and Spain some eighteen thousand years ago. They are perhaps most famous for being the possible candidates for painting the horses of Lascaux and their own hands on the walls of the Altamira Cave. Stanford argues that their tool kit, which included stone points, looks like a predecessor to the Clovis style.

"There must be fifty or sixty points of comparison," he has said.

He believes that these proto-Europeans must have been intelligent enough to make watercraft. Hugging the coast of what would have been a glacier all around the crescent edge of the northern Atlantic, they sailed away to a new land.

Other scientists are providing even more evidence that seems to support these general ideas. Several anthropologists have daringly revived the argument that examining skull shapes can reveal ethnicity. Douglas Owsley, also now at the Smithsonian, and his partner, Richard Jantz, at the University of Tennessee, have put together collections of measurements, described by *Newsweek* as a database of "2,000 or so profiles that consists of some 90 skull measurements, such as distance between the eyes, that indicate ancestry." They have developed software that allows them to input a bone's measurements and receive "ethnicity" as an output.

Among their fans and followers, there is talk of some of the peculiar skeletons found over the years. A 9,200-year-old body known as Wizards Beach Man, found at Pyramid Lake, Nevada, in 1978, was determined to be possibly of "Norse" extraction and to have "no close resemblance to modern Native Americans." Another skeleton, as Spirit Cave Man, was found in Nevada in 1940. His bones date to

7,450 BC. When his skull measurements were run through the software, out spat a finding of "Archaic Caucasoid."

Once again, there's Blumenbach's word. Only this time it's got that "oid" ending. What is the difference between Caucasoid and Caucasian?

"Caucasoid sounds more scientific," University of North Carolina anthropologist Jonathan Marks told me, laughing. Otherwise it has no more meaning or significance than Blumenbach's original. Caucasoid is a magnificent piece of pure Star Trekkery, a word meant to sound all clinical and precise, even nerdy. But the word is a rhetorical Trojan horse. Its surface meaning suggests something scientific, respectable, and learned, when in fact what we really hear are the connotations lurking inside, long-suppressed intimations of superiority, exceptionalism, and beauty.

VIII. KENNEWICK'S BIOGRAPHY

The court fight over Kennewick Man was resolved this January in favor of the scientists—in part because this is America and who can be against "open inquiry"? Yet the ramifications for Native Americans and for white Americans will be immense. In the popular market of ideas, the decision by the courts affirms a lot more than the noble virtue of open inquiry. It legitimizes the *story*—the story of the Caucasian man who came to this continent as the Authentic First American and whose bones survived the millennia to report the truth.

And the story that has been told these last eight years about this hundred-century-old man is marvelous in its perverse beauty. It begins with his name. Does anything sound more European, more positively British, than Kennewick? Native Americans had dubbed him the "Ancient One," but it didn't take. The mass media, which follows the meandering will of the popular mob, could sense where this story was trending, and so they ran with "Kennewick." Isn't that a suburb of Essex, or London's other airport? Perhaps not so ironically, the name is an anglicized version of the Indian word "kin-i-wak," meaning "grassy."*

In the few years after Sir Kennewick's discovery, his life was described and depicted in all the leading magazines. One writer on the subject, Sasha Nemecek, confessed that when she looks at the evidence "the misty images of primitive explorers evaporate" and now "I suddenly picture a single artisan spending hours, perhaps days, crafting these stone tools" whose "workmanship is exquisite, even to my untrained eye." To accompany her article, an artist rendered images of what Kennewick's ilk looked like. You might mistake him for an English professor at Bennington, but in fact he's the First American.

And his bride has the complex tool kit of her time, not to mention a nice Ann Tayloroid dress and a haircut that presages Jennifer Aniston by nearly ten millennia. She has thoughtfully shaved her legs for the artist, the better to see her lovely Caucasian skin.

Where did these pictures appear? *Scientific American.*

Right away, Kennewick was described with words that launched him millennia ahead of his primitive enemies, the Paleo-Indians. He was, as Chatters had said, probably an individual "trapper/explorer"—two words that, together, imply degrees of complex thought far in advance of his time, especially when set up against a mass of "stone age peoples." An article in the local newspaper, the *Tri-City Herald*, painted beautiful scenes of Kennewick as the "strongest hunter in his band." Paleo-Indians were still mucking around in "tribes" while Kennewick traveled with his "immediate and extended family members."

Food was important. "To keep up his strength, he and his band dined on rich, lean roasts and steaks . . ." Kennewick is, naturally, on the Atkins diet. No Type II diabetes for Kennewick.

---

*Just when Kennewick was discovered, another ancient skeleton was found on Alaska's Prince of Wales Island. This skeleton was quickly declared to be "Prince of Wales Island Man," making it seem as if the ancient forebears to the Saxon kings thought of the Pacific Northwest as a dandy vacation spot.

Kennewick Man received glamour treatment from all the major media, in which he was lauded for his near modernity. Lesley Stahl's piece on *60 Minutes* introduced Kennewick to television viewers as someone with "a tremendous amount of symmetry to his body" and therefore "handsome." (Blumenbach's notion of superiority as beauty is never really behind us.) Stahl permitted Chatters to say that Kennewick possessed "a lot of poise." The *Washington Post Magazine* took note of Kennewick's "ambition."

In a *New Yorker* article, we learn that "Some nearby sites contain large numbers of fine bone needles, indicating that a lot of delicate sewing was going on." The needles might have belonged to the Paleo-Indians, or: "Kennewick Man may have worn tailored clothing."

Swish that word around on your connotative palate. *Tailored.* Feel the force, tugging us in a certain direction.

Newsweek's cover story noted that skulls like Kennewick's are so different from what archaeologists expect that they "stand out like pale-skinned, redheaded cousins at a family reunion of olive-skinned brunettes."*

In these stories the Indians are typically ignored or they simply

---

*And these are the elegant accounts that struggle to keep the story contained inside the scientists' own cautious terms. From there the implications of Kennewick quickly became insinuated in current fashions of political opinion. John J.Miller of the *National Review* mentions a "growing suspicion among physical anthropologists, archaeologists, and even geneticists that some of the first people who settled in the New World were Europeans." Note how a tentative resemblance of skull shape, "Caucasoid-like"—always hedged by the scientists—has quickly settled into declarative certainty: "were Europeans." The politically obvious conclusion is also clear, as the writer continues: "An important part of American Indian identity relies on the belief that, in some fundamental way, they were here first. They are indigenous, they are Native, and they make an important moral claim on the national conscience for this very reason. Yet if some population came before them—perhaps a group their own ancestors wiped out through war and disease, in an eerily reversed foreshadowing of the contact Columbus introduced—then a vital piece of their mythologizing suffers a serious blow." Once you step away from the magazines and books, the story drifts into the poisonous domain of the Internet, where discussions tend toward a brutalist reduction, like this comment from shmogie1 on the alt. soc.history board: "Kennewick man is older than any known N/A [Native American] remains, and appears to be much more European than N/A, so your people stole the land from my European ancestors who were here first."

move about as a supernumerary horde brought onstage to throw the Cascade point and bring down the handsome Kennewick with his poise and ambition and all the other adjectives that will eventually lead to the abandonment of nomadism, the invention of agriculture, and on to the foundation of society that would lead us inexorably toward Western Civilization.

Which, in turn, would bring Kennewick's Caucasoid-like descendants back to America to find him and tell his story.

IX. KENNEWICK'S BACK STORY

The story of an early European presence here in America would be fascinating if it hadn't already been told so many times. The number of theories holding out Native Americans as either latecomers or Europeans in loincloths is endless. Even the earliest depictions of Indians simply used European bodies and faces with a few feathers added.

Western Europeans were stunned that the New World had so many people already in it. How could these primitives have gotten there first? They must be . . . us! Theories abounded. Some in England thought the Indians were covert Welsh families who'd slipped over on their rafts. Others wondered whether they weren't the lost people of Atlantis. A whole host of arguments had it that Indians were Jews. During the colonial era, the chief rabbi of Holland, Menashe ben Israel, claimed that all Native Americans were descended from the Lost Tribes of Israel, and the theory was confirmed by a 1650 book entitled *Iewes in America, or, Probabilities that the Americans are of that Race*. Mormons continue to believe this account of Native American origin, holding that the sons of Lehi sailed to the Americas around 600 BC and lost their traditions and knowledge of the Torah. They reverted to a state of savagery, and their descendants scattered among the plains and throughout the two continents. Thus all Indians are, essentially, Jews Gone Wild.

Most Americans rarely saw images out of books such as the rabbi's. Rather, the most widely available image was to be found on the coins in your pocket. European, if not Roman imperial.

In 1914, on a ten-dollar-gold coin, it was still possible to see in the face of the Indian the wavy-blond Nordic princess of our dreams. Practically at the same time, in 1913, an image that registered in our pattern-constructing brains as "Indian" would finally appear on the famous Buffalo nickel.

It's important to know this history and tradition when you consider the image conjured by Chatters when he asked an artist to take the Kennewick skull and reconstruct the face. Well, if only that was precisely what he did. But Chatters didn't just hand the skull to someone and ask him to reconstruct the face. Instead, he had an epiphany, as he explained once, right at home: "I turned on the TV, and there was Patrick Stewart—Captain Picard, of *Star Trek*—and I said, 'My God, there he is! Kennewick Man.'"

Forensic reconstruction is a very iffy "science." The problem is that the features we look to for identification are fleshy ones—ears, nose, and eyes—and those are the most difficult to know from a skull.* So reconstruction is more art than science, or, with its stated success rate of roughly 50 percent, about as good a predictor as a coin toss. Consider what Chatters did: by making Kennewick Man perfectly resemble one of the most famous pop-culture Brits of our time, he allows the visual cues to confirm his finding and so avoids even the need to repeat the word "Caucasoid-like."

Kennewick's skull is often described as "narrow, with a prominent nose, an upper jaw that juts out slightly, and a long narrow braincase," or, more properly, dolichocranic and slightly prognathous, marked by a lack of an inferior zygomatic projection. Yet here's the problem with looking at those vague features and declaring them "Caucasoid." We don't really know what people's skulls looked like ten thousand years ago. We have only a few, like the pre-Clovis points, so it's reckless to draw any conclusions. Skull shapes,

---

*I and every other writer call Kennewick's head a "skull." The implication is that it was found whole. In fact, it was found in parts that Chatters pieced together. When government experts put the pieces together, they built a skull whose dimensional differences from Chatters's version were deemed statistically significant. Again, at every stage of this story, the details get pushed toward the Caucasoid-like conclusion

like skin color, can change more quickly than we think, especially if there has been traumatic environmental change.

Franz Boas, the legendary anthropologist from the turn of the last century, debunked a lot of skull science in his time by proving that the skulls of immigrant children from all parts of the world more closely resemble one another than do their parents'. Rapid dietary shifts can cause major structural changes in skeletons—just ask the average Japanese citizen, who has shot up four and a half inches in height since World War II, or the average American man, who has packed on an extra twenty-five pounds since 1960. The truth is that there exists no coherent history of skull shapes back through time, so to say that a ten-thousand-year-old skull resembles a modern white-guy skull is to compare apples and oranges.

In time, Chatters tried to calm the storm of his unscientifically absurd remarks. He repeatedly said things like this: Kennewick Man "could also pass for my father-in-law, who happens to be Scandinavian."

Then one day he was suddenly insisting, "Nobody's talking about white here."* He insisted that he meant that the skull simply didn't resemble the classic "Mongoloid" features of Asia. He said that Kennewick could have been Polynesian or even ancient Japanese. It turns out that those vague Caucasoid features are also found in the Ainu people of prehistoric Japan, as well as in other non-European peoples.

Don't be confused here. The scientists themselves who fling around words like "Caucasoid" are the very ones who also admit that the "Caucasian" skull is found everywhere. That's right. This Caucasian skull shape is found all over the planet. For example, another ancient skull always brought up alongside Kennewick's is a female skull found in Brazil. Nicknamed Luzia, the skull was analyzed in a report that cited the following locations for resemblance:

---

*His contradictions are maddening. At one point, Chatters said: "I referred to the remains as Caucasoid-like . . . I did not state, nor did I intend to imply, once the skeleton's age became known, that he was a member of a European group." But then he told Elaine Dewar, the author of *Bones: Discovering the First Americans*: "I say you can say European. Who can prove you wrong?"

skulls seen among early Australians, bones found in China's Zhouk-oudien Upper Cave, and a set of African remains known as Taforalt 18. So we've narrowed it down to Australia, China, and Africa.

Another study of an ancient skeleton known as Spirit Cave Man narrowed down his skull-shape origin to: Asian/Pacific, the Zulu of Africa, the Ainu of Japan, the Norse, or the Zalawar of Hungary.

What conclusion can be drawn from finding Caucasian skulls in Asia? Or finding African skulls in Brazil? Or finding Polynesian skulls at the continental divide? Is it that these "groups" traveled a lot, or that skull shapes change radically and quickly over time? It's the latter, of course, and plenty of anthropologists have known that for some time. In the early twentieth century, Harvard anthropologist Earnest Hooten documented the wide variety of skull shapes he found among ancient Native Americans.

As Jonathan Marks explained it to me, Hooten "studied Native American skulls from precontact all the way to the eighteenth century, and he sorted them into cranial racial categories. He called them 'pseudo-Australoid' and 'pseudo-Negroid' and 'pseudo-Mediterranean' because they had those features. He was smart enough not to say, 'Well, I guess these people encountered a stray Australian aborigine on his way to Colorado.' Clearly he recognized that there was considerably more diversity in early Indian skulls than he was used to seeing."

What this suggests is not so much that Africans, Mongoloids, and Europeans were storming the American shores ten thousand years ago but rather that in any one group, at any one time, you will find all sorts of anomalies. The Center for the Study of the First Americans, at Texas A&M University, is a clearinghouse for pro-Caucasian theories of early America. The center publishes a monthly newsletter, "Mammoth Trumpet," in which one can find a set of arguments that inspire a kind of sorrow and pity. The founder, Dr. Robson Bonnichsen (like so many of these academics: the look of a Norse king with a big bushy beard), was commonly quoted stating things like this: "We're getting some hints from people working with genetic data that these earliest populations might have some shared genetic characteristics with latter-day European populations." Maybe he doesn't know that he's the direct heir to King Charlemagne.

What makes the claim all the more paltry is that once you start reading about the European connection to pre-Clovis Man here in America, you can't help but notice that the same essential story is getting told in other, completely separate fields—such as when the first Europeans evolved or when early ape creatures crossed over the line leading to humans. All of them make claims that have the contours of the same fight—the revolutionaries challenging the traditionalists, all of them finding a way to shoehorn Europeans into a story with hints of superiority and beauty.

The current theory about the beginning of mankind—the Out of Africa theory—states that an early prehuman, *Homo erectus*, evolved into *Homo sapiens*, who then left Africa some one hundred thousand years ago and eventually evolved into the modern peoples of the world. But there is a small contingent of rebel theorists—the "multiregionalists"—who hold that it was *Homo erectus* who spread out to various locations where each developed into its own transitional hominid. In Asia: Peking Man. In South Asia: Java Man. And in Europe: Neanderthal Man. Each of these specimens would eventually evolve simultaneously into *Homo sapiens*. According to the rebels, there was some gene mixing at the margins of these separately developing species to keep the general hominid ability to reproduce together. It's a serviceable theory that manages to keep all mankind barely in the same species while creating an intellectual space for racial differences and European uniqueness. It is the "separate but equal" theory of physical anthropology.

As theories go, multiregionalism can be pretty slippery, but then it has to be. New evidence constantly confounds. Not long ago, DNA tests revealed that Neanderthal made no direct genetic contribution to modern man. So multiregionalists now struggle to keep Neanderthal in the picture at all, arguing that there was some sex among the different humans and that the evidence is with us. One of the arguments is that my big nose (as well as those great beaks on Jews and Arabs) is telling evidence of Neanderthal genes. That's the theory of

Dr. Colin Groves, a very dolichocranic man who, it should be no surprise by now, sports a big beard.

There are so many theories in which the key moment of development that "makes us human" somehow occurred in Europe that I have begun to collect them, like baseball cards. Those cave paintings in Lascaux and Altamira, for instance, are often held up as the threshold event revealing "abstract" thought, which made us truly human. My personal favorite, this week, takes us all the way back to the apes. A few years ago, David Begun, a primate specialist in Toronto, announced that he'd found our last common ancestor with the great apes; i.e., the notorious missing link. Where? In Europe. His theory holds that African apes crossed into Europe, picked up those civilizing traits that would eventually lead to humanness, and then slipped back to the dark continent just under the deadline for their Out of Africa journey. Scientists are now finding these apes all over Europe. Just last winter another one was excavated near Barcelona and heralded as further proof of Begun's theory. The researchers remained tight-lipped about what it all meant, but popular outlets found ways to get the point across, such as this sentence in a recent CBS News report: "The researchers sidestepped a controversy raging through the field by not claiming their find moves great-ape evolution—and the emergence of humans—from Africa to Europe."

X. A CAUCASIAN HOMECOMING

The question of just when we became human gets answered in our popular press all the time. Was it when we assembled the first rudimentary tool kit, or when we grunted out the earliest phonemes of complex language? Was it when we made those paintings in Altamira and Lascaux, or when we left off being knuckle-dragging apelike critters and stood up? Standing up has been a particularly fertile field for this kind of musing, with theories ranging from cooling off to intimidating other species to freeing the hands. I'd always heard that we abandoned squatting because we wanted to see over the top of the grass on the African savannahs, allegedly our first habitat. One early 1980s theory was that standing evolved for "phallic display directed at females."*

Last year a British scholar named Jonathan Kingdon argued in his book, *Lowly Origin*, that our standing up probably had a lot to do with getting food and happened in undramatic stages, first by straightening the back while squatting and later by extending the legs—all of this happening in tiny incremental stages over vast swaths of time.

As theories go, that's not nearly as much fun as "seeing over the grass" or "phallic display," but it has the ring of truth to it, a ring that, let's face it, will never endear such an idea to writers of news-weekly cover lines. Which is also why you've never heard of Jonathan Kingdon.

Scientists like to invoke Occam's razor, the principle that the simplest explanation is often the most truthful. These days we have almost the opposite problem: pop thinkers tend to oversimplify in a way meant to attract attention. The first time I ever got a whiff of this was when I was a teenager reading Desmond Morris's book *The Naked Ape*. Morris theorized that the reason human females had big breasts (as opposed to the tiny sagging dugs of other primates) was because we had discovered love. In doing so we switched from copulating doggie style to the more romantic missionary position. But all those eons of looking at the round globes of the female's buttocks from behind had developed into the image stimulus required for the maintenance of erections during intercourse. Therefore, Morris argued, the human male still needed large rounded visual cues and, according to the rules of Darwin, was rewarded with great big hooters.

Even as a kid, I remember thinking, excellent, but really? Morris's simplicity makes monstrous assumptions that just so happen to yield a theory pre-edited for the short punchy demands of modern mass media. A hook, if you will. (Not that it didn't work: thirty years after reading that book, the only detail I can remember is the boob theory.)

*Were this the case, every animal in nature, down to the amoeba, would stand.

Morris's theory has little to do with truth and everything to do with selling books. Perhaps it's time to set aside Occam's razor and pick up Morris's razor, which shuns any theory that might excite a cable-television producer and elevates the plodding theory that makes a kind of dull, honest sense.

Apply Morris's razor to Kennewick Man and here's what you might get:

Chances are that Adovasio and his colleagues are right about the basic assertion of an ancient arrival of *Homo sapiens* to this continent. It easily fits in with what else is known. For instance, the archaeological record in Australia is redundant with evidence that aboriginals arrived there at least fifty thousand years ago. That journey would have required boating some eighty miles, many believe. So it's perfectly conceivable that there were multiple entries to the American continent, with at least one crew, probably Asians like the Ainu, lugging their Haplogroup X gene and following the food (not "exploring") by canoe or on foot across the Berengia bridge, possibly just after the penultimate ice age, circa twenty thousand to thirty thousand years ago, giving them plenty of time to leave some pre-Clovis fossils.

That's one story, a very Kingdon-like theory, all very probable but not a very good cable special or science-magazine cover story. Morris's razor, though, spares us the rest of the theory, according to which the First American is of an ancient tribe whose members just happen to resemble the very scientists making the claim and whose sad end came about after a genocidal campaign against these superior but outnumbered Caucasoids by hordes of Mongoloid stone age peoples. This epic extrapolation is drawn from one single Cascade spear-point—a leap about as likely as a Martian anthropologist staring at an Enfield bullet, a scrap of gray wool, and a dinged canteen, and then successfully imagining the states'-rights debate leading up to the nation's Civil War.

The same Martian anthropologist might also quarrel with the pre-Clovisites' view that the Kennewick battle is a latter-day clash between science and religion—the Indians with their mythic stories of origin and the scientists with their lithics and their scientific dates. Given the scant evidence for either, it's more accurate to see the debate as between two forms of folklore squaring off over control of our continent's creation story. In an editorial last year, the *Seattle Times* captured one side of this fight perfectly. Kennewick, the paper said, had "held onto his secrets for more than nine thousand years and now, finally, scientists will get a chance to be his voice."

Why assume the scientists' narrative in this case is closer to the empirical truth? There have been times in the history of archaeology when one could find more objective, hard factual truth in the local oral narratives than in the scientists' analysis, and this may well be one of those times. Oral legends, we increasingly learn, are often based on real events, and those myths can sometimes be decoded to reveal the nuggets of ancient journalistic truth that originally set them into play.

How do we know that the Vikings made a landing at L'anse Aux Meadows in Newfoundland? Because an obsessed lawyer named Helge Ingstad insisted that the Icelandic sagas, the oral epic poetry of his people, were based on fact. No one disputes that the *Iliad* is based on a real war, Ingstad argued, or that the *Song of Roland* derives from an actual tactical blunder by Charlemagne. This small-town lawyer analyzed the details given in the myths and spent years trying to locate the campsite for "Vinland." In 1961 he found it and overthrew the old European story about who arrived first to this continent.

There are several Indian creation stories about coming out of ice. The Paiute tell one that ends this way:

Ice had formed ahead of them, and it reached all the way to the sky. The people could not cross it. . . . A Raven flew up and struck the ice and cracked it. Coyote said, "These small people can't get across the ice." Another Raven flew up again and cracked the ice again. Coyote said, "Try again, try again." Raven flew up again and broke the ice. The people ran across.

Such accounts are myths, yes, but many Native-American origin accounts involve coming out of ice, which certainly fits into all the theories of America's human origins. So why aren't these stories studied the way Ingstad examined his own sagas? Why is the benefit of the doubt given to the scientists' story? It's quite possible that not a single fact in this new pre-Clovis story is true.

Part of the problem of reading either of these stories is that we no longer have a capacity to appreciate the real power of myth. Most of us are reared to think of myth as an anthology of dead stories of some long-ago culture: Edith Hamilton making bedtime stories out of Greek myths; Richard Wagner making art out of Norse myth; fundamentalist Christians making trouble out of Scripture.

When we read ancient stories or founding epics, we forget that the original audience who heard these accounts did not differentiate between mythic and fact-based storytelling. Nor did these stories have authors, as we conceive of them. Stories arose from the collective culture, accrued a kind of truth over time.

Today we've split storytelling into two modes—fiction and non-fiction. And we've split our reading that way as well. The idea of the lone author writing "truth" has completely vanquished the other side of storytelling—the collectively conjured account. I think we still have these accounts, but we just don't recognize them for what they are. Tiny anxieties show up as urban legends and the like. In the late 1980s, when the queasily mortal idea of organ donation was infiltrating the social mainstream, suddenly one heard an authorless story of a man waking up in a Times Square hotel room after a night of partying to find a stitched wound on his lower back and his kidney missing.

In many ways, the occasional journalistic scandal stems from this tension between the individual as author and the audience as author. The most recent case was *USA Today*'s Jack Kelley. His made-up stories are pure collective desire—stories that we, not just he, wanted to hear. He told the story of the little terrorist boy pointing at the Sears Tower and saying, "This one is mine." Perfect story, finely tuned:

The corruption of innocence. American icon as target. The anxiety that terrorism has no end.

Enduring myth can be based on fact, as in Ingstad's case. But often the collective account needs no factual basis, just a mild apprehension that the world is not quite what it seems. No one has ever found a razor blade in an apple at Halloween, nor has any doctor treated anyone for gerbiling.

The story of the Ancient European One is this kind of story, toggling back and forth between the world of fiction and (possibly) nonfiction, authored by a few curious facts and the collective anxiety of the majority.

Because we no longer read mythological stories, we no longer appreciate their immense power. We find ourselves stunned at how something so many deeply long to be true will simply assemble itself into fact right before our eyes. If the majority profoundly longs to believe that men of Caucasoid extraction toured here sixteen thousand years ago in Savile Row suits, ate gourmet cuisine, and explored the Pacific Northwest with their intact pre-Christianized families until the marauding horde of war-whooping Mongoloid injuns came descending pell-mell from their tribal haunts to drive Cascade points into European hips until they fell, one after another, in the earliest and most pitiful campaign of ethnic cleansing, then that is what science will painstakingly confirm, that is what the high courts will evenhandedly affirm, and that is what in time the majority will happily come to believe.

TOM MUELLER

Your Move

FROM *THE NEW YORKER*

When the IBM supercomputer Deep Blue defeated chess champion Garry Kasparov in 1997, it was heralded as a major turning point in the continuing struggle between man and machine. Adapting Deep Blue's approach to less powerful PCs, programmers are making up for lack of number-crunching ability with artfulness. As Tom Mueller has discovered, the results have been unexpected, with computers developing strategies grand masters have never thought of.

CHRILLY DONNINGER PREFERS TO WATCH FROM A distance when Hydra, his computer chess program, competes, because he is camera-shy, but also because he rarely understands what Hydra is doing, and the uncertainty makes him nervous. During Hydra's match against the world's seventh-ranked player, Michael Adams, in London last June, Donninger sat with three grand masters at the back of a darkened auditorium, watching a video projection of the competition on the wall behind Adams. Most of the time, Donninger, a forty-nine-year-old Austrian, had little to worry about; Hydra won the match five games to none, with one draw. But in the second game, which ended in the draw, the program made an error that briefly gave its human opponent an advantage.

The game was played at a spotlit table on a low podium. Adams sat in the classic chess player's pose—his elbows resting on the table, his chin cupped in his palms—reaching out now and then with his right hand to move a piece on a large wooden chessboard. Across from him was Hydra—a laptop linked by Internet connection to a thirty-two-processor Linux cluster in Abu Dhabi—and Hydra's human operator, who entered Adams's moves into the computer and recorded the program's replies on the board. On the laptop's screen was a virtual chessboard showing the current position in the game, as well as a pane of swiftly scrolling numbers representing a fraction of the thousands of lines of play that Hydra was analyzing, and a row of colored bars that grew or shrank with each move, according to the program's assessment of who was winning—green bars meant an advantage for white, red bars for black.

For much of the match, the bars showed Hydra comfortably in the lead. When Adams made a mistake, they spiked dramatically, but mostly they grew in small increments, recording the tiny advantages that the program was steadily accumulating. Many of these were so subtle that Donninger and the grand masters failed to grasp the logic of Hydra's moves until long after they had been made. But about twenty minutes into the second game, when Hydra advanced its central e-pawn to the fifth rank, there was a small commotion in the group. Yasser Seirawan, an American player formerly ranked in the top ten, who had coached Adams for the match, gave a thumbs-up sign. Christopher Lutz, a German grand master who is Hydra's main chess adviser, groaned. Only Donninger, who programs chess far better than he plays it, was baffled. He turned to Lutz in alarm.

"What was that? What did you see?"

"Now our pawn structure has become inflexible," Lutz replied. "Do we have anything in the program for flexibility?"

"What do you mean by 'flexibility'?"

Lutz frowned. He sensed that Hydra had hemmed itself in, giving Adams the upper hand. Bishop to b7 was the correct move, Lutz believed—the most natural way for Hydra to preserve its attacking chances and its room to maneuver. But explaining his nebulous insights to a lesser player like Donninger was a challenge.

"This position lacks flexibility," he repeated, shaking his head.

"When you can define 'flexibility' in twelve bits, it'll go in Hydra," Donninger told him, twelve bits being the size of the program's data tables.

Adams locked up Hydra's center with his next move and managed, several hours later, to eke out a draw. "Hydra didn't play badly, but 'not bad' isn't good enough against a leading grand master," Donninger said after the game. His program is widely considered to be the world's strongest chess player, human or digital, but it still has room for improvement.

LEAN AND RESTLESS, WITH A scraggly beard and a large Roman nose, Donninger says that he approaches programming less like a scientist than like a craftsman—he compares himself to a *Madonnenschnitzer,* one of the painstaking Baroque and rococo wood-carvers whose Madonna sculptures adorn the churches near Altmelon, the village in northern Austria where he lives and works. He speaks German with a thick Austrian brogue and frequently uses expressions like *"Das ist mir Wurscht!"*—"That's all sausage to me!" For the past two years, he has led the Hydra project, a multinational team of computer and chess experts, which is funded by the Pal Group, a company based in the United Arab Emirates which makes computer systems, desalinization plants, and cyber cafés. Pal's owner, Sheikh Tahnoon bin Zayed al-Nahyan, is a member of the country's royal family and a passionate chess player; he hired Donninger with the goal of creating the world's best chess program. Pal is also using the same kind of hardware that runs Hydra for fingerprint-matching and DNA-analysis applications, which, like computer chess, require high-speed calculations. The program's main hardware resides in an air-conditioned room in Abu Dhabi, and Donninger is frequently unable to access it, because the sheikh and Hydra, playing under the name zor_champ, are on the Internet, taking on all comers.

As a child, Donninger was so attached to puzzles that his mother worried that he was disturbed. At the age of four, he spent months building houses out of four colors of Lego bricks, in which no bricks of the same color ever touched; two decades later, when he was an undergraduate at the University of Vienna, he learned that this was a famous conundrum in topology—the Four-Color Problem. After completing a doctorate in statistics, he worked as a programmer for Siemens, where he earned a reputation as a bug fixer, the computer equivalent of a puzzler. In 1989, he was transferred to the Dutch city of Noordwijk. It was there, during a period of intense loneliness, that Donninger joined a local chess club and started writing his first chess program. "I found my ecological niche," he says.

He had also found the ultimate puzzle. With about 10^{128} possible unique games—vastly more than there are atoms in the known universe—chess is one of mankind's most complex activities. In an average arrangement on the board, white has thirty-five possible moves and black has thirty-five possible replies, yielding twelve hundred and twenty-five potential positions after one full turn. With subsequent moves, each of these positions branches out exponentially in further lines of play—1.5 million positions after the second turn, 1.8 billion after the third—forming a gigantic map of potential games that programmers call the "search tree."

How human beings confront this complexity and seize on a few good moves remains a mystery. Experienced players rely on subconscious faculties known variously as pattern recognition, visualization, and aesthetic sense. All are forms of educated guesswork—aids to making choices when certainty through exhaustive calculation is impossible—and may be summed up in a word: intuition. Even a novice player uses intuition to exclude most moves as pointless, and the more advanced a player becomes the less he needs to calculate. As the eminent Cuban grand master José Raúl Capablanca once told a weaker player, "You figure it out, I know it."

Computers have the advantage of formidable analytical power, but even the fastest machine is quickly overwhelmed by the sheer number of moves that it must assess. (Donninger estimates that Hydra would need 1030 years to "solve" chess, starting from the first move and analyzing all possible sequences of play.) To produce world-class chess of the sort that Hydra played against Michael Adams, programmers must somehow teach their machines intuition.

This turns out to be a highly personal task, which every programmer approaches differently. Stefan Meyer-Kahlen, a thirty-seven-year-old German who wrote the four-time world-champion program Shredder, was inspired by Anatoly Karpov, the Russian player known for his calm, ruthlessly logical play and his masterly defense. Amir Ban and Shay Bushinsky, Israeli programmers who created Junior, another four-time world champion, draw on a large collection of computer chess games to shape their program's style. "We don't use grand-master games for this, because they're too full of errors," says Ban, who made a fortune in the 1990s as an entrepreneur in flash memory. (Bushinsky is a professor of computer science and artificial intelligence, or A.I., at the University of Haifa.) Ban and Bushinsky believe that their method accounts for Junior's "speculative" play—its keen understanding of time and space, and its unrivaled knack for sacrifice—and they gleefully describe how Junior trounced an early version of Hydra two years ago, because Hydra (or, rather, Donninger) had badly misjudged a position. (Ban and Donninger detest one another, and after getting into a shouting match at a tournament in 1997, they no longer speak.)

Hydra is famous for its relentless assault on the enemy king. "It's the Rottweiler of computer chess," Donninger says proudly. "It floats like a butterfly, stings like a hornet." He says that he has tried to endow the program with the slashing, sacrificial style of the former world champion Mikhail Tal. Yet Hydra's fighting spirit is as much Donninger's as Tal's. As a boy, Donninger fought constantly in school, analyzed each of Muhammad Ali's matches, and taught his younger sister an Ali-inspired uppercut to ward off bullies. In his twenties, he fought as a junior welterweight in a top Vienna gym. Occasionally, he pulls on a worn pair of boxing gloves and hammers away at a heavy bag that hangs from a beam on the side of his house.

Hydra, Shredder, Junior, and Fritz—another top program—routinely defeat leading grand masters, each playing with a distinctive personality that reflects not only its inventor's particular approach to chess and programming, but also moves and tactics that seem to arise spontaneously from intricacies of the computer code, which the programmer himself often cannot explain. Over the past decade, these programs, which typically sell for about sixty dollars and run on a PC, have become essential tools for grand masters to analyze past games, test opening lines, and generate new ideas. (Hydra is not commercially available, in part because of its specialized hardware; some programs, including versions of the reigning world champion, Zappa, can be downloaded, free, from the Internet.) In the past several years, these programs have begun to play the kind of elegant, creative chess once thought to be the exclusive province of humans. Computers are allowing people to look more deeply into the game than ever before. They are even helping people to play more like machines.

The first chess automaton was, like Hydra, created as a diversion for royalty. In 1769, the engineer Wolfgang von Kempelen built "the Turk" for the Hapsburg ruler Maria Theresa. A robed and turbaned mannequin seated at a large desk, the Turk toured Europe and America for decades, trouncing all but the best players; according to one story, it beat Napoleon so badly that he swept the pieces from the board in disgust. Though the Turk's mechanical components were impressive—it had elaborate, whirring gears and could nod, roll its eyes, and lean over the board as if in concentration—its human component was decisive: it was secretly operated by a skilled chess player curled up inside the desk.

The first real chess-playing machine was designed in the late 1940s by the British mathematician Alan Turing, who, in 1950, in the paper in which he proposed the famous Turing Test, identified chess as an ideal proving ground for machine intelligence. Since computers were not yet widely available, Turing acted as his own central processing unit, laboriously working out each move on paper. With the advent of computers a few years later, chess became the darling of the A.I. community. The game was enormously complex, had simple rules, and, unlike many objects of scientific research, provided an unambiguous way to measure results: the more a program won, the smarter it was thought to be. In broad terms, the early programs of the 1950s and 1960s worked the way Hydra and its peers do today. They consisted of a search function, which sifted through the tree of possible moves, and an evaluation function, which applied a score to positions that arose along the way, awarding bonuses for good characteristics and penalties for bad. The move leading to the highest-scoring position would be selected.

The first chess programmers attempted to use the same intuitive strategies in search and evaluation that people employed when playing chess. However, their translations of human rules of thumb—control the center, don't move your queen too early—into programming language proved too crude to produce good chess. Worse, the more knowledge the programmers built into the search function, the slower the search became, which limited how deeply the program could see into a position—its "search horizon." The first programs were characterized by nonexistent strategy, embarrassing endgame technique, and a remarkable gift for blunders. In 1956, the MANIAC, a nuclear-weapons computer at Los Alamos, lost to a human opponent, even though the rules had been simplified and it had been spotted a queen. Mikhail Botvinnik, a former world champion, tried to write a program that thought the way he did, but it never won a game in tournament play.

A breakthrough came in the late 1970s, with the advent of "brute force" programming, which traded selectivity for speed. By paring back chess knowledge, emphasizing search algorithms like alpha-beta pruning, and exploiting faster hardware, programmers were able to consider a far broader search tree. Computers began to beat master players in the early eighties, and in 1988 Deep Thought became the first program to defeat a grand master. The brute-force approach culminated in 1997, when Deep Thought's successor, Deep

Blue, a multimillion-dollar IBM supercomputer that could evaluate two hundred million positions per second, won a six-game match against Garry Kasparov, the world champion.

Computers had triumphed at chess not by aping human thought, as most A.I. experts had expected, but by playing like machines. The analogy with flight is instructive: as long as people tried to fly by imitating birds, attaching diaphanous wings to their arms and flapping madly, they were doomed to failure; once they escaped the paradigm of the familiar, however, they were soon flying much faster than birds. Yet something still seemed to be missing. Programmers had made the most of computers' computational superiority, but many experts agreed that humans retained the edge in strategy. After Deep Blue's victory, A.I. researchers lost interest in chess, largely because brute-force methods seemed too crude and mechanical to shed much light on the nature of intelligence. " 'Brute force' was a derogatory term," recalls Jonathan Schaeffer, a computer scientist who is the author of several chess programs and the world-champion checkers program Chinook. "You were considered a heretic if you didn't try to emulate the human brain."

By THE LATE NINETIES, MOST chess programming was done not for mainframes but for much slower microcomputers and, subsequently, for PCs. Even today, the fastest PC programs can analyze only about four million positions per second, a fraction of Deep Blue's capacity. In order to achieve world-class results at these speeds, programmers needed to find ways of searching more selectively and evaluating more precisely. Over the past several years, the most gifted programmers have learned how to distill the more arcane principles of grand-master play into computer language. Some have identified principles that grand masters never imagined.

Donninger reviews Hydra's errors alone or with Christopher Lutz, trying to define each problematic position in twelve bits' worth of questions, which he can incorporate into Hydra's code. "Sometimes it would be nice to have more questions to work with," Donninger says. "But then you'd risk diluting the essential characteristics of the position with less vital information. Twelve bits is good discipline." Because these questions determine how Hydra will play, Donninger won't reveal most of them; a few, however, are more or less the same for all programs. The questions that Hydra uses to assess the value of a passed pawn are: "Is this a passed pawn?" (1 bit); "Is the square in front of it blocked?" (1 bit); "Which row is it on?" (3 bits); "Is it supported by a neighboring pawn?" (1 bit); "Is it supported by a neighboring pawn that is itself a passed pawn?" (1 bit); "Is it an advanced passed pawn?" (1 bit); "Is the enemy king inside the pawn's square?" (1 bit); and "Which phase of the game are we in?" (3 bits).

Once Donninger is satisfied that he has the right questions, he enters them into Hydra's evaluation function as a new heuristic, or chess rule. Hydra, like all other chess software, has hundreds of heuristics woven into its code, where they behave like DNA, shaping the program's personality. The Hydra code for evaluating a passed pawn, written in the computer language Verilog, looks like this:

```
if (iwPA7) begin
wBlocked_A<=!iEmptyA8;
wPassed_A<=1'b1;
wSupported_A<=iwPB6;
wDuo_A<=(iwPB7);
wBack_A<=1'b0;
wMaxRow_A<=3'h6;
wPRow_A<=3'h6;
wLever_A<=1'b0;
end
```

How the heuristics interact, reinforcing and overriding one another, is mysterious; even a slight adjustment to a single rule produces side effects that the programmer cannot predict. After Donninger adds a new rule, he runs a long series of test matches to determine whether it works, pitting the new version of Hydra against other programs. If the new Hydra wins more often than its predecessor, the new heuristic stays. Donninger says that for each new rule he needs about three months to work out unexpected kinks. (By contrast, Ban and Bushinsky sometimes tweak Junior's code right up to the start of a game. "We like to change things, take risks, improvise," Bushinsky says. "Maybe this is not so smart sometimes—it's considered a real no-no in computer science. But that's how we work. Maybe we do have an instinct for the program, sense something about how it feels.")

Today, the best programs blend knowledge and speed so effectively that even the most talented human players have little chance of defeating them. In 2003, Fritz and Junior fought Garry Kasparov to a draw in tense multi-game matches. A round-robin event in October, 2004, pitting Hydra, Fritz, and Junior against three leading grand masters, ended in an 8½–3½ victory for the computers. The machines' superiority was most obvious during the Hydra-Adams match in London. "Adams was simply pushed off the board by a much stronger opponent," says David Levy, an international master who watched the event.

Donninger is no longer interested in man-versus-machine matches. "I see the same pattern in each game," he says. "I call it Chrilly's Law: every ten moves, at the most, in complicated positions, even the strongest player will commit a slight inaccuracy—the second-best move when only the best will do. He doesn't even notice it, but Hydra does. Its evaluation bars start growing, a little taller with every move. By the time the grand master realizes the problem, it's already Game Over." Many chess players and programmers would like to see a match between Hydra and Kasparov, who has officially retired from chess to pursue a career as a politician in Russia but is still considered the ultimate opponent. "The world's greatest-ever human player against the world's greatest-ever computer player—we would all love to see it," Levy says. Donninger is indifferent to the idea. "I'm much more interested in beating Shredder, Fritz, and the other programs," he says. "I learn more from those matches."

* * *

IN FEBRUARY, I WATCHED HYDRA play Shredder in one of the most sophisticated chess games in history, during the fourteenth International Computer Chess Championship. The tournament was held in Paderborn, Germany, in a shabby, fluorescent-lit conference room whose boisterous disarray often suggested a tailgate party more than a competition. Sixteen contestants sat chatting in pairs at small tables laden with computers, chess sets, beer, coffee, and half-eaten hunks of strudel. The programs reflected their authors' whims: one sounded a gong with every move, others displayed photos—of a pet falcon in one case, a scantily clad starlet in another. "They're extensions of our egos," Vincent Diepeveen, the author of Diep, a Dutch program, said.

Donninger and Hydra sat at a table in the middle of the room, the laptop draped with a UAE flag and Donninger in his game-day outfit, which he wore on all five days of the tournament: black jeans, dirty white clogs, and a gray cardigan with deerhorn buttons. Across from him was Shredder and its inventor, Meyer-Kahlen, a round-faced man with a melodious tenor voice, who is the only professional chess programmer not affiliated with a larger organization and is widely admired by his peers. "He does everything himself—the program, the user interface, sales, technical support," Donninger says. "No one knows how he manages to stay at the top."

The game started with a handshake, a custom in matches between grand masters, and continued for about twenty minutes with a chatty congeniality unthinkable in competitive chess. Once a game begins, programmers are not permitted to adjust their programs, but there is no rule against sharing information. Donninger and Meyer-Kahlen turned their screens so that each could see from the scrolling numbers and colored bars what the other's program was thinking, and speculated aloud about their programs' prospects. When Donninger recorded the wrong move on the board, Meyer-Kahlen politely corrected it. However, as the position became complicated, both men grew quiet and stone-faced, their eyes fixed on the screens. Other programmers drifted away from their matches and gathered in a tight circle around the table.

"What a stupid sport!" Donninger snapped, as the programs jockeyed for infinitesimal advantages. "We're completely helpless. It's like riding shotgun in a Formula One race car."

Ninety minutes into the game, most of the pieces were still on the board, arranged in an intricate logjam. Shredder was happy with the position, but so was Hydra; evidently one of the programs was mistaken. Then Shredder attacked Hydra's kingside, with a risky pawn advance that seemed to expose Shredder's own king. "*Scheisse!*" Meyer-Kahlen exclaimed. "What the devil is Shredder doing?"

The situation was critical, but neither programmer knew who was winning. Nor did anyone in the crowd around the table, which included the two grand masters on the Hydra team, Christopher Lutz and Talib Mousa.

"*Unklar,*" Lutz murmured, when I asked him what he thought of the position.

Donninger's face brightened for a moment. "'Unclear' is a grand master's way of saying, 'Who the hell knows?'"

The uncertainty persisted for several more moves. Then, suddenly, it became obvious that Shredder was on the verge of being checkmated. Nevertheless, the program made a queenside pawn push, just as Hydra was cornering its king on the other side of the board.

"Oh, Shredder, what kind of a crap move is that?" Meyer-Kahlen said. Eight moves later, he reached abruptly across the board to shake Donninger's hand, resigning the game. Then he stalked away from the table.

Afterward, while Mousa recounted the match to Sheikh Tahnoon on a cell phone, Lutz and Donninger reviewed the game at the chessboard. "We're trying to understand what happened and why," Donninger said wearily.

IT IS NOW PLAUSIBLE TO argue that computers are playing subtler, more imaginative chess than the humans they have been designed to emulate. "They make a lot of counterintuitive, even absurd-looking, moves that on closer inspection can turn out to be outrageously creative," says John Watson, an international master who has written more than twenty-five books on advanced chess theory and strategy. "By generating countless new ideas, they are expanding the boundaries of chess, enabling top players to study the game more deeply, play more subtly." Viswanathan Anand, a thirty-five-year-old Indian who is currently rated the world's top active player, often uses several chess programs simultaneously when he trains. "I have Shredder, Fritz, Junior, and HIARCS"—another popular program—"running all the time so I can see their various opinions, which are often very different," he says. "When a position catches my fancy, we compare notes." In some cases, computers are rewriting the game's ground rules. "Certain endgames that for centuries were unanimously thought to be draws have actually proved to be clear wins," says John Nunn, a player formerly ranked in the top ten, whose groundbreaking books on endgames were the first to be written using extensive computer analysis. "Computers helped me to discover a number of fundamentally new positions that no one had ever expected, some of which were outstandingly beautiful," he says.

Chess programs are even having a psychological impact. Because computers feel neither nervousness nor fear, they are able to defend apparently hopeless positions, which has encouraged human opponents to persevere even when defeat seems inevitable. The seventeen-year-old American champion Hikaru Nakamura recently told the *Times* that he plays with the courage of a computer. "I'll play some of these really crazy moves that people are not going to be expecting," he said. "The way I play is not like most people. The moves are more computeresque."

Shay Bushinsky and Amir Ban believe that computeresque is better. "Many people don't like it when I say this, but I think Junior plays more creatively than humans," Bushinsky says. Ban goes further, insisting that Junior's creativity is a symptom of its inherent intelligence. "This is an emergent phenomenon of the program, not something I put into it," he says. "It's like Junior is the child and I'm the father. I may think I've taught my child everything, but it's constantly dreaming up things that surprise me."

Such claims to creativity and intelligence are not that far-fetched. In the last few decades, scholars of emergent phenomena have revealed how simple rules at work in termite mounds, traffic jams, quantum mechanics, and the structure of galaxies can give rise to sophisticated and unanticipated behavior, just as the few basic rules of chess yield the endlessly subtle game played by grand masters and chess programs. Scientists have found that the best way to understand these complex systems is often not to theorize but to build a computer model and see how it behaves, in the same way that a chess programmer writes a new version of his program and then watches it play. As the model exhibits patterns and behaviors whose existence its programmer never suspected, it is, in some real sense, creating. And while this may not constitute true machine intelligence, a growing number of cognitive scientists and philosophers see no fundamental distinction between computers and human brains. "Sure, I think the brain is a machine," Mark Greenberg, a philosopher of mind at UCLA, says. "And, likewise, that there's no reason in principle that a computer couldn't think, have beliefs and other mental states, be intelligent. Many mainstream philosophers would agree."

Some, of course, do not. John Searle has tried to disprove the notion of machine intelligence with his "Chinese Room" thought experiment, and Roger Penrose has used Gödel's ideas to the same end. The philosopher Colin McGinn argues that consciousness itself, a crucial part of intelligence, is cognitively closed to us. Yet for those who view intelligence as something essentially and almost mystically human, the analogy with flight may provide a salutary warning. In October 1903, just two months before the Wright brothers completed their first successful powered flight, the astronomer Simon Newcomb published an essay attempting to prove that airplanes would never fly. He got nearly everything right, identifying the intricate ratios of size, weight, and wing surface in birds, which proved that a man-size bird could never get airborne. Yet he overlooked one key detail—the lift effect of an airfoil—and the larger point that an airplane was not a bird. Might those who appear to require a human brain for intelligence be overlooking a broader but no less valid definition of the term?

In any event, such metaphysical matters can be neatly sidestepped with the Turing Test, which merely asks whether a machine can imitate intelligence well enough to fool a human observer. In 2000 and 2001, the leading British grand master Nigel Short played a number of speed-chess games on the Internet, against an anonymous opponent. In most games, this player put himself at a disadvantage with several bizarre opening moves, yet went on to trounce Short, who is among the world's best speed-chess players. Short became convinced that his quirky, brilliant opponent was the reclusive chess genius Bobby Fischer—who else could beat him with such superhuman ease? "I am ninety-nine percent sure that I have been playing against the chess legend," he told the London *Sunday Telegraph*. "It's tremendously exciting." He said that he treasured these games as products of Fischer's rare art. "To me, they are what an undiscovered Mozart symphony would be to a music lover."

In fact, Short's opponent was probably a computer. "It's fairly clear that the phantom Fischer was an experienced chess-program user playing a practical joke," Frederic Friedel, a founder of Chess-Base, a software company that publishes Fritz, Junior, and several other programs, says. "He made the first few absurd moves by hand to throw people off the scent, then unleashed the machine." When Friedel played through several of the games with Fritz, the program's moves were virtually identical to those of Short's mystery opponent. So a computer duped one of the world's top chess players into believing that it was a human. Friedel says that the converse also happens. "Raffael," one of the strongest players at his company's popular chess server Playchess.com, was originally thought to be a powerful computer, but was later observed making all-too-human errors. "Raffael" is now believed by many to be Garry Kasparov.

2007

Editor: GINA KOLATA

LAWRENCE K. ALTMAN

The Man on the Table Was 97, But He Devised the Surgery

FROM *THE NEW YORK TIMES*

When the legendary heart surgeon Michael DeBakey was admitted to the hospital with a heart ailment, doctors—his colleagues— had to decide whether, at his advanced age, he would survive the operation he himself created. Lawrence Altman reports on this great medical pioneer's most unexpected milestone.

IN LATE AFTERNOON LAST DECEMBER 31, DR. MICHAEL E. DeBakey, then 97, was alone at home in Houston in his study preparing a lecture when a sharp pain ripped through his upper chest and between his shoulder blades, then moved into his neck.

Dr. DeBakey, one of the most influential heart surgeons in history, assumed his heart would stop in a few seconds.

"It never occurred to me to call 911 or my physician," Dr. De-Bakey said, adding: "As foolish as it may appear, you are, in a sense, a prisoner of the pain, which was intolerable. You're thinking, What could I do to relieve myself of it? If it becomes intense enough, you're perfectly willing to accept cardiac arrest as a possible way of getting rid of the pain."

But when his heart kept beating, Dr. DeBakey suspected that he was not having a heart attack. As he sat alone, he decided that a ballooning had probably weakened the aorta, the main artery leading from the heart, and that the inner lining of the artery had torn, known as a dissecting aortic aneurysm.

No one in the world was more qualified to make that diagnosis than Dr. DeBakey because, as a younger man, he devised the operation to repair such torn aortas, a condition virtually always fatal. The operation has been performed at least 10,000 times around the world and is among the most demanding for surgeons and patients.

Over the past sixty years, Dr. DeBakey has changed the way heart surgery is performed. He was one of the first to perform coronary bypass operations. He trained generations of surgeons at the Baylor College of Medicine; operated on more than 60,000 patients; and in 1996 was summoned to Moscow by Boris Yeltsin, then the president of Russia, to aid in his quintuple heart bypass operation.

Now Dr. DeBakey is making history in a different way—as a patient. He was released from Methodist Hospital in Houston in September and is back at work. At 98, he is the oldest survivor of his own operation, proving that a healthy man of his age could endure it.

"He's probably right out there at the cutting edge of a whole generation of people in their 90s who are going to survive" after such medical ordeals, one of his doctors, Dr. James L. Pool, said.

But beyond the medical advances, Dr. DeBakey's story is emblematic of the difficulties that often accompany care at the end of life. It is a story of debates over how far to go in treating someone so old, late-night disputes among specialists about what the patient would want, and risky decisions that, while still being argued over, clearly saved Dr. DeBakey's life.

It is also a story of Dr. DeBakey himself, a strong-willed pioneer who at one point was willing to die, concedes he was at times in denial about how sick he was and is now plowing into life with as much zest and verve as ever.

But Dr. DeBakey's rescue almost never happened.

He refused to be admitted to a hospital until late January. As his health deteriorated and he became unresponsive in the hospital in early February, his surgical partner of forty years, Dr. George P. Noon, decided an operation was the only way to save his life. But the hospital's anesthesiologists refused to put Dr. DeBakey to sleep because such an operation had never been performed on someone his age and in his condition. Also, they said Dr. DeBakey had signed a directive that forbade surgery.

As the hospital's ethics committee debated in a late-night emergency meeting on the twelfth floor of Methodist Hospital, Dr. DeBakey's wife, Katrin, barged in to demand that the operation begin immediately.

In the end, the ethics committee approved the operation; an anesthesiology colleague of Dr. DeBakey's, who now works at a different hospital, agreed to put him to sleep; and the seven-hour operation began shortly before midnight on February 9. "It is a miracle," Dr. DeBakey said as he sat eating dinner in a Houston restaurant recently. "I really should not be here."

The costs of Dr. DeBakey's care easily exceeded $1 million. Methodist Hospital and his doctors say they have not charged Dr. DeBakey. His hospitalizations were under pseudonyms to help protect his privacy, which could make collecting insurance difficult. Methodist Hospital declined to say what the costs were or discuss the case further. Dr. DeBakey says he thinks the hospital should not have been secretive about his illness.

Dr. DeBakey's doctors acknowledge that he got an unusually high level of care. But they said that they always tried to abide by a family's wishes and that they would perform the procedure on any patient regardless of age, if the patient's overall health was otherwise good.

Dr. DeBakey agreed to talk, and permitted his doctors to talk, because of a professional relationship of decades with this reporter, who is also a physician, and because he wanted to set the record straight for the public about what happened and explain how a man nearly 100 years old could survive.

AS DR. DEBAKEY LAY ON the couch alone that night, last New Year's Eve, he reasoned that a heart attack was unlikely because periodic checkups had never indicated he was at risk. An aortic dissection was more likely because of the pain, even though there was no hint of that problem in a routine echocardiogram a few weeks earlier.

Mrs. DeBakey and their daughter, Olga, had left for the beach in Galveston, but turned back because of heavy traffic. They arrived home to find Dr. DeBakey lying on the couch. Not wanting to alarm them, he lied and said he had fallen asleep and awakened with a pulled muscle.

"I did not want Katrin to be aware of my self-diagnosis because, in a sense, I would be telling her that I am going to die soon," he said.

An anxious Mrs. DeBakey called two of her husband's colleagues: Dr. Mohammed Attar, his longtime physician, and Dr. Matthias Loebe, who was covering for Dr. Noon. They came to the house quickly and became concerned because Dr. DeBakey had been in excellent health. After listening to him give a more frank account of his pain, they shared his suspicion of an aortic dissection.

Dr. DeBakey and his doctors agreed that for a firm diagnosis he would need a CT scan and other imaging tests, but he delayed them until January 3.

The tests showed that Dr. DeBakey had a type 2 dissecting aortic aneurysm, according to a standard classification system he himself devised years earlier. Rarely did anyone survive that without surgery.

Still, Dr. DeBakey says that he refused admission to Methodist Hospital, in part because he did not want to be confined and he "was hopeful that this was not as bad as I first thought." He feared the operation that he had developed to treat this condition might, at his age, leave him mentally or physically crippled. "I'd rather die," he said.

Over the years, he had performed anatomically perfect operations on some patients who nevertheless died or survived with major complications. "I was trying to avoid all that," he said.

Instead, he gambled on long odds that his damaged aorta would heal on its own. He chose to receive care at home. For more than three weeks, doctors made frequent house calls to make sure his blood pressure was low enough to prevent the aorta from rupturing. Around the clock, nurses monitored his food and drink. Periodically, he went to Methodist Hospital for imaging tests to measure the aneurysm's size.

On January 6, he insisted on giving the lecture he had been preparing on New Year's Eve to the Academy of Medicine, Engineering and Science of Texas, of which he is a founding member. The audience in Houston included Nobel Prize winners and Senator Kay Bailey Hutchison.

Mrs. DeBakey stationed people around the podium to catch her husband if he slumped. Dr. DeBakey looked gray and spoke softly, but finished without incident. Then he listened to another lecture—which, by coincidence, was about the lethal dangers of dissecting aneurysms.

Dr. DeBakey, a master politician, said he could not pass up a chance to chat with the senator. He attended the academy luncheon and then went home.

In providing the extraordinary home care, the doctors were respecting the wishes of Dr. DeBakey and their actions reflected their awe of his power.

"People are very scared of him around here," said Dr. Loebe, the heart surgeon who came to Dr. DeBakey's home on New Year's Eve. "He is the authority. It is very difficult to stand up and tell him what to do."

But as time went on, the doctors could not adequately control Dr. DeBakey's blood pressure. His nutrition was poor. He became short of breath. His kidneys failed. Fluid collected in the pericardial sac covering his heart, suggesting the aneurysm was leaking.

Dr. DeBakey now says that he was in denial. He did not admit to himself that he was getting worse. But on January 23, he yielded and was admitted to the hospital.

Tests showed that the aneurysm was enlarging dangerously; the diameter increased to 6.6 centimeters on January 28, up from 5.2 centimeters on January 3. Dr. Noon said that when he and other doctors showed Dr. DeBakey the scans and recommended surgery, Dr. DeBakey said he would re-evaluate the situation in a few days.

By February 9, with the aneurysm up to 7.5 centimeters and Dr. DeBakey unresponsive and near death, a decision had to be made.

"If we didn't operate on him that day that was it, he was gone for sure," Dr. Noon said.

At that point, Dr. DeBakey was unable to speak for himself. The surgeons gathered and decided they should proceed, despite the dangers. "We were doing what we thought was right," Dr. Noon said, adding that "nothing made him a hopeless candidate for the operation except for being 97." All family members agreed to the operation.

Dr. Bobby R. Alford, one of Dr. DeBakey's physicians and a successor as chancellor of Baylor College of Medicine, said the doctors had qualms. "We could have walked away," he said.

He and Dr. Noon discussed the decision several times. "We recognized the condemnation that could occur," Dr. Alford said. "The whole surgical world would come down on us for doing something stupid, which it might have seemed to people who were not there."

Surgery would be enormously risky and unlikely to offer clearcut results—either a full recovery or death, Dr. Noon and his colleagues told Mrs. DeBakey, Olga, sons from a first marriage, and Dr. DeBakey's sisters, Lois and Selma. The doctors said Dr. DeBakey might develop new ailments and need dialysis and a tracheostomy to help his breathing. They said the family's decision could inflict prolonged suffering for all involved.

Olga and she "prayed a lot," said Mrs. DeBakey, who is from Germany. "We had a healer in Europe who advised us that he will come through it. That helped us."

Then things got more complicated.

AT THAT POINT THE METHODIST Hospital anesthesiologists adamantly refused to accept Dr. DeBakey as a patient. They cited a standard form he had signed directing that he not be resuscitated if his heart stopped and a note in the chart saying he did not want surgery for the aortic dissection and aneurysm. They were concerned about his age and precarious physical condition.

Dr. Alford, the 72-year-old chancellor, said he was stunned by the refusal, an action he had never seen or heard about in his career.

Dr. Noon said none of the anesthesiologists had been involved in Dr. DeBakey's care, yet they made a decision based on grapevine information without reading his medical records. So he insisted that the anesthesiologists state their objections directly to the DeBakey family.

Mrs. DeBakey said the anesthesiologists feared that Dr. DeBakey would die on the operating table and did not want to become known as the doctors who killed him. Dr. Joseph J. Naples, the hospital's chief anesthesiologist, did not return repeated telephone calls to his office for comment.

Around 7 P.M., Mrs. DeBakey called Dr. Salwa A. Shenaq, an anesthesiologist friend who had worked with Dr. DeBakey for twenty-two years at Methodist Hospital and who now works at the nearby Michael E. DeBakey Veterans Affairs Medical Center.

Dr. Shenaq rushed from home. When she arrived, she said, Dr. Naples told her that he and his staff would not administer anesthesia to Dr. DeBakey. She said that a medical staff officer, whom she declined to name, warned her that she could be charged with assault if she touched Dr. DeBakey. The officer also told Dr. Shenaq that she could not give Dr. DeBakey anesthesia because she did not have Methodist Hospital privileges. She made it clear that she did, she said.

Administrators, lawyers, and doctors discussed the situation, in particular the ambiguities of Dr. DeBakey's wishes. Yes, Dr. Pool had written on his chart that Dr. DeBakey said he did not want surgery for a dissection. But Dr. Noon and the family thought the note in the chart no longer applied because Dr. DeBakey's condition had so deteriorated and his only hope was his own procedure.

"They were going back and forth," Dr. Shenaq said. "One time, they told me go ahead. Then, no, we cannot go ahead."

To fulfill its legal responsibilities, Methodist Hospital summoned members of its ethics committee, who arrived in an hour. They met with Dr. DeBakey's doctors in a private dining room a few yards from Dr. DeBakey's room, according to five of his doctors who were present.

Their patient was a man who had always been in command. Now an unresponsive Dr. DeBakey had no control over his own destiny.

The ethics committee representatives wanted to follow Texas law, which, in part, requires assurance that doctors respect patient and family wishes.

Each of Dr. DeBakey's doctors had worked with him for more than twenty years. One, Dr. Pool, said they felt they knew Dr. DeBakey well enough to answer another crucial question from the ethics committee: As his physicians, what did they believe he would choose for himself in such a dire circumstance if he had the ability to make that decision?

Dr. Noon said that Dr. DeBakey had told him it was time for nature to take its course, but also told him that the doctors had "to do what we need to do." Members of Dr. DeBakey's medical team said they interpreted the statements differently. Some thought he meant that they should do watchful waiting, acting only if conditions warranted; others thought it meant he wanted to die.

The question was whether the operation would counter Dr. DeBakey's wishes expressed in his signed "do not resuscitate" order. Some said that everything Dr. DeBakey did was for his family. And the family wanted the operation.

After the committee members had met for an hour, Mrs. DeBakey could stand it no longer. She charged into the room. "My husband's going to die before we even get a chance to do anything—let's get to work," she said she told them.

The discussion ended. The majority ruled in a consensus without a formal vote. No minutes were kept, the doctors said.

"Boy, when that meeting was over, it was single focus—the best operation, the best post-operative care, the best recovery we could give him," Dr. Pool said.

AS THE ETHICS COMMITTEE MEETING ended about 11 P.M. on February 9, the doctors rushed to start Dr. DeBakey's anesthesia.

The operation was to last seven hours. For part of that time, Dr. DeBakey's body was cooled to protect his brain and other organs. His heart was stilled while a heart-lung bypass machine pumped oxygen-rich blood through his body. The surgeons replaced the damaged portion of Dr. DeBakey's aorta with a six- to eight-inch graft made of Dacron, similar to material used in shirts. The graft was the type that Dr. DeBakey devised in the 1950s.

Afterward, Dr. DeBakey was taken to an intensive care unit.

Some doctors were waiting for Dr. DeBakey to die during the operation or soon thereafter, Dr. Noon said. "But he just got better."

As feared, however, his recovery was stormy.

Surgeons had to cut separate holes into the trachea in his neck and stomach to help him breathe and eat. He needed dialysis because of kidney failure. He was on a mechanical ventilator for about six weeks because he was too weak to breathe on his own. He developed infections. His blood pressure often fell too low when aides lifted him to a sitting position. Muscle weakness left him unable to stand.

For a month, Dr. DeBakey was in the windowless intensive care unit, sometimes delirious, sometimes unresponsive, depending in part on his medications. The doctors were concerned that he had suffered severe, permanent brain damage. To allow him to tell day from night and lift his spirits, the hospital converted a private suite into an intensive care unit.

Some help came from unexpected places. On Sunday, April 2, Dr. William W. Lunn, the team's lung specialist, took his oldest daughter, Elizabeth, 8, with him when he made rounds at the hospital and told her that a patient was feeling blue. While waiting, Elizabeth drew a cheery picture of a rainbow, butterflies, trees, and grass and asked her father to give it to the patient. He did.

"You should have seen Dr. DeBakey's eyes brighten," Dr. Lunn said. Dr. DeBakey asked to see Elizabeth, held her hand and thanked her.

"At that point, I knew he was going to be O.K.," Dr. Lunn said.

Dr. DeBakey was discharged on May 16. But on June 2, he was back in the hospital.

"He actually scared us because his blood pressure and heart rate were too high, he was gasping for breath" and he had fluid in his lungs, Dr. Lunn said.

But once the blood pressure was controlled with medicine, Dr. DeBakey began to recover well.

AT TIMES, DR. DEBAKEY SAYS he played possum with the medical team, pretending to be asleep when he was listening to conversations.

On August 21, when Dr. Loebe asked Dr. DeBakey to wake up, and he did not, Dr. Loebe announced that he had found an old roller pump that Dr. DeBakey devised in the 1930s to transfuse blood. Dr. DeBakey immediately opened his eyes. Then he gave the doctors a short lecture about how he had improved it over existing pumps.

As he recovered and Dr. DeBakey learned what had happened, he told his doctors he was happy they had operated on him. The doctors say they were relieved because they had feared he regretted their decision.

"If they hadn't done it, I'd be dead," he said.

The doctors and family had rolled the dice and won.

Dr. DeBakey does not remember signing an order saying not to resuscitate him and now thinks the doctors did the right thing. Doctors, he said, should be able to make decisions in such cases, without committees.

Throughout, Dr. DeBakey's mental recovery was far ahead of his physical response.

When Dr. DeBakey first became aware of his post-operative condition, he said he "felt limp as a rag" and feared he was a quadriplegic. Kenneth Miller and other physical therapists have helped Dr. DeBakey strengthen his withered muscles.

"There were times where he needed a good bit of encouragement to participate," Mr. Miller said. "But once he saw the progress, he was fully committed to what we were doing."

Now he walks increasingly long distances without support. But his main means of locomotion is a motorized scooter. He races it around corridors, sometimes trailed by quick-stepping doctors of all ages.

Dr. DeBakey said he hoped to regain the stamina to resume traveling, though not at his former pace.

Dr. William L. Winters Jr., a cardiologist on Dr. DeBakey's team, said: "I am impressed with what the body and mind can do when they work together. He absolutely has the desire to get back to where he was before. I think he'll come close."

Already, Dr. DeBakey is back working nearly a full day.

"I feel very good," he said Friday. "I'm getting back into the swing of things."

JENNIFER COUZIN-FRANKEL

Truth and Consequences

FROM *SCIENCE*

When a scientist is accused of falsifying data, what happens to that scientist's lab? As Jennifer Couzin-Frankel reports, the lab's post-docs and young researchers can pay as much of a price as the wrongdoer.

IN THOSE FIRST DISORIENTING MONTHS, AS FALL LAST year turned to winter and the sailboats were hauled out of nearby lakes, the graduate students sometimes gathered at the Union Terrace, a popular student hangout. There, they clumped together at one of the brightly colored tables that look north over Lake Mendota, drinking beer and circling endlessly around one agonizing question: What do you do when your professor apparently fakes data, and you are the only ones who know?

Chantal Ly, 32, had already waded through seven years of a Ph.D. program at the University of Wisconsin (UW), Madison. Turning in her mentor, Ly was certain, meant that "something bad was going to happen to the lab." Another of the six students felt that their adviser, geneticist Elizabeth Goodwin, deserved a second chance and wasn't certain the university would provide it. A third was unable for weeks to believe Goodwin had done anything wrong and was so distressed by the possibility that she refused to examine available evidence.

Two days before winter break, as the moral compass of all six swung in the same direction, they shared their concerns with a university administrator. In late May, a UW investigation reported data falsification in Goodwin's past grant applications and raised questions about some of her papers. The case has since been referred to the federal Office of Research Integrity (ORI) in Washington, D.C.

Goodwin, maintaining her innocence, resigned from the university at the end of February. (Through her attorney, Goodwin declined to comment for this story.)

Although the university handled the case by the book, the graduate students caught in the middle have found that for all the talk about honesty's place in science, little good has come to them. Three of the students, who had invested a combined sixteen years in obtaining their Ph.D.s, have quit school. Two others are starting over, one moving to a lab at the University of Colorado, extending the amount of time it will take them to get their doctorates by years. The five graduate students who spoke with *Science* also described discouraging encounters with other faculty members, whom they say sided with Goodwin before all the facts became available.

Fraud investigators acknowledge that outcomes like these are typical. "My feeling is it's never a good career move to become a whistleblower," says Kay Fields, a scientific investigator for ORI, who depends on precisely this occurrence for misconduct cases to come to light. ORI officials estimate that between a third and half of nonclinical misconduct cases—those involving basic scientific research—are brought by postdoctoral fellows or graduate students like those in Goodwin's lab. And the ones who come forward, admits ORI's John Dahlberg, often suffer a "loss of time, loss of prestige, [and a] loss of credibility of your publications."

Indeed, Goodwin's graduate students spent long hours debating how a decision to alert administrators might unravel. Sarah LaMartina, 29, who gravitated to biology after its appeal outshone her childhood plan to become a veterinarian, had already spent six years in graduate school and worried whether all that time and effort would go to waste. "We kept thinking, 'Are we just stupid [to turn Goodwin in]?'" says LaMartina, whose midwestern accent reflects her Wisconsin roots. "Sure, it's the right thing to do, but right for who? . . . Who is going to benefit from this? Nobody."

GOODWIN, IN HER LATE 40S, had come to the University of-Wisconsin in 2000 from Northwestern University in Evanston, Illinois, and was awarded tenure by UW soon after. Landing in Wisconsin was something of a homecoming for her; she had done a postdoc under Judith Kimble, a prominent developmental geneticist in the same department. Goodwin studied sex determination in worms during their early development and has published more than twenty papers on that and other subjects in various prominent journals (including, in 2003, *Science*). Goodwin was also the oldest of a crop of female faculty members hired in recent years by genetics department chair Michael Culbertson. "She was the role model," he says.

In the beginning, the Goodwin lab had a spark. Students recall being swept up in its leader's enthusiasm when, seeking a lab in which to settle, they rotated through for a month during their first year of graduate school. Goodwin pushed her students to believe that compelling scientific results were always possible, boosting their spirits during the low points that invariably strike Ph.D. hopefuls. She held annual Christmas parties at her home west of Madison. Once, she took the entire lab on a horseback-riding trip.

Then, last October, everything changed. One afternoon, in the conference room down the hall from the lab, Ly told Goodwin she was concerned about her progress: The project she'd been working on, Ly felt, wasn't yielding usable results. Despite months of effort, Ly was unable to replicate earlier observations from the lab.

"At that time, she gave me three pages of a grant [application]," Ly recalled recently. The proposal, which was under review at the National Institutes of Health (NIH), sought to broaden a worm genetics project that another student, third-year Garett Padilla, had begun. Goodwin, Ly says, told her that the project, on a new, developmentally important worm gene, was "really promising, but there's so many aspects of it there's no way he can work on everything." Goodwin urged Ly to peruse the pages and see whether the gene might interest her as a new project.

Reading the grant application set off alarm bells for Ly. One figure, she quickly noticed, was represented as unpublished data even though it had appeared in a 2004 paper published by Goodwin's lab.

Ly and Padilla sat back to back at desks in the corridor outside the lab. When she showed him the pages from the grant application, he too was shaken. "There was one experiment that I had just not done," as well as several published and unpublished figures that seemed to have been manipulated, he says. Two images apparently identical to those already published were presented as unpublished and as representing proteins different from the published versions. "I remember being overwhelmed and not being able to deal with it at that moment," says Padilla.

A bearish twenty-five-year-old with a closely cropped beard and wirerimmed glasses, Padilla speaks softly, with deliberation. Bored by bench work, he was considering leaving biology research for law school and had discussed the possibility with Goodwin. She had urged him to "stick it out," he says. "Everybody goes through a phase where they don't want to be here," he recalls Goodwin telling him.

At a loss after seeing the grant application, Padilla consulted two scientists for advice: his fiancée's adviser, a physiology professor at the university, and Scott Kuersten, a former postdoc in Goodwin's lab who had been dating LaMartina for several years and who happened to be in town. Kuersten and Padilla talked for about an hour and together examined the pages of the proposal. Kuersten, now at Ambion, a biotechnology company in Austin, Texas, advised Padilla to ask Goodwin for an explanation, as did the physiologist.

Padilla steeled himself for a confrontation. On Halloween day, he paced nervously outside Goodwin's office, summoning the courage to knock. The conversation did not go well, says Padilla.

In a computer log of events he had begun to keep at Kuersten's urging, which he shared with *Science*, Padilla wrote that Goodwin denied lifting a Western blot image from a published paper and presenting it as unpublished work, although, he added in the log, "She became extremely nervous and repeatedly said, 'I fucked up.'" Padilla also noted: "I left feeling that no issues were resolved." His confusion deepened when Goodwin later that day blamed the problem on a computer file mix-up.

Meanwhile, word was leaking out to others in the lab that something was terribly wrong. Two days later, Padilla called a meeting of all current lab members: six graduate students and the lab technician. To ensure privacy, the group, minus Ly, who had recently had a baby girl, convened in the nearby engineering library. Padilla laid out the grant papers for all to see.

In that meeting, ensconced in the library, the grad students hesitated at the thought of speaking with the administration. "We had no idea what would happen to us, we had no idea what would happen to Betsy, we had no idea how the university would react," says LaMartina, who admits to some distrust of authority and also a belief that people who err deserve a second chance.

Ly felt less charitable toward Goodwin but confesses that at first she considered only her own predicament. In many ways, just reaching graduate school was a triumph for Ly, and she badly wanted that doctorate. In 1981, when Ly was eight years old, her family fled Cambodia for the Chicago suburbs. Around Ly's neck hangs a goldplated French coin, a 20-franc piece her curator father had collected before he was killed in his country's civil war.

In Chicago, Ly's mother worked long hours and put her daughter through Wellesley College in Massachusetts. When Ly moved to Madison, so did her husband, now an anesthesia resident, and her mother, who speaks little English and cannot drive. "Here I am, I've invested so much time in grad school, and this happens. If we let someone know . . ." she says, her voice trailing off.

The students decided that Padilla needed to speak with Goodwin a second time, in hope of extracting a clear account of what went wrong or even a retraction of the grant application. Four days after his first nerve-wracking encounter, Padilla was in Goodwin's office again. This time, the conversation put him at ease. Padilla says Goodwin asked for forgiveness and praised him for, as he wrote in the log, "pushing this issue." She told him that the grant application was unlikely to be funded—an assertion that turned out to be untrue given that NIH approved it—but offered to e-mail her NIH contact citing some of the problems in the application. Goodwin subsequently sent that e-mail, on which Padilla was copied. He left the encounter relieved.

"At that point, I was pretty content to leave it alone," he says. "I felt like we had compromised on a resolution."

ANOTHER STUDENT, HOWEVER, WAS FINDING little peace. Mary Allen, 25 and in her fourth year of graduate school, couldn't shake a sense of torment about what her mentor might have done. A bookworm who squeezed three years of high school into one and entered college at age 15, Allen is guided by unambiguous morals and deep religious convictions, attending a local church regularly and leading a youth group there. She could not fathom that Goodwin had falsified data; at one point, Allen refused even to examine another suspect grant application. But, concerned because Goodwin seemed to have admitted to some wrongdoing, Allen felt she needed to switch labs.

Allen alerted Goodwin that she would likely be moving on. Their mentor then began offering additional explanations for the grant application, say Allen and the others. Goodwin told them that she had mixed up some files and asserted that the files had come to her unlabeled. In a private conversation with Allen, she adamantly denied faking data.

As November wore on, the lab's atmosphere grew ever more stressful and surreal. When Goodwin was present, she chatted with the students about their worm experiments and their families—the same conversations they'd always had.

Yet the strain was taking its toll. LaMartina's appetite declined, and she began losing weight, shedding 15 pounds before the ordeal was over. Padilla called former postdoc Kuersten nearly weekly for advice, and the students talked obsessively with one another. Careful to maintain confidentiality, "the only people we could bounce ideas and solutions off of were each other," says Padilla. The tension even penetrated Goodwin's annual Christmas party. For the first time, several lab members didn't show up.

Deeply worried about how speaking with administrators might impact the more senior students, lab members chose not to alert the university unless the desire to do so was unanimous. Gradually all, including Ly and LaMartina, the most senior among them, agreed that their mentor's denials left them uncomfortable and concerned that she might falsify data in the future. "My biggest worry was what if we didn't turn her in . . . and different grad students got stuck in our position," says Allen.

Two days before exams ended, on December 21, Ly and Padilla met together with Culbertson and showed him the suspect grant pages. Culbertson didn't know what to think at first, he says, but "when somebody comes to me with something like that, I have to investigate."

CULBERTSON QUICKLY REFERRED THE MATTER to two university deans, who launched an informal inquiry to determine whether a more formal investigation was warranted. As is customary, Goodwin remained on staff at the university during this time. She vigorously denied the charges against her, telling Culbertson and the students in a joint meeting that the figures in question were placeholders she had forgotten to swap out. According to Padilla's log of that meeting, Goodwin explained that she "was juggling too many commitments at once" when the proposal was submitted.

Two biology professors ran the informal inquiry, conducting interviews with Goodwin and her students. One of the two, Irwin Goldman, was also a dean, and he became the students' unofficial therapist and news source. At their first meeting in January, Goldman reassured the six that their salaries would continue uninterrupted.

The informal inquiry wrapped up a few weeks later, endorsing a more formal investigation. Three university deans, including Goldman, appointed three faculty scientists to the task.

At about this time, says Goldman, the university grew uneasy about possible fraud not only in the first grant application that the students had seen but also in two others that had garnered funding, from NIH and the U.S. Department of Agriculture. The school canceled all three grants. After a panicky two weeks during which the lab went unfunded, Goldman drew on money from both the college of agricultural and life sciences and the medical school. (Goodwin had a joint appointment at the two.) The students peppered Goldman regularly with questions, seeking advice on whether to talk to a local reporter or how their funding might shake out.

Still, because privacy rules prevented sharing the details, "we felt isolated up on our floor," says Padilla. "There were faculty nearby, but they didn't really know what was going on." Goodwin, meanwhile, all but disappeared from the lab, appearing only once or twice after the investigation began. The students tried to keep up with their projects as they'd always done. They held lab meetings alone before being invited to weekly gatherings with geneticist Philip Anderson's lab.

Most faculty members were aware that an investigation had been launched, and some had heard that Goodwin's students were the informers. That led to disheartening exchanges. A faculty member, asked by one of the students whether they'd done the right thing, told her he didn't know. Rumors reached the students that Goodwin had had "to fake something because her students couldn't produce enough data," says Ly.

In late February, Goodwin resigned. The students say they learned of her departure from a biologist who worked in a neighboring lab. Three months later, the university released its investigation report, which described "evidence of deliberate falsification" in the three applications for the cancelled grants, totaling $1.8 million in federal funds. In the school's report, which university officials shared with *Science*, investigators also raised questions about three published papers, in *Nature Structural and Molecular Biology*, *Developmental Biology*, and *Molecular Cell*.

None has been retracted or corrected so far. "We are considering the implications" of the university report, said Lynne Herndon, president and CEO of Cell Press, which publishes *Molecular Cell*, in a statement. The editor of *Nature Structural and Molecular Biology* said she was awaiting the results of the ORI investigation, and the other authors of the *Developmental Biology* paper are reviewing the relevant data, says the journal's editor in chief, Robb Krumlauf of the Stowers Institute for Medical Research in Kansas City, Missouri.

The university investigators also noted other problems in the Goodwin lab. "It appears from the testimony of her graduate students that Dr. Goodwin's mentoring of her graduate students included behaviors that could be considered scientific misconduct—namely, pressuring students to conceal research results that disagreed with desired outcomes and urging them to over-interpret data that the students themselves considered to be preliminary and weak," they wrote in their report.

Goodwin's lawyer in Madison, Dean Strang, disputes the reliability of the school's report. The investigation was "designed under the applicable UW rules to be an informal screening proceeding," and, because Goodwin resigned, "there was no adjudicative proceeding at the administrative level or elsewhere," Strang wrote in an e-mail message. He added that "there are no problems with the three published papers cited in the report (or any others)." Strang declined to address whether Goodwin pressed students to overinterpret data. "Dr. Goodwin will not respond at all to assertions of students in this forum," he wrote.

Culbertson distributed the investigating committee's report to all department faculty members; it even appeared on Madison's evening news. Still, the rapprochement some of the students had hoped for never materialized. "No one ever came up and said, 'I'm sorry,'" Padilla says.

As the graduate students contemplated their futures this spring, they did have one point in their favor: Ironically enough, the sluggish pace of their projects meant that almost none had co-authored papers with Goodwin. But when several of them sat down with their thesis committees to assess their futures, the prognosis was grim. Only one student of the six, who did not reply to *Science*'s request for an interview, was permitted to continue with her original project. She has moved to another Wisconsin lab and hopes to complete her Ph.D. within about a year, according to the others.

Thesis committees and faculty members told Ly, LaMartina, and fourth-year Jacque Baca, 27, that much of their work from Goodwin's lab was not usable and recommended that they start over with a new doctoral project. The reason wasn't necessarily data fraud, the students say, but rather Goodwin's relentless optimism that some now believe kept them clinging to questionable results. Allen, for example, says she sometimes argued but gave in to Goodwin's suggestions that she stick with molecular data Allen considered of dubious quality or steer clear of performing studies that might guard against bias. Ly, on her third, floundering project, says, "I thought I was doing something wrong experimentally that I couldn't repeat these things."

Despite her setback, Baca has chosen to stay at Wisconsin. "It's kind of hard to say" how much time she'll lose, says Baca, who notes that her thesis committee was supportive in helping her find a new lab.

The other four—Ly, LaMartina, Padilla, and Allen—have scattered. Only Allen plans on finishing her Ph.D. Determined to leave Wisconsin behind, she relocated in late March to the University of Colorado, Boulder, where she hopes to start fresh. Members of her church, her husband, and her parents persuaded her to stay in science, which she adores, but she still wonders about the future. "We unintentionally suffer the consequences" of turning Goodwin in, Allen says, noting that it will now take her eight or nine years in all to finish graduate school. To her husband's disappointment, their plans for having children have been deferred, as Allen always wanted to wait until she had completed her degree.

For Padilla, the experience cemented the pull of the law. In late July, a month after his wedding, he and his wife moved to Minneapolis-St. Paul, Minnesota, not far from where Padilla grew up, because his wife's adviser, the physiologist, had shifted his lab there. Padilla began law school in the city last week.

LaMartina spent two months in a different Wisconsin genetics lab, laboring over a new worm project she'd recently started under Goodwin. That project, however, fell apart in June. She then spent three weeks in Seattle and Alaska with Kuersten. During the trip, LaMartina abandoned her Ph.D. plans, and in July, she left Wisconsin for Texas, joining Kuersten at Ambion as a lab technician.

When Ly learned from her thesis committee that her years in the Goodwin lab had come to naught, she left the program and, as a stopgap, joined a cancer lab as a technician. "I decided that I had put my life on hold long enough," Ly says. She intends to leave science altogether and is considering business school.

For Goldman, the dean who supported the graduate students, the experience was bittersweet. Impressed by the students' professionalism and grace under trying circumstances, he came to believe strongly that science needs individuals like them. And although he admits that it's "horrible" that so many of the students were told to start over, "I don't see us changing our standards in terms of what a Ph.D. means," he says.

Still, Goldman does plan to craft formal policies for students who might encounter this situation in the future. The policies, he says, would guarantee that the university protects students from retribution and that their funding remains secure. He hopes that codifying such safeguards will offer potential whistleblowers peace of mind.

In a building with a lobby graced by a fountain shaped like DNA, the Goodwin lab now sits deserted on the second floor. Incubators, pipettes, and empty plastic shoeboxes that once held worms litter its counters. Ly's original fear months before, that something bad would happen to the lab, had proved more prescient than she had imagined.

2008

Editor: SYLVIA NASAR

JEROME GROOPMAN

What's Normal?

FROM *THE NEW YORKER*

A child exhibits quicksilver changes in behavior, euphoric and gran-
diose one minute, morose the next. A child merely acting like a kid?
Or symptoms of bipolar disorder? Jerome Groopman investigates the
controversy in diagnosing bipolar disorder in the very young.

IN APRIL 2000, STEVEN HYMAN, A PSYCHIATRIST WHO AT
the time was the director of the National Institute of Mental
Health, convened a meeting of nineteen prominent psychiatrists
and psychologists in order to discuss bipolar disorder in children.
The disorder has long been recognized as a serious psychiatric illness
in adults, characterized by recurring episodes of mania and depression. (It is sometimes called manic depression.) People with bipolar
disorder are often unable to hold down jobs; require lifelong treatment with powerful medications, many of which have severe side
effects; and have high suicide rates. The disorder is thought to afflict

between 1 and 4 percent of Americans and tends to run in families, although no genes for it have been identified. At the time of the meeting, few children had been given a diagnosis of the illness, and it was considered to begin, typically, in adolescence or early adulthood.

In the late 1990s, however, there was an increase in awareness of bipolar disorder in children, first in medical journals and then in places like BPParents, a Listserv founded by the mother of an eight-year-old boy who had been diagnosed with the disorder. Hyman himself had been consulted by parents of children who, he told me, were "really suffering and extremely disruptive, having violent outbursts at school and at home, and hard to contain under any circumstances."

Many of the parents told Hyman that they believed their child had bipolar disorder, and they cited a book called *The Bipolar Child: The Definitive and Reassuring Guide to Childhood's Most Misunderstood Disorder*. The book, which was written by Demitri Papolos, a psychiatrist affiliated with the Albert Einstein College of Medicine, in New York City, and his wife, Janice, the author of several how-to manuals, had been published in 1999. (It has sold more than 200,000 copies, and a third edition came out last summer.) "The first parents who visited me came with the Papolos book in hand," Hyman said.

The Papoloses argued that bipolar disorder was often overlooked in children. In 1998, according to *The Bipolar Child*, nearly four million children were given Ritalin or other stimulants for hyperactivity; of that number, the Papoloses contended, more than a million would eventually receive a bipolar diagnosis. They also cited researchers' estimates that anywhere from a third to half of the 3.4 million children thought to suffer from depression were actually experiencing the early onset of bipolar disorder. The book detailed the negative effects of bipolar disorder on patients (disruptive behavior, drug abuse, suicide attempts) but also prominently featured what might be described as its paradoxical benefits:

This illness is as old as humankind, and has probably been conserved in the human genome because it confers great energy and originality of thought. People who have had it have literally changed the course of human history: Manic-depression has afflicted (and probably fueled the brilliance of) people like Isaac Newton, Abraham Lincoln, Winston Churchill, Theodore Roosevelt, Johann Goethe, Honoré de Balzac, George Frederic Handel, Ludwig van Beethoven, Robert Schumann, Leo Tolstoy, Charles Dickens, Virginia Woolf, Ernest Hemingway, Robert Lowell, and Anne Sexton.

(These claims are similar to those made about other serious psychiatric disorders, particularly depression.) The Papoloses' research was based on responses to questionnaires that they distributed through BPParents, whose several hundred members are parents who suspect that their children have the disorder. "These children seem to burst into life and are on a different time schedule from the rest of the world right from the beginning," the Papoloses wrote. "Many are extremely precocious and bright—doing everything early and with gusto. They seem like magical children, their creativity can be astounding, and the parents speak about them with real respect, and sometimes even awe." The book included some parents' observations:

She was always ahead of her time. She started talking at eight months with the words "kitty cat." She walked at nine months and was speaking in complete sentences by a year. She was writing small novels in the second grade. She acted and danced and sang way beyond her years.

At eighteen months he climbed out of the baby bed in the middle of the night, opened the fridge, got out three dozen eggs (it was Easter time), and proceeded to sit in his booster chair and crack three dozen eggs onto our hardwood floors. (He wanted to bake a real cake—he didn't like the toy mixing bowl I had given him to play with.) After the insurance company quit laughing they did pay to refinish our floors.

During the meeting at the NIMH, the psychiatrists and psychologists argued about whether bipolar disorder existed in children, and, if it did, how it could be distinguished from other syndromes affecting mood and behavior, such as attention deficit hyperactivity disorder (ADHD) and autism. One psychiatrist, Barbara Geller, a professor at Washington University in St. Louis, had published articles about children whose moods often fluctuated rapidly. In the course of a single day, the children were extremely sad, even suicidal, and then, suddenly, they became elated and "grandiose"—a term that psychiatrists use to mean an inflated sense of one's abilities. Geller believed that some of these children who matched several specific and narrow criteria had bipolar disorder. Joseph Biederman, a child psychiatrist at Massachusetts General Hospital, in Boston, who also attended the meeting, had treated children suffering from extreme symptoms of irritability and aggressive behavior and, often with a colleague, Janet Wozniak, had published several articles in medical journals asserting that these children met the criteria for bipolar disorder described in the *Diagnostic and Statistical Manual of Mental Disorders (DSM-IV)*, the reference book for psychiatric illnesses. Hyman encouraged the group to arrive at a consensus, in part to create a uniform set of criteria that could be used to enroll children in studies of the disorder.

In August 2001, the results of the meeting were published in the *Journal of the American Academy of Child and Adolescent Psychiatry*, and it was concluded that "bipolar disorder exists and can be diagnosed in prepubertal children," though the article went on to say that not all children who appeared to have the disorder satisfied the *DSM* criteria. The vagueness of the definition offered few guidelines for practical diagnosis.

Meanwhile, articles inspired by the Papaloses' book had begun appearing in newspapers and magazines, promoting the idea that there was a new diagnosis for troubled children. In August 2002, *Time* published a cover story titled "Young and Bipolar," with the tagline "Once Called Manic Depression, the Disorder Afflicted Adults. Now It's Striking Kids. Why?" The article featured a list of behaviors—adapted from the Papaloses' book—that was intended to help parents "recognize some warning signs" of the disorder. Among those were "poor handwriting," "complains of being bored," "is very intuitive or very creative," "excessively distressed when separated from family," "has difficulty arising in the A.M.," "elated or silly, giddy mood states," "curses viciously in anger," and "intolerant of delays." The magazine also published a sidebar listing prominent writers and musicians who may have suffered from bipolar disorder, including Lord Byron, Edgar Allan Poe, and Kurt Cobain. Although the article cited external factors such as stress and drug use, it also noted that the disorder is "hugely familial," as one doctor put it. (One mother, who was afflicted with bipolar disorder, claimed that she knew before her son was born that he would be bipolar, because he was restless even in the womb.)

Not long after the article came out, a research team at Massachusetts General Hospital, led by Biederman and Wozniak, began an eight-week comparative study of the antipsychotic drugs olanzipine (marketed under the name Zyprexa) and risperidone (Risperdal) for thirty-one children between the ages of four and six who had been given a diagnosis of bipolar disorder based on *DSM* criteria. During the trial, the children gained an average of six pounds and experienced sharp increases in prolactin, a pituitary hormone, which, when elevated, might interfere with sexual development. But their symptoms of severe irritability and aggression were markedly muted by the treatment, and the researchers, while noting the adverse effects, concluded that the drugs could be beneficial to bipolar children.

There are few reliable statistics on the incidence of pediatric bipolar disorder, but according to a national study of community-hospital discharge records, led by Brady Case, a research assistant professor of psychiatry at New York University, and Anthony Russo, a child psychiatry fellow at Bradley Hospital, in Providence, the percentage of mentally ill children under eighteen who have been given a diagnosis of the disorder increased more than fourfold between 1990 and 2000. Many doctors fear that the media, in drawing attention to bipolar disorder, may have exaggerated its prevalence in children and pre-sented a misleading picture of the disorder. The situation has some similarities to the overdiagnosis of attention deficit disorder in the first half of the 1990s, during which the prescription of stimulants such as Ritalin tripled for children between the ages of two and four, according to a study published in February 2000, in the *Journal of the American Medical Association*. Some children do, of course, suffer from bipolar disorder, but it is important to recognize that the con-sequences of its treatment can be dire, particularly when parents are unaware of or ignore the dangerous side effects of the medications.

In December 2006, a four-year-old girl in Massachusetts, who had received a bipolar diagnosis at the age of two and a half, died from an apparent overdose of Clonidine, a blood-pressure medicine used to sedate hyperactive children. She was also taking Seroquel, an antipsychotic, and Depakote, an antiseizure medication that helps regulate mood. (Her parents have been charged with murder and have pleaded not guilty.)

"The diagnosis has spread too broadly, so that powerful drugs are prescribed too widely," Hyman told me. "We are going to have hell to pay in terms of side effects."

ONE OF THE EARLIEST ACCOUNTS of bipolar disorder comes from Aretaeus the Cappadocian, a Greek physician who is believed to have practiced in Alexandria and Rome in the second century A.D. He wrote of the afflicted, "They are prone to change their mind readily; to become base, mean-spirited, illiberal, and in a little time, perhaps, simple, extravagant, munificent, not from any virtue of the soul, but from the changeableness of the disease. But if the illness becomes more urgent, hatred, avoidance of the haunts of men, vain lamentations; they complain of life, and desire to die." However, the disorder was not clearly recognized for centuries, and it wasn't until January 1854, at a meeting of the French Imperial Academy of Medi-cine, in Paris, that a physician named Jules Baillarger cited a mental illness that involved recurring oscillations between mania and depression: Baillarger described it as *folie à double forme* (dual-form insanity). The following month, another French doctor, Jean-Pierre Falret, described a similar illness to the academy, calling it *folie circulaire* (circular insanity). The term "manic-depressive psychosis" was introduced in 1896 by Emil Kraepelin, a German psychiatrist, who observed that periods of acute mania and depression were usually separated by longer intervals during which the patient was able to function normally.

Doctors made little progress in treating the disorder until after the Second World War, when John Cade, an Australian psychiatrist working at a veterans' hospital, set out to test the hypothesis that mania was related to a toxic buildup of urea in the bloodstream. By chance, he discovered that the lithium urate he injected into guinea pigs had a calming effect. After testing lithium carbonate on himself, he began administering it to his manic patients. It became the first successful drug therapy for a psychiatric disorder. (Lithium remained the only treatment for bipolar disorder for decades, and is still the most prevalent, but in recent years anticonvulsants and some antipsychotics have also proved effective.) In 1980, the term "bipolar disorder" replaced "manic-depressive disorder" as a diagnostic term in the *DSM*, but it was applied only to teenagers and adults.

"Until about ten years ago, it was considered quackery to talk about bipolar disorder in children," Barbara Geller told me. "The overwhelming number of adult and child psychiatrists believed that this was just a hyperactive child." Geller first encountered a child she believed exhibited the classic symptoms of bipolar disorder in the early '90s, a thirteen-year-old girl from a white middle-class family who was in the juvenile-correction system in the southern United States. The girl was euphoric despite her incarceration. "She seemed elated, grandiose, and infectiously funny, in spite of being in reform school," Geller recalled. Geller wondered whether the girl might be experiencing a manic episode, similar to those seen in adults with bipolar disorder. She began to interview other school-age and young adolescent children, seeking similar cases. One eleven-year-old girl harbored romantic fantasies about her teacher that led her to routinely disrupt class. She was also "delightfully euphoric" in an interview session with Geller, but as the questioning progressed she said that she had a loaded gun hidden at home, and had prepared a suicide note. Her parents searched their home, and found both the gun and the note. Geller was struck by the young girl's simultaneous grandiosity and depression; the two states are hallmarks of adult bipolar disorder, but they are rarely seen in such quick succession.

Geller found that the manner in which symptoms appeared in children with bipolar disorder was significantly different from that of most adults who had the illness. The episodes of mania and depression in most adults tend to subside after a few weeks or several months; children's episodes generally last longer, and cycle on a daily basis through a more extreme set of moods. "We have these kids who look so sad it hurts to watch them. And a moment later it looks like they've had a snort of coke," Geller said. "For four hours, they will be high: they are giggling, they are laughing, they are hypersexual, they want to touch the teacher, they want to undress in church, they talk too much, they sleep too little, and they think they are in charge of things. Then they switch. In the same day, they can suddenly become suicidal and depressed."

In 1995, with a grant from the NIMH, Geller began a longitudinal study of three groups of children: those she had diagnosed as having bipolar disorder using more precise categorical criteria than those specified in the *DSM*; those with attention deficit hyperactivity disorder; and a control group of children who had no known behavioral disorders. There were about ninety subjects in each group, and the average age was ten. Based on interviews with their parents and close relatives, Geller and her colleagues found that adult bipolar disorder was relatively common in the family members of the children who suffered from the disorder but not in those who had ADHD, or those in the control group. Geller concluded that there is a strong genetic basis for bipolar disorder in children, and that, among those diagnosed as having the disorder, more than 80 percent might also have ADHD.

Experts now agree that bipolar disorder can occur in children, but there is disagreement about which symptoms clearly indicate a diagnosis. Geller maintains that inappropriate euphoria and grandiose behavior must accompany symptoms of irritability or depression. Biederman and Wozniak contend that extreme irritability, including aggression, should compel a clinician to consider a diagnosis of pediatric bipolar disorder, in keeping with *DSM* criteria. However, Ellen Leibenluft, who heads the pediatric bipolar-disorder research program at the NIMH, told me that there is no certain way to classify even severe irritability as normal versus aberrant, particularly as children develop. Geller uses the analogy of sore throats: "Strep infection causes sore throat, but only 5 percent of all sore throats are due to strep, and 95 percent are due to viruses. Irritability is akin to the symptom of a sore throat: children with bipolar disorder are extremely irritable, but they comprise only a small subset of all irritable children."

Despite these differences, most researchers use the *DSM* criteria as a guideline. Demitri Papolos, however, argues against applying these categorical criteria, saying that their vagueness can cause confusion. "The diagnostic category in and of itself doesn't really capture the condition," he said. He prefers to make a diagnosis based on whether a patient's behavior matches the "core phenotype" he has developed, which includes mania and depression, among several other symptoms. "Once you see what this"—pediatric bipolar disorder—"looks like, you can't mistake it," he told me. "They call it the View. If you have the View, you get it. It's not apocalyptic, it's a very clear picture." Papolos, who is not a child psychiatrist, said that he has had children referred to him from all over the country, as many as two a week in the past seven years. He could not immediately recall any child in this group who did not have a bipolar diagnosis, because, he said, "the people who come to see me have read the book."

The need to establish diagnostic criteria is particularly urgent because many of the drugs given to bipolar children are relatively new and have not been tested extensively, especially in children. Depakote, the most common brand name for valproate, is an antiseizure medication for adults and children over the age of ten, which is also used to treat acute mania in adults; it can cause obesity and diabetes and has been associated with polycystic ovarian disease. The antipsychotic drug Risperdal can result in involuntary distorted movements, or "tardive dyskinesia." Lithium can cause decreased thyroid function and kidney failure. "Most important, we don't understand their long-term effects on the developing brain," Geller said. Failing to correctly diagnose pediatric bipolar disorder has its own dangers, since treating a bipolar patient with a selective serotonin reuptake inhibitor like Paxil or Zoloft, as if he were simply depressed, or with a stimulant like Ritalin, as if he had ADHD, might worsen his symptoms. Like other serious psychiatric illnesses, bipolar disorder is diagnosed largely by observing the patient's behavior. There is no blood test, or other clinical diagnostic tool, for the disorder; although brain scans have been performed on children who have been given the diagnosis, none have shown a definitive pattern.

Some books and articles on bipolar disorder in children and adolescents have suggested that a positive response to a drug like Risperdal, which can be effective in adults with manic bipolar disorder, indicates that the child is bipolar. In fact, the drugs typically given to bipolar children are what doctors call "nonspecific," which means that their apparent efficacy is not diagnostic of the syndrome. "All the medicines that work in bipolar cases also work in kids who are just aggressive," Geller said. "Children with mental retardation who acted aggressively were treated with drugs like lithium, and it helped to mute their behavior. But it also made them very thirsty, so they started drinking from toilet bowls and engaging in other kinds of unsuitable behavior. The contention that treatment with these drugs 'makes' the diagnosis is frightening—and completely untrue."

In January 2007, the American Academy of Child and Adolescent Psychiatry published a paper to guide clinicians in their assessment and treatment of children and adolescents with bipolar disorder.

The paper cited a survey of members of the Illinois-based Child and Adolescent Bipolar Foundation, in which 24 percent of the children from 854 families who had been given a diagnosis of bipolar disorder were between the ages of zero and eight. (A more recent survey conducted by the foundation puts the number at 15 percent.) "The validity of diagnosing bipolar disorder in preschool children has not been established," the academy's paper noted. "Until the validity of the diagnosis is established in preschoolers, caution should be taken before making the diagnosis in anyone younger than age six. The evidence is not yet sufficient to conclude that most presentations of juvenile mania are continuous with the classic adult disorder." Biederman and Wozniak have given the diagnosis to preschool children and have included them in drug trials. But other experts, Geller and Leibenluft among them, contend that bipolar disorder cannot yet be accurately diagnosed in a child younger than six, because there is currently no consensus on what constitutes aberrant behavior at that age. In addition, they say, symptoms of manic behavior must be elicited through an interview not only with the parents but also with the children themselves; those younger than six may lack the language to describe what they are experiencing.

IN THE EARLY '90S, IN an effort to insure that children were receiving the correct diagnosis, Geller established a second-opinion clinic for bipolar disorder at Washington University. "Following the publication of the Papoloses' book, we began to have a greater influx of people into the clinic," she said. The positive effect of the book, she added, was that "parents realized it was OK to take their kids to a child psychiatrist." At the same time, the book could lead to false diagnoses. Geller went on, "In the clinic, the first question we have learned to ask of parents is 'Have you read the Papoloses' book?' And 'What in the book resembles your child?' And we will get answers like 'My child is irritable and he likes sweets.'" Geller's team developed stringent criteria to characterize mania as abnormal elation and grandiosity—such as inappropriate bouts of extreme giddiness, or hyperbolic statements of one's importance or ability—so that irritability alone was not adequate to establish a diagnosis of bipolar disorder. Many parents, she said, cling to a bipolar diagnosis when, in fact, the child is suffering from an autistic developmental disorder: "Wouldn't you rather have your child grow up to be Ted Turner," who has bipolar disorder, "than Rain Man?"

April Prewitt, a child psychologist who trained at Harvard and practices in Lexington, Massachusetts, also spends a good deal of time "undiagnosing" children who have been told they are bipolar. In the past three years, Prewitt says, she has seen thirty children and adolescents diagnosed as having bipolar disorder. In her opinion, only two had the malady. "It has become a diagnosis *du jour*, as ADHD was five years ago," Prewitt told me. "Not only is the diagnosis being made incorrectly but it's being made in younger and younger children." She said that parents routinely arrive at her office with the Papolos book, and with lists of behaviors like the one featured in *Time*. "Each one of these could be behaviors due to something completely different," she said. "I could score twenty on this list on a bad day."

Prewitt recalled a seven-and-a-half-year-old boy she saw, who lived in an affluent Boston suburb. Max (a pseudonym) had trouble concentrating and was refusing to go to school. His pediatrician had diagnosed bipolar disorder and begun treating him with Risperdal and Seroquel. "It turned out that the diagnosis was 'a divorce situation,'" Prewitt said. Max's parents had separated and were undergoing bitter divorce negotiations. "Max had put on twenty pounds because of the medication, while he was being shuttled back and forth, one week with mom and one week with dad." Prewitt believed that the parents' feuding was causing Max to oscillate between being sullen and withdrawn and aggressive and hyperactive. She recommended that Max be evaluated by a neuropsychologist, who found that he had only some minor attention deficits. During the following six months, his parents went into mediation in an effort to settle their divorce more amicably, and Max was weaned off his medications.

Prewitt maintains that it may not be possible to diagnose bipolar disorder with certainty in a preadolescent child. "After all these years, I am not sure of the diagnosis of bipolar disorder until a child is well into adolescence," she told me. "I've never seen a seven- or eight-year-old that I would be comfortable definitively diagnosing with bipolar disorder. The changes that children undergo, both in the biology of their development and in the need to adapt to changes in environment at home and at school—interactions with parents, siblings, and other children—all can trigger behaviors with rapid and wild swings of mood."

PHILLIP BLUMBERG, A PSYCHOTHERAPIST IN Manhattan, told me, "Psychological diagnosis is, in essence, a story. If you have a mood disorder, there is the fear, the shame, and the confusion—the stigma—associated with it, so you want to grab on to the most concrete and clear story you can. There is something about the clarity of bipolar disease, particularly its biological basis, which is incredibly soothing and seductive."

Blumberg, who for two years was a vice president at ABC Motion Pictures, believes that advertising by pharmaceutical companies has influenced the public's view of bipolar disorder. (Eli Lilly, in particular, has come under fire for its marketing practices. The drug company is currently the subject of lawsuits that claim that the company attempted to hide Zyprexa's side effects, and promoted the drug for off-label uses. Lilly has denied the accusations.) Blumberg described recent ads, for drugs like Zyprexa, that include a list of symptoms characteristic of the disorder. "But, of course, we all have these symptoms," he said. "Sometimes we're irritable. Sometimes we're excited and elated, and we don't know why. With every form of advertising, the first goal is to make people feel insecure. Usually, they are made to feel insecure about their smell or their looks. Now we are beginning to see this in psychiatric advertising. The advertisements make frenetic, driven parents feel insecure about the behavior of their children."

Blumberg noted that he had seen instances of the disorder in some children, and that it was a real and serious diagnosis. But he also cited the mounting pressure on children, particularly in the middle and upper classes, to succeed, first at private or selective public schools, and then at exclusive colleges and universities. "These kids become very well turned-out products," he said. "They live to have résumés. They don't have résumés because they live." Parents may fear that children who behave in an eccentric way are at a disadvantage, and in turn pressure the pediatrician or the psychiatrist to come up with a diagnosis and offer a treatment. "Then an industry grows up around it. This, then, enters as truth in the popular imagination."

The debate over pediatric bipolar disorder will likely extend to the next edition of the *Diagnostic and Statistical Manual of Mental Disorders*. "*DSM* always has an out in its definitions, a category called NOS—'not otherwise specified,'" Steven Hyman said. "The problem with describing a kid who is up-and-down and irritable and sullen and wild and then grandiose is that he could indeed be rapidly cycling between mania and depression, but it could be an awful lot of other things, too. Bipolar disorder in children represents the intersection of two great extremes of ignorance: how to best treat bipolar disorder and how to treat children for anything. It's really important that we define the kids with bipolar disorder and treat them, but it's also important that we not begin to diagnose kids with excess exuberance or moodiness as having the disease. We have to realize that we are risking treating children who could turn into obese diabetics with involuntary movements. There is something very real about the kids with devastating and disruptive symptoms, but the question is still the boundaries. You can do more harm than good if you treat the wrong kid."

AMY HARMON

Facing Life with a Lethal Gene

FROM *THE NEW YORK TIMES*

> *Now that genetic testing is becoming more common, people at risk*
> *for hereditary disease are struggling with whether to find out their*
> *genetic fates. Amy Harmon follows one young woman whose test*
> *results have changed her life.*

THE TEST, THE COUNSELOR SAID, HAD COME BACK positive.

Katharine Moser inhaled sharply. She thought she was as ready as anyone could be to face her genetic destiny. She had attended a genetic counseling session and visited a psychiatrist, as required by the clinic. She had undergone the recommended neurological exam. And yet, she realized in that moment, she had never expected to hear those words.

"What do I do now?" Ms. Moser asked.

"What do you want to do?" the counselor replied.

"Cry," she said quietly.

Her best friend, Colleen Elio, seated next to her, had already begun.

Ms. Moser was twenty-three. It had taken her months to convince the clinic at New York-Presbyterian Hospital/Columbia University Medical Center in Manhattan that she wanted, at such a young age, to find out whether she carried the gene for Huntington's disease.

Huntington's, the incurable brain disorder that possessed her grandfather's body and ravaged his mind for three decades, typically strikes in middle age. But most young adults who know the disease runs in their family have avoided the DNA test that can tell whether they will get it, preferring the torture—and hope—of not knowing.

Ms. Moser is part of a vanguard of people at risk for Huntington's who are choosing to learn early what their future holds. Facing their genetic heritage, they say, will help them decide how to live their lives.

Yet even as a raft of new DNA tests are revealing predispositions to all kinds of conditions, including breast cancer, depression, and dementia, little is known about what it is like to live with such knowledge.

"What runs in your own family, and would you want to know?" said Nancy Wexler, a neuropsychologist at Columbia and the president of the Hereditary Disease Foundation, which has pioneered Huntington's research. "Soon everyone is going to have an option like this. You make the decision to test, you have to live with the consequences."

On that drizzly spring morning two years ago, Ms. Moser was feeling her way, with perhaps the most definitive and disturbing verdict genetic testing has to offer. Anyone who carries the gene will inevitably develop Huntington's.

She fought her tears. She tried for humor.

Don't let yourself get too thin, said the clinic's social worker. Not a problem, Ms. Moser responded, gesturing to her curvy frame. No more than two drinks at a time. Perhaps, Ms. Moser suggested to Ms. Elio, she meant one in each hand.

Then came anger.

"Why me?" she remembers thinking, in a refrain she found hard to shake in the coming months. "I'm the good one. It's not like I'm sick because I have emphysema from smoking or I did something dangerous."

The gene that will kill Ms. Moser sits on the short arm of everyone's fourth chromosome, where the letters of the genetic alphabet normally repeat C-A-G as many as thirty-five times in a row. In people who develop Huntington's, however, there are more than thirty-five repeats.

No one quite knows why this DNA hiccup causes cell death in the brain, leading Huntington's patients to jerk and twitch uncontrollably and rendering them progressively unable to walk, talk, think, and swallow. But the greater the number of repeats, the earlier symptoms tend to appear and the faster they progress.

Ms. Moser's "CAG number" was forty-five, the counselor said. She had more repeats than her grandfather, whose first symptoms— loss of short-term memory, mood swings, and a constant ticking noise he made with his mouth—surfaced when he turned fifty. But it was another year before Ms. Moser would realize that she could have less than twelve years until she showed symptoms.

Immediately after getting her results, Ms. Moser was too busy making plans.

"I'm going to become super-strong and super-balanced," she vowed over lunch with Ms. Elio, her straight brown hair pulled into a determined bun. "So when I start to lose it I'll be a little closer to normal."

In the tumultuous months that followed, Ms. Moser often found herself unable to remember what normal had once been. She forced herself to renounce the crush she had long nursed on a certain firefighter, sure that marriage was no longer an option for her. She threw herself into fundraising in the hopes that someone would find a cure. Sometimes, she raged.

She never, she said, regretted being tested. But at night, crying herself to sleep in the dark of her lavender bedroom, she would go over and over it. She was the same, but she was also different. And there was nothing she could do.

Lesson in Stigma

Ms. Moser grew up in Connecticut, part of a large Irish Catholic family. Like many families affected by Huntington's, Ms. Moser's regarded the disease as a curse, not to be mentioned even as it dominated their lives in the form of her grandfather's writhing body and unpredictable rages.

Once, staying in Ms. Moser's room on a visit, he broke her trundle bed with his violent, involuntary jerking. Another time, he came into the kitchen naked, his underpants on his head. When the children giggled, Ms. Moser's mother defended her father: "If you don't like it, get out of my house and go."

But no one explained what had happened to their grandfather, Thomas Dowd, a former New York City police officer who once had dreams of retiring to Florida.

In 1990, Mr. Dowd's older brother, living in a veteran's hospital in an advanced stage of the disease, was strangled in his own restraints. But a year or so later, when Ms. Moser wanted to do her sixth-grade science project on Huntington's, her mother recoiled.

"Why," she demanded, "would you want to do it on this disease that is killing your grandfather?"

Ms. Moser was left to confirm for herself, through library books and a CD-ROM encyclopedia, that she and her brothers, her mother, her aunts, an uncle, and cousins could all face the same fate.

Any child who has a parent with Huntington's has a 50 percent chance of having inherited the gene that causes it, Ms. Moser learned.

Her mother, who asked not to be identified by name for fear of discrimination, had not always been so guarded. At one point, she drove around with a "Cure HD" sign in the window of her van. She told people that her father had "Woody Guthrie's disease," invoking the folk icon who died of Huntington's in 1967.

But her efforts to raise awareness soon foundered. Huntington's is a rare genetic disease, affecting about 30,000 people in the United States, with about 250,000 more at risk. Few people know what it is. Strangers assumed her father's unsteady walk, a frequent early symptom, meant he was drunk.

"Nobody has compassion," Ms. Moser's mother concluded. "People look at you like you're strange, and 'What's wrong with you?'"

Shortly after a simple DNA test became available for Huntington's in 1993, one of Ms. Moser's aunts tested positive. Another, driven to find out if her own medical problems were related to Huntington's, tested negative. But when Ms. Moser announced as a teenager that she wanted to get tested one day, her mother insisted that she should not. If her daughter carried the gene, that meant she did, too. And she did not want to know.

"You don't want to know stuff like that," Ms. Moser's mother said in an interview. "You want to enjoy life."

Ms. Moser's father, who met and married his wife six years before Ms. Moser's grandfather received his Huntington's diagnosis, said he had managed not to think much about her at-risk status.

"So she was at risk," he said. "Everyone's at risk for everything."

The test, Ms. Moser remembers her mother suggesting, would cost thousands of dollars. Still, in college, Ms. Moser often trolled the Web for information about it. Mostly, she imagined how sweet it would be to know she did not have the gene. But increasingly she was haunted, too, by the suspicion that her mother did.

As awful as it was, she admitted to Ms. Elio, her freshman-year neighbor at Elizabethtown College in Pennsylvania, she almost hoped it was true. It would explain her mother's strokes of meanness, her unpredictable flashes of anger.

Ms. Moser's mother said she had never considered the conflicts with her daughter out of the ordinary. "All my friends who had daughters said that was all normal, and when she's twenty-five she'll be your best friend," she said. "I was waiting for that to happen, but I guess it's not happening."

When Ms. Moser graduated in 2003 with a degree in occupational therapy, their relationship, never peaceful, was getting worse. She moved to Queens without giving her mother her new address.

WANTING TO KNOW

Out of school, Ms. Moser soon spotted a listing for a job at Terence Cardinal Cooke Health Care Center, a nursing home on the Upper East Side of Manhattan. She knew it was meant for her.

Her grandfather had died there in 2002 after living for a decade at the home, one of only a handful in the country with a unit devoted entirely to Huntington's.

"I hated visiting him growing up," Ms. Moser said. "It was scary."

Now, though, she was drawn to see the disease up close. .

On breaks from her duties elsewhere, she visited her cousin James Dowd, the son of her grandfather's brother who had come to live in the Huntington's unit several years earlier. It was there, in a conversation with another staff member, that she learned she could be tested for only a few hundred dollars at the Columbia clinic across town. She scheduled an appointment for the next week.

The staff at Columbia urged Ms. Moser to consider the downside of genetic testing. Some people battle depression after they test positive. And the information, she was cautioned, could make it harder for her to get a job or health insurance.

But Ms. Moser bristled at the idea that she should have to remain ignorant about her genetic status to avoid discrimination. "I didn't do anything wrong," she said. "It's not like telling people I'm a drug addict."

She also recalls rejecting a counselor's suggestion that she might have asked to be tested as a way of crying for help.

"I'm like, 'No,'" Ms. Moser recalls replying. "'I've come to be tested because I want to know.'"

No one routinely collects demographic information about who gets tested for Huntington's. At the Huntington's Disease Center at Columbia, staff members say they have seen few young people taking the test.

Ms. Moser is still part of a distinct minority. But some researchers say her attitude is increasingly common among young people who know they may develop Huntington's.

More informed about the genetics of the disease than any previous generation, they are convinced that they would rather know how many healthy years they have left than wake up one day to find the illness upon them. They are confident that new reproductive technologies can allow them to have children without transmitting the disease and are eager to be first in line should a treatment become available.

"We're seeing a shift," said Dr. Michael Hayden, a professor of human genetics at the University of British Columbia in Vancouver who has been providing various tests for Huntington's for twenty years. "Younger people are coming for testing now, people in their twenties and early thirties; before, that was very rare. I've counseled some of them. They feel it is part of their heritage and that it is possible to lead a life that's not defined by this gene."

Before the test, Ms. Moser made two lists of life goals. Under "if negative," she wrote *married*, *children*, and *Ireland*. Under "if positive" was *exercise*, *vitamins*, and *ballroom dancing*. Balance, in that case, would be important. Opening a bed-and-breakfast, a goal since childhood, made both lists.

In the weeks before getting the test results, Ms. Moser gave Ms. Elio explicit instructions about acceptable responses. If she was negative, flowers were OK. If positive, they were not. In either case, drinking was acceptable. Crying was not.

But it was Ms. Elio's husband, Chris Elio, who first broached the subject of taking care of Ms. Moser, whom their young children called "my Katie," as in, "this is my mom, this is my dad, this is my Katie." They should address it before the results were in, Mr. Elio told his wife, so that she would not feel, later, that they had done it out of a sense of obligation.

The next day, in an e-mail note that was unusually formal for friends who sent text messages constantly and watched *Desperate House wives* while on the phone together, Ms. Elio told Ms. Moser that she and her husband wanted her to move in with them if she got sick. Ms. Moser set the note aside. She did not expect to need it.

"IT's TOO HARD TO LOOK"

The results had come a week early, and Ms. Moser assured her friends that the *Sex and the City* trivia party she had planned for that night was still on. After all, she was not sick, not dying. And she had already made the dips.

"I'm the same person I've always been," she insisted that night as her guests gamely dipped strawberries in her chocolate fountain. "It's been in me from the beginning."

But when she went to work the next day, she lingered outside the door of the occupational therapy gym, not wanting to face her colleagues. She avoided the Huntington's floor entirely, choosing to attend to patients ailing from just about anything else. "It's too hard to look at them," she told her friends.

In those first months, Ms. Moser summoned all her strength to pretend that nothing cataclysmic had happened. At times, it seemed easy enough. In the mirror, the same green eyes looked back at her. She was still tall, a devoted Julia Roberts fan, a prolific baker.

She dropped the news of her genetic status into some conversations like small talk, but kept it from her family. She made light of her newfound fate, though often friends were not sure how to take the jokes.

"That's my Huntington's kicking in," she told Rachel Markan, a coworker, after knocking a patient's folder on the floor.

Other times, Ms. Moser abruptly dropped any pretense of routine banter. On a trip to Florida, she and Ms. Elio saw a man in a wheelchair being tube-fed, a method often used to keep Huntington's patients alive for years after they can no longer swallow.

"I don't want a feeding tube," she announced flatly.

In those early days, she calculated that she had at least until fifty before symptoms set in. That was enough time to open a bed-and-breakfast, if she acted fast. Enough time to repay seventy thousand dollars in student loans under her thirty-year term.

Doing the math on the loans, though, could send her into a tail-spin.

"I'll be repaying them and then I'll start getting sick," she said. "I mean, there's no time in there."

Finding New Purpose

At the end of the summer, as the weather grew colder, Ms. Moser forced herself to return to the Huntington's unit.

In each patient, she saw her future: the biophysicist slumped in his wheelchair, the refrigerator repairman inert in his bed, the one-time professional tennis player who floated through the common room, arms undulating in the startlingly graceful movements that had earned the disease its original name, "Huntington's chorea," from the Greek "to dance."

Then there was her cousin Jimmy, who had wrapped papers for the *New York Post* for nineteen years until suddenly he could no longer tie the knots. When she greeted him, his bright blue eyes darted to her face, then away. If he knew her, it was impossible to tell.

She did what she could for them. She customized their wheelchairs with padding to fit each one's unique tics. She doled out special silverware, oversized or bent in just the right angles to prolong their ability to feed themselves.

Fending off despair, Ms. Moser was also filled with new purpose. Someone, somewhere, she told friends, had to find a cure.

It has been over a century since the disease was identified by George Huntington, a doctor in Amagansett, New York, and over a decade since researchers first found the gene responsible for it.

To raise money for research, Ms. Moser volunteered for walks and dinners and golf outings sponsored by the Huntington's Disease Society of America. She organized a Hula-Hoop-a-thon on the roof of

Cardinal Cooke, then a bowl-a-thon at the Port Authority. But at many of the events, attendance was sparse.

It is hard to get people to turn out for Huntington's benefits, she learned from the society's professional fund-raisers. Even families affected by the disease, the most obvious constituents, often will not help publicize events.

"They don't want people to know they're connected to Huntington's," Ms. Moser said, with a mix of anger and recognition. "It's like in my family—it's not a good thing."

Her first session with a therapist brought a chilling glimpse of how the disorder is viewed even by some who know plenty about it. "She told me it was my moral and ethical obligation not to have children," Ms. Moser told Ms. Elio by cellphone as soon as she left the office, her voice breaking. In lulls between fundraisers, Ms. Moser raced to educate her own world about Huntington's. She added links about the disease to her MySpace page. She plastered her desk at work with "Cure HD" stickers and starred in a video about the Huntington's unit for her union's Web site.

Ms. Moser gave blood for one study and spoke into a microphone for researchers trying to detect subtle speech differences in people who have extra CAG repeats before more noticeable disease symptoms emerge.

When researchers found a way to cure mice bred to replicate features of the disease in humans, Ms. Moser sent the news to friends and acquaintances.

But it was hard to celebrate. "Thank God," the joke went around on the Huntington's National Youth Alliance e-mail list Ms. Moser subscribed to, "at least there won't be any more poor mice wandering around with Huntington's disease."

In October, one of Ms. Moser's aunts lost her balance while walking and broke her nose. It was the latest in a series of falls. "The cure needs to be soon for me," Ms. Moser said. "Sooner for everybody else."

A CONFRONTATION IN COURT

In the waiting room of the Dutchess County family court house on a crisp morning in the fall of 2005, Ms. Moser approached her mother, who turned away.

"I need to tell her something important," Ms. Moser told a family member who had accompanied her mother to the hearing. He conveyed the message and brought one in return: unless she was dying, her mother did not have anything to say to her.

That Ms. Moser had tested positive meant that her mother would develop Huntington's, if she had not already. A year earlier, Ms. Moser's mother had convinced a judge that her sister, Nora Maldonado, was neglecting her daughter. She was given guardianship of the daughter, four-year-old Jillian.

Ms. Moser had been skeptical of her mother's accusations that Ms. Maldonado was not feeding or bathing Jillian properly, and she wondered whether her effort to claim Jillian had been induced by the psychological symptoms of the disease.

Her testimony about her mother's genetic status, Ms. Moser knew, could help persuade the judge to return Jillian. Ms. Maldonado had found out years earlier that she did not have the Huntington's gene.

Ms. Moser did not believe that someone in the early stages of Huntington's should automatically be disqualified from taking care of a child. But her own rocky childhood had convinced her that Jillian would be better off with Ms. Maldonado.

She told her aunt's lawyer about her test results and agreed to testify.

In the courtroom, Ms. Moser took the witness stand. Her mother's lawyer jumped up as soon as the topic of Huntington's arose. It was irrelevant, he said. But by the time the judge had sustained his objections, Ms. Moser's mother, stricken, had understood.

The next day, in the bathroom, Ms. Maldonado approached Ms. Moser's mother.

"I'm sorry," she said. Ms. Moser's mother said nothing.

The court has continued to let Ms. Moser's mother retain guardianship of Jillian. But she has not spoken to her daughter again.

"It's a horrible illness," Ms. Moser's mother said, months later, gesturing to her husband. "Now he has a wife who has it. Did she think of him? Did she think of me? Who's going to marry her?"

FACING THE FUTURE

Before the test, it was as if Ms. Moser had been balanced between parallel universes, one in which she would never get the disease and one in which she would. The test had made her whole.

She began to prepare the Elio children and Jillian for her illness, determined that they would not be scared, as she had been with her grandfather. When Jillian wanted to know how people got Huntington's disease "in their pants," Ms. Moser wrote the text of a children's book that explained what these other kinds of "genes" were and why they would make her sick.

But over the winter, Ms. Elio complained gently that her friend had become "Ms. H.D." And an impromptu note that arrived for the children in the early spring convinced her that Ms. Moser was dwelling too much on her own death.

"You all make me so happy, and I am so proud of who you are and who you will be," read the note, on rainbow scratch-and-write paper. "I will always remember the fun things we do together."

Taking matters into her own hands, Ms. Elio created a profile for Ms. Moser on an online dating service. Ms. Moser was skeptical but supplied a picture. Dating, she said, was the worst thing about knowing she had the Huntington's gene. It was hard to imagine someone falling enough in love with her to take on Huntington's knowingly, or asking it of someone she loved. At the same time, she said, knowing her status could help her find the right person, if he was out there.

"Either way, I was going to get sick," she said. "And I'd want someone who could handle it. If, by some twist of fate, I do get married and have children, at least we know what we're getting into."

After much debate, the friends settled on the third date as the right time to mention Huntington's. But when the first date came, Ms. Moser wished she could just blurt it out.

"It kind of just lingers there," she said. "I really just want to be able to tell people, 'Someday, I'm going to have Huntington's disease.'"

"A Part of My Life"

Last May 6, a year to the day after she had received her test results, the subject line "CAG Count" caught Ms. Moser's attention as she was scrolling through the online discussion forums of the Huntington's Disease Advocacy Center. She knew she had forty-five CAG repeats, but she had never investigated it further.

She clicked on the message.

"My mother's CAG was 43," it read. "She started forgetting the punch line to jokes at 39/40." Another woman, whose husband's CAG count was forty-seven, had just sold his car. "He's 39 years old," she wrote. "It was time for him to quit driving."

Quickly, Ms. Moser scanned a chart that accompanied the messages for her number, forty-five. The median age of onset to which it corresponded was thirty-seven.

Ms. Elio got drunk with her husband the night Ms. Moser finally told her.

"That's twelve years away," Ms. Moser said.

The statistic, they knew, meant that half of those with her CAG number started showing symptoms after age thirty-seven. But it also meant that the other half started showing symptoms earlier.

Ms. Moser, meanwhile, flew to the annual convention of the Huntington's Disease Society, which she had decided at the last minute to attend.

"Mother or father?" one woman, twenty-three, from Chicago, asked a few minutes after meeting Ms. Moser in the elevator of the Milwaukee Hilton. "Have you tested? What's your CAG?"

She was close to getting herself tested, the woman confided. How did it feel to know?

"It's hard to think the other way anymore of not knowing," Ms. Moser replied. "It's become a part of my life."

After years of trying to wring conversation from her family about Huntington's, Ms. Moser suddenly found herself bathing in it. But for the first time in a long time, her mind was on other things. At a youth support group meeting in the hotel hallway, she took her place in the misshapen circle. Later, on the dance floor, the spasms of the symptomatic seemed as natural as the gyrations of the normal.

"I'm not alone in this," Ms. Moser remembers thinking. "This affects other people, too, and we all just have to live our lives."

SEIZING THE DAY

July 15, the day of Ms. Moser's twenty-fifth birthday party, was sunny, with a hint of moisture in the air. At her aunt's house in Long Beach, New York, Ms. Moser wore a dress with pictures of cocktails on it. It was, she and Ms. Elio told anyone who would listen, her "cocktail dress." They drew the quotation marks in the air.

A bowl of "Cure HD" pins sat on the table. Over burgers from the barbecue, Ms. Moser mentioned to family members from her father's side that she had tested positive for the Huntington's gene.

"What's that?" one cousin asked.

"It will affect my ability to walk, talk, and think," Ms. Moser said. "Sometime before I'm fifty."

"That's soon," an uncle said matter-of-factly.

"So do you have to take medication?" her cousin asked.

"There's nothing really to take," Ms. Moser said.

She and the Elios put on bathing suits, loaded the children in a wagon, and walked to the beach.

More than anything now, Ms. Moser said, she is filled with a sense of urgency.

"I have a lot to do," she said. "And I don't have a lot of time."

Over the next months, Ms. Moser took tennis lessons every Sunday morning and went to church in the evening.

When a planned vacation with the Elio family fell through at the last minute, she went anyway, packing Disney World, Universal Studios, Wet 'n Wild, and Sea World into thirty-six hours with a high school friend who lives in Orlando. She was honored at a dinner by the New York chapter of the Huntington's society for her outreach efforts and managed a brief thank-you speech despite her discomfort with public speaking.

Having made a New Year's resolution to learn to ride a unicycle, she bought a used one. "My legs are tired, my arms are tired, and I definitely need protection," she reported to Ms. Elio. On Super Bowl Sunday, she waded into the freezing Atlantic Ocean for a Polar Bear swim to raise money for the Make-A-Wish Foundation.

Ms. Elio complained that she hardly got to see her friend. But one recent weekend, they packed up the Elio children and drove to the house the Elios were renovating in eastern Pennsylvania. The kitchen floor needed grouting, and, rejecting the home improvement gospel that calls for a special tool designed for the purpose, Ms. Moser and Ms. Elio had decided to use pastry bags.

As they turned into the driveway, Ms. Moser studied the semiattached house next door. Maybe she would move in one day, as the Elios had proposed. Then, when she could no longer care for herself, they could put in a door.

First, though, she wanted to travel. She had heard of a job that would place her in different occupational therapy positions across the country every few months and was planning to apply.

"I'm thinking Hawaii first," she said.

Then they donned gloves, mixed grout in a large bucket of water and began the job.

2009

Editor: NATALIE ANGIER

KAREN OLSSON

The Final Frontier

FROM *THE TEXAS MONTHLY*

Two astronomers based in Texas want to study the secrets of the universe. But it costs money. To raise that money, they look beyond the federal-grant system, to wealthy individuals and others. Karen Olsson watches as two scientists become salesmen——and in Texas, no less.

ONE EVENING LAST OCTOBER, A UNIVERSITY OF TEXAS at Austin astronomer named Gary Hill stood behind a lectern at Miss Hattie's Café and Saloon, which occupies a restored nineteenth-century bank building in downtown San Angelo, and cheerfully proclaimed his ignorance. "We really don't understand the universe," he said. "We thought we did, but it turns out we only understand about four percent of it."

A dozen or so people, among them businessmen, the editor of the local newspaper, a school librarian, and a couple of college professors, had assembled at Miss Hattie's, where the lace curtains and rose-print wallpaper harked back to a time when the universe was no larger than our own galaxy and Newton's laws seemed to explain it and a tunnel linked the building where we sat to a nearby bordello.

There was something old-fashioned too about the fact that a bespectacled, British-born scientist had traveled from the state capital to give a talk to the curious and that the curious had turned out to hear what he had to say. His subject, on the other hand, was the very future of cosmology and physics and how they might be affected by one telescope in particular, located 212 miles farther west.

Galileo stuck lenses onto either end of an organ pipe; today's research telescopes, while considerably more elaborate, still perform the same fundamental task of collecting and focusing light. It's all astronomers have to go on: electromagnetic radiation from distant objects, whether it arrives in the form of X rays or visible light or radio waves. "We're detectives, but we can only use what light will give us," Hill had said to me earlier that day. "So we get fairly ingenious in the ways we analyze light to look for clues." They rely, for instance, on spectroscopy, the process of separating light emitted by an object in space into its component wavelengths, as a prism does, then analyzing those components. And they invent new tools to analyze the light. To probe deeper and deeper into space, scientists must design better and better detectors, sensitive to the faintest of emissions.

Such instruments don't come cheaply, which is why Hill and his colleague Karl Gebhardt have periodically taken to the road over the past three and a half years: They've been promoting an ambitious $34 million overhaul of a telescope at UT's McDonald Observatory, in the Davis Mountains of West Texas. Speaking to potential donors in Houston or a luncheon group in Abilene, they've been publicizing an endeavor called HETDEX, or the Hobby-Eberly Telescope Dark Energy Experiment, the aim of which is to help attack what some have labeled one of the most important problems in science.

Hill grew up in England but left to go to where the telescopes were, first as a graduate student in Hawaii, then as a postdoctoral researcher in West Texas, in 1988. Finding that certain instruments at the observatory weren't sensitive enough, he designed and built a new spectrograph on the cheap, still in use today. He is now the observatory's chief astronomer. At Miss Hattie's he applied his knack for innovative thinking to the problem of business attire—he wore a striped green shirt and a pink tie—and as he spoke, he grinned and nodded infectiously. "We have a huge opportunity to lay the groundwork in Texas for understanding how the universe has changed through time," he said. He outlined the goals of the experiment: to conduct the largest survey of other galaxies ever completed and to use that information to measure how the scale of the universe has evolved—and to reinvent the telescope in the process. By doing so, Hill, Gebhardt, and their collaborators hope to better understand what astronomers call dark energy, though no one really knows what the term means: "Dark energy" is a label for a mystery. "The thing is," Hill told his audience, "it may not be dark and it may not be energy."

After the presentation had ended and most of the audience had departed, Hill was subjected to a more rigorous interrogation at dinner from Ken Gunter, a tall, poker-faced San Angelo businessman and a member of the McDonald's Board of Visitors, a statewide group of observatory supporters. This turned into a debate between the gruff West Texan and the polite but impassioned British scientist, while half a dozen others at the table looked on. Though he supports the experiment, Gunter was skeptical as to whether he could raise funds for it. "What is the pragmatic end product, except exciting a bunch of astronomy Ph.D.'s in Austin? Give me something I can identify with. If you want to raise some honest-to-God money, you better start raising some honest-to-God tie back to medicine or energy." That, said Hill, wasn't the point. The most practical argument he could make for the telescope was that it might excite students in a country where science education was failing and draw better faculty to the university. Gunter seemed unconvinced. "My sense is that most people don't give two hoots in hell whether the universe is expanding or contracting or moving sideways!" he said, and drew out a cigar.

Earlier that day I'd ridden in a rented Suburban with Hill; David Lambert, the director of the observatory; and Joel Barna, its development director, from Midland to Abilene to San Angelo. The flat landscape was staked by the technology of energy production: near Midland the pump jacks kowtowed to the brush, while farther south a line of soaring silver windmills receded toward the horizon. (One question often posed by lay audiences in Texas, Hill told me, is "How can we harness dark energy for human use?") It was a warm, hazy morning, and as we'd all risen early to catch a seven o'clock flight from Austin to Midland, a soporific air had fallen over the car, leaving me in a state of sleepy wonderment at one of astronomy's fundamental principles, that light can ripple for billions of years through the vast universe and collide with nothing else during that unfathomably long journey, reaching our planet with information about its place of origin. How can that be, I asked. "There's a lot of empty space out there," Hill said. "The fraction of the area of the sky with stuff is not very great, so the chances of a photon of light hitting anything long its route other than your telescope are actually very small."

I fell silent. All that void. A little while later I asked something else, then mulled over the answer, and that's pretty much how the ride went, as I surfaced every so often with another question for the patient professors, then let my head spin for a while. It's humbling to stumble up against the edifice of astronomy, the massive and intricate body of knowledge humans have built up over the millennia, and then all the more humbling—if somehow also reassuring—to contemplate how much more we don't know. And how much we can't possibly see, since only 4 percent of the stuff in the universe is thought to be visible matter. That includes you and me and microorganisms and other galaxies, at least 100 billion of them. As one scientist put it recently, "we're just a bit of pollution," while most of the universe is made of something else.

"Nature and nature's laws lay hid in night" goes the famous epitaph Alexander Pope composed for Isaac Newton. "God said, 'Let Newton be!' and all was light." But as it turns out, almost all is, in fact, dark, and a crucial portion of those laws remain hidden. Theorists first ventured into the "dark" to resolve a problem concerning the motions of galaxies and the stars within them. The trouble was, there just weren't enough visible stars out there. Matter far away from the center of a galaxy tended to move much faster than could be explained by the net gravitational attraction of all the visible matter. So in order to save Newton's laws of gravity, astronomers invented a new type of matter that was dark but plentiful: dark matter. The universe is littered with it, they concluded. Which might seem like cheating—the invisible check is in the mail—yet the theory has helped explain the motions of other cosmic entities, and there are high hopes that dark matter will be detected in experiments this year at CERN, the particle physics laboratory in Geneva, Switzerland.

Then scientists discovered another anomaly, this one not limited to objects like galaxies but pertaining to the entire cosmos. And they came up with something even stranger to explain it. The problem was the way in which the universe was growing. Until the twentieth century, the universe was generally thought to be static, neither expanding nor contracting. But along came Edwin Hubble (who, late bloomers take note, taught high school and coached basketball in Indiana before returning to school for his Ph.D.). In the twenties he made measurements of how far away galaxies were and how fast they were moving, and he discovered that the farther away they were, the faster they were receding. The universe, this implied, was expanding, everything moving away from everything else. (Albeit with negligible impact locally. In *Annie Hall*, Alvy Singer's mother is basically correct when she tells her existentially morose son that "Brooklyn is not expanding.") The concept of an expanding universe in turn suggested that at one time, everything was closer together. Thus Hubble's discoveries were a prod to the subsequent development of the big bang theory.

Meanwhile, a decade before Hubble, Einstein had revised Newton's idea of gravity—an attractive force between massive objects—

with his theory of general relativity, in which gravity depends on the curvature of four-dimensional space-time. The twentieth century saw the Newtonian model of a fixed, orderly universe supplanted by that of a warping, expanding space with unimaginably chaotic origins. This universe had a beginning and would perhaps come to an end as well: If the expansion of space was indeed due to the propulsion from the big bang, then it stood to reason that because the gravitational pull of all the matter in the universe would be retarding that outward growth, one of three things would ultimately happen: Gravity would win out and the universe would collapse, the initial propulsion from the big bang would win and the universe would expand forever, or—and this is the most accepted case—the two would be perfectly balanced.

But in 1998, two groups of researchers independently arrived at a surprising result, so surprising that members of each originally believed that they had made a mistake. Both teams had been studying a class of exploding stars called type 1a supernovae, measuring their distances and speeds. What each team found was that the most distant supernovae were fainter than expected, fainter than they would have appeared in a decelerating or even a coasting universe. The expansion of the universe, this meant, seemed not to be slowing down but rather speeding up. And no one had a good explanation for it. What phenomenon could possibly be pushing space outward?

"Theorists have been guiding observers for ten thousand years," said Edward "Rocky" Kolb, a professor of astronomy and astrophysics at the University of Chicago. "Now they've observed something that we don't understand. We desperately need a better idea of what's going on." The notion that some form of mass energy might pervade all of space dates back to Einstein, but it gained widespread acceptance only in response to the observed acceleration of the universe. But what sort of energy? Has it changed over time? Or could it be that there really is no such thing as dark energy and that our understanding of gravity is actually wrong? These questions demanded new experiments, which in turn would require new telescopes or modifications to existing ones.

* * *

KARL GEBHARDT ARRIVED AT THE University of Texas in 2000, an expert on nearby galaxies and black holes. But in 2004 he attended a meeting on the future of U.S. telescopes, where much of the talk was about dark energy.

"It really hit home: everyone is pushing on this," he told me when I visited him in his office. "All the dark energy missions were beginning to take root, and I said, 'Hey, look, I think we can do this at Texas.' I came back from the meeting all excited. So one day in the hall I was talking to Gary Hill about it, and I said, 'Can we do this? Can we study dark energy?' It turned out he was working on an instrument design with Phillip [MacQueen, the observatory's chief scientist and a senior researcher at UT-Austin], and we decided we can make a really nice instrument to look at the problem."

For the next few weeks, Gebhardt and Hill traded ideas about how to proceed, and MacQueen and Hill consulted about whether the instrument they'd conceived would be up to the task. "We went back and forth for a few months until we came up with a nice design," Gebhardt said. "But it's easy to come up with designs. The hard part is finding the money and the telescope to do it on." Here, though, the team had two advantages: the Hobby-Eberly Telescope and a recent grant from the Air Force.

Not long afterward, they began trying to raise the $34 million, more than the cost of the original telescope. The financial end was both a burden and a potential edge: the Texas scientists would not be bound by the same sort of bureaucratic limitations that they might have encountered using a federally administered facility or depending heavily on government grants. "The National Science Foundation won't go off the beaten path until they've beaten the path," said Gary Bernstein, a professor of physics and astronomy at the University of Pennsylvania. "If you have your own facility and can do what you want to do, you have more freedom." Or as Hill said to me, "In Texas, if you have the idea and you have the money, you can do it." And the $34 million, while hardly a small sum, was much lower than the costs of other proposed dark-energy experiments.

A plan to put together a world-class instrument on the cheap might sound an alarm in the mind of anyone familiar with the observatory's history, for a cost-saving design had been trumpeted once before, in building the Hobby-Eberly Telescope itself. Though less expensive than other telescopes of comparable size, the HET had suffered technical problems for several years after it was dedicated, in 1997. While it was one of the largest telescopes in the world, it had gained a reputation for poor image quality. Now, at last, it was functioning properly, and here came some upstart astronomers with a proposal to chop off its top half and replace the detector with a novel apparatus. Could grand ambitions get the better of the observatory a second time?

If the scientists themselves had such doubts, they kept them quiet. Their concerns were more concrete: raise the money and get results before anyone else. Among the other proposed dark-energy experiments, only one will employ the same technique as HETDEX, and that's a collaboration between scientists in Japan and the United States to build something called the Wide-Field Multi-Object Spectrograph, which would be installed on the Japanese-operated Subaru Telescope, in Hawaii. "This is a strange game, in that you don't know exactly how much data you have to take before you can make a great discovery," Kolb said. "Timing is of the essence. It's sort of a race between the Japanese and Texans. This is such a hot topic that many people are interested in it. There is the potential of great discoveries to be made, and so you just can't sit on it and wait."

The HETDEX researchers, led by the Texas group and further supported by two universities in Germany and the consortium that operates the HET, are the mavericks of the dark-energy industry, relying on a small number of people and a relatively low-cost instrument. So far they've raised $20.1 million—enough to build a prototype for the elaborate new spectrograph and to rebuild the HET to give it a much wider field of view—and they're gunning to finish their upgrade and their observations by 2013. "We are dwarfed by these other teams," Gebhardt said. "They have the ability to go out there and barrage everybody at conferences. We can't do that. We are working all-out just to get our instrument built. But it never hurts to be the underdog. I think people are a little scared of HETDEX because we're going to finish soon now. We are really moving."

IF YOU WERE TO LOOK at a nighttime satellite image of Texas, you would see large splotches of light produced by Dallas–Fort Worth and Houston, smaller ones for Austin and San Antonio, and a grid of glowing points as you move west from Austin, the most prominent strand of them following Interstate 10. Gradually the lights trail away; in West Texas south of the interstate, the map goes almost completely dark. It's one of the darkest spots in the continental United States, making it a natural place for an observatory.

The location was identified in the summer of 1932 by two astronomers who drove a Chevrolet nearly eight thousand miles— roughly one third of the earth's circumference—all within Texas. They ranged from Galveston to El Paso and as far north as Amarillo, stopping to peer through a small telescope, make notes, and take photographs at prospective sites. An East Texas banker named William McDonald had bequeathed his fortune to the University of Texas so that it could build an astronomical observatory (for the stated purpose of "seeing closer the gates of heaven"), and the university, which had no astronomy department, contracted with scientists from the University of Chicago to supply the expertise—the first order of business being to choose a location. They selected the Davis Mountains, a choice approved by Otto Struve, the Russian émigré who became the observatory's first director, after he spent several nights camping on Mount Locke with his wife.

Today, as you drive from the interstate to the town of Fort Davis and on to the observatory, the elevation rises, the land begins to buckle and swell, and having passed over miles of desert plains, you find yourself driving through cedar-sprinkled hills and finally up

Mount Locke, where most of the observatory is located. At first you see two white domes resembling centurion helmets at the summit.

They are the observatory's older telescopes, the Struve telescope, or "the 82-inch," after the diameter of its primary mirror, which was built in 1939, and the Harlan J. Smith 107-inch, completed in 1968. Each in its time was one of the most powerful telescopes in the world, only to be eclipsed, inevitably, by technology's advance. (They are still in use, but they are no longer considered cutting-edge.) Higher up the hill a silver-mirrored dome resembling a giant bucky-ball comes into view: this, situated on an adjacent peak, is the Hobby-Eberly Telescope.

With its own water supply, fire marshal, staff homes, and lodge for visitors, formerly called the Transients' Quarters (now the Astronomers' Lodge), the observatory is its own little campus on a hill, one that abides by strange customs. People drive around at night with only their parking lights on, for instance, to keep things dark. It's a quiet place, where an influential portion of the population sleeps during the day and works at night, and the sky commands attention—not just from astronomers but from anyone who finds herself on the mountain. The night I arrived at the observatory, a woman passing me on the road told me to be sure to take in the stunning sunset; the next night another person bid me look out at the storms to the west.

But there's the sky we see, and then there's the sky astronomers investigate. Enter through a side door of the HET building, and it's as if you've stepped into a small manufacturing plant, with a concrete loading area and a flight of metal stairs leading to the site manager's spare office. The manager in this case is Bob Calder, who worked for the Subaru telescope, in Hawaii, and the Smithsonian Astrophysical Observatory, in Cambridge, Massachusetts, before moving to Texas to oversee the operation and maintenance of the HET—though "maintenance" is perhaps too plain a word, too reminiscent of boilers or car engines, to convey the kind of care one has to take with a major telescope. Even cleaning is a delicate task. To focus on the very thin slices of sky required for astronomical work, the telescope's large primary mirror must be absolutely smooth, free of any imperfections larger than one tenth the wavelength of the light hitting it. The aluminum coatings on the HET's mirrors are the thickness of oil on water; they are cleaned on Mondays, Wednesdays, and Fridays by a four-person team that applies a carbon dioxide "snow" with a wand.

As site manager of the HET, Calder also greets the dignitaries and potential donors who come to tour the telescope, a duty that has, on occasion, served to remind him that he is not in Cambridge any longer. "We had a guy one time who tried to give me a wad of bills after the tour," Calder recalled. "He goes, 'Let me do something for your family.' I suggested he donate to the observatory instead, and he said he was going to, but he still wanted to give me some money too." (Calder declined the gift.)

He escorted me down through the control room, where the telescope is manipulated via computers and electronics, and inside the dome. It is a sort of cross between a science cathedral and a science factory, given over to one giant piece of industrial equipment aimed at the heavens: the HET. While it calls to mind some sort of futuristic vehicle poised to be launched into space, the telescope actually rotates on a fixed base, letting space come to it. Ninety-one hexagonal pieces form the primary mirror, a silver dish inside a steel cage; the light from the night sky hits this and then is relayed to an instrument above the mirror called the tracker. Itself a complex piece of machinery that took two years to build, the tracker can follow the image of a particular object as that image crosses the mirror. (Due to the rotation of the earth, the sky and its contents shift, relative to the position of the telescope, over the course of the night.)

Calder flipped a switch, engaging the air bearings below the telescope, and like a big hovercraft, it rose a few inches and then began to rotate. Moments later, a recording of squawking birds began to play, which is supposed to ward off real birds that might fly in through the ventilation shafts or through the top of the dome. Speaking over the sounds of the machinery and the squawking, Calder summarized the changes planned for the HET. "There's one camera up there right now," he said. "That whole top end is going to be replaced with a new top end that supports on the order of one hundred and fifty cameras, one hundred and fifty spectrographs." Those spectrographs, he told me, would be deployed, over the course of 140 nights, to record one million galaxies.

LATER THAT EVENING I CROUCHED on a platform below the Smith telescope, where Hill, MacQueen, and graduate student Josh Adams were bustling about a prototype of the instrument that is slated to be put on the HET. The instrument is called VIRUS, for Visible Integral-field Replicable Unit Spectrograph, and it will incorporate more than 145 copies of a simple spectrograph, each of which registers data from at least 246 fibers arrayed within something called an integral-field unit. Scattered on the floor of the platform were scissors and cables and screws and Allen wrenches, as if the scientists were fixing a motorcycle rather than testing a highly engineered piece of equipment, which was contained within an irregularly shaped black box about four feet wide and attached to the underside of the telescope's shaft by a metal harness. I watched as they checked the connections between the telescope and the box, cooled a crucial part with liquid nitrogen, and installed a glass plate, all in preparation for an observing run.

"There are four big links in the chain of observational astronomy," MacQueen explained as he connected the liquid nitrogen tank to the device. "Collecting the light, processing the light, detecting the light, and all the software side of analyzing the light." HETDEX will, if all goes smoothly, increase by about thirty-fold the area of sky that can be observed at any one time, speeding up the first three steps and thereby transforming the HET into a far more efficient and comprehensive cartographer of the skies. Rather than pointing at and shooting known objects, the upgrade will allow the research team to methodically obtain spectra from a giant celestial swath, taking information from more than 40,000 pixel-like sections of sky per exposure. Those will be captured by an 800-megapixel camera whose technology is similar to that of any vacationer's digital camera. "This is just a super-duper digital camera of sorts," MacQueen said.

Yet this is a camera that takes pictures of the remote past. Imagine a man in California trying to construct a map of the United States, using only the information brought to him by slow-moving (but long-lived) ants, creeping along at a hundred yards per year. The ants from New Jersey would have departed more than 50,000 years ago, before humans arrived in North America; the Midwestern ants some tens of thousands of years ago; the central California ants just a few years ago—so the map would record the East Coast as wild and uninhabited while the West Coast would contain highways and burger joints. This is the sort of map astronomers construct of the universe: The light that arrives from greater distances relays information about earlier eras.

If the big-bang model of the universe is correct, though, we cannot receive any messages from the earliest time periods, any more than our Californian mapmaker could learn about France. For some 380,000 years after the big bang, the universe was so hot that particles couldn't form atoms; electrons whizzed around every which way, and light couldn't travel any distance without colliding with those electrons. While this early fireball of a universe remains opaque to us, it is theorized that there must have been random variations in how densely its particles were distributed. Some areas were more dense than average, creating hot spots that drove matter out to cooler regions, which in turn caused waves to travel at what in that primordial plasma was the speed of sound—about sixty percent of the speed of light. The result was a series of ripples through the sea of particles.

When the universe cooled down enough for atoms to form and light to escape, the oscillations ceased. At that particular moment in the history of the cosmos, the ripples were frozen into the density distribution of matter—so that now when astronomers map the heavens, they find the imprints of the early ripples in the way that galaxies are clustered. (It's as if you drew a pattern on a balloon and then inflated it. As the balloon expanded, the pattern would persist though its scale would change.) These imprints are what the HETDEX team plans to measure, to learn how they might have grown over time. By comparing the traces of the oscillations at different epochs, both with one another and with a pattern already discovered in something called the cosmic microwave background—which gives us a picture of the universe just after the light first escaped—they will be able to evaluate the changes in the scale of the universe and from that infer whether dark energy has made a constant contribution to the universe's expansion or has varied over the eons.

Some cosmologists have questioned whether a concerted push to do dark-energy experiments would be detrimental to the wider field of astronomy, hindering discoveries in other areas and relegating too many scientists to supporting roles on large-scale endeavors. After all, maybe there isn't any such thing as dark energy. Maybe no one really understands how gravity works. Or maybe the universe is not as homogenous as theorists have assumed. Maybe "dark energy" is the wrong way to frame the problem.

But even the possibility that dark energy might be a mistaken notion is no cause for pessimism, according to Gebhardt. "That would be the most exciting answer—if we're just so completely out to lunch," he said. "It means there is something fundamental about the nature of our universe that we don't understand. So whatever the answer is, it's going to be a fundamental shift in our understanding.

"In other words, it's not going to be a boring answer, and who knows where it will lead?"

MARGARET TALBOT

Birdbrain

FROM *THE NEW YORKER*

> *Alex, the African gray parrot who died in 2007, exhibited some re-markable traits—language skills and communication that went well beyond what one expects of parrots. For Alex's owner, Irene Pepperberg, Alex proved that animals are far more intelligent than we think. Other scientists are not convinced. Margaret Talbot tries to make sense of it all.*

As the crowd at the Midwest Bird Expo waited for the cognitive scientist Irene Pepperberg to take the podium, the hum of human chatter was punctuated by the sound of parrots whooping it up—twittering and letting loose with wolf whistles, along with the occasional full-out jungle squawk. The birds, many of them for sale, were displayed in cages just beyond the curtained-off stage, which was inside the main hall of the DuPage County Fairgrounds, in Wheaton, Illinois. Nobody seemed particularly distracted by the commotion. People were too busy pulling out their cell phones and showing one another photographs of their cockatiels back home. It was a warm Saturday afternoon in early April, and a woman in the folding metal chair in front of me, who was wearing large parrot earrings, said that she had driven all the way from Florida to see Pepperberg. Indeed, if this were a political rally, the audience would be Pepperberg's base. Here were admirers who had sent in ten-dollar bills to help support her research with Alex, the African gray parrot that she worked with for thirty years; and here were people who, after Alex died, unexpectedly, of heart arrhythmia, on September 6, 2007, helped form an online community that comes together on the sixth day of every month to reflect about him.

Pepperberg, arriving onstage, picked up a microphone and said, "I have a feeling you all know how smart Alex was." Everyone clapped in assent. (The parrot had appeared on television many times, mainly on PBS and the Discovery Channel.) She explained to the audience, which was largely middle-aged and female, that, in the late nineteen-seventies, when she started working with Alex—whose name was an acronym for Avian Learning Experiment—other scientists had been dismissive of her ambition to communicate with him. As she put it, "My grant proposals came back basically saying, 'What are you smoking?'" The woman from Florida laughed heartily, her parrot earrings bobbing.

Pepperberg, who is fifty-nine years old, has imposing cheekbones and an abundance of long, dark hair; she wears smoky eye makeup, short skirts, and an armful of silver bangles. In Wheaton, she quietly worked the crowd into a pleasurable state of shared outrage. At one point, she said that colleagues had admonished her, "Birds can't do what you say he can do. They just don't have the brainpower." Linnea Faris, a woman from Michigan who was wearing a "Remember Alex" T-shirt, shook her head in disbelief. Faris told me, "My husband doesn't really understand it. I can't fully explain it myself. But I've spent hours crying over that damn bird." She went on, "People used to think birds weren't intelligent. Well, they used to think women weren't intelligent, either. They talked about the smaller circumference of our skulls as though it made us inferior to men! You know what? They were wrong on both counts."

Pepperberg has had an unconventional academic career: she rents a small lab at Brandeis, and holds a part-time lecturer position at Harvard. That afternoon, she was delivering what she calls her "It's a Wonderful Life" speech, so named because it's about how surprised and touched she was to learn, after Alex died, that he had meant so much to people. "You all are my Clarences," she said, referring to the angel who shows Jimmy Stewart the sorry state of a Bedford Falls without him in it.

It wasn't just parrot people who had found themselves moved by Pepperberg's three-decade relationship with Alex: obituaries of the bird ran everywhere from *The Economist* to the *Hindustan Times*. Within a few days of his death, Pepperberg told the audience, she had received some six thousand messages of condolence via e-mail.

As everyone knows, parrots are remarkably good at mimicking human speech, but they tend to repeat randomly picked-up phrases: obscenities, election slogans, "Hey, sailor." Many parrots kept as pets also imitate familiar sounds, like the family dog barking or an alarm clock beeping. But Pepperberg taught Alex referential speech—labels for objects, and phrases like "Wanna go back." By the end, he knew about fifty words for objects. Pepperberg was never particularly interested in teaching Alex language for its own sake; rather, she was interested in what language could reveal about the workings of his mind. In learning to speak, Alex showed Pepperberg that he understood categories like same and different, bigger and smaller. He could count and recognize Arabic numerals up to six. He could identify objects by their color, shape ("three-corner," "four-corner," and so on, up to "six-corner"), and material: when Pepperberg held up, say, a pompom or a wooden block, he could answer "Wool" or "Wood," correctly, about eighty per cent of the time. Holding up a yellow key and a green key of the same size, Pepperberg might ask Alex to identify a difference between them, and he'd say, "Color." When she held up two keys and asked, "Which is bigger?" he could identify the larger one by naming its color. Looking at a collection of objects that he hadn't seen before, Alex could reliably answer a two-tiered question like "How many blue blocks?"—a tricky task for toddlers. He even seemed to develop an understanding of absence, something akin to the concept of zero. If asked what the difference was between two identical blue keys, Alex learned to reply, "None." (He pronounced it "nuh.")

Pepperberg also reported that, outside training sessions, Alex sometimes played with the sounds he had learned, venturing new words. After he learned "gray," he came up with "grain" on his own, and after learning "talk" he tried out "chalk." His trainers then gave him the item that he had inadvertently named, and it eventually entered his vocabulary. (When Alex devised nonsense words—like "cheenut"—Pepperberg and his other trainers did not respond, and he quickly stopped saying them.) In linguistic terms, Alex was recombining phonemes, the building blocks of speech. Stephen Anderson, a Yale linguist who has written about animal communication, considers this behavior "apparent evidence that Alex did actually regard at least some of his words as made up of individual recombinable pieces, though it's hard to say without more evidence. This is something that seems well beyond any ape-language experiments, or anything we see in nature."

Pepperberg told me that Alex also made spontaneous remarks that were oddly appropriate. Once, when she rushed in the lab door, obviously harried, Alex said, "Calm down"—a phrase she had sometimes used with him. "What's your problem?" he sometimes demanded of a flustered trainer. When training sessions dragged on, Alex would say, "Wanna go back"—to his cage. More creatively, he'd sometimes announce, "I'm gonna go away now," and either turn his back to the person working with him or sidle as far away as he could get on his perch. "Say better," he chided the younger parrots that Pepperberg began training along with him. "You be good, see you tomorrow, I love you," he'd say when she left the lab each evening. This was endearing—and the *Times*'s obituary made much of the fact that these were the bird's last words—although, as Anderson points out, it was during such moments that Alex was, most likely, merely "parroting." It helped Alex's charisma quotient that he made all his remarks in an intonation that was part two-year-old, part Rain Man, part pull-string toy. His voice, at once tinny and sweet, was easy to understand. Pepperberg tended to speak to Alex in the singsong "motherese" that doting parents use with young children, and he replied in a voice that seemed to convey a toddlerish pride.

Diana Reiss, a professor of cognitive psychology at Hunter College, is a dolphin researcher and a friend of Pepperberg's. (She was a co-author of the first studies to show that dolphins and elephants, like some primates, recognize themselves in a mirror.) Reiss recalls that when she first met Alex, "I was left alone with this bird I'd never seen. And I'm not really a bird person. Irene had said, 'Just do what you want with him.' After a few minutes, he said, 'Wanna go knee.' So I put out my hand, and he walked onto my knee. Then he said, 'Tickle,' and he put his head down to be tickled. I thought, I'm communicating with this bird! This is amazing! Then I thought, O.K., I'll test him. I knew Irene's paradigm. I knew she'd hold an object up really close to his beak. So I pick up a little red toy car and ask, 'What's this?,' and out he comes with 'Truck.' Now, if I were unconsciously cuing him with, say, subvocal speech—some subtle movement of my vocal cords or lips—I'd have said, 'Car.' But the label Alex had learned was 'truck.' The whole encounter knocked my socks off."

All children grow up in a world of talking animals. If they don't come to know them through fairy tales, Disney movies, or the Narnia books, they discover them some other way. A child will grant the gift of speech to the family dog, or to the stray cat that shows up at the door. At first, it's a solipsistic fantasy—the secret sharer you can tell your troubles to, or that only you understand. Later, it's rooted in a more philosophical curiosity, the longing to experience the ineffable interiority of some very different being. My eight-year-old daughter says that she wishes the horses she rides could talk, just so she could ask them what it feels like to be a horse. Such a desire presumes—as Thomas Nagel put it in his 1974 essay "What Is It Like to Be a

Bat?"—that animals have some kind of subjectivity, and that it might somehow be plumbed. In any case, Nagel explained, humans are "restricted to the resources" of our own minds, and since "those resources are inadequate to the task," we cannot really imagine what it is like to be a bat, only, at best, what it is like to behave like one—to fly around in the dark, gobble up insects, and so on. That inability, however, should not lead us to dismiss the idea that animals "have experiences fully comparable in richness of detail to our own." We simply can't know. Yet many of us would be glad for even a few glimpses inside an animal's mind. And some people, like Irene Pepperberg, have dedicated their lives to documenting those glimpses.

Pepperberg will never really know what it is like to be a parrot, and she is careful not to claim that Alex learned a language. She calls what he learned a "two-way communication system," and prefers the more conservative term "labels," rather than "words," to describe his vocabulary. "I wouldn't say it was as much conversation as you'd have with a five-year-old," she said when I asked her about Alex's limits. "But maybe with a two-year-old. It wasn't like he was going to say, 'Hi, how are you, how was your day?' But if you came in and asked him what he wanted, where he wanted to go, and asked him questions within the context of labels he knew, you could talk to him."

At the Bird Expo, she told a story about the time an accountant was working on some tax forms near Alex's cage, and was more or less ignoring him. Peering down at the visitor, he asked her, "Wanna nut?" No, she said, not looking up. Want some water? No. A banana? No. And so on, through his repertoire of nameable desires. At last, Alex asked, in a tone in which it was hard not to detect a note of impatience, "What do you want?"

FOR CENTURIES, THE IDEA OF intelligent animals struck most intelligent people as ridiculous. In 1637, René Descartes marveled that all humans—"without even excepting idiots"—can "arrange different words together, forming of them a statement by which they make known their thoughts, while there is no other animal, however perfect and fortunately circumstanced it may be, which can do the same." Two centuries later, Charles Darwin took a radically different view. The theory of evolution suggested that men and animals were separated not by an unbridgeable mental gulf but, rather, by developmental gradations. In *The Descent of Man*, Darwin contended that "there is no fundamental difference between man and the higher mammals in mental faculties." Chimps, he noted, used tools, and dogs had a capacity for abstraction—a poodle, seeing a German shepherd in the distance, knows it to be a fellow canine. Discussing language, Darwin observed:

> That which distinguishes man from the lower animals is not the understanding of articulate sounds, for, as everyone knows, dogs understand many words and sentences. In this respect they are at the same stage of development as infants, between the ages of ten and twelve months, who understand many words and short sentences, but cannot yet utter a single word. It is not the mere articulation which is our distinguishing character, for parrots and other birds possess this power. Nor is it the mere capacity of connecting definite sounds with definite ideas; for it is certain that some parrots, which have been taught to speak, connect unerringly words with things, and persons with events. The lower animals differ from man solely in his almost infinitely larger power of associating together the most diversified sounds and ideas.

Darwin undermined these observations, however, with romantic overreaching about emotion in animals—he even made a claim for parental affection among earwigs. In 1881, Darwin's protégé George Romanes went still further; his book *Animal Intelligence* compiled hundreds of anthropomorphizing anecdotes about uxorious ostriches, passionate pike, and prudent alligators. Such excesses inspired a backlash. In 1894, the British psychologist C. Lloyd Morgan established what came to be known as Morgan's canon: "In no case may we interpret an action as the outcome of the exercise of a higher psychical faculty, if it can be interpreted as the outcome of the exercise of one which stands lower in the psychological scale." If instinct could explain why your dog growled at your suitcase, then there was no need to cast about for a richer interpretation, one that might, as Morgan put it, "savour of the prattle of the parlour tea table rather than the sober discussion of the study." As sensible as Morgan's canon sounded, it essentially censored the question "Do animals think?"

The reigning theory for the new era of animal studies—especially in America—was the behaviorism of John Watson and B. F. Skinner. It was firmly rooted in the laboratory, in psychology rather than in biology departments, in the metaphor of animal as machine, and in the use of mazes and the Skinner box. Behaviorists tested the capacities of animals not through naturalistic observation but through highly controlled stimulus response experiments. Speculation about the subjective experiences or thought processes of animals seemed unscientific: animals didn't think, they reacted. As Gregory Radick writes in *The Simian Tongue: The Long Debate About Animal Language* (2007), the idea of animal cognition "came to be regarded as belonging to the sentimental nineteenth century."

Meanwhile, the tale of the horse Clever Hans gave a chill to any scientist still hoping to demonstrate that animals were thinking creatures. Around the turn of the century, Wilhelm von Osten, a German schoolmaster, bought a horse, named it Hans, and supposedly taught him arithmetic—addition, subtraction, even fractions and decimals—along with some spoken and written German. When von Osten asked Hans, for example, "What is twelve divided by three?" Hans tapped his hoof four times. Von Osten gave regular demonstrations of his horse's astonishing abilities, until a psychologist named Oskar Pfungst pointed out that von Osten was unconsciously cuing the animal with subtle movements of his head and eyes. One lesson to have drawn from this episode was that, although Hans may not have been so clever at arithmetic, he was, in fact, quite clever at reading the body language of humans, a talent that could have warranted further investigation. Another—and this was the one that took—was that anybody studying animal communication had to be extremely careful about accidental cuing.

By the mid-nineteen-sixties, the behaviorist paradigm was being challenged by the field of ethology, which emphasized the role of instincts and of underlying biology, and relied more on naturalistic observation of animals than on laboratory experiments. A prominent Harvard zoologist named Donald Griffin—he had discovered that bats navigate through echolocation—began pushing his colleagues to acknowledge that animals had thoughts and emotions. He wrote, "The customary view of animals as always living in a state comparable to that of human sleepwalkers is a sort of negative dogmatism." Wasn't it possible that a chimpanzee who scoured the rain forest for a chunk of granite, then used it to crack open a nut, was consciously thinking about that tasty morsel inside, rather than executing rote movements? And did we really know enough to say whether animals had consciousness or not?

In the late seventies, the ethologists Robert Seyfarth and Dorothy Cheney reported some of the first evidence of what appeared to be a referential communication system among animals. Cheney and Seyfarth had gone to Kenya to study the vervet monkey, which is hunted by multiple predators—pythons, leopards, and eagles. The vervets, it seemed, had developed alarm calls that referred to specific predators—a phenomenon that Cheney and Seyfarth were able to demonstrate by playing recordings of the calls, and watching what the monkeys did upon hearing them. If the call was the one for "Python!" they stood on their hind legs and started looking for it; if the call was "Leopard!" the vervets climbed the nearest tree; if they were already in a tree and they heard "Eagle!" they scrambled for the bushes.

For some researchers, though, the vital question was not so much "Can animals talk to each other?" as "Can they talk to us?" In the fifties, a chimp named Viki, who had been raised by a psychologist and his wife in their Florida home, and treated as much like a human child as possible, was taught to say four words—"mama," "papa," "cup," and "up"—in a hoarse whisper. And, in the late sixties, Beatrice and Allen Gardner, researchers at the University of Nevada, decided to teach a chimp American Sign Language. Chimps, they reasoned, were notably expressive with their hands, and so a gestural language would probably be easier for them to adopt than a spoken one. The Gardners' success with a chimp named Washoe—she reportedly learned nearly three hundred signs before her death, last year—ushered in a busy era of ape-language studies. In the seventies and eighties, Koko the gorilla, Kanzi the bonobo, and the mischievously named Nim Chimpsky all became simian celebrities. (Noam Chomsky, the renowned linguist, has argued that language is the exclusive endowment of *Homo sapiens*.) The ape studies seemed to appeal to a vague hope that animals might be gurus of sorts, offering humankind a salutary humbling. Francine Patterson, a California-based researcher who worked with Koko, published popular children's books about the gorilla and her love of felines ("soft good cat cat," Koko once signed), and Nim Chimpsky made appearances on "Sesame Street" and on David Susskind's talk show.

The prominent ape studies tended to be time-consuming and strife-ridden—Nim was quite bitter, with the attention span of, well, a chimpanzee—and the results were mixed. Several apes acquired respectable vocabularies, but, unlike most toddlers, they did not learn to produce sentences combining more than two or three words. (A few did seem to comprehend more complicated sentences: Kanzi, who communicates with the aid of a keyboard, reportedly can distinguish, for instance, between the commands "Make the doggie bite the snake" and "Make the snake bite the doggie"—don't worry, these were toys.) When the apes did combine words, the second word was often a nongrammatical intensifier, as in "open hurry." And, when they produced a longer utterance, it tended to be a string of repetitions of the sort rarely encountered outside a Gertrude Stein poem. (A quote from Nim Chimpsky: "Give orange give me eat orange me eat orange give me eat orange give me you.") In 1979, Herbert Terrace, a psychologist at Columbia University who initiated the Nim Chimpsky research, published an article in *Science* in which he essentially declared the project a failure. Nim knew individual words, and, like Hans the horse, he responded ably to his teachers' cues, but he wasn't really using language. In 1980, a conference in New York seemed to seal Terrace's verdict. Called "The Clever Hans Phenomenon: Communication with Horses, Whales, Apes, and People," it was convened by the semiotician Thomas Sebeok, who invited a magician, the Amazing Randi, and an expert on the psychology of circus animals to make the point that animal-language studies involved an element of deception. Diana Reiss, the dolphin researcher, attended the conference and first met Pepperberg there. Reiss remembers it as a strange and disheartening gathering, in which "Sebeok started off by saying that asking whether animals had language was like asking if elephants could fly."

In the aftermath of the conference, an aura of failure and even chicanery clung to animal-language studies. This was unfortunate, Stephen Anderson suggests in his 2004 book, *Dr. Dolittle's Delusion: Animals and the Uniqueness of Human Language*. The ape-language projects, however flawed, had demonstrated abilities that "had not been previously suspected and about which it would be exciting to learn more." Did apes acquire full-blown expressive language? No. Could they learn to communicate their wants and needs? Yes. Poignantly, even after Nim had been retired to a Texas ranch where most of the employees didn't know sign language, he continued to sign. According to a new book, *Nim Chimpsky: The Chimp Who Would Be Human*, by Elizabeth Hess, when Bob Ingersoll, an old teacher of Nim's, came to visit him, the chimp, who was in a cage at the time, eagerly signed "Bob," "out," and "key." And, when Nim was joined at the ranch by another chimp, Sally, with whom he became quite close, he taught her signs for a couple of his favorite things, such as "gum" and "banana," and signed "sorry" after a quarrel. As Reiss told me, "Nim Chimpsky learned a lot—just not, perhaps, language."

WHEN IRENE PEPPERBERG WENT TO New York for the Clever Hans conference, she was thirty-one, and had owned Alex for three years. She had arrived in the world of animal communication from "out of left field," as Diana Reiss puts it. Pepperberg has a Ph.D. from Harvard in theoretical chemistry, not psychology or zoology. But in the midst of her thesis work, which involved modelling chemical-reaction rates, it suddenly hit her, she recalls, that "(a) we don't know enough at this point to do this exactly right and (b) in the future, what it's taking me seven years to do with a mathematical model is going to take a computer hours, or seconds." She decided to pursue something different. In any case, the prospects for women in her field hadn't been encouraging. Speaking of her class at Harvard, she recalled, "My year was the first year that graduate-school draft deferrals for men were cut way back. So they let in a lot of women for a change. But the women were asked in their job interviews things like 'What kind of birth control are you using?'"

In 1974, Pepperberg watched two programs on PBS, one about Washoe and one about dolphin and whale intelligence. "And it sort of clicked for me that this was real science, that you could be a scientist and study this," she said. "I didn't want to give up science—I loved the scientific method." She also realized that "nobody was doing this kind of research with birds." Pepperberg suspected that this was a mistake, because, unlike apes, some birds were proficient at mimicking human speech. And, based on personal experience, she felt certain that birds could be smart. Pepperberg was born in 1949, and grew up in an apartment above a store in Brooklyn. She was an only child. Her father, Robert Platzblatt, was a frustrated biochemist who passed on his love of science, bringing home *The Microbe Hunters* and biographies of Marie Curie for his daughter to read. But, when Irene was little, her father was simultaneously teaching middle school in Bedford-Stuyvesant, studying for his master's degree, and taking care of his sick mother.

"He'd wake me up and kiss me good morning, and then sometimes I wouldn't see him till the next morning," she recalls. Her mother had been happy working as a junior bookkeeper before she had Irene, and resented staying home, as young mothers were expected to do in the fifties. "For me, there were no other children at home to play with, and for her there was no respite," Pepperberg says.

When Pepperberg was four years old, her father bought her a budgie, to keep her company. She ended up owning a series of budgies, and training them all to speak, at least a little; when she went off to M.I.T. as an undergraduate, one of the birds went with her to her dorm room.

Despite her graduate-school epiphany at Harvard, she continued with her Ph.D. in theoretical chemistry, receiving her degree in 1976; but she also started attending courses in departments relevant to the bird research she now hoped to do. "I was spending forty hours a week learning psychology and biology and forty hours finishing my doctorate," she recalls. In 1977, her husband at the time, David Pepperberg, a neuroscientist, got a professorship at Purdue University, and they moved to Indiana. Pepperberg started looking around for a parrot—preferably an African gray. Among parrot owners, grays have a reputation for being good talkers, and Pepperberg had come across German studies that found them to be adept at numerical and other cognitive tasks. Meanwhile, some recent theorizing about animal intelligence had suggested that the important factor was not absolute brain size but brain size relative to body weight—and on that score, the so-called "encephalization quotient," "birds were surprisingly high up there," Pepperberg said. In her 1999 book, *The Alex Studies*, published by Harvard, Pepperberg writes about becoming excited by an idea that Donald Griffin, the zoologist, had articulated; namely, that "researchers might benefit from studying animals the way that anthropologists study a previously undiscovered primitive tribe." He recommended that scholars attempt "to establish two-way communication and use this communication to determine how they process information and interpret the events in their world."

In 1977, Pepperberg went to a Chicago-area pet store and bought a thirteen-month-old African gray parrot for six hundred dollars. Like all African grays of the Congo subspecies, he was the color of a storm cloud and about a foot tall, with a shiny, scimitar-shaped black beak, a white face, and a lipstick-red tail. She named him Alex. (Luckily for science, when she and her husband divorced, twenty years later, David Pepperberg suggested that she keep the parrot and he keep the dog.)

Pepperberg wasn't sure how to train Alex, although she knew that she didn't want to pursue a behaviorist model. These paradigms had been tried on talking birds, with poor results. (In one 1967 experiment, mynah birds were placed in soundproof boxes where they heard tape-recorded words, followed by the dispensing of food pellets; the birds did not learn to mimic the words. Meanwhile, mynahs that had been left out of the experiment, and turned into pets by the lab assistants, talked fluently.) To Pepperberg, the Skinnerian approach made no sense: "I mean, you don't take a preschooler and put him in a Skinner box! You give him all this enrichment and social interaction." In some ways, a smart bird wasn't so different. Gray parrots are social animals. In the wild, they settle down for the night in roosts with hundreds of other parrots, forage for food in small groups, may have a dominance hierarchy, and mate for life. For mates, imitating one another is a big part of their vocalizing. With their mates, they sing—or squawk—a duet that is unique to that couple. "A single parrot in the wild is a dead parrot," Pepperberg said. "It cannot forage and look for predators at the same time. I was in Australia a number of years ago, and there was this little juvenile rosella at the top of the trees, screaming its head off. Your first reaction is, It's screaming its head off, it's gonna be eaten. And your second reaction is, It might be eaten, but it's got to find its flock."

Pepperberg was further influenced by two papers, one by the primatologist Alison Jolly, in 1966, and one by the psychologist Nicholas Humphrey, in 1976. In different ways, both made the novel argument that the evolutionary pressures fostering intelligence in animals were not the primal demands of subsistence but the more abstract ones of living within a complex social hierarchy. The more intricate the social system, the more evolution would select for intelligence. Pepperberg noted that longevity also played a role. The longer a bird lived, the more it would have to remember—not only about which birds in the flock could dominate which other birds but also about "which trees are blossoming and fruiting, and which trees have died and which paths have now been taken over by leopards, and where the elephants are now going to make their wallows, so it can go and get water."

Pepperberg needed a method for teaching a parrot that played to its particular strengths. She came across something called the model/rival technique, which a German ethologist named Dietmar Todt had tried in a 1975 study of parrots. Todt had reasoned that, since parrots learn to squawk by watching each other vocalize, they might be able to learn German by observing people talk. So he developed a system in which one person was the trainer and one was the model for the bird—and its rival for the trainer's attention. Pepperberg tweaked the protocol: in her version, the model/rival and the trainer periodically exchanged roles, so the bird could see that one person wasn't always in charge. Parrots started the process by learning referential labels for things they wanted, rather than dialogues of the "Hello, how are you? I am fine" variety, which, Pepperberg figured, didn't mean much to a parrot. There were no extrinsic rewards. If the parrot named an object, he'd get to play with that object, and, if he didn't want it, he got the right to ask for something else. Pepperberg explained, "Let's say you're the model/rival and I'm the trainer. I have this object that the bird wants, and I show it to you and I say"—she adopted a singsong voice—"'What's this?,' and you say, 'Cork.' I say, 'That's right,' and you say, 'Cork, cork, cork,' while you're holding it and the bird is practically falling off the perch because he wants it. And he hears that this weird noise is what mediated the transfer of this object. So we change roles, and then, instead of saying 'Cork,' I go, '*Raaaawkk*,'"—an uncannily accurate screech—"and you go, 'No, no, you're wrong,' so the bird sees that not just any weird noise transfers the cork."

The system worked. At first, a parrot might make a sound more like "erk" than "cork." He'd need practice. Certain sounds are nearly impossible to produce without lips—Alex was never able to say "purple," for instance, even after he nailed all his other colors. Still, as Reiss says, "Irene really found the appropriate method based on what we know about these birds. If you can tap into what these birds do in their own environment—in this case, the way these birds pair-bond—then you can set up a powerful learning paradigm."

As it happens, the model/rival method may have some utility for another species: humans. Diane Sherman, who works with autistic children in Monterey, California, has had some preliminary success in encouraging speech in her clients using Pepperberg's protocol. In an article published in *The International Journal of Comparative Psychology*, Sherman and Pepperberg say that, in two studies of children in Sherman's private practice, the model/rival method led to "significant gains" in the children's "communication and social interaction with peers and adults." (Behavioral changes were measured by reports from parents and teachers, and included criteria like demonstrations of empathy, improved eye contact, saying hello to people, and speaking in sentences.)

When Pepperberg started publishing papers on Alex, Reiss recalls, many of her colleagues were nonplussed: "I can remember being at a psychology conference in the early eighties where Irene was giving a paper about Alex, and people were saying, 'I see it but I don't believe it.' A lot of the work being presented was pretty Skinnerian and I remember that, at her talk, some people in the back row got up and walked out. Now she gets a radically different reception. I was at a comparative-cognition conference recently, and many of those same people were there. And I heard a number of people talking about Irene's work and referring to it as groundbreaking."

A FEW WEEKS AFTER PEPPERBERG'S speech at the Bird Expo, I saw her in a more properly scientific guise, teaching an undergraduate seminar and an evening extension course on animal cognition at Harvard. At the evening course, she lectured about one of her favorite subjects—the songbirds known as oscines, which learn their melodies much like human children learn language. They have an innate predisposition to learn song; they have an initial period of babbling; they have specific brain areas for song-learning, just as we have for speech; and they have a sensitive phase in childhood for acquiring song, just as humans have for acquiring language. The parallel is striking, Pepperberg told her students, partly because so few other species actually learn to communicate vocally, as opposed to making primal sounds instinctually. "Besides humans, it's dolphins and certain birds—and maybe, we think now, elephants," she said.

An innate predisposition isn't enough for oscine songbirds to learn their repertoire, Pepperberg said. They need tutoring from members of their own species—usually, from their fathers or the dominant males in their flock, since it is males who tend to sing, in order to attract mates or defend territory. Pepperberg spoke of songbirds with prodigious repertoires—the adult brown thrasher can sing two thousand songs. In a voice that had a faint trace of her native Brooklyn, she said, "You can raise some birds in social isolation and give them audiotapes of their own species singing, but it doesn't work very well. And, if you keep them alone in a little tiny box during their sensitive phase, they will sing, but it will be a kind of tentative, crummy song." She urged her students to "go out and listen to the dawn chorus. It's cacophony. A beautiful cacophony, but nonetheless." She argued that, in order for a songbird to recognize the music of its own species, it must be able to make distinctions between same and different—just as Alex did.

In speaking about animal intelligence, Pepperberg has tried to strike a balance between what the ecologist James Gould has called "the unprofitable extremes of blinding skepticism and crippling romanticism." Pepperberg has published widely in peer-reviewed scientific journals, even as she raises funds for her research with a Web site that sells adorable Alex tote bags, key chains, and mugs.

Still, for many years, Pepperberg felt that she and Alex were, in intellectual terms, out on a limb. In the past decade, though, dozens of studies have buttressed Pepperberg's claims about avian intelligence. Alex's brain was the size of a shelled walnut, as Pepperberg often observed. Yet Nathan Emery, a cognitive biologist at the University of London, points out that, "in relation to their body size, parrots have brains as big as those of chimpanzees." Emery has taken to calling certain of the brighter birds the "feathered apes in your garden." And Erich Jarvis, a neuroscientist at Duke University, argues that avian brains, long regarded as primitive, are not so different from mammalian brains after all. Birds, Jarvis explains, "have a cortical region that developed, in fact, from the same substrate as in humans." Soon enough, "birdbrain" may no longer be a viable insult.

One important set of studies centers on the clever corvid family of birds, which includes crows, ravens, jays, and magpies. (Perhaps it's no coincidence that crows or ravens often appear as cunning tricksters and problem-solvers in Native American legends and Aesop's fables.) A 1998 study suggested that these birds have a surprising capacity for "episodic-like memory." Scrub jays hide food and retrieve it later, and in the study the birds were allowed to cache two kinds of food: peanuts and wax-moth larvae, which they much prefer (though only when the larvae are fresh). Some of the jays were then sent to their cages for four hours, and some for five days, after which they were given access to their stashes. The birds that were released first went for the larvae, while the ones let out later settled for the peanuts, apparently having remembered not only when and where they had hidden their food but how long it took for the larvae to go bad. Further studies noted that, if a scrub jay realized that it was being spied on by another jay as it cached its food, it was more likely to come back later and hide the goodies elsewhere. Moreover, jays that had previously stolen from another's stash were more prone to move their food to a different hiding place. (It takes a thief to know one, apparently.) Such behavior suggests that jays not only have a Machiavellian streak; they also possess a "theory of mind," and can guess, to some degree, what other birds are thinking. The husband-and-wife team of Nicola Clayton and Nathan Emery, who are largely responsible for this work, argue that it shows some birds have "the same cognitive tool kit" that apes have: "causal reasoning, flexibility, imagination, and prospection." They believe that evolution created multiple paths to intelligence—and that "complex cognitive abilities had evolved multiple times in distantly related species."

Alex Kacelnik, a professor at Oxford, studies another corvid, the New Caledonian crow, which has a rare ability to make tools (a talent once thought to be limited to primates). It will tear a strip off a leaf, and then use the strip to poke into insect-harboring crevices. In 2002, Kacelnik and his colleagues presented a group of birds with the challenge of making a tool, with a material not found in nature, to solve a novel problem. In one room, which the birds could enter freely, was a length of wire and a cylindrical container that had something tasty, like a piece of pig's heart, at the bottom. One of the crows, a female named Betty, figured out how to bend the wire with her beak, so as to fashion a hook for retrieving the meat. Did Betty look at the wire and have an insight about what to do? Not exactly.

"The crows don't fully understand what they are doing," Kacelnik told me. "And yet neither can you say it's explainable as purely mechanical repetition." To insure that Betty wasn't somehow acting on instinct, Kacelnik and his colleagues "gave her a task that was the opposite. We gave her a piece of metal that was bent so it was too short. Would she be clever enough to unbend it? She was. So that implied some understanding of the physical requirements of the task." Though some crows, like Betty, cracked the challenge quickly, others took many tries; still others never mastered it. Watching videos of Betty on Kacelnik's Web site, I noticed that she seemed to have a particularly focussed and alert way about her. Even Kacelnik, who is loath to anthropomorphize, confessed to me, "An element of our finding that still puzzles me is that while Betty was not chosen or treated in any special way, she was different. She showed a readiness to coöperate and solve problems that none of the other animals in our study have replicated. We have no idea why."

How representative are Betty and Alex of their species? For science, one remarkable bird is not enough. Kacelnik told me, "We study multiple animals for a reason: if you want to characterize a species, you need to try similar ideas on different subjects, to examine how much is due to exceptional circumstances and how much is a property of your method and your experiments." I asked him why more researchers weren't working with African grays, trying to replicate Pepperberg's achievements with Alex. "The problem with these animals is that they are the opposite of fruit flies," he said, meaning that parrots live a long time—often, fifty to sixty years in captivity. "Alex was still learning when he died, and he was thirty." He later elaborated: "Irene's work could not really have been planned ahead, as nobody knew what was possible. Alex's development as a unique animal accompanied Irene's as a unique scientist. Hers is not a career trajectory one would advise to young scientists—it's too risky."

Pepperberg told me that there are now a few groups of researchers studying cognition in African grays: one group in Prague, where the parrots are learning Czech; one in Milan, where they are learning Italian; and one outside Paris, where they are studying "referential communication" that does not involve language. In the end, though, it may be Pepperberg herself who has the greatest drive and capacity to replicate her own work, although she has suffered from funding shortfalls; over the decades, she has received eight grants from the National Science Foundation, but she does a lot of fund-raising on her own. At the Brandeis lab, she is training and testing her two remaining parrots, Griffin and Arthur. Griffin, who is thirteen, shows more promise than Arthur, who is nine. Both seem shyer and less confident than Alex. Pepperberg's lab manager, Arlene Levin, describes Griffin as "a timid guy, and a plucker." (Anxious parrots pluck out their feathers.) And Griffin grew up in Alex's shadow; he was the one whom Alex interrupted and corrected—"Say better," "Pay attention," "Bad parrot." Griffin currently knows about a dozen words for objects; Alex knew fifty. "I'm not saying that Griffin won't get there," Pepperberg told me. "I think he will. He's smart. It's just a matter of convincing him that, no, Alex is not going to give you the answer. Don't just sit there waiting!" She admits that there's pressure on her, too: "It's important to show that Alex was not some unique individual."

Even Nathan Emery, the cognitive biologist, who is otherwise admiring of Pepperberg's work, thinks it is possible that Alex might have been an exceptionally bright bird. Pepperberg notes that she picked him at random at the pet store, precisely to forestall the suspicion that she'd gone hunting for the avian Einstein. She says, "I think that what made Alex special was that, for the first fifteen years of his life, he was an only bird, and he had people with him talking with him eight hours a day—interacting with him, treating him like a toddler. When he said something, you reacted in some way or another, so he learned that his vocalizations could control the environment."

Clive Wynne, an animal psychologist at the University of Florida, is suspicious of most animal-communication projects. (He writes papers with titles like "The Perils of Anthropomorphism" and "Pets Aren't Us.") He is no less dubious about Pepperberg's work. "An African gray parrot is an expensive pet, but it's not expensive compared with, say, a dolphin, which costs tens of thousands of dollars," he says. "Why is Alex the only parrot in the history of parrotdom to have done these things? If there's really something going on here—I mean, he lived thirty years—then somebody else, somewhere along the line, would have replicated this. If we really want this to be science and not just some sort of adjunct to the entertainment industry, we shouldn't be relying on one animal."

LAST MONTH, I VISITED PEPPERBERG and her two remaining birds at Brandeis. Her lab is a windowless, fluorescent-lit room, ten feet by fifteen feet, with white cement walls. One wall is lined with shelves stacked with bags of nuts and kibbles, boxes of bite-size Shredded Wheat, and plastic jars full of colored wooden blocks, plastic letters, and pompoms. There are newspapers on the floor, and three big cages, one of them empty. Alex, it's clear, was not simply a pet or a laboratory subject. For thirty years, he was the center of Pepperberg's life: a little like a child, a little like a significant other, very much like a collaborator. When Alex died—a technician discovered his body—she was devastated. "I always felt I was working toward the next stage with him," she told me. "And I thought I had at least a decade more." When two close friends of Pepperberg's—a nuclear-submarine commander named Carl Hartsfield and his wife, Leigh

Ann—heard the news, they drove up from Washington, D.C., along with their own African gray, Pepper, to be with her.

My first glimpse of Griffin made me glad that I'm not a parrot who has to identify my life's mate in a flock. Griffin, who was shuffling down one side of his cage in a parroty version of the Electric Slide, looked just like the photographs of Alex that I'd seen, and just like Arthur, who was over in a corner, quietly preening. Griffin is named, in part, for Donald Griffin, and in part for the gryphon he reminded Pepperberg of when she first bought him—"He was all talons and beak." Now he's grown into himself, and, when he's not plucking, is full-feathered and handsome, just like Alex. I did notice that, when Griffin spoke, his voice was softer than the Great One's, which is preserved on dozens of YouTube clips.

One of the odd things about observing Griffin speak was the contrast between his face—goggle-Eyed and masklike, and much less expressive than a dog's—and his ability to make his wishes clear.

"Wanna go chair," Griffin said, and Arlene Levin, the lab manager, picked him up and placed him on a perch next to her office chair. Then Levin showed me a little of what the new boy could do. "What matter?" she asked, holding up a small block of wood close to Griffin's beak, so he could tap it if he wanted. This was how the parrots were queried about what material an object is made of.

"Wood," Griffin said.

"You want the wood?"

Griffin didn't pick up the block.

"What do you want?"

"Nut." Griffin was given an almond, and he snarfed it down.

"What matter?" Levin asked, holding a stone.

"Rrrr-ock," Griffin said.

"Want the rock?"

No—he wanted another nut. (Nuts are offered only in training sessions.)

"What color?" Levin asked, showing him a plastic cup.

"Green," Griffin announced correctly, in an uninflected tone, and then "yellow" when shown another cup.

A while later, two Brandeis undergraduates, Shannon Cabell and Michelle Barras, came in to do a training session, and it didn't go quite as smoothly. Pepperberg was sitting at a desk in the corner, thumbing through the latest issue of *Animal Cognition*. The two young women were perched on tall stools, and Griffin was on a perch across from them.

"What shape?" Cabell asked. She had to repeat it four or five times, as Griffin wasn't saying a thing.

From the corner, Pepperberg instructed, "All right, model it for him." Cabell picked up a square object and asked Barras what shape she was holding. With a theatrical display of pride, Barras responded, "Four-corner!"

"Right," Cabell said. "She's such a good bird. She gets a four-corner for that."

"Wanna nut," Barras said, in convincing parrotese. Cupping the square in her hand, she gamely mimed eating it.

"What color?" Cabell asked about a yellow pompom, a material that the birds identify as wool.

"Wool," Griffin chimed.

Pepperberg sighed, distractedly pulled a piece of sandwich bread out of a plastic bag on the shelf, and began eating it. "Right," she told Griffin. "It's wool. What *color* wool?"

"Yellow." There were a few more exchanges like this, as well as some long silences during which Pepperberg murmured, "C'mon, Griffs," and Barras said, "All these nuts can be yours."

Watching this exchange, I indulged in my own anthropomorphic speculation—I imagined that Griffin was thinking that he'd like to be back where he was half an hour ago, sitting quietly in Pepperberg's lap, having his head tickled.

Barras pulled out a green block and asked Griffin what color it was. The parrot stared at his feet.

"See if he'll do it for a bean," Pepperberg suggested. Barras took an orange jelly bean out of a bag. "No," Pepperberg prompted. "A bean the same color." Barras dug out a green one. In the fall, candy corn is the major training treat; in the winter, it's candy hearts; in the spring, there are jelly beans; in the summer, the parrots get Skittles. "Half a jelly bean once in a while is acceptable for his diet," Pepperberg told me. It's also a powerful motivator.

"*Green*," Griffin said immediately.

This parrot is good, even impressive. But he's not Alex. Not yet.

About the Contributors

LAWRENCE K. ALTMAN, M.D., one of the few medical doctors working as a reporter, joined the *New York Times* in 1969. An award-winning journalist, he began his career at the Centers for Disease Control and Prevention, and as chief of the Public Health Service's division of epidemiology and immunization. A graduate of Harvard and Tufts University School of Medicine, Dr. Altman is a professor at New York University Medical School, a Master of the American College of Physicians, a Fellow of the American College of Epidemiology and the New York Academy of Medicine, and a member of the Institute of Medicine of the National Academy of Sciences. In addition to reporting, he writes "The Doctor's World" column in *Science Times*.

MICHAEL BENSON is a journalist, filmmaker, and photographer. His most recent book, *Far Out: A Space-Time Chronicle* (Abrams, fall 2009), is a companion volume to his award-winning *Beyond: Visions of the Interplanetary Probes* (Abrams, 2003). Benson has written features and Op-Ed pieces for *The New Yorker,* the *Atlantic Monthly,* the *New York Times* and the *Washington Post,* among many other venues. His film *Predictions of Fire* (1995) premiered at the Sundance and Berlin international film festivals and won several best documentary awards internationally. Benson is currently working with director Terrence Malick on space sequences in two new Malick films. He lives in New York City with his wife, Melita Gabric, and son, Daniel.

"My respect, and even awe, for the achievements of the engineers and planetary scientists at NASA's Jet Propulsion Laboratory in Pasadena has only waxed since the publication of my *New Yorker* piece on the extraordinarily resilient *Galileo* Jupiter probe of 1989–2003," he writes. "Operated by CalTech, JPL has to be the most cost-efficient government-funded organization in the republic. For a tiny percentage of what's spent on human spaceflight, they whip up such astonishing creations as the Mars Rovers *Spirit* and *Opportunity*, still going strong on opposite sides of the Red Planet, six years and five mission-extensions later. As for *Galileo*'s legacy, the discovery that Jupiter's ice-skinned moon Europa almost certainly contains a vast unitary global ocean raises the remarkable prospect that life could have arisen across eons in the outer solar system. Further exploration of Europa should be NASA's top priority."

JENNIFER COUZIN-FRANKEL is a staff writer for *Science* magazine, where she covers various topics in medicine, basic biology, and the scientific community. Her work has also been published in *U.S. News & World Report*, *Newsweek*, and the *Washington Post*, among other publications. She appeared in *The Best American Science Writing* in 2005 and 2007, and she previously won the Evert Clark/Seth Payne Award, given annually to a young science journalist. She grew up in Toronto, Canada, and lives with her husband and son in Philadelphia, PA.

"Some stories stay with you after they're written, and for me, this was one of them," she says. "It was a case in which, by all accounts, graduate students did what they had been trained to do in reporting potential misconduct, but then suffered serious consequences. The Wisconsin students spoke to me for hours with great candor and showed me around Madison, reliving an experience several would have preferred to leave behind. Since this difficult time they've moved on, some sticking with scientific research and others leaving it for other pursuits. Their professor, Elizabeth Goodwin, was later cleared of scientific misconduct on three published papers about which the university had raised concerns."

FREEMAN DYSON is a physicist who has worked in many areas, including particle physics, condensed matter, nuclear engineering, climate studies, astrophysics and biology. He is a retired professor at the Institute for Advanced Study in Princeton. Beyond his professional work in physics, he writes books for the general public about the human side of science and the human consequences of technology. His two most recent books are *The Scientist as Rebel* and *A Many-Colored Glass*. In the year 2000 he was awarded the Templeton Prize for progress in religion.

"The main change in my life as a writer since 2001 has been a regular assignment as reviewer for *The New York Review of Books* (NYRB)," he reports. "This magazine has a policy of printing long reviews. Each review is about 4,000 words long, giving me a chance to write essays covering a wider field than a single book. Many of my reviews are included in the collection, *The Scientist as Rebel*, published by NYRB in 2006. My latest review published in July 2009, reviewing *The Age of Wonder* by Richard Holmes, returns to the theme of my article, 'Science, Guided by Ethics, Can Lift Up the Poor,' reprinted in this volume."

ATUL GAWANDE is a general and endocrine surgeon at the Brigham and Women's Hospital in Boston, a staff writer for *The New Yorker*, and an associate professor at Harvard Medical School and the Harvard School of Public Health. He is the author of *Complications*; *Better*; and, forthcoming, *The Checklist Manifesto*.

"This was hardly the first article in which a physician confronted his mistakes," he recalls. "But it came at a time when it was becoming acceptable, and finally necessary, to think hard about failure in medicine. It also launched my career in multiple ways. This was my foot in the door at *The New Yorker*—I became a staff writer with this article. And it prompted what has become more than a decade of thinking about and researching how danger and complexity are handled in an endeavor like medicine—as both a practical matter and a moral matter."

JEROME GROOPMAN holds the Dina and Raphael Recanati Chair of Medicine at the Harvard Medical School and is Chief of Experimental Medicine at the Beth Israel Deaconess Medical Center. He serves on many scientific editorial boards and has published more than 150 scientific articles. His research has focused on the basic mechanisms of cancer and AIDS and has led to the development of successful therapies. His basic laboratory research involves understanding how blood cells grow and communicate ("signal transduction"), and how viruses cause immune deficiency and cancer. Dr. Groopman also has established a large and innovative program in clinical research and clinical care at the Beth Israel Deaconess Medical Center. In 2000, he was elected to the Institute of Medicine of the National Academy of Sciences. He has authored several editorials on policy issues in *The New Republic*, the *Washington Post*, the *Wall Street Journal* and the *New York Times*. He has published four books; his most recent, the bestseller *How Doctors Think*, came out in a paperback edition in March, 2008. For his comments on "What's Normal?" please see his introduction to this volume.

AMY HARMON is a National Correspondent for the *New York Times* who writes about how science and technology shape the lives of ordinary people. She has won two Pulitzer Prizes, the first in 2001 as part of a team for a stories about race in America, the second in 2008 for her series "The DNA Age," about genetic tests that reveal more than we may be prepared to learn about who we are, where we came from, and what our future might hold. She continues to practice long-form journalism in the stubborn belief that it, and newspapers, will survive on the Web.

"Katie Moser continues to pack all she can into a life that she knows will almost certainly be shorter than most," she writes. "She dated a fireman who at first seemed unfazed that she has the genetic mutation that causes Huntington's disease. But when it didn't work out, she began to plan to have children on her own. With a new job as a Huntington's patient advocate for a drug company, she is saving to afford a procedure that tests embryos, to ensure she does not pass on the disease gene. She travels often. 'Katie Moser,' reads a recent Facebook update, 'is on the log flume.' She remains estranged from her mother."

ROBIN MARANTZ HENIG has written eight books, most recently *Pandora's Baby: How the First Test Tube Babies Sparked the Reproductive Revolution*. Her articles have appeared in the *New York Times Magazine*, where she is a contributing writer, as well as *Civilization, Discover, Scientific American*, and just about every woman's magazine in the grocery store. She is on the board of directors of the National Association of Science Writers, and in 2009 was awarded a Guggenheim Foundation grant.

"We're not post-racial yet, despite the election of Barack Obama," she says. "In the five years since my article appeared, a cottage industry has sprung up to help people track their origins through mitochondrial DNA. You can't do that unless you presume that the genes of Africans are different somehow from the genes of, say, northern Europeans. And scientists are still looking for genetic fingerprints of racial identity and pursuing the dream of race-based medicine—but they're doing so with caution, and their work is being watched closely (I hope) by bioethicists and politicians."

JACK HITT is a Peabody Award–winning writer for the *New York Times Magazine, Harper's* magazine, and the public radio program, *This American Life*. He is the author of *Off the Road: A Modern-Day Walk Down the Pilgrim's Route into Spain*, in paperback from Simon & Schuster. He is currently at work on a book about amateurs in America.

"Kennewick Man has been, as the culinary aphorist Irma Rombauer said of saints and pigs, 'more honored in death than in life,'" he admits. "His bones are maintained in a climate-controlled reliquary. His story is hymned by a chorus of hagiographers. And his exploits are more imaginatively embroidered than Quixote's. The greatest of his scriveners is the divinely named James Chatters, who now plies the extremist Internet-radio circuit gushing about 'European' shapes he discerns in 10,000-year-old skeletons. Meanwhile, his edgy audience has found a new euphemism for 'white victimhood' and a new shibboleth, typically uttered in tones quivering with the sorrow and the pity, in what the hosts now call 'Solutrean Pride.'"

WILLIAM LANGEWIESCHE, a former airplane pilot, has contributed to major magazines, including the *Atlantic Monthly* and *Vanity Fair*, and is the author of seven books: *Cutting for Sign, Sahara Unveiled, Inside the Sky, American Ground, The Outlaw Sea, The Atomic Bazaar,* and *Fly by Wire.* He lives in France.

ERNST MAYR, one of the most influential evolutionary theorists of our time, was Alexander Agassiz Professor of Zoology, Emeritus, at Harvard University, at the time of his death in 2005. Born in Germany in 1904, Mayr received his doctoral degree in zoology from the University of Berlin in 1926; five years later he emigrated to the United States, taking up a position at the American Museum of Natural History in New York City. His work focused on the evolution of new species by sharpening the definition of the species concept through the introduction of population thinking and by establishing the principle that genetic and, most often, geographic isolation are the key elements in speciation. He put forward these views in several important books, including *Systematics and the Origins of Species* (1942) and *Animal Species and Evolution* (1963). He was also the author of books on the history and philosophy of evolution and biology, including *Growth of Biological Thought, One Long Argument: Charles Darwin and the Genesis of Modern Evolutionary Thought,* and *This Is Biology: The Science of the Living World.* He was the recipient of numerous honorary doctorates and awards, including the Darwin-Wallace Medal, the Darwin Medal of the Royal Society, the Benjamin Franklin Medal, and the Balzan Prize.

TOM MUELLER earned his bachelor's degree at Harvard and his doctorate at Oxford, where he was a Rhodes Scholar. He writes freelance for *The New Yorker, National Geographic,* the *Atlantic Monthly,* the *New York Times,* and other publications.

"Since writing 'Your Move,' I have continued to publish stories in *The New Yorker, National Geographic* and elsewhere," he reports. "I've also completed my first novel, a historical thriller about the building and rebuilding of Saint Peter's in the Vatican and the mystery of Peter's tomb, forthcoming in 2010. I am now at work on a nonfiction book about the culture, aesthetics, science and crime of olive oil, to be published by W. W. Norton in 2010."

DANIELLE OFRI's newest book is *Medicine in Translation: Journeys with my Patients* (Beacon, 2010), which examines the challenges that immigrants face in the American health-care system, as well as her own experience as a patient in a foreign country. She is the author of two essay collections about life in medicine: *Incidental Findings* and *Singular Intimacies*. Ofri practices medicine at Bellevue Hospital and is on the faculty of New York University School of Medicine. She is editor-in-chief and co-founder of the *Bellevue Literary Review*. Her writings have also appeared in the *New York Times*, the *LA Times, Best American Essays,* the *New England Journal of Medicine,* the *Lancet,* and on *National Public Radio.*

Because she feels the comments she offered about "Common Ground" when it appeared in *The Best American Science Writing 2003* are still relevant, we reprint them here: "If it is unsettling to write about the private affairs of a patient, it can be agonizing to write about one's own. For my patients, I am acutely cognizant of, and troubled by, the ethical issues and so take pains to alter names and identifying characteristics. For myself, this is not so easy. Before I'd written 'Common Ground,' I'd never shared this episode with anyone, save one close friend. Well into my late thirties, married, with children and several advanced degrees, I still hadn't told my parents about what had occurred when I was seventeen. When I'd initially written this essay, I created two versions: one with, and one without, my own experience contrasted to the patient's. I wrestled with which version to publish, then finally decided to include myself. As a writer, I realized that I have no choice but to seek the truth, and that overrode my personal queasiness and lingering doubts. And as a physician who brings the agonies and deepest vulnerabilities of her patients to paper, I can be no less brutal with myself. If my patients have their guts revealed to the world, how can I hide behind a white coat or a writer's pen?"

A native of Washington, D.C., KAREN OLSSON lives in Austin, Texas. She is an editor-at-large for *Texas Monthly* and the author of the novel *Waterloo.*

"One of the perks of reporting in Texas," she relates, "is stumbling across unexpected cultural collisions, i.e. a couple of astronomers driving from one west Texas town to the next to promote a dark energy experiment to locals. The HETDEX scientists' fundraising efforts served as a reminder of how much extrascientific work is required to bring such a big, expensive experiment to fruition. Presumably it's not the sort of thing they studied in graduate school, yet public relations seemed to come fairly naturally to Gary, Karl, and their collaborators, thanks to their enthusiasm for the project.

"The McDonald Observatory itself is a beautiful spot; the combination of natural beauty and helpful interview subjects made this article a really enjoyable one to research. Since it appeared, the HETDEX team has passed a couple of reviews and obtained more than two-thirds of the needed funds. They plan to start making observations in 2011."

DAVID QUAMMEN is a science journalist and author, based in Montana, who travels widely on assignment, often to jungles, deserts and swamps. His usual beat is ecology and evolutionary biology, and he writes frequently about field biologists—including eminent field biologists of the past, such as Darwin and Wallace. Quammen is a contributing writer for *National Geographic*, and has three times received the National Magazine Award. His books include *The Song of the Dodo* and *The Reluctant Mr. Darwin*. He's presently at work on a book about the ecology and evolution of scary viruses.

"During the year that followed first publication of this essay, efforts by religious conservatives to confuse and dilute the teaching of biology in America's public schools came famously to a climax in Dover, Pennsylvania," he writes. "The court case now known as *Kitzmiller v. Dover* was argued there, in autumn 2005, over the question of whether a local school board had the constitutional right to compel teachers to read a disclaimer about evolutionary theory in ninth-grade biology classes at Dover High School. The essence of the disclaimer was that evolution is a theory, 'not a fact,' and that the notion of 'intelligent design' is an alternative explanation for the same observed phenomena. The presiding judge in the case was John E. Jones III, a Republican appointed by George W. Bush. On December 20, 2005, Judge Jones issued his heroically clear-sighted and thorough decision, finding that 'intelligent design' has no place in a science curriculum, since it isn't science, and that forcing science teachers to read the disclaimer was unconstitutional. With that, the evolution-deniers had failed in their latest gambit against public science education. But we can assume that they will be back."

FLOYD SKLOOT is the author of fifteen books, most recently the memoir *The Wink of the Zenith: The Shaping of a Writer's Life* (University of Nebraska Press, 2008), the poetry collection *The Snow's Music* (LSU Press, 2008), and *Selected Poems: 1970–2005* (Tupelo Press, 2008), winner of a Pacific NW

Book Award. He has won three Pushcart Prizes and lives in Portland, Oregon, with his wife, Beverly Hallberg.

"My mother died in April 2006, almost four years after I wrote 'The Melody Lingers On,'" he reports. "There was a moment, at the end of 2004, as she failed to appear for her performance at a talent show in the nursing home, when I knew song had left her. She would only hum, or recite 'Three Blind Mice.' At the end, when she stopped eating and lay on her side, I sang her favorite songs back to her. Suddenly her eyes opened, moved across the space between us, across my face, then shut. I knew then it was time for silence."

LAUREN SLATER is a psychologist and the author of six books: *Welcome to My Country, Prozac Diary, Lying, Love Works Like This, Opening Skinner's Box*, and *Blue Beyond Blue*. Her work has appeared in several major publications and has been widely anthologized.

SHERYL GAY STOLBERG has been a reporter for the *New York Times*, where she is now a White House correspondent, and formerly covered medicine and health policy, since 1997. Prior to that she worked for the *Journal-Bulletin* in Providence, Rhode Island, and then spent nearly ten years with the *Los Angeles Times*.

"It has been ten years since Jesse Gelsinger died, setting off a slew of lawsuits and federal investigations," she says. "Paul Gelsinger spent several years fighting for better patient protections, but eventually withdrew from public advocacy, saying he grew weary of the constant reminders of his loss. Steve Raper has left the fulltime practice of medicine and enrolled in law school. Mark Batshaw and Jim Wilson are still researching potential gene-therapy treatments for OTC Deficiency. Wilson was barred for a time from conducting studies in humans; he still runs his lab at Penn but limits his experiments to test tube and animal studies and has urged colleagues not to rush into human testing. As part of a settlement with the Justice Department, Wilson recently authored an academic journal article reflecting on the lessons learned; in it, he accepted 'full responsibility" for flaws in the experiment that cost Jesse his life, and concluded that families like the Gelsingers 'deserve better.'"

MARGARET TALBOT has been a staff writer for *The New Yorker* since 2003. She lives in Washington, D.C., with her husband, writer Arthur Allen, and their children, Isaac and Lucy, both of whom can now do excellent imitations of Alex the parrot.

"One of the ironies that strikes me when I look back on this story," she reflects, "is that researching sociability and communication in animals can be a fairly lonely pursuit. Irene Pepperberg's work with Alex was something that earned her a lot of skepticism and isolated her from other scientists to some degree, and getting parrots to talk in a meaningful way required her to devote a huge amount of time and emotional energy to cultivating a relationship with them. And African Grays are needy, sensitive birds—the Woody Allens of the avian world."

GARY TAUBES is the author of *Good Calories, Bad Calories: Challenging the Conventional Wisdom on Diet, Weight Control, and Disease* (Knopf, 2007). Taubes began his science journalism career at *Discover* in 1982 and became a contributing correspondent for *Science* a decade later. Along the way, he has written for the *Atlantic Monthly,* the *New York Times Magazine, Esquire, Slate,* and other publications. Since the mid-1980s, Taubes has focused his reporting on controversial science and the tools and methodology needed to establish reliable knowledge. His particular obsession is the intersection of science, health and public policy.

"I followed up on 'The Soft Science of Dietary Fat' with a controversial July, 2002, cover story in the *New York Times Magazine*—'What If It's All Been a Big Fat Lie?'—arguing that dietary fat doesn't make us fat, but the carbohydrates we've been advised to eat instead probably do," he explains. "That in turn led to my 2007 book, *Good Calories, Bad Calories: Challenging the Conventional Wisdom on Diet, Weight Control, and Disease,* which does exactly what the subtitle suggests—challenging virtually everything we think we know about the nature of a healthy diet."

Permissions